AMAZING NORTHEAST

MEGHALAYA

AMAZING NORTHEAST

MEGHALAYA

Edited & Compiled by
Aribam Indubala Devi

Vij Books India Pvt. Ltd.
(Publishers, Dustributors & Importers)

4675-A, 21, Ansari Road, Darya Ganj,
New Delhi-110002

Published by
Vij Books India Pvt. Ltd.
(Publishers, Distributors & Importers)
4675-A, 21, Ansari Road, Darya Ganj,
New Delhi-110002
Phone: 91-11-65449971, 91-11-43596460
Fax: 91-11-47340674
E-mail: vijbooks@rediffmail.com

First Edition: 2010

ISBN: 978-93-80177-27-4

Contents

Preface

In India, the Northeastern region is quite charming and interesting enough to be known about. Among the eight Northeastern States, Meghalaya is basically an agricultural state in which about 80 per cent of its population depends primarily on agriculture for their livelihood. The State has a vast potential for the development of horticulture, due to the agroclimatic variations, which offer much scope for cultivation of temperate, subtropical and tropical fruits and vegetables. Besides major food crops of rice and maize, Meghalaya is renowned for its oranges, pineapples, bananas, jackfruits, temperate fruits, like plum, pear and peach, etc. Cash crops, popularly and traditionally cultivated include, potato, turmeric, ginger, black pepper, arecanut, betelvine, tapioca, short staple cotton, jute and mesta, mustard and rapeseed. Special emphasis is presently being laid on non-traditional crops like oilseeds (groundnut, soyabean and sunflower), cashewnut, strawberry, tea and coffee, mushroom, medicinal plants, orchids and commercial flowers.

Meghalaya was created as an autonomous state within the State of Assam on 2 April 1970. The full-fledged State of Meghalaya came into existence on 21 January 1972. It is bound on north and east by Assam and on south and west by Bangladesh. Meghalaya, which literally means 'the Abode of Clouds' is essentially a hilly state. It is predominately inhabited by Khasi, Jaintia and Garo tribe communities. The Khasi Hills and Jaintia Hills, which form the central and eastern part of Meghalaya, from an imposing plateau with rolling grassland, hills and river valleys. The southern face of the plateau is marked by deep gorges and abrupt slopes, at the foot of which, a narrow strip of plain land runs along the international border with Bangladesh.

This small but comprehensive and compact book on this northeastern state, offers all information, within one cover. Hopefully, it would serve all those working on or interested in knowing about northeastern India, be they scholars, researchers, journalists, students or general readers. This is in fact, 'Knowledge in Nutshell'.

— *Editor*

Meghalaya
An Overview

Governor	:	Ranjit Shekhar Mooshahary
Chief Minister	:	Dr. D.D. Lapang
Speaker	:	Charles Pyngrope
Chief Secretary	:	M.S. Pariat
Capital	:	Shillong
High Court	:	Guwahati (Bench at Shilong)

Brief Description

Meghalaya or the abode of the clouds is situated between 89.46° to 94.36° East longitude and 25.05° to 26.41° North latitude. It is bounded on the north by Goalpara, Kamrup and Nagaon districts, on the east by Karbi Anglong and North Cachar Hills districts, all of Assam, and on the south and west by Bangladesh. It shares a 443 km long international border with Bangladesh. Spread over a geographical area of 22,429 sq km, Meghalaya comprises 0.68 per cent of India's landmass and 8.55 per cent of that of the North-East.

Meghalaya was created as an autonomous state within the state of Assam on 2 April 1970 and was

Facts and Figures

- *Area:* 22,429 sq km (8.5% of total area of North-East)

- *Geographical Location:* Situated between latitude 20° 1' N to 26° 5' N & longitude 85° 49' E to 92° 52'

- *Capital:* Shillong

- *Population:* 2,318,822 (2001 Census) (6% of population of North-East)

- *Density (per sq km):* 103 (National Figure: 324)

- *Principal Languages*: Khasi, Garo and English

Contd...

declared a state of the Indian Union on 21 January 1972. Shillong, the capital of Meghalaya, is located at an altitude of 1496 metres above sea level. It is currently divided into seven districts. The districts are further divided into eight subdivisions and 39 blocks. The blocks are further subdivided into 15 Gram Sevak Circles. The local administration of the state is run through the Autonomous District Councils, set up under the Sixth Schedule of the Indian Constitution. There are three such councils: the Garo Hills Autonomous District Council at Tura, the Khasi Hills Autonomous District Council at Shillong and the Jaintia Hills Autonomous District Council at Jowai.

Meghalaya is home to two main tribal formations: Hynniewtreps and the Achiks. The Khasi, Jaintia, Bhoi, and War tribes, belonging to the Proto-Austroloid Monkhmer race, are collectively known as the Hynniewtrep people, who predominantly inhabit the East Meghalaya districts. The Garos, who prefer to call themselves as Achiks, predominantly inhabit the Garo Hills. They belong to the Tibeto-Burman race and are said to have migrated from Tibet. The literacy rate of Meghalaya is 63.61 per cent.

Due to its rugged terrains, the state of Meghalaya is sparsely populated. According to Census 2001, Meghalaya has a total population of 2,306,069, thus, constituting 0.22 per cent of the population of India and 5.91 per cent of the North-East. It has a density of

- *Sex Ratio:* 972 females to 1,000 males (National figure: 933 females to 1,000 males)
- *Population below Poverty Line:* 33.9% (National Figure: 27.5%)
- *Literacy Rate (2007):* 72.1% (National Figure: 67.6%)
- *Per Capita income (in Rs.) (2006-07):* 2,4672 (National Figure: Rs. 29,901)
- *Net State Domestic Product (NSDP) (Rs. in crore) (2007-08):* 6,707 (National Figure: 38,11,441)
- *Per Capita NSDP (2007-08):* Rs. 26,636 (National Figure: Rs. 33,283)
- *Per Capita GSDP (2004-05):* Rs. 20,775 (National Figure: Rs. 25,944)
- *Birth Rate (2006):* 24.7 (National Figure: 23.1)
- *Death Rate (2006):* 8 (National Figure: 7.4)
- *Infant Mortality Rate (2007):* 56 (National Figure: 55)
- *No. of Villages (as per 2001 Census):* 6,026
- *No. of Towns (as per 2001 Census):* 16
- *State Bird:* Hill Myna
- *State Animal:* Clouded Leopard
- *State Flower:* Lady Slipper Orchid
- *Forest Area:* 8,510 sq km
- *Average Rainfall:* 1,200 cm per annum
- *Highest Point:* Shillong Peak (1965 m)
- *No. of Districts:* (07) East Garo Hills, East Khasi Hills, Jaintia Hills, Ri-Bhoi, South Garo Hills, West Garo Hills, West Khasi Hills.

Contd...

103 persons per square kilometre. The people are predominantly Christians.

Agriculture is one of the basic means of subsistence in this tribal state. This sector provides employment to about 65.89 per cent of the total working population. The state has a vast potential for developing horticulture due to agro-climatic variations, which offer much scope for cultivation of temperate, subtropical and tropical fruits and vegetables. The per capita Gross State Domestic Product (GSDP) in rupees 20,775 and the per capita Net State Domestic Product (NSDP) in 1999-2000 is rupees 11,678. Meghalaya ranks 24th in the human resource development index and 28th in the poverty index in India, according to the Human Development Report, 2001.

- *Major Towns:* Shillong, Jowai, Nongpoh, Tura, William Nagar, Baghmara, Nongstoin
- *Major Crops:* Rice, Maize, Jute, Rape seed, Mustard
- *Major Plantations:* Rubber, Coffee
- *Major Fruits, Vegetables & Spices:* Banana, Pineapple, Guava, Jackfruit, Cashew, Tomato, Brinjal, Potato, Sweet potato, Chilli, Cabbage, Turmeric, Ginger, Tapioca, Pear
- *Major Minerals:* Coal, Limestone, Petroleum, Granite, Sillimanite, Iron ore, Clay, Quartzite, Feldspar
- *Airport:* Umroi (Shillong)

Meghalaya is rich in natural resources. However, the growth of industries in the state is still in the rudimentary stage. Insurgency movements have sprang up in the state, claiming to represent the interests of the Hynniewtreps and the Achiks. In fact, there exists a divide between the Khasis and the Garos and this is well reflected in the politics of the state. In addition, Meghalaya's rugged mountains and its proximity with Bangladesh have been exploited by insurgents of various neighbouring states to set up transit camps and safe houses.

Area, Population and Headquarters of Districts

S.No.	District	Area (sq km)	Population	Headquarters
1.	East Khasi Hills	2,820	6,60,923	Shillong
2.	West Khasi Hills	5,247	2,96,049	Nongstoin
3.	Ri-Bhoi	2,448	1,92,790	Nongpoh
4.	Jaintia Hills	3,819	2,99,108	Jowai
5.	East Garo Hills	2,603	2,50,582	Williamnagar
6.	West Garo Hills	3,677	5,18,390	Tura
7.	South Garo Hills	1,887	1,00,980	Baghmara

[Based on Latest Official Data Available]

Meghalaya

M E G H A L A Y A

Outline Map

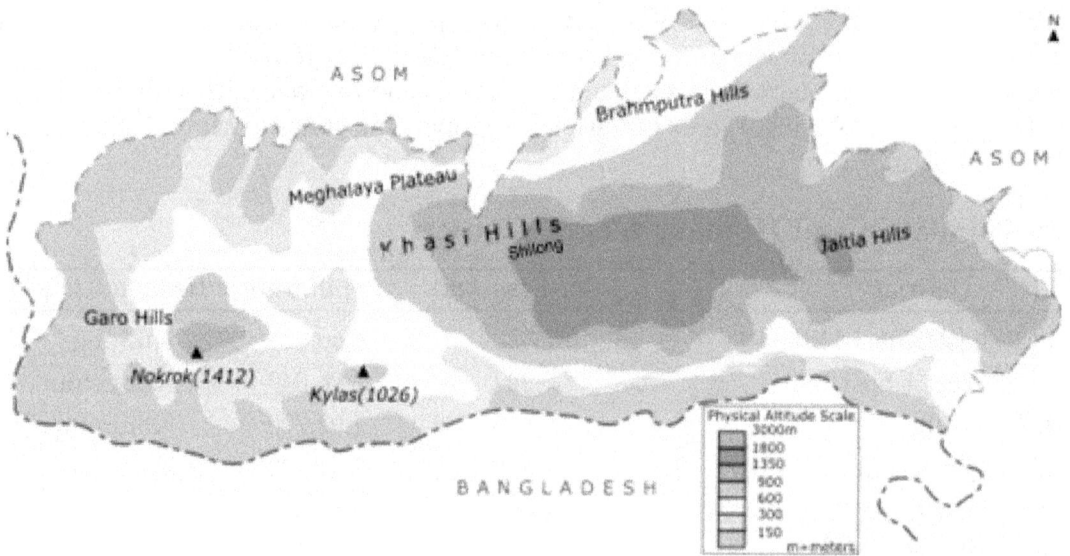

A S O M

Brahmputra Hills

A S O M

Meghalaya Plateau

Khasi Hills
Shilong

Jaitia Hills

Garo Hills

Nokrok(1412)

Kylas(1026)

Physical Altitude Scale
3000m
1800
1350
900
600
300
150
m=meters

B A N G L A D E S H

Geographical Map

Tourist Map

Districts of the State

$$\boxed{1}$$

Introduction

- -

Meghalaya is a small state in Northeastern India. The word "Meghalaya" literally means "The Abode of Clouds" in Sanskrit and other Indic languages. Meghalaya is a hilly strip in the eastern part of the country about 300-km-long (east-west) and 100-km-wide, with a total area of about 22,429 sq km. The population numbered 2,318,822 in 2001. The capital is Shillong, which has a population of 260,000.

About one-third of the state is forested. The Meghalaya subtropical forests ecoregion encompasses the state; its mountain forests are distinct from the lowland tropical forests to the north and south. The forests of Meghalaya are notable for their biodiversity of mammals, birds, and plants.

"Abode of the Clouds", this is Meghalaya, the destination which soothes the minds of weary travellers. Clouds are always found during the monsoon season nestling in the tropical forest valleys of Garo Hills or in the temperate pine forests of the Khasi and Jaintia Hills. Situated in the northeastern corner of India, Meghalaya is bounded by Assam in the north and east, and the plains of Bangladesh in the south and west. The state covers an area of 22,429 sq km with a population density of 102.8 per sq km.

The name describes the climatic phenomenon that brings torrential rain to its hills and forests, these same hills and mountains are responsible for this climatic experience as they force rain clouds coming in from the Bay of Bengal to move up — resulting in heavy rain. The Cherrapunji belt receives the highest rainfall in the world.

The higher ranges of the Khasi/Jaintia Hills enjoy a cool, bracing, temperate climate while the winters can be cold. The Garo Hills on the other hand, is at a lower altitude, and has tropical vegetation. The summer months in Tura, the administrative capital of Garo Hills, are warm and humid whereas winters are pleasant with a slight chill.

Meghalaya became the 21st State of the Indian Union, when it achieved full-fledged Statehood in 1972. Home to the Khasi, Garo, Jaintia and some lesser known tribes, Meghalaya boasts of a unique matrilineal lineage system practised by all the three major tribes with some degree of variation. Property is inherited by the women, and the youngest daughter is the heiress of the ancestral property in the Khasi/Jaintia tradition. The Garos have a slight variation, if the youngest daughter is found not worthy, the property may be given to any of the other daughters.

The Khasis and the Jaintias predominantly inhabit the districts of Eastern Meghalaya. They are known to be amongst the earliest ethnic group of settlers belonging to the Proto Austroloid, Mon-Khmer race. The Jaintia Kingdom was a known kingdom in bygone years with mention in the Ahom chronicles. The Garo Hills are predominantly inhabited by the Garos, or as they prefer to call themselves, the Achiks. Belonging to the Tibeto-Burman race, they are said to have migrated from Western China via Tibet.

Traditionally, the Khasis believe that their religion is God-given and not founded by man. It is Mono-Theistic based on the belief of One Supreme God who is called 'U Blei Nongthaw'. Respect is paid to ancestors as they are believed to keep a watch over the family. To the Khasi, life is God's greatest gift and he therefore has to account for it in the hereafter.

The Garos, like the Khasis, believe in One Supreme God called 'Rabuga' who is the Sustainer and Commander of the world. The spirits connected to the agricultural life are very important to them and are appeased only by sacrifices and never worshipped. However, many members of the Khasi, Garo and Jaintia communities profess Christianity which was introduced in the middle of the 19th century. Today, one can see churches, temples, mosques, gurudwaras and monasteries in Meghalaya. By nature, the people of Meghalaya are cheerful, hospitable, peaceful and social; something reflected in their music, dance and sports.

Historical Aspects

Meghalaya's history illustrates that Meghalaya had an eventful past. The history deals with the various incidents and illustrations that are witness to the rise of Meghalaya as an autonomous state. To begin with it can be said that the Meghalaya has been the homeland of a number of tribes, namely the Garo, Khasi and Jaintia. Till the 19th century, each of the three tribes had their independent rule in the different territories of state. But the arrival of the Britishers in the political scenario of India changed the plight of these tribal communities.

In the 19th century, Meghalaya became a counterpart of the British Empire in India. During the British Raj, the state was annexed under the British Empire. Further in 1935, it became a part of Assam. Yet, it enjoyed a semi-independent status due to the treaty that was signed between Meghalaya and the British Crown.

Moreover, after the Partition of Bengal in 1905, Meghalaya was made a part of the new province that was culled out of Bengal. In 1905, the state became a part of Eastern Bengal and Assam. Again, in 1912, when the partition was reversed, it was clubbed with Assam as a single territory. The history proves that although Meghalaya had been a part of Assam in 1947; yet it enjoyed an autonomous power within the territory of Assam. In fact, two districts of Assam were also put under the jurisdiction of Meghalaya in 1947.

The modern history maintains that with the Parliament passing the Northeastern Areas (Reorganisation) Act, 1971 conferred autonomy on Meghalaya. On January 21, 1972, it became an autonomous state, housing a Legislative Assembly of its own.

Khasi Kingdom

Originally, the Khasi Kingdom consisted of 25 independent Khasi chiefdoms in the mid-sixteenth century. Around 1815, the Khasi states came under British rule. There was very limited cultural relations between the Khasi states prior to British rule. Frequent wars between the states and villages, trading and raiding in the Brahmaputra and Sylhet valleys were the chief characteristics of the Khasi Kingdom.

The Khasi Kingdom became an integral part of the British Empire in 1765, when the Sylhet markets were considered a part of the economy of British. Around 1790, there were raids in the Khasi regions and finally the British fortified the foothills and stopped trading of the Khasi goods in the markets of Sylhet.

The mutual enmity between the Khasi Kingdom and the British ended when a road was put up in 1837 to connect Kolkata with the Brahmaputra Valley across the state of Nongkhaw. The antagonism officially ended with all the Khasi states and the British signing some treaties in 1862. These treaties allowed the Khasis autonomy and freedom from paying taxes to the British.

The Khasi Kingdom of Meghalaya exhibited a great deal of cultural change after Shillong was declared the capital of Assam. These changes include decreasing popularity of traditional culture, increase in wealth, the acceptance of intermarriage and showing progress in education.

An autonomous tribal region was established in 1947, which was answerable to the governor of Assam, who functioned like an agent of Indian President. Nevertheless, the state system of the native Khasis remained undisturbed, that is, the different functionaries of their state system were not altered. Currently, the Khasis form a predominant tribe in Meghalaya, which is their own state.

Garo Kingdom

The Garo Kingdom of Meghalaya originated from Tibet, from where they went to the present Cooch Behar and then to Dhubri. Then they moved on to Jogighopa, present Kamakhya Hills or Kamagre, along the Brahmaputra valley and finally spread in

Goalpara or the Habraghat Pargana. The Garos prospered in the Habraghat Pargana neighbourhood. The first Garo Kingdom was created here and its first Ruling Prince was Abrasen. He had his capital and palace at Sambol Ading, a lonely hill close to the Dakaitdol village near the Goalpara town.

In the medieval period, the kingdom of the Garos in the hills were at hostility with the Zamindars of the estates, located on the plains near the foot the hills. Some of the important estates are Bijini in the Eastern Duars, Kalimalupara, Karaibari, Habraghat and Mechpara in Rongpur and Sherput and Susang in Mymensing in Bengal. The Garos still belonged to a few small Nokmaships, while the estates were fewer in number and larger in area.

In the later part of the 18th century, the British East India Company started establishing contact with the Garos, after acquiring the Diwani of Bengal from the Mughal Emperor. The British won overall the semi-independent estates that bordered the Garo Hills. But the internal administration of the estates was not disturbed. They were given the responsibility of keeping the power of the Garos in check, as in the time of the Mughals. Hence, the enmity between the Garos and the zamindars grew stronger and the British had to finally intervene. Finally, this chaos ended when the Garo Hills were annexed in 1873. The first Deputy Commissioner of Garo Hills District was Williamson. In 1979, it was divided into two districts, that is, West Garo Hills and East Garo Hills.

Jaintia Kingdom

The district of Jaintia Hills is an integral part of the Jaintia Kingdom, which is otherwise called Sutnga Kingdom. In the society of Jaintia Kingdom the villages that were located in a particular region formed a single political unit. The villages of this political unit were termed 'elakas'. The chief of each area (elaka) was termed Doloi. He was elected from the senior population and could be expelled for his inefficiency or immorality.

A collection of many elakas constituted a Jaintia Syiemship or a kingship. The chief of the Kingdom of Jaintias was the Raja. The Dolois represented their respective people in the Raja's durbar. This old governmental setup excepting the Raja still exists. The respective durbars checked the power of the Doloi and the Raja. The durbar, in turn, checked the government power. Initially, Jaintia Hills was called 'Ka Ri Khadar Doloi' or ' the land of the twelve tribal chiefs'. Initially, in Jaintia Hills there were twelve Dolois, who ruled twelve separate elakas.

The British abolished the Syiem office in the Jaintia Kingdom though they kept the concepts of Doloi and village headman or Waheh Chnong unchanged. The British brought the entire Jaintia Hills and a few other Khasi Hills villages under one administrative system. These regions were directly ruled by the British.

In 1972, after Meghalaya was declared a separate state, the Jaintia Hills and the Khasi Hills were put under the same administrative unit. In 1952, the concept of district council was introduced in these hilly regions. Consequently, both Jaintia Hills and Khasi were given separate district councils, though they remained parts of the same state.

British Rule

The current state of Meghalaya primarily consisted of the Khasi Kingdom, the Garo Kingdom and the Jaintia Kingdom before the advent of the British East India Company. The nature of British rule in each of these crucial parts is described below.

The British rule made the Khasi Kingdom an integral part of their empire in 1765 by considering the Sylhet markets as an integral part of the Company's economy. The raids in the Khasi localities around 1790 finally led the British to fortify the foothills and did not allow further trading of Khasi goods at the Sylhet markets.

The antagonism between the Khasis and the British came to an end with the construction of a road in 1837 in Nongkhaw. The hostility finally ended when the Khasi states and the British signed a few treaties in 1862. These treaties made the Khasis autonomous and free from paying taxes to the Company.

The British rule won overall the semi-independent estates bordering the Garo Hills. But the British did not alter the internal administration of the estates. The zamindars were supposed to check the power of the Garos, as during the rule of the Mughals. Hence, the hostility between the Garos and the zamindars became even stronger. Finally, the British annexed the Garo Hills in the year 1873.

The British rule at Meghalaya abolished the Syiem office in the Jaintia Kingdom but they did not modify or eradicate the posts of Doloi and village headman or Waheh Chnong. They put the whole Jaintia Hills and a few other Khasi Hills villages under the same administrative system. The British directly governed these regions.

Post Independence

On 2nd April 1970, Meghalaya became an autonomous state and on 21st January 1972, it was declared a full-fledged state with capital at Shillong. It stands at a height of 1,496 metres above sea level. It remained the capital of Assam from 1874 to 1972. Shillong owes its name from its creator named Shyllong. The Jaintias, the Khasis and the Garos form the majority of the population of the state.

All the actions of the State Government follow the laws formed by the Parliament after independence. The Union has the right to give directions to the State Government as and when necessary. The basic structure of post-independent is given below:

Council of Ministers: In post-independent Meghalaya, the council of ministers execute the functions of the State Government. The Chief Minister is the head of the council. The governor appoints the Chief Minister and the rest of the ministers. The council of ministers is answerable to the state legislative assembly.

It is made up of ministers, comprising of the Cabinet members and the state ministers. The Cabinet Ministers finalise the government policies. When required, the rest of the ministers have to attend Cabinet meetings.

The governor carries out all the executive functions. He is the constitutional head of the State Government. All the actions of the governor are based on the decision of the ministers. In case of a few exceptions, he can exercise his authority.

Advocate General is the topmost State Government legal adviser. His advise is often taken in case of interpretation of laws, other rules and the Constitution. He is present in the supreme court in case of important cases as a representative of the government. He can actively participate in the Legislative Assembly proceedings.

Geographical Aspects

Geographically, the state of Meghalaya is also known as the "Meghalaya Plateau". It consists mainly of archean rock formations. These rock formations contain rich deposits of valuable minerals like coal, limestone, uranium, sillimanite, etc. It has many rivers. Most of these are rainfed and are therefore seasonal. The important rivers in the Garo Hills Region are Daring, Sanda, Bandra, Bhogai, Dareng and Simsang, Nitai and the Bhupai. In the central and eastern section of the plateau the important rivers are Umkhri, Digaru, Umiam, Kynchiang (Jadukata), Mawpa, Umiew or Barapani, Myngot and Myntdu. In the southern Khasi Hills Region, these rivers have created deep gorges and some of the most beautiful waterfalls.

The elevation of the plateau ranges between 150 m to 1961 m. The central part of the plateau comprising the Khasi Hills has the highest elevations, followed by the eastern section comprising the Jaintia Hills Region. The highest point in Meghalaya is Shillong Peak, which is also a prominent IAF station in the Khasi Hills overlooking the city of Shillong. It has an altitude of 1,961 m. The Garo Hills Region in the western section of the plateau is nearly plain. The highest point in the Garo Hills is the Nokrek Peak with an altitude of 1,515 m.

Flora and Fauna

As per the state of Forest Report 2003, published by the Forest Survey of India, Meghalaya has a forest cover of 9,496 sq km, which is 42.34 per cent of the total geographical area of the state. The Meghalayan subtropical forests have been considered among the richest botanical habitats of Asia. These forests receive abundant rainfall and support a vast variety of floral and faunal biodiversity. A small portion of the forest area is under what is known as "sacred groves". These are small pockets of ancient forest that have been preserved by the communities for hundreds of years due to religious and cultural beliefs.

These forests are reserved for religious rituals and generally remain protected from any exploitation. These sacred groves harbour many rare plant and animal species. The Nokrek biosphere reserve and the Balaphakram National Park, both in the West Garo Hills are considered to be the most biodiversity rich sites in the state. In addition, Meghalaya has three Wildlife Sanctuaries. These are the Nongkhyllem Wildlife Sanctuary, the Siju Sanctuary and the Bhagmara Sanctuary, which is also the home of the insect eating pitcher plant *Nepenthes khasiana*.

Due to the diverse climatic and topographic conditions, Meghalayan forests support a vast floral diversity, including a large variety of Parasites and Epiphytes, Succulent plants and shrubs. Two of the most important tree varieties include: Shorea robusta or Sal and the Tectona grandis or teak. The state is also the home to a large variety of fruits, vegetables, spices and medicinal plants. Meghalaya is also famous for its large variety of orchids – nearly 325 of them. Of these the largest variety is found in Mawsmai, Mawmluh and Sohrarim forests in the Khasi Hills.

It also has a large variety of mammals, birds, reptiles and insects. The important mammal species include elephants, bear, civets, mongooses, weasels, rodents, gaur, wild buffalo, deer, wild boar and a number of primates. Meghalaya also has a large variety of bats. The limestone caves such as the Siju cave are home to some of the rarest bat species.

The prominent bird species include the Magpie-Robin, the Red-vented Bulbul, the Hill Myna is usually found in pairs or in flocks in the hill forests the Large Pied Hornbill and the Great Indian, which is the largest bird in state. Other birds include the Peacock Pheasant, the Large Indian Parakeet, the Common Green Pigeon and the Blue Jay. It is also home to over 250 species of butterflies, nearly a quarter of all the species found in India.

The common reptile varieties in Meghalaya are lizards, crocodiles and tortoises. It also has a number of snakes including the python, the Copperhead, the Green Tree Racer, the Indian Cobra the King Cobra, the Coral Snake and Vipers.

Lakes

Ward's lake is synonymous to Shillong as the Qutub Minar is to Delhi and Tulips are to Holland. Situated in the heart of the city it is an artificial lake crafted with beauty in those laid-back days of the British Raj. Thadlaskein Lake, 56 km from Shillong, is a beautiful spot for outing, boating and picnics. Umhang Lake, another tourist spot, is popular among tourists for picnics and weekend visits. The facilities of water sports are also available at the lake site: from kayaking and water skiing for the adventurous to water cycling and simple boating for the less brave.

Districts

Meghalaya currently has 7 districts. These are: East Garo Hills, East Khasi Hills, Jaintia Hills, Ri-Bhoi, South Garo Hills, West Garo Hills and West Khasi Hills.

The *East Garo Hills District* was formed in 1976 and has a population of 250,582 as per the 2001 census. It covers an area of 2,603 square kilometres. The District Headquarters are located at Williamnagar, earlier known as Simsangiri.

The *East Khasi Hills District* was carved out of the Khasi Hills on 28 October 1976. The district covers an area of 2,820 square kilometres and has a population of 660,923 as per the 2001 census. The headquarters of East Khasi Hills are located in Shillong.

The *Jaintia Hills District* was created on 22nd February 1972. It has a total geographical area of 3,819 square kilometres and a population of 299,108 as per the 2001 census. The district headquarters are located at Jowai. Jaintia Hills District is the largest producer of coal in the state. Coal mines can be seen all over the district.

The *Ri-Bhoi District* was formed by further division of East Khasi Hills District on 4th June 1992. It has an area of 2,448 square kilometres. The total population of the district was 1,92,790 as per the 2001 census. The district headquarters are located at Nongpoh. It has a hilly terrain and a large part of the area is covered with forests. The Ri-Bhoi District is famous for its pineapples and is the largest producer of pineapples in the state.

The *South Garo Hills District* came into existence on 18th June 1992 after the division of the West Garo Hills District. The total geographical area of the district is 1,857 square kilometres. As per the 2001 census the district has a population of 1,00,980. The district headquarters are located at Baghmara.

The *West Garo Hills District* lies in the western part of the state and covers a geographical area of 3,677 square kilometres. The population of the district is 5,18,390 as per the 2001 census. The district headquarters are located at Tura.

The *West Khasi Hills District* is the largest district in the state with a geographical area of 5,247 square kilometres. The district was carved out of Khasi Hills District on 28th October 1976. The district headquarters are located at Nongstoin.

Climate

The climate of Meghalaya is moderate but humid. With average annual rainfall as high as 1,200 cm in some areas, it is the wettest state of India. The western part of the plateau, comprising the Garo Hills Region with lower elevations, experiences high temperatures for most of the year. The Shillong area, with the highest elevations, experiences generally low temperatures. The maximum temperature in this region rarely goes beyond 28 degrees, whereas winters temperatures of subzero degrees are common. The town of Cherrapunji in the Khasi Hills south of capital Shillong holds the world record for most rain in a calendar month, while the village of Mawsynram, near town of Cherrapunji, holds the distinction of seeing the heaviest yearly rains. Best time to visit Meghalaya is during the months of March to July. Originally the British and Assam Tea Estate owners would shift here during the summer months to escape the heat of the Indian Plains.

Social Aspects

The original inhabitants of this state are Khasis, Jaintias and Garos who are a predominantly tribal lot. A common cultural tradition of all the tribes of Meghalaya is the matriarchal law of inheritance by which, custody to property and succession of family position runs through the female line, passing from the mother to the youngest daughter, instead of the male line as is common elsewhere in the country.

Animism (the worship of nature deities and other spirits), Hinduism, and Christianity are the main religions. There is also a small minority of Muslims and even smaller groups of Buddhists and Sikhs. Traditional customs are maintained, and religious festivals include varied forms of dance, an important element in the local culture. Khasi and Garo are the principal languages; together with Jaintia and English they are also official languages.

The area is rich in tribal culture and folklore. Drinking and dancing to the accompaniment of music from buffalo horn singas, bamboo flutes, and drums are integral parts of religious ceremonies and social functions. Marriages are exogamous. The advent of Christianity in the mid-19th century, along with its strict morality, has disrupted many of the tribal and communal institutions.

Festivals vary according to the region and tribe. Festivals, apart from those of the Christian faith, are held annually. This is a time when the ancestral spirits are appeased, following sowing and harvesting. Ka Pomblang Nongkrem, or the Nongkrem dance, is one of the most important Khasi festivals. Shad Sukmynsiem is another important festival of the Khasis. Behdiengkhlam, the most significant festival of the Jaintias is celebrated in July. Wangala, is the prominent festival of the Garos and is dedicated to the Sun God.

People

The Khasi, Jaintia, Bhoi, War collectively known as the Hynniewtrep people predominantly inhabit the districts of East Meghalaya, also known to be one of the earliest ethnic groups of settlers in the Indian subcontinent, belonging to the Proto Austroloid Monkhmer race.

The Garo Hills is predominantly inhabited by the Garos, belonging to the Bodo family of the Tibeto-Burman race, said to have migrated from Tibet. The Garos prefer to call themselves as Achiks and the land they inhabit as the Achik-land.

The Khasi-Pnars: The Khasis inhabit the eastern part of Meghalaya, in the Khasi and Jaintia Hills. Khasis residing in Jaintia Hills are now better known as Jaintias. They are also called Pnars. The Khasis occupying the northern lowlands and foothills are generally called Bhois. Those who live in the southern tracts are termed Wars. Again among the Wars, those living in the Khasi Hills are called War-Khasis and those in the Jaintia Hills, War-Pnars or War-Jaintias. In the Jaintia Hills we have Khyrwangs, Labangs, Nangphylluts, Nangtungs in the northeastern part and in the east. In the Khasi Hills the Lyngngams live in the northwestern part. But all of them claim to have descended from the 'Ki Hynniew Trep' and are now known by the generic name of Khasi-Pnars or simply Khasis. They have the same traditions, customs and usage with a little variation owing to geographical divisions.

Dress: The traditional Khasi male dress is 'Jymphong' or a longish sleeveless coat without collar, fastened by thongs in front. Now, the Khasis have adopted the western dress. On ceremonial occasions, they appear in 'Jymphong' and dhoti with an ornamental waistband. The Khasi traditional female dress is rather elaborate with several pieces of cloth, giving the body a cylindrical shape. On ceremonial occasions, they wear a crown of silver or gold on the head. A spike or peak is fixed to the back of the crown, corresponding to the feathers worn by the menfolk.

Food and Drinks: The staple food of Khasis is rice. They also take fish and meat. Like the other tribes in the North-East, the Khasis also ferment rice-beer, and make spirit out of rice or millets by distillation. Use of rice-beer is a must for every ceremonial and religious occasion.

Social Structure: The Khasis, the Jaintias and the Garos have a matrilineal society. Descent is traced through the mother, but the father plays an important role in the material and mental life of the family. While, writing on the Khasi and the Jaintia people, David Roy observed, "a man is the defender of the woman, but the woman is the keeper of his trust". No better description of Meghalayan matrilineal society could perhaps be possible. In the Khasi society, the woman looks after home and hearth, the man finds the means to support the family, and the maternal uncle settles all social and religious matters. Earlier in the conservative Jaintia non-Christian families, however, the father only visits the family in the night and is not responsible for the maintenance of the family.

Inheritance: Khasis follow a matrilineal system of inheritance. In the Khasi society, it is only the youngest daughter or 'Ka Khadduh' who is eligible to inherit the ancestral property. If 'Ka Khadduh' dies without any daughter surviving her, her next elder sister inherits the ancestral property, and after her, the youngest daughter of that sister. Failing all daughters and their female issues, the property goes back to the mother's sister, mother's sister's daughter and so on.

The Ka Khadduh's property is actually the ancestral property and so if she wants to dispose it of she must obtain consent and approval of the uncles and brothers.

Among the War-Khasis, however, property passes to the children, male or female, in equal shares but among the War-Jaintias, only the female children get the inheritance.

Marriage: Marriage within a clan is a taboo. Rings or betel-nut bags are exchanged between the bride and the bridegroom to complete the union. In the Christian families, however, marriage is purely a civil contract.

Religion: The Khasis are now mostly Christians. But before that, they believed in a Supreme Being, The Creator – U Blei Nongthaw and under Him, there were several deities of water and of mountains and also of other natural objects.

The Garos: The virile and vibrant ethnic people who reside in the Garo Hills are known as the Garos. The *Garo* word has been coined after the name of a small group of the Garos residing in the central part of the southern hills. Besides the Garo Hills, there are Garo settlements in the plains of Assam and Bangladesh.

The Garos call themselves *Achik-mande.* In the Garo language *Achik* means Hills and *mande*, Man. So, *Achik-mande* means the *hills people.*

Dress: The Garo women used to wear a piece of cloth around their waists and puts on a blouse or vest. The men usually wear, in addition to cloth, a turban. On all festive occasions, the Garos, irrespective of sex, wear head dresses with rows of beads stuck with feathers of hornbill. Males and females – both wear bangles and earrings. Educated and well-to-do Garos in the towns wear western dress.

Food and Drink: The Garos have no inhibitions about food. Their chief meals consist of rice with onions, capsicum and salt thrice a day. Practically all types of animal foods are taken. Drinks are almost an everyday affair. The liquor is not distilled, but prepared by brewing food grains.

Birth, Marriage and Death: Birth is a matter of joy not only to the family, but also to the community. Till death the newborn baby belongs to the mother's family, irrespective of sex, even after marriage. Lineage is always matrilineal like the Khasis and the Jaintias. Except amongst the Nayars in Kerala, this system is not found anywhere in the country. It is unique among the Meghalayans in the North-East.

Marriage within the clan is completely prohibited and severely punishable. Marriage is however, arranged with the formal sanction of the parents.

Death of a person is not only a loss to the family, but is also mourned by the entire community. Elaborate rituals are held. Before embracing Christianity, they used to cremate the dead body, in the presence of all relations of the deceased. Nowadays, according to Christian practice, the body is buried.

Bachelors' Dormitories: Till now, the institution of Bachelors' Dormitories which is gradually disappearing amongst the tribes of Northeastern Region, are found in the Garo villages. In such dormitories, young people stay and live together till they are married. They receive various training in the dormitories like protection of crops, construction of roads, organising festivals, sports and ceremonies.

Meghalaya Tribes: There are many races of people in the state, mainly the region is inhabited by tribes, the tribes from Mizoram, tribes from Nagaland and other tribes that have migrated from the neighbouring states.

Taking Meghalaya tribes into account, they are broadly classified into the Hynniewtrep people and the Garos.

The Hynniewtrep Tribe: Known to be the earliest ethnic group of settlers in the Indian subcontinent, the Hynniewtrep inhabit the districts of east Meghalaya. The Hynniewtrep are composed of the tribes of Khasi, Bhoi and War and they belong to the Proto Austroloid Monkhmer race. The three subtribes belong to the group Khasi but are known according to the place they belong to. The Khasis that inhabit along the southern tracts are known as War and those living in the Khasi Hills are known as War-Khasis and in the Jaintia Hills as War-Pnars and War-Jaintias. The Khasis settling in the northern lowlands and foothills are known as Bhois. And lastly the Khasis who inhabit the eastern part of Meghalaya, i.e., the Khasi Hills and the Jaintia Hills are known as Jaintias or Pnars. All of them claim to be the descendants of the "Ki Hynniew Trep" or commonly known as Khasi-Pnars or Khasis. They collectively have the same traditions and customs.

Dress: Though they have a traditional dress by the name 'Jymphong', they usually wear it during ceremonial celebrations. These male dresses are longish sleeveless coat without collar, fastened by thongs in front. During the occasions, they appear in Jymphong and Dhoti (long cotton cloth) with an ornamental waistband. Women dresses are elaborate with several pieces of clothes, giving the body a cylindrical look.

Food and Drinks: The Khasis staple food is rice. Fish and meat is also eaten in these areas. During every celebration, rice beer is a must.

Social Structure: The tribes in these places have a peculiar feature. The Khasis, the Jaintias and the Garos have a matrilineal society. The name and the property of descendant is traced through the mother. In the Khasi society, it is only the youngest daughter or 'Ka Khadduh' who is eligible to inherit the ancestral property.

Marriage: Marriage within a clan is prohibited and regarded as a taboo. During the marriage, they have a tradition to exchanged rings or betel-nut bags between the bride and the bridegroom to complete the union. In the Christian families, however, marriage is purely a civil contract.

Religion: The religion of the people is mostly Christians. Before Christianity came, they believed in 'The Creator' — U Blei Nongthaw and under 'Him', there were several deities of water, of mountains and also of other natural objects.

Demographics

Tribal people make up the majority of Meghalaya's population. The Khasis are the largest group, followed by the Garos. These were among those known to the British as "hill tribes". Other groups include the Jaintias, the Koch and the Hajong, Dimasa, Hmar, Kuki, Lakhar, Mikir, Rabha, Nepali, etc.

Meghalaya is one of three states in India to have a Christian majority with 70.3 per cent of the population practising Christianity; the other two (Nagaland and Mizoram) are also in the North-East of India. Hinduism is the next sizeable faith in the region with 13.3 per cent of the population practising it. A sizeable minority, 11.5 per cent of the population follows an ancient Animist philosophy (classified as other on the census). Muslims make up 4.3 per cent of the population as well.

As per the census of India 2001, the sex ratio in the state was 972 females per thousand males which was much better than the national average of 933. It has grown steadily from a 1981 level of 954. Traditionally the sex ratio in the rural areas has been higher than that in the urban areas. However, as per the census figures for 2001, the urban sex ratio of 985 was higher than the rural sex ratio of 972. This has often been attributed to the belief that, unlike most other parts of India, there is no special preference for a male child in Meghalaya.

Costumes

Nestled in the peaceful hills of the northeastern part of India, the beautiful state of Meghalaya houses the three famous hill tribes of India, namely, the Khasi, Jaintias and Garos.

It is interesting to note that the Garos are the most skilled weavers of the region. Probably, every family earns their livelihood through weaving.

Indeed, the traditional costume for women, called *Jainsen*, is an unstitched garment wrapped around to cover the body. It is woven from mulberry silk cultivated in the local region. The crowning glory of the costume of Meghalaya is the Endi silk shawl. Sonidan is the hub of Endi or Errandi silk-production in Meghalaya. The hill communities rear Philosamia ricini, the silkworm, feeding on castor leaves. These nature's artists, the silkworms produce rich protein fibre and accordingly spin round the open-ended cocoon. It is from this fibre that the coveted silk is generated. Endi silk is the product of the domesticated silkworm, Philosamia ricini that feeds mainly on castor leaves. Sericulture is a popular small-scale industry of Meghalaya. The silk-weavers use the Endi silk threads to weave splendid shawls, that are not only warmth-retentive or supple, but assets to boast of. These shawls are invested with natural soothing shades of creme, white, brown, beige and gold. They are favourites of not only the local tribal, but also of any fashion-addict of India.

The weaver-ace Garos, cater to different forms of costume, in keeping with the air of the ambience they are residing in. In the remote areas of Garo Hill villages, the women drapes eking, a short cloth round the waist, while the men put in a loincloth.

But the Garo women, go for a longer version of cotton attire in the crowded zones. A Garo woman dons a blouse, and wears a "Lungi" like mantle of unstitched cloth called

Dakmanda, by fastening it round the waist. The Dakmanda is an example of hand-woven cotton fabric. Its speciality is the six to ten inch broad borders embellished with attractive motifs or floral patterns.

The Khasi sect comprising 50 per cent of the total population in the state, emits a discrete aura, owing to the costume they wear. The traditional costume of the Khasi man in Meghalaya is an unstitched lower apparel, akin to Dhoti, completed by a jacket and headgear or turban. However, in the recent times, men display themselves in traditional garments only on social festivals and ceremonies, to keep the flame of tradition, glowing.

Western concept of dressing has entered the realms of costume-design in Meghalaya. However, the element of tradition is much alive in the costume of the Khasi women. It entails a Jainsen, concealing till the ankles, which is topped-off by a blouse. Above these garments, she ties the edges of tap-moh khlieh, a chequered cotton shawl, round her neck or pins at the shoulders, to serve somewhat like an apron.

During occasions, Ka Jainsem Dhara, a long piece of Assam muga silk, is added to this attire, so as to assume a radiant appearance. But the base-material for these costumes are mill-manufactured, as the Kashis are not so much attached with weaving today. Another srtip of woollen cloth called *Jainkup*, is used by the senior women. Jainkup is not so much in vogue among the younger generation. Khasi women, have the affordability to deck themselves in ornaments of pure gold and silver, made by local jewellery-smiths. The costume of the male members of the Jaintia tribe bears similarities with that of the Khasi men.

However, the costume of the Jaintia women in Meghalaya is a little different from the other groups. A Jaintia woman, envelops her head with a cloth-piece with checks called "Kyrshah", at the times of harvest-work in the field. She covers herself from the shoulders to the ankles, with a velvet blouse, along with a sarong called *Thoh Khyrwang* wrapped round her waist. She also ties round her shoulders an Assam muga silk cloth, flowing down to the ankles. There exists a practice among Jaintia men and women, to present themselves in gaudy, resplendent costumes, on festive and gay occasions.

Dressing without the embellishments of ornaments, is lustreless for Jaintia women. They adorn themselves with earrings and other ornaments of gold and silver. It is a custom to dress in head ornaments, like a silver circlet worn round the head as a forehead decoration. Both the Khasis and the Jayantis, flaunt themselves in a pure gold pendant known as *Kynjri Ksiar*. The elegance and grace inherent to the ethnic costumes of Meghalaya complements the scenic beauty of the picturesque landscape of Meghalaya.

Economic Aspects

Meghalaya's economy is predominantly an agrarian-based economy. Agriculture and allied activities engage nearly two-thirds of the total workforce in Meghalaya. However, the contribution of this sector to the state's NSDP is only about one-third. Agriculture in the state is characterised by low productivity and unsustainable farm practices, giving rise to a high incidence of rural poverty. As a result, despite the large percentage of population engaged in agriculture, the state is still dependent upon imports from other states for most food items such as meat, eggs, food grains, etc. Infrastructural constraints have also prevented the economy of the state from growing at a pace commensurate with that of the rest of the country.

Meghalaya is considered to have a rich base of natural resources. These include minerals such coal, limestone, sillimanite, Kaolin and granite among others. The state also has a large forest cover, rich biodiversity and numerous water bodies. The low level of industrialisation and the relatively poor infrastructure base in the state acts as an impediment to the exploitation of these natural resources in the interest of the state's economy. However, in recent years two large cement manufacturing plants with production capacity more than 900 MTD have come up in Jaintia Hills District and several more are in pipeline to utilise the rich deposit of very high quality limestone available in this district. Meghalaya also has much natural beauty and the State Government has been trying to exploit this for promoting tourism in the state. However, infrastructural constraints and security concerns have hampered the growth of tourism in the state.

Incidence of Poverty

Planning Commission, the apex planning body under the Government of India, has estimated the percentage of population below poverty line in Meghalaya at nearly one-third the total population of the state in 2000. The incidence of poverty in rural areas at about 55 per cent is almost double the percentage of poverty in the urban areas.

Agriculture

Nearly 10 per cent of the total geographical area of Meghalaya is under cultivation. Agriculture in the state is characterised by limited use of modern techniques and low productivity. As a result, despite the vast majority of the population engaged in agriculture, the contribution of agricultural production to the state's GDP is low and most of the population engaged in agriculture remains poor. A substantial portion of the cultivated area is under the traditional shifting agriculture known locally as "Jhum" cultivation.

Food grains are the most important crop in Meghalaya. These are grown in over 1,330 sq km, nearly 60 per cent of the state's cultivated area. The production of food grains is over 230 thousand tonnes. Rice is the dominant food grain crop accounting for over 80 per cent of the food grain production in the state. Other important food grain crops are maize, wheat and a few other cereals and pulses.

Oilseeds such as rape and mustard, linseed, soya bean, castor and sesame are grown on nearly 100 sq km. Rape and mustard are the most important oilseeds accounting for well over two-thirds of the oilseed production of nearly 6.5 thousand tonnes.

Fibre crops such as cotton, jute and mesta had traditionally been among the only cash crops in Meghalaya, grown almost exclusively in Garo Hills. These have been losing popularity in recent years as indicated by their declining yield and area under cultivation.

Climatic conditions in Meghalaya also permit a large variety of horticulture crops including fruits, vegetables, flowers, spices and medicinal plants. These are considered to be higher value crops but traditional values and food security concerns have prevented farmers at large from embracing these crops.

The important fruits currently grown in the state include citrus fruits, pineapple, papaya, banana, etc. The mandarin orange grown in Meghalaya is considered to be of very high quality. In addition to this, a large variety of vegetables are grown in the state including cauliflower, cabbage and radish.

Areca nut plantations can be seen all over the state, especially around the road from Guwahati to Shillong. Other plantation crops like tea, coffee and cashew have been introduced lately and are becoming popular. A large variety of spices, flowers, medicinal plants and mushrooms are also grown in the state.

Industries

Compared to agriculture, this aspect of the economy of Meghalaya is less developed. In spite of the fact that Meghalaya has not been untouched by the influence of industrialisation; yet the development of the industries is not up to the mark.

But, it goes without mention that Meghalaya is rich in minerals. Some of the important minerals that support the economy are:

- Limestone,
- Coal,
- Granite,
- Silimanite, etc.

Moreover, in recent times, real estate and tourism is supporting the economy of Meghalaya. With the arrival of foreign tourists and NRIs tourism, as well as real estate has taken a gigantic leap; thus, influencing the economy of the land.

Thus, it is evident that the state economy largely depends on agriculture, industries, tourism and the real estate: although, agriculture is the predominating faculty in the economy of Meghalaya.

Transport

The partition of the country has created severe infrastructure constraints for the Northeastern Region, with merely 2 per cent of the perimeter of the region adjoining the rest of the country. A narrow strip of land, often called the Siliguri Corridor, or the

Chicken's Neck connects the region with the state of West Bengal. Meghalaya is a land locked state with a large number of small settlements in remote areas. Road is the only means of transport within the state. While the capital Shillong is relatively well connected, road connectivity in most other parts of the state is relatively poor. A significant portion of the roads in the state are still unmetalled. Most of the arrivals into the Meghalaya take place through Guwahati in neighbouring Assam, which is nearly 103 km away. Assam has a major railhead as well as an airport with regular train and air services to the rest of the country. The state still has a large number of old timber bridges.

Meghalaya does not have any railhead. It has a small airport at Umroi, about 40 km from Shillong on the Guwahati-Shillong highway. The small size of the airport does not allow the operations of large aircraft and only small aircraft operate from Kolkata and Agartala, capital of the neighbouring state of Tripura.

Political Aspects

State Government

Like most other states in India, Meghalaya has a unicameral legislature. The ceremonial head of the state is the Governor appointed by the Government of India. However, the real executive powers are held by the Chief Minister.

Meghalaya does not have a high court of its own. The Guwahati High Court has jurisdiction in Meghalaya. A Circuit Bench of the Guwahati High Court has been functioning at Shillong since 1974.

Autonomous District Councils

In order to provide a local self governance machinery to the rural population of the country, provisions were made in the Constitution of India and accordingly the Panchayati Raj institutions were set up. However, on account of the distinct customs and traditions prevailing in erstwhile state of Assam (of which Meghalaya and most of the North-East was a part), it was felt necessary to have a separate political and administrative structure in Assam. Moreover, some of the tribal communities in the region also had their own traditional political systems and it was felt that Panchayati Raj institutions may come into conflict with these traditional systems.

To provide a simple and inexpensive form of local self governance to the tribal population, the Sixth Schedule was appended to the Constitution on the recommendations of a subcommittee formed under the leadership of Gopinath Bordoloi. The Sixth Schedule provided for the Constitution of Autonomous District Councils (ADCs) in certain rural areas of the North-East including some areas that now fall in Meghalaya. The Sixth Schedule carries detailed provisions for the Constitution and management of Autonomous District Councils (ADCs) and laid down the powers of the ADCs. At present Meghalaya has three ADCs, viz., Khasi Hills Autonomous District Council, Garo Hills Autonomous District Council and the Jaintia Hills Autonomous District Council.

Traditional Political Institutions

All the three major ethnic tribal groups, namely, the Khasis, Jaintias and the Garos also have their own traditional political institutions that have existed for hundreds of years. These political institutions were fairly well developed and functioned at various tiers, such as the village level, clan level and state level. In the traditional political system of the Khasis, each clan had its own council known as the "Durbar Kur", which was presided over by the clan headman. The council or the durbar managed the internal affairs of the clan. Similarly, every village had a local assembly known as the Durbar Shnong, i.e., village durbar or council, which was presided over by the village headman. These councils or durbars played an administrative role in issues of common interest, such as sanitation, water supply, health, roads, education and conflict resolution. However, the inter-village issues were dealt with through a political unit comprising adjacent Khasi villages. This political unit was known as the Raid. The Raid had its own council the Raid Durbar, which was presided over by the elected headman known as Basans, Lyngdohs or Sirdars. Above the Raid was a supreme political authority known as the Syiemship. The Syiemship was the congregation of several raids and was headed by an elected chief known as the "Syiem" (or the King). The Syiem ruled the Khasi state through the State Assembly, known as the Durbar Hima. Most of the elections were through adult male suffrage.

The Jaintias also had a three tier political system somewhat similar to the Khasis. The supreme political authority was the Syiem. The second tier of this structure was the congregation of Jaintia villages known as Raids. These were headed by "Dolois", who were responsible for performing the executive, magisterial, religious and ceremonial functions at the Raid level. At the lowest level were the village headmen. Each administrative tier had its own councils or durbars. Most elections were through adult male suffrage.

In the traditional political system of the Garos a group of Garo villages in the traditional political system of the Garos a group of Garo villages comprised the Akhing. The Akhing functioned under the supervision of the Nokmas, which was perhaps the only political and administrative authority in the political institution of the Garos. The Nokma performed both judicial and legislative functions. The Nokmas also congregated to address inter-Aching issues. There were no well-organised councils or durbars among the Garos.

Tourism Aspects

Earlier, foreign tourists required special permits to enter the areas that now constitute the state of Meghalaya. However, the restrictions were removed in 1955. Today it is considered to be one of the most picturesque states in the country. It has enough tourism content to attract tourists of many different interests.

Tourism Content

Meghalaya has some of the thickest surviving forests in the country and therefore constitutes one of the most important ecotourism circuits in the country today. The subtropical forests support a vast variety of flora and fauna. It has 2 National Parks and 3 Wildlife Sanctuaries.

Meghalaya also offers many adventure tourism opportunities in the form of mountaineering, rock climbing, trekking and hiking, water sports, etc. The state offers several trekking routes, some of which also afford an opportunity to encounter some rare animals such as the slow loris, assorted deer and bear. The Umiam Lake has a water sports complex with facilities such as rowboats, paddleboats, sailing boats, cruise-boats, water-scooters and speedboats.

Meghalaya has an estimated 500 natural limestone and sandstone caves spread over the entire state including most of the longest and deepest caves in the subcontinent. Krem Liat Prah is the longest cave and Synrang Pamiang is the deepest cave, both located in the Jaintia Hills. Cavers from United Kingdom, Germany, Austria, Ireland and the US have been visiting the area for over a decade exploring these caves. Not many of these have, however, been developed or promoted adequately for major tourist destinations.

Important Tourist Spots

Cherrapunji, may well be regarded as one of the most popular tourist spots in North-East of India. It lies to the south of the capital Shillong. The town is very well known and needs little publicity. A rather scenic, 50-kilometre-long road, connects Cherrapunji with Shillong.

The popular waterfalls in the state are the Elephant Falls, Shadthum Falls, Weinia Falls, Bishop Falls, Nohkalikai Falls, Langshiang Falls and Sweet Falls. The hot springs at Jakrem near Mawsynram are believed to have curative and medicinal properties.

Meghalaya also has many natural and man-made lakes. The Umiam Lake (popularly known as Bara Pani meaning big water) on the Guwahati-Shillong road is a major tourism attraction for tourist besides several parks like Thangkharang Park, the Eco-park, the Botanical Garden and Lady Hydari Park to name a few. Dawki, which is located at about 96 kilometres from Shillong is the gateway to Bangladesh and affords a scenic view of some of the tallest mountain ranges in Meghalaya and the Bangladesh border lands.

Problems and Constraints

The state has a relatively poor road and communication network. While some of the major circuits such as Shillong-Jowai, Shillong-Tura and Shillong-Sohra are well developed;

the internal road networks are rather poor and inadequately maintained. There are few markets outside capital Shillong. Banking facilities are also missing and few establishments in the state accept credit cards. The Garo Hills region which has some of the most important tourist spots is not well connected with the rest of the state.

Tourism in the North-East in general has also suffered on account of years of insurgency and the resulting security concerns. Many governments had in the past issued advisories against travelling to the North-East of India, worsening the security perception. It may, however, be mentioned that Meghalaya is perhaps the least affected by insurgency in the North-East Region. The current ground scenario for Shillong is one in which tourist are welcome to come and enjoy the beauty of nature.

Capital of the State: Shillong

Shillong (Khasi Shillong) is the capital of Meghalaya, one of the smallest states in India. It is also the district headquarters of the East Khasi Hills District and is situated at an average altitude of 4,908 ft (1,496 m) above sea level, with the highest point being "lum shyllong" at 1,965 m. Shillong has steadily grown in size and significance in its own traditional way from a mere village as it used to be when it was made the new civil station of the Khasi and Jaintia Hills in 1864 by the British. It remained the summer capital of Eastern Bengal and Assam for many years.

In 1874, on the formation of Assam as a Chief Commissioner's Province, it was chosen as the headquarters of the new administration because of its convenient location between the Brahmaputra and Surma Valley and more so because the climate of Shillong was much cooler than tropical India. Shillong remained the capital of undivided Assam until the creation of the new state of Meghalaya on January 21, 1972 when Shillong became the capital of Meghalaya and Assam moved its capital to Dispur.

Geography

Shillong is located at 25°34' N 91°56' E. It is on the Shillong Plateau, the only major pop-up structure in the northern Indian shield. The city lies in the centre of the plateau and is surrounded by hills, three of which are revered in Khasi tradition: Lum Sohpetbneng, Lum Diengiei and Lum Shillong.

Due to its latitude and high elevation, Shillong has a subtropical climate with mild summers and chilly to cold winters. Shillong is subject to vagaries of the monsoon. The monsoons arrive in June and it rains almost until the end of August. October-November and March-April are the best months to visit Shillong.

Connectivity

This is one of the few hill stations with motorable roads all around. Shillong has no rail lines. There is a small airport at Umroi, around 30 km from Shillong; most flights into Umroi are only on certain days of the week. The nearest major airport and railway station is at Guwahati, approximately 120 km from Shillong. The tourist towns of Cherrapunji (around 56 km) and Umiam Lake (around 16 km) are close to the city.

Demographics

As of 2001 India census, Shillong had a population of 232,876. Males constitute 50 per cent of the population and females 50 per cent. Shillong has an average literacy rate of 80 per cent, higher than the national average of 65.5 per cent: male literacy is 83 per cent, and female literacy is 78 per cent. In Shillong, 11 per cent of the population is under 6 years of age.

Khasis make up the majority of the population though the percentage of Khasi people in the city continues to fall as a result of the large number of migrants from other Indian states. All the other North-East Indian tribes are represented here as well as significant numbers of Bengali, Nepali, Assamese, Biharis and Marwaris making it a fairly cosmopolitan city.

Christianity is the dominant religion in the city. Protestants make up three-fourths of the population of Shillong and Catholics make up the remaining one-fourth. A sizable proportion of the population follow the original Khasi religion. Other religions found in India are also represented in significant numbers in the city.

Area, Population and Headquarters of Districts

S.No.	District	Area (sq km)	Population	Headquarters
1.	East Khasi Hills	2,820	6,60,923	Shillong
2.	West Khasi Hills	5,247	2,96,049	Nongstoin
3.	Ri-Bhoi	2,448	1,92,790	Nongpoh
4.	Jaintia Hills	3,819	2,99,108	Jowai
5.	East Garo Hills	2,603	2,50,582	Williamnagar
6.	West Garo Hills	3,677	5,18,390	Tura
7.	South Garo Hills	1,887	1,00,980	Baghmara

Salient Features

Significance of State

History and Geography

Meghalaya was created as an autonomous state within the state of Assam on 2 April, 1970. The full-fledged state of Meghalaya came into existence on 21 January, 1972. It is bound on the north and east by Assam and on the south and west by Bangladesh. Meghalaya literally meaning the abode of clouds is essentially a hilly state. It is now divided into seven administrative districts. They are:

- Jaintia Hills.
- East Garo Hills.
- West Garo Hills.
- East Khasi Hills.
- West Khasi Hills.
- Ri-Bhoi.
- South Garo Hills.

These are predominantly inhabited by the Khasis, the Jaintias and the Garos. These tribal communities are the descendants of very ancient people having distinctive traits and ethnic origin. The Khasi Hills and Jaintia Hills which form the central and eastern parts of Meghalaya is an imposing plateau with rolling grassland, hills and river valleys. The southern face of this plateau is marked by deep gorges and abrupt slopes, at the foot of which, a narrow strip of plain land runs along the international border with Bangladesh.

A number of rivers, none of them navigable, drain the mountainous state. In the Garo Hills, the Manda, the Darming and the Jinjiram flow towards the north while the Ringge and the Ganol flow in the western direction. Rivers flowing to the south are the Simsang which is the biggest river in Garo Hills and the Bugi. In the Khasi and Jaintia Hills, the rivers that flow in a northern direction include the Khri, the Umtrew, the Umiam, the Umkhen besides the Kupli on the border between Jaintia Hills and North Cachar hills. The Kynshi, the Umiam Mawphlang and the Umngot flow to the south into Bangladesh.

Natural Boundaries

Meghalaya, a separate geographical entity becomes an autonomous state. The political experiment of an autonomous state within the state of Assam is being tried for the first time in India.

With the advent of the new state the long aspiration of the people for political autonomy has been satisfied and now it would be expected that new state should serve as a shining outpost of Indian democracy.

The new state Meghalaya is bounded by the Brahmaputra Valley on the North, East Pakistan in the South and West and the Mikir, North Cachar hills on the East.

The area covered by Meghalaya is roughly about 8,500 sq miles, comprising two of the five hill districts of Assam, i.e., the Garo and the united Khasi Jaintia Hill districts.

Meghalaya have an estimated population of more than 900,000 hill tribals, predominantly Khasis, Garo and Jaintias. Density of population is 90 persons per sq mile, about three times lower than the Indian average. Racially, these tribals belong to the mongoloid stock while their dialects are Tibeto-Burman in origin. They are the descendants of the great Baro clan which ruled a large part of Assam at one time. Their ancestors came via Bhutan numbering 4 lakhs.

At present most of the tribals are peace loving peasants practising Jhum cultivation after clearing the land by slash and burn method. They are also adept in fishing wherever possible. In general, people are brave, intelligent and colourful. Culturally, they possess a distinctive form of social organisation in which descent and inheritance are recognised through women rather than through men. Residence after marriage shifts to inlaws' house so that a man goes to live with his wife's family. This kind of matrilineal arrangements have, of course, undergone some modification among the educated and urbanised Khasis and Garos but there are important points of difference in the culture and social organisation of Khasis and Garos.

Geologically Meghalaya belongs to archean group of rock (550 million years) over which lies the alluvium of Ganga and Brahmaputra. The whole terrain was below sea and was lifted up from the floor of the sea. The geological movement was slow and free from backing that the sedimentary beds retained the horizontal character and gave rise to structural platforms, well developed in Cherrapunji. The presence of many rapids and waterfalls is the neighbourhood of Shillong indicates that this region has a youthful topography perhaps to recent uplift.

Physiographically and administratively also the central and eastern parts of Meghalaya can be grouped together under the name Khasi and Jaintia Hills and the western Part Garo Hills.

Garo Hills covers an area of 300 sq miles lower in elevation and rise gently from southern plains. Tura range (a typical horst) and Simsang Valley are the main physiographic units.

Khasi and Jaintia Hills covers an area of 5,500 sq miles and it is mainly in the form of Plateau. Here general elevation varies within 4,000-6,000 ft. (1,219.2 to 1,824.0 m). The Shillong hills towering above Shillong town contain the highest pineapples surface. South of Shillong lies the structural platform of Cherrapunji which are built up of sandstorm and limestones. From Cherrapunji the plateau slopes very gently southwards for about 6 km and then falls rapidly to the plains. The easternmost section of Meghalaya is the Mikit hills. The hills are rugged and thinly populated due to the presence of barren sandstones of Surma series.

Climatically, Meghalaya experience two seasons — the mild Summer and the Winter. The climate is noted for its coolness and humidity. Here Cherrapunji receives the word's highest rain fall (600 inches) in a year. Whereas Shillong located 50 miles away receives only 80-100 inches rainfall. This is primarily due to Shillong's position in rain-shadow area. The Monsoon laden with heavy moisture knocked at the Cherrapunji plateau just before reaching plateau. Garo Hill located in the west receives only 43 inches of rainfall.

Politically the new state will have a full Judged Legislative Assembly of 38 members and a council of 5 Ministers for the present. It will have a common Governor and a common High Court with Assam. At present, the overall responsibility for law and order in Meghalaya remains with the Assam Government, the new state will have its own village and town police. It will also have enforcement powers to cover the 61 subjects out of 65 in its state list.

As Meghalaya will be normally within the state of Assam, the present Assam Legislative Assembly constituencies in Meghalaya area will still find representation in the Assam Legislative Assembly even after the formation of the new state. At present, there are 16 Assembly constituencies in the hilly areas of Assam, reserved for Scheduled tribes of these, nine are from the proposed Meghalaya area. As far as the Meghalaya areas are concerned the Government and Legislative Assembly of Assam will have Jurisdiction in respect of only certain subjects of common interest including state high ways, major industries and hydroelectricity power. Again the Assam and Meghalaya states will have concurrent powers requiring notification both by state Assemblies in 13 subjects including the acquisition of land.

Economically, Meghalaya is one geared to agriculture with rice as the staple food of the people. Many fruits are also found in the area such as apples, pears, peaches and oranges, the last being the most abundant. Apart from this short staple variety of cotton is grown especially in the Garo Hills.

With a heavy rainfall the flora of the hill is regarded as the richest in the Indian subcontinent. There are about two hundred varieties of orchids in the area and few rarest species are potential Exchange earners. Soft woods are another valuable resource of the state.

From the point of view of minerals, the state has rich deposits of coal (1% of India), limestones, silimanite, felspar (quartz) glass sand and china clay. Geological Survey of India has located strains of uranium and zinc. Further investigations are continuing.

In respect of industries also the new state have high potentiality since most of the hydel power stations of North-East India, i.e., the Uiam, Umtru and Kopili are located in this region. At present small handicraft industry such as weaving of silk, muga and endi are flourishing but there are immense possibility of setting up a few new industries like paper, and cement by utilising the local coal, limestone and timber. In Cherrapunji a cement factory has now gone into production with a capacity of 250 ton per day or less than one lakh ton annually.

In the field of education the new state have the higher percentage of literacy (31.5%) than the rest of Assam (27.4%). This is mainly due to the service of Christian Missionaries. Like everywhere else the main activity of the Christian Church has been to promote education so that many of the tribes know Latin and not an Indian script. Fascination of tribal peoples for western dress, top music, English movies and novels projects an image of the average educated tribal of the region.

In hill areas where topography is rough, rainfall is copious, transport becomes a problem. Here also one faces such difficulty of transport. Trains are non-existent in hill areas. Only means of transport is therefore motor vehicles. But services are quite efficient. The National highway, the life line of Meghalaya connecting Guwahati with Shillong extends up to Dawki on the East Pakistan Border. Garo Hills on the other hand is linked with only one all weather road from Goalpara.

The new state have very few cities and towns. Only Shillong and Tura are the cities that have considerable importance. Shillong the charming hill station located at an altitude of 1961 metres above sea level is the Capital of the new state. The natural setting of Shillong has provided it with attractions for tourists which can well be developed.

Tura, the headquarters of the Garo Hills is located in the extreme west of Meghalaya. It is about 1412 metres above sea level and have over 30,000 population. So far as tourists are concerned this small but very beautiful and clean town has also a special appeal.

A Long Journey

Meghalaya was created as an autonomous State within the state of Assam on 2 April 1970. The full-fledged State of Meghalaya came into existence on 2 January 1972. It is bound on the north and east by Assam and on the south and west by Bangladesh. Meghalaya, literally meaning the abode of clouds, is essentially a hilly state. It is predominantly inhabited by the Khasis, the Jaintias and the Garos tribal communities. The Khasi Hills and Jaintia Hills which form the central and eastern parts of Meghalaya is an imposing plateau with rolling grassland, hills and river valleys. The southern face of the plateau is marked by deep gorges and abrupt slopes, at the foot of which, a narrow strip of plain land runs along the international border with Bangladesh.

Religious Features

The Meghalaya religion is based on the fear and dread of the supernatural powers. Although, traditionally the religion is not animistic; yet the people celebrates a presiding God, known as 'Dakgipa Rugipa Stugipa Pantugipa' or 'Tatora Rabuga Stura Pantura'. The religion is basically monotheistic, yet has many polytheistic stages. In fact, the genesis of the religion shows that it was purely monotheistic; gradually it became polytheistic.

Moreover, the Garos believe in the creation of the universe, earth, living beings, seas, heavenly bodies, rain, storm, thunder, wind — this constitute the essence of the religion in Meghalaya. Besides, the nature worship, the religion also constitutes many lesser gods and many ceremonies and festivities are attached to it.

In the recent years, most of the Garos have turned Christians. Yet, talking about the religion of the Garo clan in Meghalaya, it can be said that the religion is a combination of Hinduism and Pantheism. The Garos, like the Hindus and the Buddhists, believe in the 'Spirit of Man': this incarnation is based on sin. Some of the important deities are Tartar-Robunga, Choradubi, Saljong, Goers, Susine, etc.

Furthermore, sacrifices are a part of the religion. The titular deities are invoked on many occasions, such as birth, illness marriage, death, harvesting of crops, welfare of the community, protection from danger, etc. Like most of the Hindu religion, state religion also shows reverence towards their ancestors.

But, according to the generalisation of many scholars and researchers, the religion of Meghalaya does not have a concrete base, as it is devoid of any logic. The nature worship or sacrificial rituals rank among the illogical human practices. Therefore, as it is evident, basically the religion of the Garos, show a cultural pattern, which is unlike any other religious practices of any other part of India.

Cultural Features

The Khasi, Garo and Jaintia are people with a rich cultural heritage. The important crafts of the Khasi and the Jaintia districts are artistic weaving, woodcarving and cane and bamboo work. Carpet and silk weaving and the making of musical instruments, jewellery and pineapple fibre articles are among its minor craft.

The popular handicrafts of the Garo Hills District are artistic weaving, cane and bamboo work including poker work (in which designs are burnt into the bamboo with a red-hot pointed rod), woodcarving, jewellery and making of clay toys and dolls and musical instruments.

Festivals

Meghalaya literally means the 'land of clouds'. The state is believed to be the home of dances and music. The festivals are associated with their different dance forms and hence they are to be enjoyed throughout the year. Each tribe has its own set of festivals in which they actively participate to enhance their festive spirit and to come of their monotonous life. In fact the indigenous festivals of this beautiful state mirror its diverse heritage during the celebration of the seasonal cycle of sowing and harvesting. Most of the festivals revolve around agriculture, which is the prime occupation of the state people. Although some religious and spiritual sentiments are interwoven into secular rites and rituals, the predominant themes of the festivals is to offer prayers to the Supreme Being who is known by different names in different Naga dialects. But participation of all in these festivals is compulsory.

Religious Festivals:

Behdienkhlam: This is one of the most popular festivals of Meghalaya. It is celebrated during the monsoon season in the month of July at Jowai and Tuber in the hills of Jaintia. This grand festival is characterised by religious ceremonies and dancing at a pool called *'eit nar'* and also includes a football game called *'datlawakor'*. This festival is essentially celebrated to seek the blessings of the Almighty for a bounteous yield of crops in the following year and also to chase away various kind of diseases and plague.

Shad Suk Mynsiem: This colourful festival of Meghalaya is in fact a thanksgiving festival celebrated during the season of spring all over Khasi Hills. The beautiful maidens adorn themselves in traditional finery and men-folk in vibrant coloured costumes participate with much enthusiasm in the traditional dance to the accompaniment of drum beats and other musical instruments.

Wangala: This is a major festival of the Garo tribes in the state and is gaily celebrated after the harvest season. During this festival, the locals hold propitiation ceremonies in honour of the deity Patigipa Rarongipa in almost every village of the state. The people of the state follow the religious rites and rituals with much veneration for a consecutive period of four days and nights accompanied by unrestrained jollity. The conclusion of the festival is marked by the warrior's dance which is indeed a magnificent and enchanting spectacle to observe.

Ka Pomblang Nongkrem: Ka Pomblang Nongkrem is one of the most famous festivals of Meghalaya. This much-awaited festival takes place at Smit, the capital of Kheyrem Syiemship, near Shillong. This is usually a harvest festival and is considered to be the most eminent festival of the 'Khasi' community. There are several religious rites and rituals associated with this festival among which the offering of goats (also known as Pomblang ceremony) to the administrative head is the most important one. The first day of the festival is marked by a royal dance performance which takes place at the dawn. Besides the traditional dances the sword dances, music, colourful costumes and stunning jewellery enhance the spirit of the festive celebrations.

Umsan Nongkharai: This is one of the most special festivals of Meghalaya and is grandly celebrated in the months of April/May according to the Christian calendar. It commences on Sugi Lyngka with a ceremonial sacrifice of a goat and two cocks before the supreme deity of the Khasis-Lei Shyllong. After the prayers are offered to establish the person-to-person contact between the finite and infinite, male dancers dance to the rhythmic beats till sunrise. On the second day of the festival ritualistic prayers are offered whereas on the third day divine blessings are sought. A symbolic "fertility" ritual is enacted on the fourth day whereas on the fifth and final day public worship is done and fish from the Umran River are offered as special gifts.

Saram Cha'A: This is a post-harvest festival of the Attongs celebrated around the same time as the Wangala festival. It is also a thanksgiving festival but does not involve the extreme merriment as of the Wangala festival. This much-awaited festival of the Attongs is celebrated in the months of September/October. The priests chant religious hymns and an offering of an egg; a chicken, boiled rice and curry are made to the local Deity. Domestic animals are also killed on this auspicious occasion for the purpose of feasting.

Dance Festivals:

Doregata: This is a very popular dance festival held in the state of Meghalaya. In this dance the female members try to knock-off the turbans of their male counterparts. While dancing if the women are able to knock-off the turbans successfully it is followed by a peal of laughter.

Lahoo: This dance festival in the state is performed with much excitement and exuberance with the sole purpose of entertaining the locals. It is performed by both males and females. Both the men and women folks are dressed in vibrant coloured outfits. In this dance two young men on either side of a woman hold arms together and dance in step. Lahoo dance festival is thus one of the most famous festivals.

Chambil Mesara or Pomelo: This is one of the very popular dance festivals of Meghalaya. This solo dance form requires great skill. In this dance, the performer hangs a pomelo on a cord tied to his waist and then makes a thrusting forward movement without any perceptible motion of the hips.

Shad Beh Sier: This deer hunting dance festival is solely dedicated to occupational merriment and is one of the most cherished festivals of state. During the season of off-harvest, the male folks wander about the dense forests to prey for deer. When one or two deer are killed it becomes a local celebration. The youth of the village mount the slain deer on a bamboo pier and parade it through villages. The very hunting adventure turns out to be a stunning spectacle.

Lingual and Literary Features

Meghalaya language is a reflection of the rich culture. Although the state language is English; but the principal languages are Khasi, Garo and Jaintia.

To begin with the Meghalaya language, it can be said that Khasi is one of the chief languages. Khasi, which is also spelled Khasia, Khassee, Cossyah and Kyi, is a branch of the Mon-Khmer family of the Austroasiatic stock; and is spoken by about 900,000 people. It is interesting to know that many words in the Khasi language have been borrowed from Indo-Aryan languages, the most important being Hindi and Bengali languages. Moreover, the Khasi language had no script of its own in its onset. But, it is said that William Carey was the first person to pen the language in Eastern Nagari script in the 18th century. Garo also deserves a special mention in the languages of Meghalaya. In fact, it is noteworthy that Garo, like Khasi, is also the official language. However, the language has a close affinity with the Bodo language, the official language of Assam.

Garo, spoken by the majority of the population, is spoken in many dialects such as A'we, Chisak, A'beng, Ganching, Kamrup, A'chick, Dacca and Matchi. Another language at Meghalaya, which deserves special mention among the languages is the language spoken by the people of the Jaintia Hills. This language, as matter of fact, is a variation of the standard Khasi language. The Jaintia language is spoken, along with the Khasi language, by the tribal groups, viz., Khynriam, Bhoi, Pnar and War. Thus, we find that the languages in Meghalaya shares the characteristic traits of the sociocultural pattern of the different regions.

Khasi Language

Khasi is the official language of Meghalaya and is spoken by about 900,000 people. The language spoken by the Khasi tribes hails from the Mon-Khmer family of the Austroasiatic society. Khasi is spoken by the people in the surrounding areas of the Khasi and Jaintia Hills. In fact, the Khasi is also spoken by the inhabitants of the adjoining areas such as Assam and Bangladesh.

It is noteworthy that on its very onset, this Khasi language had no script of its own. But in the 18th century, William Carey tried to introduce a formal script for the language, following the Eastern Nagari script. Later many variations in the script was introduced; but the Roman script, which is akin to the Khasi language, was adopted.

Khasi is a language that is rich in folklore and folktale. The language, in fact, reflects the sociocultural vitality of Meghalaya. Therefore, many stories related to the ancestors, nature, wildlife and mythology are found in the Khasi language.

In fact, it is through a study of the Khasi language that we can trace the ethnicity, culture and traditions of the Meghalayan culture. As such it can be said that the Khasi language is an integral part of state.

Garo Language

Garo (also spelled as Garrow, or else known by the people's own name for themselves, Mande) is the language of the majority of the people of the Garo Hills. Garo is also used in Kamrup, Dhubri, Goalpara and the Darrang districts of Assam, as well as in neighbouring Bangladesh. Garo uses the Latin alphabet and has a close affinity to Bodo, the language of one of the dominant communities of the neighbouring state of Assam.

Dialects include A'beng (A'bengya, Am'beng), A'chick (A'chik), A'we, Chisak, Dacca, Ganching, Kamrup, Matchi. The Achik dialect predominates among several inherently intelligible dialects. The Abeng dialect is in Bangladesh, closest to Koch.

The Department of Garo, the only one of its kind in the world, was established in response to popular demand in 1996 at the inception of Northeastern Hill University. The Department documented in audio and videotapes parts of A'chick (Garo) epic poetry of "Katta Agana", the legend of "Dikki and Bandi", some folktales, folk songs, and traditional oral poetry.

Academic Features

Although the state of Meghalaya does not occupy a mammoth portion of the Indian turf but it is developing into one of the most advanced and technically sound states. Education has played a major role in this metamorphosis. In fact, according to the data collected in the 2001 census, approximately 63.31 per cent of the occupants of the state are literate. This is a homogeneous achievement in itself despite of the limited number of resources that are provided to it.

The central university that coordinates the actions of all the smaller educational institutions of the state is located in its functional capital of Shillong. To add that touch of modernisation and sophistication to education quite a few number of colleges are being put up to provide a platform to the youth of the state. These colleges are equipped with the latest state of the art facilities to procure assistance to the students in all the various fields. They include 'Shillong Engineering and Management College' which is positioned at a venue known as Mawlai.

To keep up with the other neighbouring states the policy of free and compulsory education for all the children under the age group of 14 years has also been espoused by the state in the sphere of education. The 10+2 system of education that exists in all the other states has also penetrated into the state of Meghalaya.

As a part developmental programme in Northeastern States ministry of human resource development opened seventh Indian Institute of Management in Shillong which is named as Rajiv Gandhi Indian Institute of Management. This institute started admissions from the academic year 2008.

Schools

Different Kinds of Schools: Several primary, middle and high schools function in Meghalaya. The schools are either affiliated to the state education board, the CBSE board or ICSE board.

Number of Schools: As per a survey conducted in the year 2004-05, the total number of schools in Meghalaya is 8,321 (approx.). This includes primary and junior basic schools, middle and senior basic schools and high and higher secondary schools.

Medium of Teaching: English is generally the medium of instruction in ICSE and CBSE schools. Regional languages are also taught in most of the schools either as first or as second language.

Dropouts: Midday meals are provided in the government schools to increase the rate of retention and reduce the dropout rate as well. Apart from this, the State Government has also taken up several initiatives for the overall development of education in Meghalaya.

Famous Schools: Some of the CBSE affiliated schools in Meghalaya are Kendriya Vidhyalaya, Laitkorpeak; Kendriya Vidhyalaya NEHU Permanent Campus, Umshing; Kendriya Vidhyalaya, Tura; Kendriya Vidhyalaya, Nepa and Kendriya Vidhyalaya, Umroi Cantonment Barapani. Students can also take admission in several other schools like St Edmund's School, Shillong; St Edmund's High School, Shillong; Mawkhar Christian High School, Shillong; St Anthony's Higher Secondary School (A Don Bosco Institution), Laitumkhrah Shillong; St Peter School, Shillong and Assam Rifles Public School Laitkor.

Central Board of Secondary Education

Quite a few schools in the state are affiliated to the Central Board of Secondary Education or (CBSE). These CBSE schools are well-equipped with all sorts of facilities that aid the students to earn knowledge in a very interesting way. Another advantage possessed by the Central Board of Secondary Education is that its syllabus has a lot of resemblance with the syllabus of the various competitive examinations. Hence, the pupils have an edge over their contemporaries descending from other boards.

The major schools in Meghalaya under Central Board of Secondary Education are mentioned below:

- *Kendriya Vidhyalaya:* This school has three branches across the state. These branches are situated at the following venues of Laitkor Peak in the capital of Shillong, Upper Shillong and Happy Valley in Shillong. All these schools are coeducational.

- *Assam Rifles Public School:* This school is positioned in the picturesque locale of Laitkor. This school is dedicated to the boys only.

The Central Board of Secondary Education has procured quality schools and other related educational institutions that have over the years nurtured brilliant pupils and transformed them into successful human beings. The abbreviated form of the Central Board of Secondary Education is 'CBSE'.

Colleges

Meghalaya Colleges have made their mark in terms of providing quality education to the various aspiring doctors, engineers and businessmen who desire to make their mark. The colleges procure all sorts of courses that aid them to choose between different options. They can also seek the advise of elite professors in these colleges to choose the correct and most suitable stream for them.

The different colleges are enlisted below:

- *Engineering Colleges:* The state of Meghalaya only houses a sole college dedicated to the engineering students known by the name of Shillong Engineering and Management College. The AICTE or All India Council of Technical Education has also approved all the courses offered by this college.

- *Management Institutes:* Shillong Engineering and Management College that is located at Mawlai.

- *Nursing Colleges:* Repsbun School of Nursing is the sole nursing school in the state. It is located in East Khasi Hills.

- *Polytechnic Institutes:* There three polytechnic institutes including Jowai Polytechnic, Shillong Polytechnic and Tura Polytechnic. All these colleges are AICTE approved.

- *Law Colleges:* Department of Law, Northeastern Hill University, Khad-Ar-Doloi Law College, Tura College and Shillong Law College.

- *Biotechnology Colleges:* St Anthony's College and Department of Biotechnology.

- *Hotel Management:* Institute of Hotel Management in Shillong is the only college that offers a course in Hotel Management.

- *Computer Institutes:* St Edmund's College and St Anthony's College at Shillong.

- *Mass Communications:* Department of Mass Communications in St Anthony's College in the venue of Shillong provide courses in Mass Communication.

Universities

The two major universities are the Northeastern Hill University and the Indira Gandhi National Open University. The Northeastern Hill University is one of the leading universities established on 19th July, 1973. The Shillong regional centre of Indira Gandhi National Open University is as old as 1998. Currently, the Shillong regional centre manages and controls all the curricular activities across entire Meghalaya.

The Northeastern Hill University is counted among the most renowned universities as its main campus is located in the capital city of Shillong. An additional campus was set up at Tura in February 1996.

The university offers courses in almost all the major branches of education. The university is divided into seven schools and all the departments of the university come under these schools. There are as many as fifty-three undergraduate colleges that are affiliated to this renowned university. There are 8 colleges under the university that provide professional courses.

Indira Gandhi National Open University is one of the most popular universities. The courses offered here are varied – diploma, certificate and degree courses. The educational activities of the Indira Gandhi National Open University spans to various training programmes, research oriented work and extension education.

Education is offered at the Indira Gandhi National Open University in two different ways — open learning and distance education. Both these modes of education have become very popular among the young professionals of the state.

Distance Education

Meghalaya distance education is gradually gaining in popularity after initial circumspections following their introduction within the academic structure of the state. The inhabitants have slowly but surely awoke to the fact, that pursuing higher education with some other vocation is almost always a wonderful option. Apart from the major universities, there are many institutions for distance education that specialise in distance learning.

State of Meghalaya Distance Education: Like everywhere else in India, distance education at Meghalaya was not greeted with great enthusiasm at its inception. Students were doubtful about its worth. Most preferred a regular education system to distance education and often left for universities outside the state, to be enable to pursue some job alongside their education. However, soon a change in the mindset was noticed, as the inhabitants of the state realised the fact that the same facilities could be availed from within the state. The distance education opened up the possibilities of education for all interested students who were not able to take up education as a full time engagement because of various constraints.

IGNOU and NEHU: Indira Gandhi National Open University and the distant programme of the Northeastern Hill University (NEHU) are the most popular of all Meghalaya distance education programmes. While IGNOU offers a wide range of courses to the students to choose from, the NEHU course offers degrees and diplomas more on the lines of the university curricula. Most universities of India have been presently forced to offer distance learning courses as a part of the diversification programmes of their operations. NEHU is also a great attraction for the research scholars because of their M.Phil. and Ph.D. programmes.

Vocational Education

Meghalaya Vocational Education is extremely popular because it opens up plenty of placement opportunities for its students. The rapid growth of industrialisation has increased the demand for skilled and semi-skilled labours to a great degree, consequently making Vocational Education all the more lucrative. The vocational education is greatly encouraged by the government. The state directorate for employment and craftsman training is committed towards the optimisation of the human resources of the state through the distance education facilities offered by the various institutions of the state.

Facilities in the Polytechnic Colleges: The polytechnic colleges take a major role in imparting Meghalaya Vocational Education, apart from the various degree courses. The students of these colleges are equipped in various technical capacities, which help them to play an important part in the many industries of the state, as well as to explore possibilities of self-employment. The polytechnic colleges which offer vocational education are:

- Jowai Polytechnic in the Jaintia Hills;
- Shillong Polytechnic in Shillong; and
- Tura Polytechnic in the Garo Hills.

Other Vocational Courses: Apart from the semi-professional and Vocational Education as offered by the various polytechnic colleges, there are various other vocational courses on offer by other institutes as well. Vocational education plays a very important role in the economic empowerment of the womenfolk of the state. They are trained in various skills of the technical as well as the craftsmanship to secure jobs in the big as well as small scale industries of the state, which are fundamental to the state's economy.

High Seats of Learning

1. North Eastern Hill University, P.O. NEHU Campus, Mawkynroh Umshing, Shillong.

Economy

Industries

The Meghalaya Industrial Development Corporation Limited, as the Industrial and Financial Institution of the State, has been rendering financial assistance to the local entrepreneurs. The District Industries Centres have been working in the field of promotion and development of the small scale, village, tiny and cottage sector of industries. A number of industrial projects have been set up for the manufacture of iron and steel materials, cement and other consumer products.

Agriculture

Meghalaya is basically an agricultural State in which about 80 per cent of its population depends primarily on agriculture for their livelihood. The State has a vast potential for developing horticulture due to agrodinamatic variations which offer much scope for cultivation of temperate, sub-tropical and tropical fruits and vegetables. Besides the major food crops of rice and maize, Meghalaya is renowned for its oranges (Khasi Mandarian), pineapple, banana, jackfruits, temperate fruits like plum, pears and peaches, etc. Cash crops, popularly and traditionally cultivated include potato, turmeric, ginger, black pepper, arecanut, betel-vine, tapioca, short staple cotton, jute and mesta, mustard and rape. Special emphasis is presently laid on non-traditional crops like oilseeds (groundnut, soya bean and sunflower), cashewnut, tea and coffee, mushroom, medicinal plants, orchids and commercial flowers. The estimated irrigation potential of the state both from surface and ground water is about 2.13 lakh hectare, the potential created so far is 55,182 hectare.

Farming

Meghalaya is basically an agricultural state. Eighty three per cent of the total population depend primarily on agriculture for their livelihood. The topography, physical features and land conditions as prevailing in the state provide extremely limited scope for extensive cultivation or to bring additional area under wet cultivation. Rice and maize are the major food crops. Wheat has been introduced a few years back and the result is quite encouraging. Potato, jute, mesta, cotton, mustard, arecanut, ginger, turmeric, betel-vine, black pepper, tezpata, etc., are some of the cash crops. Orange, pineapple, banana, lemon, guava, litchi, jackfruit and temperate fruits such as plum, pear and peach are some of the important horticultural crops grown in Meghalaya. Apart from the above crops, the state has achieved success in the cultivation of tea, mushroom and tomato.

Irrigation and Power

The state has power potential for nearly 1,200 mw. It could tap about 186.71 mw up to 1992-93. It is a power surplus state. About 36 per cent of electricity generated in the state is supplied to the neighbouring states. The per capita consumption is only 143.80 kw as in 1990-91. By the end of March 1991-92, 47.22 per cent of the villages in the state have been electrified.

Industries and Minerals

The public sector cement factory at Cherrapunjee has been reactivated to raise the production to 1,65,000 mt per annum. The tantalum capacitor unit of the Meghalaya

Electronics Development Corporation at Umiam-Khwan is in production. The mini cement plant, one at Damas in East Garo Hills district and the other at Sutnga in Jaintia Hills district have also gone into production. The number of small scale industrial units covering service industry, bakeries, furniture-making, iron and steel fabrication, tyre retreating, spice, etc., is increasing and the government is giving greater thrust on entrepreneurship development. The Meghalaya Industrial Development Corporation (MIDC) is assisting the industrial units by way of term loans and also by participating in equity capital.

Natural Wealth

Forests

The total forest area in the state is 8,510 sq km with only 993 sq km under the control of the State Government and the rest under the district councils and private managements. The principal timber species are: teak, titachap, gomari, bola, pine, birch, and makrisal. Principal forest products include timber, bamboo, reed, cane, ipecac, medicinal herbs and plants, cinnamon and thatch grass. Azaleas and rhododendrons grow wild in the forest of Khasi and Jaintia Hills and many kinds of beautiful orchids are found in the woods.

Pitcher plant, the insect-eating plant of botanical wonder, is found in plenty in the South Garo Hills and West Khasi Hills district and it is said that such a plant is found nowhere else in the world. Many rare and interesting plants are also found endemic to the state like wild citrus and pygmy lily.

Wildlife

Meghalaya is also rich in wildlife. There are elephants, tigers, bears, wild boars, leopards, golden cats, leopard cats and jungle cats, deer of various kinds, bintorongs, slow loris, monkeys of different types including capped langurs, golden langurs and hoolocks, flying squirrels and giant squirrels. There are also many rare and interesting birds including the hornbills, patridges, pheasants, teals, snipes, geese, ducks and quails. All these are protected by law. The state has two national parks, viz., the Nokrek National Park and the Balpakram National Park and two wildlife sanctuaries, namely, the Nongkhyllem Wildlife Sanctuary and Siju Wildlife Sanctuary.

Minerals

Mineral wealth of Meghalaya include coal, silimanite, limestone, dolomite, fire-clay, felspar, quartz and grass-sand. The total estimated reserve of coal in the state is 562 million tonnes and that of limestone is around 4,500 million tonnes.

Housing Pattern

The Khasis who dwelled in the upland region built houses with the help of stones and wooden planks. Such houses had to be elevated from the ground to a height of about

2 to 3 feet with the support of a plinth. They were devoid of any window. To protect from the effect of strong wind, such houses were built in the shape of egg. These thatched houses were not tall enough and hence the roof was not much higher from the ground.

An average house in the Khasi region includes three separate segments – a living room, a resting room and a verandah (balcony). The roof resembled one half of an umbrella. The house was protected from the outside with a fence, which was open only at the entrance. The entrance generally faced the main road of the respective village. An average house of the War-Khasis stood on stilts. A Bhoi or a Lyngngams house is built on an elevated platform. This platform was made up of bamboos.

Architecture in Meghalaya also includes the houses of Cherrapunji which are unique. They had stone walls, so that they could protect the houses from continuous rains. The houses of the Jaintia Hills exhibit plastered walls. The plaster was actually mud. Even these mud walls were painted with bright colours.

Art and Crafts

Regarded as the 'abode of the clouds' in Hindi, the state of Meghalaya is dowered with some adept artists who have been producing some quality artwork. The monuments and mansions of state reflect the true architectural brilliance of the engineers of who had consecrated their mind and soul behind the construction of each building.

The handlooms constitute another major wing of the art. Primarily, cane along with bamboo are used as the chief ingredients for the manufacture of baskets, sieves, furniture, decorative articles and many more intriguing items. The baskets are a speciality of the Garo Hills. They are even bestowed with a completely new name — 'meghum khoks'. Musical instruments, exotic carpets, various intricately designed ornaments, hats constructed from bamboo which are round in shape, umbrellas hailing from the Khasi Hills which are referred to as 'kurups' by the locals are all examples of art from Meghalaya.

The art also includes attires worn by the women which are indeed exquisitely designed and made from very tender but at the same time very durable materials. The ladies descending from the various tribes have devised their own trenchant fashion of dressing up. The woman from the Khasi Hills just love to put on 'Jainsem', that is basically a modification of a skirt that extends down to the ankles. Then, there is 'Ka Jainsem Dhara' that is principally manufactured from muga silk and again stretches from the shoulders to the knees. The ladies belonging to the Garo tribes dress themselves in all sorts of clothing like 'Dakmanda', Daksari and 'Mekhla'. All these attires are draped like a skirt and extends till the ankles.

One rarely comes across the kind of houses that originally constituted the Meghalaya architecture. They have found place in the showcases of the museum in the interior rural villages. The remnants of the fortress in Jaintiapur and Nartiang and the Jaintia Hills and Khasi stone bridges bear testimony of the Jaintia and Khasi architecture.

Crafts

Weaving is an ancient craft of the tribals of Meghalaya — be it weaving of cane or cloth. The Khasis are famous for weaving cane mat, stools and baskets. They make a special kind of cane mat called *'Tlieng'*, which guarantees a good utility of around 20-30 years. The Garos weave the material used for their costumes called the *'Dakmanda'*. Khasis and Jaintias also weave cloth. The Khasis have also been involved in extracting iron ore and then manufacture domestic knives, utensils and even guns and other warfare weapons using it.

Handlooms

The Garo women are engaged in weaving handlooms. Their only cotton textile product is Dakmandes, which is traditionally worn to cover the body till the knees from the waist. The other items woven by the Garos include tablecloths, shirting, bed sheets and bed covers. One of the most famous handlooms of Meghalaya is the endi silk. It is known across the region for its durability and texture. Endi is chiefly woven at Sonidan, though the women folk of other villages are also involved in weaving it.

Mulberry silk is another popular handloom material, which is largely used to prepare Jainsen, the most commonly worn attire among the women of Meghalaya, in particular the communities of Khasi and Khynrium. The local people are trained to weave silk. This has led to a gradual progress in the commercial production of silk items. The chief handloom attires used by the people are:

Mekhla: The women of Mikir, Man and Assam wear mekhla. It is a lower garment, that is not stitched.

Jainsem: It is the attire worn by the Khasi lady, which is an ankle-length dress. This is one of the most important of the handlooms at Meghalaya.

Ka Jainsem Dhara: It is an attire worn on formal occasions over the Jympien. It is actually quite a long piece of muga silk belonging to Assam. It is a knee-length dress pinned up over the shoulders.

Thoh Khyrwang: Occasionally, Jaintia women wear a striped cloth termed Thoh Khyrwang. It is made up of Assam muga silk, one of the major handlooms in Meghalaya. The attire is worn around the waist and touches the ankles.

Dakmandes: The Garo women wear a Dakmandes made up of raw cotton. It is similar to a 'Lungi'.

Songs and Music

The Garos generally sing folk songs relating to birth, marriage, festivals, love and heroic deeds sung to the accompaniments of different types of drums and flutes. The Khasis and Jaintias are particularly fond of songs praising the nature like lakes, waterfalls, hills, etc. and also expressing love for their land. They use different types of musical instruments like drums, duitara and instruments similar to guitar, flutes, pipes and cymbals.

Dances

Shad Sukmynsiem (Dance of the Blissful Heart): This dance is popularly known as Shad Weiking and is so called after the name of the ground where the dance used to be held every year. Being a thanksgiving festival, Shad Sukmynesiem is a symbolic offering of salutations to God, homage to their ancestors and proclamation of unity of the Khasi people. It is organised by the Seng Khasi (Khasi Religion). The dance lasts for three days. Only unmarried men and women are allowed to take part in the dance. The dancers dance rhythmically making regular movements and keeping time with the beat of the drum and pipe (Tanguari). Damsels (unmarried) dressed colourfully.

Nongkrem: 'Nongkrem' is the name of an important folk dance from Meghalaya, which is performed by the Khasis tribe. This dance is performed in the Nongkrem dance festival. The tribal people celebrate the ripening of paddy for threshing by singing and dancing. Though, the Nongkrem dance had a purpose of celebration, it is also performed for community peace and there is no age limit to participate in the same.

The Nongkrem dance festival is a multi-purpose event. With the reason of this event, all tribes of this hilly region area people meet together from their scattered hamlets. They strongly believe in group prayers or community gathering. Through this dance performance, all these people offer their thankfulness to the gods for a bountiful harvest. They also pray to nature to keep up the timely delivery of rain and ward-off evil disasters.

Shad Nongkrem: Another folk dance of the Khasis, Shad Nongkrem is associated with Ka Pomblang Nongkrem. Like all other ceremonies it is performed to propitiate the all powerful Goddess Ka Blei Synshar for a rich bounteous harvest and prosperity of the people (subject). There is no fixed date for this festival. It is generally celebrated in November of every year.

Doregata: Another dance among the Khasis is Doregata in which the women try to knock-off the turbans of their male partners, using their heads. Another dance that the performer dangles a pomelo or any other fruit on a cord tied to his waist and then whirls it round and round after the initial impetus with a barely perceptible movement of his hips. Some experts can control two separate pomelos in this way.

Do Dru-su'a: The Garos have traditional dance called Do Dru-su'a in which two women dance like doves pecking each other.

Laho: For entertainment, the Pnars have their Laho dance, in which members of both sex participate in their festival finery. Usually two young men on either side of a girl, linked together in arms, dance in steps. While in place of pipe and drum there is a 'Cheer leader', usually a man with the gift of impromptu recitation.

IT Features

The Information Technology (IT) vision, mission, objectives, plans and strategies of the Government of Meghalaya as enunciated below have been formulated keeping in view the desirability for accelerating the state's economic development and maximising the people's benefits through its widespread application in various spheres.

The Vision

The Government envisages: i) to make IT as a tool for attaining all round development in the state; and ii) to fully participate in the IT revolution to bring prosperity to people. The goal is creation of wealth, employment generation and IT led economic growth.

The Mission

The Government would: i) use IT based applications to manage development programmes for all round development of the state; ii) take necessary steps to make the state a favoured destination for IT business, industry, education and services; iii) apply IT tools and infrastructure to aid the process of good governance and efficient administration.

Objectives

In order to actualise the vision and mission, the government's thrust is to make IT the vehicle for productive growth in the state. Productive growth will be classified into three categories: i) IT for all round developmental growth (IT as an aid for Development); ii) Developmental activities leading to IT related growth (Development of IT Sector); and iii) Improved performance in governance and administration.

- *IT for Economic and all round Developmental Growth:* In order to make IT an engine for the growth and economic development in the state, the government will strive to:
  — use IT to effectively manage the implementation of development programmes in the state;
  — make use of IT to enhance the performance and effectiveness of development programmes in the context of economic development;
  — facilitate and promote usage of IT to attain economic, productive and developmental growth.
- *Development of IT Sector:*
  — *Creation of an Environment Conducive to IT related Activities*
    – The State Government would make an effort to create the right environment and atmosphere conducive for promoting the IT Industry in the state by way of the following:
    – Making Meghalaya a favoured IT industrial destination in the country, attracting investments from within and outside the country.

- Promoting the growth of *e*-Commerce and software exports.
- Facilitate the establishment of IT enabled service centres in the state.
- Use IT to increase the employment potential for the educated youth of Meghalaya.
- Provide special incentives to the entrepreneurs and investors and to remove bottlenecks, problems encountered by them.
- Take steps to create a conducive environment for development of IT sector.
- Endeavour to establish basic infrastructure for the development of IT industry in the state through its own resources or with the help of the Government of India, financial institutions and other IT organisations.

— *Human Resource Development:* In order to provide quality manpower for the growth of the IT industry in the state and also for the support of various services:

- The Government will facilitate and play a proactive role in ensuring professional and quality IT education in the state. In doing so, Government would take steps to ensure that organisations/institutions imparting IT education meet the standards and certifications requirements.
- With the help of the IT industry, Government would encourage setting up of IT institutions of repute in the state.

- *IT in Governance and Administration:* Providing good governance and efficient administration in the fast growing and competitive world is a challenge. IT infrastructure and tools would be utilised in overcoming the challenge by:

— applying IT in the process of attaining good governance through *e*-Governance and related concepts.

— providing quality and speedy services to the citizens of the state.

— addressing and managing security issues, cyber crimes, formulation of IT related rules and procedures and other matters relating to effective implementation of this policy.

— evolving an effective model for process re-engineering which will guide and drive the future development of *e*-Governance projects and applications.

— ensuring that a robust *e*-Governance backend is established including establishing an integrated *e*-Government systems.

— establishing a data hub and a data centre for facilitating data exchange between departments in a structured manner.

- *IT for Masses:* Making IT as a tool to play a pivotal role for uplifting the citizens through *digital unite* and bringing economic prosperity to all sections of people. The Government will use IT to the extent possible, for providing quality services to the citizens in the following areas:

  — Basic Citizen Services Interface.

  — Basic Citizen Utilities Billing Payment Interface.

  — Basic Business Services Interface.

  — Government Internet-working Interface.

    The objective is to make SMART (Simple, Moral, Accountable, Responsive, Transparent) Governance a reality, which will bring transparency, accountability and responsibility through the use of IT and achieve the following benefits:

  — Better Government Citizen services facilities.

  — Better Government Citizen transactions facilities.

  — Better Government Office automation facilities.

  — Better Government Communication facilities.

Strategy

In order to achieve the above-mentioned objectives, the government proposes to take up the following measures:

- Facilitating the creation of basic and related IT infrastructure, a prerequisite for attracting the private sector to invest in the state.

- Expediting the setting up of a Software Technology/ IT Park in the state and improving the communications network and Internet bandwidth.

- Take steps to provide last mile connectivity to the villages of the state to participate and leverage IT revolution.

- Facilitating entry of the private sector in areas like creation of IT infrastructure, creation of bandwidth, setting up of IT enabled services, software exports, etc., in furtherance of the objectives of this policy subject to rules and regulations in force.

- Forging strategic partnerships with global leaders in specific thrust areas of IT like IT infrastructure, IT education and so on.

- Spreading mass awareness about IT in the state through use of mass media such as Internet, radio, television, newspapers, workshops, exhibitions, etc.

- Giving overriding importance to Human Resource Development by investing adequately on quality training and education and by collaborating with reputed educational private sector firms within and outside the country for enhancing the marketability/employability of the IT manpower of the state.

- Promoting the use of IT in distance education and the growth of virtual classrooms and widening of opportunities for undergoing IT related vocational courses apart from strengthening the existing computer literacy programme in the schools.

- Quickening the pace of bringing about *e*-Governance which should ultimately lead to SMART (Simple, Moral, Accountable, Responsive, Transparent) Governance through:

  — encouraging an integrated government system for the purpose of grants management, budget preparation and execution and government accounting in order to enhance efficient use of resources;

  — preparation of a plan to make government services citizen-friendly and capable of being transacted through the Internet, including setting up of a mechanism for electronic delivery of citizen services in lines of *e*-Seva and other applications;

  — earmarking of up to 5 per cent of the budget by each government department for back office automation, training and capacity building, etc.;

  — introduction of web enabled citizen centric services by government departments;

  — making computer literacy a desirable qualification for recruitments in government;

  — making all the existing staff of the government computer literate at the earliest, preferably within the next three years;

  — encouraging functionaries in the government to play a proactive role in the implementation of this policy, through constant upgradation of their IT awareness and skills using IT enabled learning tools;

  — creating appropriate forum for regular interaction among the government, the academia, the industry/business and other key players in the field of IT promotion and development;

  — setting up of an IT Implementation Committee in each department for drawing up a suitable IT plan for the department, examining the problems faced during implementation and suggesting remedial action with a view to propagating IT. The IT Implementation Committee will work within specified target implementation and deadlines in order to ensure that actual solutions get implemented in a desirable timeframe;

  — designating one senior officer in each department as a Nodal Officer for IT for more effective liaison on all IT related matters with the IT department;

  — encouraging functionaries in the government to play a proactive role in the implementation of this policy, through constant upgradation of their IT awareness and skills;

  — putting in place mechanism for removal of hurdles and bottlenecks.

Incentives and Investment Promotion

In pursuance of the goals and objectives enunciated in the foregoing paragraphs, the State Government has decided to offer investors the incentives as specified in the State Government's Industrial Policy 1997 as amended from time to time or its successor policy.

- *Special Incentives for IT Enabled Industries:* Over and above the benefits provided to the IT industries in terms of the State Industrial Policy, an additional 10 per cent subsidy would be provided to the IT enabled services in respect of power, captive generating set including non-conventional energy generating set, state capital investment subsidy and subsidy on rented infrastructure.

- *Priority for Disbursement:* The disbursement of the incentives by the implementing agency would be in accordance with the chronological order of approved claims. Priority would, however, be given to 100 per cent export oriented units.

- *Interpretation:* The decisions of the Department of Information Technology, Government of Meghalaya as regards to interpretation of this policy including the incentive schemes shall be final.

- *Inter-connectivity of International Call Centres/IT Enabled Services:* The Government would permit inter-connectivity between call centres or other units of IT Enabled Services. This includes load sharing between the centres for optimum utilisation of expensive resources (International Bandwidth), interconnecting two facilities through fibre optic cable to help companies to establish customer/expertise specific centres of excellence, international call centre, etc.

- *Single Window Clearance:* To facilitate and expedite the various clearances and government approvals required by entrepreneurs, as also to promote investments in the state, the government would set up a single window agency for all IT related investments in the state.

- *Working Capital from Banks:* Government will encourage lead Banks to set up special cells to provide working capital to IT enabled services units.

Role of the IT Department

The Information Technology Department would perform a nodal, catalytic and facilitating role in all matters relating to IT and also in the implementation of this IT policy. The policy shall come into effect from the date of notification and until further orders. The Government reserves the right to make any amendments to the policy. All departments would consult and inform IT department in IT related matters.

Significant Festivals

A five-day-long religious festival of the *Khasis Ka Pamblang Nongkrem* popularly known as *Nongkrem* dance is held annually at village Smit, 11 km from Shillong. *Shad Sukmynsiem*, another important festival of the Khasis, is held at Shillong during the second week of April. *Behdiengkhlam,* the most important and colourful festival of the Jaintias, is celebrated annually at Jowai in Jaintia Hills in July. *Wangala* festival is observed for a week to honour Saljong (Sungod) of the Garos during October-November.

Ka Pomblang Nongkrem popularly known as Nongkrem dance is one of the most important festivals of the Khasis. It is a five-day religious festivals held annually at Smit village 11 km from Shillong, the headquarters of the syiem (chief) of Khyrim. The festival is held as a thanks-giving ceremony to God Almighty for harvest and to pray for peace and prosperity. Shad Sukmynsiem is another important festivals of the Khasis.

It means 'Dance of the Joyful Heart and is also a thanks-giving dance. Maidens dressed in traditional fineries and men folk in colourful costumes participate in the dance to the accompaniment of drums and flute. It is held in Shillong sometime during the second week of April every year and lasts for three days.

Behdiengkhlam, the most important festival of the Jaintias is celebrated annually at Jowai in Jaintia Hills during the month of July. It is a very popular and colourful festival where men, young and old take part in the dancing to the tune of drums and flute. Wangala, one of the most important festivals of the Garos is held during October-November, and it lasts for a week.

This festival is observed to honour and offer sacrifice to their greatest God called Saljong (Sungod). The occasion is initiated, right in the field by simple but impressive ceremony known as RUGULA. After that the ceremony of incense known as Sasat Soa is celebrated. This is performed inside the house of the chief of the village. On this occasion people-young and old, boys and girls in their colourful costumes with feathered headgear dance to the tunes of music played on long oval-shaped drums.

Transportation

Roads: Six national highways pass through Meghalaya. The State has 7,328 km of both surfaced and unsurfaced roads under PWD.

Aviation: The only airport in the state at Umroi, 35 km from Shillong, is yet to function.

Railways: The state is not connected by railway network.

Aviation: Shillong is the only airport in the state. Vayudoot service caters to this airport.

Sports

Meghalaya, cosily nestled on the lap of Himalayas, has not been the seat of traditional and popular games like cricket or football. Meghalaya sports demand a higher adrenaline rush and tensing of the nerves. Some of the sports that commensurate with the vibrant topography and climate of the place are:

- *Trekking:* Trekking in Meghalaya is like an adventurer's dream come true. The state challenges the trekkers with its diverse flora and fauna, rare orchids, rolling rivers and towering mountains. It is preferred by the trekkers over, say, Rotang Pass or Pelling for being snow-ridden. Though rainfall poses a serious threat to them, yet the terrain is irresistibly alluring.

- *Caving:* Meghalaya can boast of abundant stalagmite and stalactite caves that are not easy for general tourists to explore. That is why expert cavers round the globe flock into Meghalaya to map and classify them. Caving provides a cutting edge to the tourism industry of the state. Some of the caves available for caving are Siju, Mawsynram, Syndai and Mawsmai.

- *Archery:* Archery is the most prominent source of recreation of the ethnic groups of the state, and it also plays a vital role in their festivals. Locally it is known as 'Teer'.

- *Golf:* Golf is also a popular game. The United States Golf Association Library and Museum has titled the Shillong Golf Course as the "Gleneagle of the East". But unlike archery, golf in Meghalaya is usually played by the upper-middle class.

Football

The prospect of Indian football is too bleak, so is the case with state football. Though the passion and excitement of the game keeps the football-lovers on their toes, it is listed far down, among all the football playing states of India. Its neighbouring state, Manipur, has left its mark in the domain of football. Football is still to make its impact felt.

In the national games football has made its debut only recently. None of its team appear in the National Football League. It does not have any 1st division clubs either. Teams like Lajong Sports Club, Shillong, and Laitumkhrah Football Club, Shillong, plays only in the 2nd division, but Meghalaya junior football team had won the Junior Football Championship way back in 1989.

It is true that the climate is not at all conducive for football because round the calendar it is washed-off by heavy downpour. Even the topography of the place does not support the game. Even the management called the Meghalaya Football Association is hardly furnished to bring some drastic change.

In spite of these drawbacks, the state over the years have produced some great players of the game. But the saddest part of the story is that these players from Northeastern India migrate either to West Bengal or Goa for adequate exposure and also to earn a livelihood. Consequently, Meghalaya football has never excelled as a State Unit. The recent victory of Meghalaya over the stalwart of Indian football, West Bengal by 4-1 margin, is now considered as the epiphany of its football.

Tourism

Meghalaya is dotted with a number of lovely tourist spots where nature unveils herself in all her glory. Shillong, the capital city, has a number of beautiful spots. They are: Ward's Lake, Lady Hydari Park, Polo Ground, Mini Zoo, Elephant Falls and Shillong peak overlooking the city and the golf course which is one of the best in the country.

Tourist Centres

Meghalaya is dotted with a number of lovely spots where nature unveils herself in all her glory. Shillong, the capital city has a number of beautiful spots. They are: Ward's Lake, Lady Hydari Park, Polo Ground mini stadium. Elephant Falls and Shillong Peak overlooking the city and the golf course which is one of the best in the country.

3

History

- -

Khasi linguistically represents the Mon-Khmer speeches spoken in South East Asia. Mon-Khmer, it is well known, belongs to the Austro-Asiatic family included in the Austric super-family. Khasi as survived as a distinct island of its own owing to its past connection with the number of Mon-Khmer speeches which exist in the far-flung South-Eastern Asia, still spoken in Laos, Cambodia, Vietnam and as far as Malaysia, and which include mainly the Khmeric and the Bahnaric. A belief may have subsisted that Mon-Khmer although now current in the Asiatic mainland, must have at one time, belonged to some other Languages spoken more westwardly whose home lay originally in the Middle East or the Mediterranean World. Language is a very important factor to determine the ethnological, cognate, cultural relations of the races with whom the Khasis were related. Ethnologically the Mon-Khmer speaking people are believed to originally represent the Negrito or Dravidic substratum of physical formation which subsequently gave way to the Mongoloid complex in a series of racial inter-mixture.

Old Settlers

The Khasis ascribed to be the earliest immigrants possessed a culture which up-till the medieval time, had shown a transformation from palaeolithic to neolithic and rteolithic to chalcolithic (with a developed techno-economic pattern of its own): the theory of their migration from the once known Mon-Khmer abodes has been receiving its proper corroboration. Their migration must have been caused by many factors. DGE Hall subscribes to the view that the Mon-Khmer were among the first to discover the irrigated rice irrigation as conforming to wet-rice farming and this practice was adopted in the great delta of Red river in Tonking. This led to the foundation of new centres of wet rice cultivation on the mouths of the Mekong, the Menam and the Irrawadi.

The Tonking later on was preponderated by the Vietnamese for which the majority of the wet-rice cultivators went up the Red river to Yunnam and owing to the severe cold climate, followed the Red river to its source South of Tali. "Made their way across northern Burma to Khasi in the plain of East Assam where they established a new centre".

Luce's theory must have been partly corroborated by the local tradition which recounts that their ancient forefathers came here from the coastal region through the long, arduous journey in search of rice lands. In their new centres great rice markets, such as law-dai-ja were established which symbolised the greatness of ancient kingdoms such as Malnoiang and Shillong and great rice bowls (pliang ja) highly symbolic of kingdom's power in the ancient Sutnga. The first batch among the immigrants who touched the flat rice lands, squatted them where they established an entity; the next following batch having found such rice lands deficient, were compelled to develop a rice terraced farming on the hills' bases and the valley about them; the next batch due to the paucity of good arable lands, pushed themselves to the higher hills to develop a dry rice cultivation and the last batch pushed southward to develop horticulture on the southern flanks. Along, the Sutnga syiem, tradition suggests, having been hard pressed by the deficiency of rice lands, later on descended down to Jaintiapur near Sylhet and by means of a strategy and conquest, annexed Sylhet to Sutnga which became the dominion of his kingly dynasty till 1835.

States in Ancient Period

The ancient kingdoms were confined to the contiguous plain comprised mostly in the Kamrup and Nowgong districts, Assam and eastward. Glimpses to their ancient kingdoms located in Assam have also flashed themselves. The kingdoms evidently were Kamakhya (after Ka meikha, the ancient mother), Kolong or Kapli, Mahadem and others. The Ka raeikha kingdom later on was known as Nongwah or Rani which survived till the middle of the last century.

A fully reconstructed history has come out. It presents a detailed account of socio-economic, cultural and political events and focuses the state chronology of all the Khasi kingdoms. A condensed History as should suit with our purpose here, therefore, is deduced. The glimpses of their ancient history can now be considered. In condensing this form of history, only the most important landmarks will be made use. The history in its own fashion has revealed many formative events more especially in the field of statesmanship and other auspicious events. They have bearing on the romantic, or otherwise the realistic and intellectuous life-styles of the people.

About the Khasis, Allan Wilson writes: "There is some reason to believe that they sent an embassy to China, sometimes in the 16th century, for it has on the record that an embassy came to Peking headed by a man named U All which is essentially a Khasi name, and some twelve years ago, a small metal slab was obtained in Nowgong the district which adjoins the north side of the Khasi Hills which is a Chinese credential of some sort.

It is made of copper, thickly plated with gold, in the shape of the knifeboard about five inches long, two and half wide and one inch thick.

It is evidently formed of a pair; because an inscription had been engraved round the edges of the two placed together and this cannot be read in the absence of the second slab as every letter is cut in half. It seems likely that after these slabs were prepared, the ambassador was given one, the other being retained in Peking so that if later another ambassador, came, bearing the credential given to the former man, the two could be placed together he has properly accredited person". Wilson upon this finding (subject to further corroboration) concludes." In the ancient times the Khasis were a much more powerful people than they have ever been since the British had any connection with India, and their customs are enforced or copied by neighbouring tribes.

In this regard we find also that the Rajmala mentioned that the Kingdom Kupli or Kolong, Nowgong also called *Hidimba* (in Khasi Mahadem) as its earlier King being Yu-Chai (Khasi U All) who sent a mission in 428 AD to Peking. This is corroborated by the finding of a sculpture of an ancient piece of embroidery with the familiar Chinese twig and flower designs along with a few inscriptions of a local or mixed character at Raitong, the hill headquarter of a great and extensive kingdom. About 200 years ago, Lindsay said that he saw a trade caravan descending the hills to modern Bangladesh bringing numerous hill goods consisting of the coarsest silk from the confines of China.

Yet a few stories mention a few Khasi kingdoms on North Cachar and Nowgong. I got one story which says that the troops of a Kashmiri conqueror who, after having subjugated many kingdoms in India, came to invade Assam. The troops arrived at the bank of Kolong river in Nowgong. A Khasi Kingdom has extended as far as Loom-Ding (now Lumding railway junction) on its eastern limits. The Khasis dropped the offensive and adopted a stratagem for maintaining their defence.

The stratagem they employed was simple by which a large number of eastern wares were floated down the river. The enemy took this sight as a warning and bad portent. The Kashmirian opened negotiation which led to an intermarriage held and for which in return, the Kashmirians gave the Khasis a turban, or Pagri in Khasi Khor or Kliriant of embroidered colours used till this day by princes, officials and even dancers. Thus through tactful means the Khasis defended themselves without any loss. We find one reference to Laladitya's invasion of Assam which occurred in the 8th century AD. In that account we find the Laladitya with his troops were successfully repulsed by the Queen of Jaintia.

The corroborative evidence reads as follows:

"The next invasion of importance was the invasion of the country by Laliditya, the kind of Cashemre whose reign extended from 714 to 750 AD. He seems to have bent for acquiring the sovereignty of all over India, for having made the circuit of Hindustan ....he directed his steps to Assam the city of Pragjyotishpore was empty on his arrival, and he turned thence to the country of Jaintia called the Stri Rajya, because it was governed by a Queen. The Queen and her subjects, it is said, triumphed over the monarch and his soldiers by other weapons than those of a war".

As regards Kamakhya, it was occupied by a Khasi King for ages. It remained under the British a much small kingdom till the last century; the kingdom according to record lapsed because there was no more heir to succeed to it. The Garos also say that they stayed at Kamakhya for sometime. However, a tradition claims that the Khasis rescued the Garos during their sojourn on the Brahmaputra bank. In fact Kamakhya in Garo means victory to my mother where at its precinct a Garo maiden was married to a Khasi Prince and where since then, the common matrilineal laws of succession (with deviations as tantamount to their conditions) were adopted by them. Many treaties of friendship and allegiances were since then adopted by them. Bulk of Nowgong comprising Raha, Neli, Sahara, Khela, Dimurka, Gobhat till precisely 1835 was ruled by the Jaintia King and westward part of Dimurua, Beltola, Khanapara were ruled by the King of Shillong and areas extending more westward to Goalpara by the other Syiems. The Khasis, subsequently fought against the Muslim invaders who sought passage to Assam and repulsed them. The tradition also recounts that the ancient Khasis came here in search of rock traps for building, their stone culture with its vast and variegated manifestations or facets as well as the iron pyrites and various metals.

Some of the cultural and economic factors which determined the stages of settlement can be reiterated briefly below:

"Agriculture among other activities predominated the scene. Agriculture had hitherto confined itself to the fertile valleys and lower ranges but even the southern mountain terrain had accommodated farming of several tropical fruits and crops. A variegated system of agriculture had sprung."

Some megalithic- constructions evidently were connected with agricultural festivals; they were as well connected with the funerary customs and practices of the people.

The first hordes of immigrants spread first in lower Assam and the adjoining region that was northern Meghalaya where, they practised wet rice cultivation. In course of time, ironsmelting had dwindled in Bhoi or the north and the ever increasing population stood in need of more arable land for paddy and crops; this caused a transmigration process from Bhoi on the north to the central plateau where considerable works in ironsmelting, iron industry and other kinds of metallurgy were boosted for the long ages. The population made inroads into the narrow, southern terrain for fruit cultivation and lime excavation. The first northern Bhoi kingdoms evidently had emerged which subsequently were absorbed to the central kingdoms where mining and iron-smelting were actively undertaken. Iron-smelting recently appears lately have dwindled on account of the heavy deforestation which had upturned the series of hills and had made them permanently barren. Most of the plain tracts where the earliest population was confined were the integral part of the Khasi kingdoms and the arrangement lasted until the first British administrators in keeping with their administrative interest, bifurcated bulk of those tracts and transferred them to the plain districts of Assam.

The commercial considerations as such loom large in which the priority of economic importance is stressed. We find that the iron industry had effectively played its role in causing the type of economic viability which accounted for a huge scale transaction of steel, iron and other blacksmithery implements, instruments and other products which had shaped the mercantile character of the people. Gold and Silver as well had been actively mined in the hills located in the vicinity of centres of iron-smelting which occurred at the rainiest terrain. Goldsmithery and Blacksmithery as such, once were extant.

Historical Retrospective

Evidently the Khasis had established kingdoms which comprised the hills and plain tracts. There were other events which became the great, illustrious landmarks. With regard to the historical retrospective, the earliest Bhoi Kingdom were renowned and had equally displayed many creative attainments in the field of culture, society and statesmanship. The exemplary kingdoms are named Mu-Ksiar, Mahadem, Thaiang, Nongtluh, Myrwet, Iapngar, Mawthoh, Nongbri and many others. They were superseded by the great central kingdom and till today, the Syiems of those reduced principalities owe their allegiance and acknowledge their overall jurisdiction. A few other Bhoi principalities such as Jirang and Nongpoh retain their old identity and are not subordinate to the big kingdoms. Some large kingdoms of old went extinct. The commercial jurisdiction of such states had become enhanced and trade links were maintained with the distant lands such as China, Bengal and the great plains of Hindustan.

Most of the Khasi States recognised till 1947 (the date on which the transfer of power by the British to the National Government occurred), are still retained and the continuity of their traditional system of administration is now maintained under the Autonomous District Council. Some of the kingdoms already came to limelight during the Anglo-Burmese war which took place between 1818 and 1824. This event laid the antecedent for the British occupation of the North-East. In 1824 and 1826, U Ram Singh Rajah of Jaintia and U Tirot Singh, the King of Nongkhlaw signed an agreement with the East India Company represented by David Scott, Agent to the Governor General which sought to facilitate a road construction through the hills to connect Bengal and Assam and stipulated other terms of a trade treaty. The parties agreed to reinforce mutual assistance in the event of a war against any other party. In 1829 the Khasis rose in insurrections against the British

Government which with certain gaps lasted till 1839. The contemporary situation provides the important clue to the Khasi kingdoms and their territorial jurisdictions. The situation can be reiterated on the basis of a publication entitled U Tirot Singh, Syiem Nongkhlaw — an illustrious Khasi Hero and Personage published in 1984.

The article contained therein is properly authenticated and loaded by sources quoted from the records lying in the Archives. One of the quotations in 1834 says: "Some of the Khasi Rajahs in the plain are Rajahs over the independent communities in the hills or are relations of the chieftains", Ferdinand Jenkins Agent to Governor General made that statement. The review of the states is relevant to our understanding which is mentioned below:

Nongstoin: The western most state bounded on the north by Kamrup, Jyrngam and Goalpara, on the south by Mymensing, on the east by Rambrai, Muriaw, Nobsohphoh and Langrin and on the west by the Garo Hills. Its westward boundary once had stretched far into the interior of Goalpara District. But the power of the state was slowly declining after the coming of the East India Company. In 1831, a large tract of the Kala Rajah of Nongstoin lying in Goalpara was removed from his possession and merged into the British District consequent on the raid he carried out into Assam besides which a fine was imposed by an Agreement executed in August 1832. However, uptill 1863 Rambrai and Nongstoin still held a smaller tract in Goalpara. The state comprised the western plateau in which its southern boundary had stretched to Mymensing. The Nongstoin people use to cite instances of the fabulous vastness of their kingdom and the many days' journey it took to cover the distance north to south and east to west.

Raanbrai: Located northeast of Nongstoin, south of Myriaw and west of Nongkhlaw. Besides the hills, this state comprised three tracts in Lower Assam known as Pantan, Bogy and Bungang which lie north of Boko and west of Matrapur. These tracts were heavily exposed to the havocs which followed the invasion of Assam in 1830-31. David Scott wrote on a raid perpetrated by Rambrai on the lowlands of Pantan, Bogy and Bungang in January 1831 that "The estates in question were under our attachment, the first in consequence of the part which the Rajah had taken against us and the two latter for the recovery of the arrear of revenue". These tracts however had been seized from Rambrai in consequence of the war fought with Government.

Myriaw: Myriaw lies south of Rambrai and west of Nongklaw. Both the traditions and records associate Myriaw with Mawrapur as being one kingdom, the passage being made through Bardwar. Mawrapur means perhaps the modern Matrapur situated east of Pantan and west of Rani Kudam.

Nongkhlaw: Nongkhlaw lies west of Nongpoh, Nongwah and Sohiong, south east of Jirang and north of Nongspung. Its outlying territory was know as Bardwar.-The statement of Rijon Singh, the Syiem of Nongkhlaw and Bardwar from 1833 to 1848 is: "Our door is in the jurisdiction of Nucklow which is proved by the para papers of the Assam Rajah, and previous orders passed by you".

Jyrngam or Joreegham: Jyrangam lies north of Nongstoin and west of Barwar and Rambrai. Its Syiem ruled Jyrngam in the hills and Luki in Assam. But Luki was also governed by the Nongstoin Syiem or Rungshu Rajah, both maintaining control over it.

Mokut and Bungong: A plain tract administered by a vicegerent of Nongstoin. In 1834 Simtoo Singh and Jubbur administered it.

Bee Sing: A small territory in the plain and was administered by a Hill Chief.

Panbari: Lying north of Nongstoin under the Panbari or Nongkumah Syiem administered by U Long.

Boko: Lying east of Panbari and south of Pantan, administered by U Ru.

Nonglong: One of the hill principalities ruled by U Youngmah Syiem. He was the nephew of U Ru; therefore Boko and Nonglong formed one kingdom.

Nongkumah: The Nongkumah Syiem ruled this state in which Nongkuman and Nongbaji areas were comprised which thence adjoined itself to a plain known as Panbari. Lamkah was inhabited mainly by the Assamese and Durunghree and Dumran were its main stations.

Dimah: The Dimah Syiem exercised jurisdiction over Narung-mah and Ringsi which thence stretched itself to Hahym.

Jirang: Lying east of Bardwar and west of Rani was ruled by U Jah Lyngkut.

Nongwah: Comprising Pat Syiem, Mawtymmur, Mawtymmar and Hill villages and adjoining itself to Ranigoan, thence further north to Patganj and Palasari: it lies east of Matrapur and west of Beltola. The kingdom originally was known as Ka Mei Kha with its headquarter located near Maliganj. U Lanai or U Sib known in the record as Bolaram was then the Nongwah Syiem.

Nongpoh: Bounded on the north, south and east by Shillong and on the West by Nongkhlaw and Nongwah, Nongpoh or Ka Hima Knadar Lyngdoh appears to have no territory adjoined to the Assam plain, being sandwiched between Shillong and neighbouring States.

Shillong: The far-eastern kingdom bounded on the north by the river Brahmaputra and Guwahati, on the south by Sylhet, on the east by Jaintia and on the west by Rani Nongwah, Nongpoh, and Sohiong. The four tracts since time immemorial in Assam over which the Syiem exercised sovereignty were the western part of Gobha, Doomoreah or Dimurua, Khanapara and Beltola. The first Anglo-Khasi war in fact broke out in August 1828 when Bor Manick and his force attacked the Doomoreah revenue station and confiscated the revenue which had been collected by the government officials. This event provided an antecedent to the beginning of a Khasi movement which commenced on April 4, 1829.

Southern Region

On the foot of the southern hills in the plain tract conforming now to northern Bangladesh west to east, we find that the area contiguous to Sushang and Mymensing was under Nongstoin. The Langrim Syiem eastward occupied a tract near Buglee Chowrah.

The Mawiang Syiem exercised jurisdiction in Nolikhata. The Maharam Syiem occupied a tract near Sunamgani in which Ranikor and Balat in the foothills formed the main state outlets. Then eastward Shella possessed a tract which according to the tradition included Chattack which formed a state entrepot. The tract in which Panduah, Bholaganj, Fatehpur and Angajur were comprised, was under the possession of the Syiem of Sohra. The latter two tracts Angajur and Fatehpur of course were transferred from Mawsmai to Sohra after the former had ceased to be the state. Angajur and Fatehpur originally belonged to Jaintia which later on were ceded to Mawsmai in recognition of the latter's help to Jaintia against their enemy. Besides Bhowal, Mawlong, Sohbar, Nongtrai, Mawdon, Dwara Nongtyrnem, Malai Sohmat were in possession of the other smaller tracts. In 1866 the survey located an area south of Theria to Sohbar, Paran Saspoor and Chantukh under Maharani and the-position of the other states was indicated. The Khasi movement evidently centred round the possession of the plain tracts. Events were changing fast from 1824 to 1829. It was known that just before the occurrence of the Nongkhlaw massacre, some markets in Sylhet were seized from the Syiem's possessions. It was rightly put up that the coming of the British in Bengal had forced "The Khasis to retire to their native fastness to leave the town of Sylhet, the villages of Panduah, Chattack and many others which were once their possessions in the hands of their powerful neighbours."

The other states are Nobosohphoh, Mawsynram and Nongspung. Matvsynram is a southern State located between Sohra and Shella on the east, Maharam on the west, Pamsangut on the north and Mawdon on the south. Nobosohphoh located centrally and facing the flanks of the southern hills is bounded on the north by Mawiang and the south by Langrin on the east by Maharani on the west by Nongstoin. Nongspung lies west of Mawphlang and Sohiong and east of Mawiang. The three above were Syiemships. The coming of the British administration had other repercussions.

The contemporary states were the following: Nongstoin, Rambrai, Myriaw, Nongkhlaw, Jyrngam, Mokut Bongang, Panbari-Nong-Kumah, Boko-Nonglong, Jirang, Nongwah Rani, Langrin, Mawiang, Maharam, Sohra-Mawsmai, Malai-Sohmat, Nobosohphoh, Phowal, Mawsynram and Shillong. The land was called Ka Ri Ki Laiphew syiem or the land of Thirty Syiems. The earliest British officials in 1832 described that there was a confederation of chiefs by whom "the Khasiya mountains have been held. They are said to be thirty in number".

The Khasi kingdoms had extended more than they are today. Circumstances impelled the Syiems to station Vicegerent or Deputy Syiems in the plain. For instance, the Nongstoin Syiem stationed a Deputy Syiems at Mokut and Bungong. Panbari and Nongkumah were jointly governed by the Panbari and Sheba Syiems. In Boko U Ru was the principal Syiem while U Youngmah was his Deputy at Nonglong. Nongstoin in conjunction with the Jyrngam Rajah administered Luki. The Myriaw Syeim stationed a Deputy Syiem at Mawrapur and so did the Rambari at Pantan. Nongkhlaw used to place a junior Prince at Bardwar. The Shillong Syiem stationed a local Rajah at Dimurua but the tradition has it that besides him, one vicegerant was kept at Beltola. In 1834 Jenkins reported that "the Ryuuts are with a few exceptions all of the Kassiah origin and more Kassiah in their manners, than the Hindoos".

The most important Syiems' headquarters in Assam were Bardwar, Bhologanj, Mawrapur, Luki dwar, Pantan, Bungong, Vagatwar, Beltola, Dimurua and Rani. Some of them formed the great trade depots.

Transitional Phase: Some of the dwars had already been dislocated consequent on the Burmese invasion. The establishment of the British administration caused some adverse repercussions. For instance Bungong up-till 1825 was ruled by Obdiah who perhaps assisted the Burmese against the British and thereafter ran away after the British made their entry. In 1827 Mawrapur likewise was detached from the hold of a Syiem. Other tracts were taken consequent on the war the Khasis fought with the British. In 1836 F. Jenkins advocated that at least seven of the Dwars in Assam should be restored viz; 1. Mawrapur, 2. Bardwar, 3. Pantan, 4. Bogayee, 5. Boko, 6. Bungong and 7. Luki. Jenkins partially succeeded in that Bardwar was reinstated to a boy named Rijon who succeeded Tirot Singh in March 1834 while Boko was restored to U Ru and Bogayee was also granted to Rijon of Nongkhlaw. These Dwars when restored, the Syiems holding them had to fulfil some obligations for having accepted the British Protectorate. It was on this ground that Jenkins insisted that the above Dwars should be restored. He however omitted Bhologanj and Chhuyong (detached from Rambrai).

We find that Captain F. G. Lister located the Rajahs of the Dwars as follows:

- *Meorapur or Matrapur:* Rajah of Morreal or Myriaw.
- *Doomooreah:* Bur Manick or Bor Manick.
- *Burdwar:* Rujjon or Rijon of Nongkhlaw.
- *Boko:* Nonglong and Panbari Rajahs.
- *Boga or Boka:* Kyndoor Singh.
- *Lookee or Luki:* Rajahs of Joringam and Rungshee.

In the light of the repretensions, a communication from the Court of Directors in 1837, reads:

"The claims of certain Cosseah Chiefs to hold lands in the Doors of Assam adjacent to the Hill territories of which it is alleged, they were dispossessed of had been referred to the Commissioner of Assam. The matter immediately under consideration was a petition from the Rajah of Khyram and Moleem claiming to enter into immediate agreements with the government for the revenue of Desh Dumoora, to the exclusion of the party now enjoying the immunity, on the score of long hereditary possession. The claim of the Rajah was supported by Captain Lister, advocated by Captain Jenkins and strongly opposed by Captain Bogle".

Over the controversy raging the final ruling from the Supreme Government reads. "The Governor General requests no change of the existing state of things be made by ousting Assamese in present possession of any Door, without his previous sanction, whenever you may think it advisable to transfer any Door to a Cossya chief, you will be please to submit a special report upon the proposed arrangements, stating especially the extent of cultivated and culturable land ...the number of families inhabiting it, and their caste and tribe, and the extent of trade passing there, together with a rough delimition of the tract of country in question exhibiting the distance from the River and its bearing from Guwahati. Further it should be shown what Revenue has been here-to-fore paid for the Door and how much it is intended to demand from the Cossyas upon report drawn in this manner. His Lordship will be able to pass prompt and definite orders with satisfaction to himself". Lister and Jenkins were of course sorry for this state of things. To the Khasis it was a bolt from the blue. In these circumstances, the Khasis bade goodbye to most of their Dwars and in fact, the bulk of Lower Assam was wrested, directly from the Khasi and the Jaintia. The Khasi plain tracts were slowly being sliced from their parent kingdoms when they were annexed to the British Districts of Goalpara, Kamrup, Nowgong and Sylhet.

The gist to the decisive events which took place and which opened a new age may now be examined. In the past, however, the relations with the neighbouring kingdoms eminently the Ahom, the Kachari and Auslim had centred mostly on border skirmishes of trade pacts and, had not opened any scope for anything like political subjugation as could be carried out amongst them. With the English who had established themselves at Sylhet obtained from the Mughals as a Diwani, the relations became more effectively consolidated which had their permanent impact. The English acquired Sylhet in 1765 and this placed them very close to the southerners. The relations from the first time became strained. As early as March 1772, a punitive expedition of the East India Company advanced Jaintiapur from Sutnga or Jaintia Kingdom's capital in modern Bangladesh and exacted punishment upon them for plundering the boats laden with merchandise on the Surma. This led to the hill men's raids causing great ravages and havocal situations which complicated the administrative machinery. These raids were repeatedly conducted. In the winter of 1783, the Shella warriors raided the plain. The sardars of 137 villages at Sylhet plain perpetrated outrageous raids against their neighbours. In 1795 another conflict occurred. Almost all the southerners repeated such raids. They played fears upon the local zamindars who were faced difficulties to rendering regular revenue to Government. Some of the villages of course were taken on rent from the zamindars which was hardly returned.

We find mention to the eruption of the tribes men's raids which occurred in places lying contiguous to Sylhet in 1778, 1779, 1787 and 1795 besides the other hitherto unrecorded ones. The record corroborates the tradition which says that the Khasi freedom movement had occurred before Tirot Singh emerged as the champion of freedom struggle from 1829 to 1833 and in which U Syiem Sngap Rajah of Maharam played a similar role till 1839. Many Kings formed an alliance to protect their dominion in the plains as also trade and commerce in pre-Tirot Singh period; they took steps also to collect the revenue from their plain subjects as they had hiterto been prone to do so. In conducting the raids U Buh of Mawsmai, Kongka, Sumer and U Ksan Wahdadar of Shella and other sovereigns of Mahararn, Nongstoin arid Langrin, had their shares. The English administration at times resorted to closing the markets to the tribesmen; but it brought about the adverse result since it led to retaliations from them with repeated raids caused upon the inhabitants of the plain. The British subjects later on were prohibited from going up to the hills or supplying arms to the turbulent highlanders. This condition continued up-till the Anglo-Burmese war which also brought about the conclusion of a treaty between the East India Company and King Ram Singh and then with Tirot Singh in the years already stated. The forging of the anti-British alliance when Tirot stepped up as their champion was facilitated greatly on the similar antecental grounds laid down earlier by their predecessors.

Tirot Singh's championing of freedom movement has repeatedly been mentioned in the historical treatises. The over repetition of facts is unwarranted. The very interesting and instructive glimpses can be drawn below:

> Scott in 1826 saw to the Khasi mode of sitting of council when in person he visited Nongkhlaw to pledge a treaty with Tirot just then installed on the throne. An official attending him leaves his remark: "I was struck with astonishment at the order and decorum which characterised these debates. No shouts of exultation or indecent attempts were raised to put down the orator of the opposite party. On the contrary every speaker was fairly heard out. I have often witnessed the debates in St Stephen's Chapel, but those of the Cossya Parliament appeared to me to be conducted with more dignity of manner". It was an open door State Durbar when 500 or 600 members were present. The first ever concluded treaty was approved despite the vigorous opposition tendered and presented by the great orators.

Tirot had reasons to grow hostile to Scott and his assistants. As the road construction across the hills progressed on under the English men's supervision, relations became unpleasant. Tirot resented the oppression meted out to the road labourers. He resented some unpleasant behaviours from the sepoys posted at Nongkhlaw. To jeopardise the situation, U Bor Manick of Shillong and Tirot's ally had quarrelled the East India Company as regards his jurisdiction and authority over Desh Dimurua and in March 1828, he marched down to the dwars where he seized the revenue from the revenue officers posted by the government.

Similarly, Tirot Singh had disputed with David Scott with regard to jurisdiction over Bardwar in which Mr. Scott had proposed to restore it to the Nongkhlaw Syiem which from time immemorial belonged to them, thus Tirot announced to Government revenue superintendent at Bardwar: 'Mr. Scott made friendship with me 'previously saying your enemy is Company's enemy and that he would relinquish the Bardwar revenue, both in money and pikes. He has not done it and has the wish to give troops to my enemy'. Tirot Singh was disgusted with the refusal of the Company to furnish him military assistance against the Nongwah Syiem (Rani King), Bolaram against whom he and Bor Manick made a common stand. These circumstances led to the war fought among them from 1829 to 1833.

Initially the war struck its victory after Lts. Burlton and Beddingfield guarding the road were killed. Scott at Nongkhlaw in time miraculously escaped to Sohra and was sheltered by U Duwan the Sohra Syiem. The English indeed counted on Duwan's help for their victory. An alliance of Syiems at Tirot's behest care to exist which among others, included U Muken of Mawsmai, U Suk of Sohbar, U Ador of Mawsynram, U Ksan of Malai Sohmat, U Phar of Bhowal, U Jibor of Rambrai and many others. Later on the Nongstoin, Jyrngam, Boko and other Syiems joined the alliance. U Tirot had contrived a plot to overthrow the British power in the region and was seeking to secure adherences from his neighbours, the Assamese, the Garo, the Singpho and even the Tibetan. The English made quick and effective responses. The besieging of the hills commenced immediately, but Tirot held his ground as the war would henceforth last for four years. A book entitled Builders of Modern India — U Tirot Singh published by Publications Division 1985, New Delhi contains all the particulars in a series of exciting and interesting episodes of a great struggle; hence in our context the story needs not how to be prolonged.

Many strongholds as such were stormed and principalities reduced. Sohra became a base of operation resulting from a treaty in which Duwan Syiem handed over plots of lands in exchange with those located in the plains. Within one year, many, treaties were accepted by the southern states such as the Wahadadars of Shella (on September 3, 1829), Lar Singh of Myriaw (on September 12, 1829), Jibor of Rambrai (on October 17, 1829), Sirdar of Mawdon (in November 1829), Sirdar of Nongshken, Nongjrong and Sohbar villages and Bor Manick of Mylliem (January, 1830). They provided that the State Durbars were to settle cases except murder which had to be transferred the agent with headquarters at Sohra. The Syiems were required to grant passage to the troops and Government personnel across their kingdoms; they were required to hand over limestone quarries to the government on lease basis of returning half the dividend accruing from trade. Further, the belligerent states were imposed fines and in default, the Company took away some villages from their hold converted into British areas, discernible from states. Rambrai and Mylliem had to bear the brunt of the heaviest punishment in this respect.

Except Cherra, Langrin, Nongstoin, Nongspung and Khyrim classed as Independent, other states were treated as semi-Independent but in subsequent years, the distinction was done away with.

Back to 1829, we find that whereas the heads of States were curtailed, the large mass of people, connived with U Tirot Singh. This led to the murder of Jibor, Syiem of Rambrai for having accepted such conditions. Other states had furnished support to Tirot Singh with weapons, arms and men.

Tirot Singh conducted guerrilla operations. Many stories told are of Monbhut of great physical prowess who covered up long marches in a day. The guerrilla warfare was continued against various hindrances. The Government blockaded the hills and resorted to meting out punishment by burning many villages to the ground. With Duffa Gam, the Singpho chieftain, arrangement was made to divide their respective spheres with a view to jeopardise Government position in the hills. Rambrai made desperate stand to the last, when during 1830 and 1831 warriors of the state, on various occasions, marched down to the plains and destroyed the company's posts. At the height of these battles, David Scott died in August 1831. In 1832, the Supreme authority from Fort William, Calcutta, directed the Agent to adopt conciliatory methods and to declare amnesty to those who would submit. It was Singh Manick of Khyrim who at the last stage sought to affect a compromise between the East India Company and U Tirot Singh. During the suspensions of the operation, Tirot Singh appeared before Lister, Rutherford and Ensign Brodie in September, 1832 who assured to restore him provided he would agree to the terms and conditions. Tirot Singh demanded the abandonment of the road through his kingdom. Nothing came out, these negotiations dragged on in 1832. The British offered the throne to Jidor Singh, Tirot Singh's legitimate heir but he rejected so, long a System was there. However, during an armistice on January 13, 1833 Tirot Singh was handed over to Captain H. Inglis. He was deported to Dacca. From Dacca he was once recalled to Nongkhlaw but he rejected because he desired 'to die in a prison like a King than sit on the throne as a slave'. Not long after, he passed away.

Small States including Mawsynram, Bhowal, Malai Silmat in 1831-32 were also impelled to recognise the British paramountcy and accept the treaty imposed on them. But U Sngap Syiem of Maram prolonged the war to 1839. It was vigorously fought from 1835 to 1839. The war was waged because he refused to return the revenue collected from their lands in Sylhet to Government. U Phan Maram, U Tep Shiak and U Moit Kliaw, who commanded, held the field for long. But Maram was small and less resourceful. Nongnah, a stockaded village, remained unstormed as the three stockades were guarded day and night. But the soldiers later on learnt of an exit which was unguarded and got into it at night. Thus Maram fell and treaty was imposed.

The British creation of non-states was another characteristic of annexation, each placed under a headman whose appointment was confirmed by the Agent. They were directly responsible to him. These villages returned the annual house tax or land revenue. When Jaintia Hills were converted into British area in 1835, the Dalois, heads of elakas, were reduced to the position of petty chiefs as in the case of the other British villages. The Dalois and village headmen like laskars could levy fines up to Rs. 50 only and settle cases within the limited powers prescribed to them.

While the annexation of Khasi Hills was completed in 1839, the Jaintia Hills came under British occupation in 1835. Rajendra Singh, successor of Ram Singh, the King of Jaintia, failed to comply with some additional demands of the government to whom, he refused to pay a tribute of Rs. 10,000 in exchange for the protection conferred by the East India Company upon his kingdom; he also challenged the right of the Company to raise a new Chokey ghat at Chuppermukh in Nowgong, the boundary of his kingdom.

Moreover, he failed to produce the culprits who kidnapped and killed three British subjects who were sacrificed at the altar of the Kali goddess in Jaintiapur. For these reasons the ancient Jaintia Kingdom was annexed to the East India Company's dominion in 1835. The Viceroy at first announced to Rajendra that the government had in mind the scheme of annexing the plain portions of Jaintia Kingdom located in Cachar, Sylhet and Nowgong but Rajendra was not gratified with a partial hold of the hills and rejected it outright. Some think that his rejecting amounted to his true patriotic inclination while others suggest that he considered the hills of smaller importance as he could not exercise full authority whereas all the plains portion were counted as his personal property over which he exercised his power just like a Zamindar and drawing direct revenue from the vast estates. When the proposal was rejected, the government took the entire kingdom and since then, Jaintia Hills was classed as the British Area. Dalois were retained as the autonomous local heads.

The kingdom was sliced into the neighbouring districts, Jaintiapur and the 24 Jaintia Parganahs located in Sylhet and extending to Bodarpur were integrated into the Districts in that region whereas Chuppermukh was taken into Nowgong and the rest of the dominions in the hills was integrated into the Khasi District. The order of annexation was promulgated on February 23, 1835 and in consequence, Jaintiapur was occupied. But the Dnars and the Jaintias were not silent at the sudden turn of events. They staged an insurrection in which the regiments of the Company were moved into the hills to suppress the revolt. The insurrection was badly organised and their hills were not given a status of statehood equal to the Khasi States then.

Imposition of Tax

In 1857-58, the government imposed a house tax in Jaintia. At the same time, many crown-lands were seized upon by the administration. The people not being accustomed to paying taxes, so took it as a challenge to their custom. But the revolt in reality was aimed at the restoration of their ancient Independence. Their position was weakened by the non-availability of help. In March and April, 1860 the revolt took place and the rebels caused untold trouble to the government, they poured down to Jaintiapur where police stations located around it were burnt. Troops brought from Dacca, Sylhet and other places then were engaged to quell the revolt. Within two months, the insurrection was completely subdued. Government officials were directed to confiscate the weapons and police measures were adopted to wipe out all signs of unrest. This measure caused more hostility to the government and brought about the outbreak of the final Anglo Jantia War (1861-63). In consequence of the suspicion that Rajendra had a hand in the matter, Government ordered for his deportation to Sylhet and thence Dacca where he died in 1862.

Final Revolt

In December 1861, the final revolt broke out. The immediate cause was due to police interference in a dancing festival of the people of Jalong. The police from Jowai attended the festival and confiscated home-made weapons used during the ceremony. In these circumstances, the people of Jowai staged an insurrection and sought to furnish adequate strength in the field. The foremost leader was U Kiang Nongbah. The Pnars at first operated against the military station but it was relieved by a garrison dispatched from Cherra, the movement aiming at the attainment of full freedom. The Dalois conducted a large scale operation and the struggle took a serious turn. It continued for two years. Insurrectionary leaders were Giri Daloi of Shangpung, Bang Daloi of Nartiang, Suwar Daloi of Sutnga and many others. Other rebel leaders were Manick, Ex-Daloi from Jowai, Kiang Pator, Khro Kmah Longlah and other residents from Jowai.

Other veterans from Amwi in the south and Bhoi in the North threw solid support to Nongbah. The other names in the annals are Kma Lyngdoh and Shan Lalu of Jalong, U Smon, U Long Lyngdoh of Shangpung, U Os Daloi of Mynso, U Sati of Nongjngi, Shai Daloi of Barato and others. Terrorist methods were adopted to enlist people to the insurrectionists. Military centres were stationed. Regiments were brought from many places in view of the protracted warfare. Richardson, during the first stage, had distinguished himself in capturing many posts and locations. Yet the insurrectionaries resorted to bellicose steps to harass the government. All the warriors left their homes and were camped in the desolate jungles where they operated against Government troops and mobilised their force with lightning speed. In the middle of March 1862, General G. B. Showers proclaimed an amnesty to those who would submit but warned that the British Government would inflict a severe penalty upon those who got themselves involved with the rebels. The proclamation had no great effect. The rebels became more stubborn, the war dragged on for months and no pacification seemed possible. Both sides lost a good number of men. The Government even employed the Syiems of Sohra and Khyrim to negotiate with the rebels in thrashing over a solution to terminating this long protracted warfare and settle the differences in other ways. The insurrectionists responded that they would have nothing short of Independence.

Violent Methods

In the border areas, the Pnars adopted violent methods and from January to May 1862, campaigns were conducted into Nowgong and North Cachar Hills when villages were looted, causing great disturbances to the administration. Hundreds of warriors would appear without, warning and terrify the inhabitants. However, with the arrival of the regiments under Captain Scott and Lieutenant Inglis, they were forced to retreat.

Like U Tirot Singh, U Kiang Nongbah was captured through treachery. It is said U Long Sutnga, and U Bur Daloi on offer of money (which amounted to Rs. 1,000), gave information to the troops about U Kiang's hide-out at Umkarai village (Nartiang Daloiship). There U Kiang who was alone in his solitary residence owing to illness, was surprised by the soldiers (commanded by Lieutenant Soldier). U Kiang tried to fire them with a pistol but the weapon misfired and he was pounced upon and seized. He was arrested and taken to Jowai by devious paths in the cover of the night, and at Jowai he was tried and found guilty. Kiang gave a brave response that he had incited people because of the government's interference in their religious customs. He was hanged on December 30,1862, near the market in the heart of Jowai. Mounting up the scaffold, U Kiang made the following unforgettable dying words: "If my face turns towards the east when I die, the country will became free again. But the reverse shall happen when my face turns to the west" and when he died, it faced Eastward. Among those dead were Giri, Suwar, Mon and Kat Daloi of Nartiang. The majority of residents afterwards all came to submit. Yet it was not until November 1863, that the last of the rebels (viz., U Myllon Daloi of Mynso, U Kiang Pator of Shangpung and Bukher of Raliang) came out to tender their submission.

Shortly, after this upsurge had passed away, Jaintia Hills was consolidated into a subdivision in the charge of a Subdivisional Officer and the allegiance of the Dalois was directed to him. He was responsible to the Deputy Commissioner stationed at Shillong. Appeals from him lay with the Deputy Commissioner.

Since 1858-59, Sunnads were replaced for the old treaties conducted with the Independent and Semi-Independent States. In the arrangement in 1875, additional provisions were laid down which sought to establish Government rights to rent lands for the purpose of road-construction, raising of military and civil sanitaria and acquiring mineral rights on condition that the dividends were shared among the States and Government. The Syiem enjoyed, under the provision, judicial powers except death sentence, exile, murder and more than five years' imprisonment.

New Headquarters

In 1864, the headquarters from Sohra were transferred to Shillong after Meelay Rajah Bahadur the Syiem of Mylliem, leased out certain plots in the Shillong Town while a proportion of land needed for Government buildings was taken from private holders on rent. In 1874, Shillong was chosen to be the provincial Headquarter. In 1940, the area ceded to the Government of Assam either partially or in full was described to comprise Shillong Rifle Range and Shillong (Umlong) Cantonment. But by another arrangement, the Municipal area as, formed part of Mylliem Statue was, for the purpose of administration, under the Assam Government.

The Deputy Commissioner enjoyed almost the unlimited powers in matters relating both to the Native States and British Areas and was vested with the authority to extend Acts and other laws in the District although a few of them were not accepted. He was vested with collectorate, executive, magisterial and police functions. Most of proposals with regard to new developments were initiated by him for approval of the higher authority like the Chief Commissioner of Assam and the Governor later on. The police force acted in coordination with his advice and recommendation.

Some political parties played their role, seeking to augment the position of the states in their relations with the government. The Khasi National Durbar was one of such parties which from inception old some work until it was merged into the Eastern Tribal Union in 1955. The durbar tried to lay down rules for the codification of the diverse customs, land tenure and laws of inheritance but it was not a full success. The durbar put forward the proposal for amendment in the treaties and the abrogation of some additional clauses in the sunnads but that too was not accepted. It pressed the government to transfer some powers from the Deputy Commissioner to the state authorities but the government did not work out any change in that line. With the enforcement of the Money-Minto reforms in 1919, the Khasis got one member to represent them in the Governor's Council of Assam but the electoral constituency was confined only to those residing in Shillong's Municipal Area. It was in 1927-28 that the public representation for reserving three seats from the District in the Governor's Constituency was entertained by the Simon Commission, but the electorate comprised only the British Areas including the Jowai Subdivision and Shillong Municipality in the District.

Federation of States

In 1932, the Khasi States' Federation was formed; its objective was to act as a representative and administrative organ of the Khasi States and put forward a claim for securing greater judicial power. They urged on the transference of some departments from the Deputy Commissioner to their own management. They insisted that when any alteration of policy and administration was planned, they should be consulted. This point was pressed when a deputation from the party met Lord Wellingdon, the Viceroy of India during his visit to Shillong in 1933. But a few enlightened people, at that time thought that there should be certain scope of compromise between modernity and traditionality and that there should be some progressive efforts for expediting important reforms which should discard wrong points in the tradition, preserve good ones and introduce such administrative measures causing an all-round advancement especially in the field of Municipal administration, Higher and College Education, Public Health, Transport and Industry and Agricultural improvement. Incomplete adherence to the traditional and customary laws, some demerits were noticed such as the intricate laws of succession to State offices and others. There was further a struggle to secure a seat in the Chamber of Princes in India which the government, however, did not entertain.

On the eve of the British departure, the country became hectic as to the constitutional adjustment that should serve best for the people. In 1944, at the First Hills Youth Union formed with representatives from Naga, Lushai, Garo and Khasi communities, sought to evolve a separate pattern of administration for the Assam Tribes in a constitutional set-up. Later on, a few Ahoms joined and the said Union adopted the title of the Hills and Tribes' Conference. But soon it died down during the election issue in 1946 as misunderstanding cropped in as to the choice of an election ticked by one candidate.

Interim Period

The Interim period in India was eventful for during that time, the Khasi States' Federation managed the affairs of the states, according to the powers derived from the Instrument of Accession. The party supporting this Institution was the Khasi States People's Union. Important portfolios of administration were opened excluding those which vested on the Dominion Legislature whereas other concurrent matters fell under the joint control of the Federation and either the Dominion or the Government of Assam. When the Federation was set up, the point was also pressed that British Areas be merged into their respective parent States or assign them a separate state status. The Court of the Federation was set up which was to be the highest authority in respect of customary law, whereas in appeals not concerned with customary law, the Assam High Court would have the appellate jurisdiction. This Court was even empowered to pass death sentence, transportation and life-imprisonment, subject to the revision and confirmation of the High Court of Assam. Its subordinate courts were given powers not exceeding those of a Magistrate of the First Class as defined in the Code of Criminal Procedure. No appeal was recommended to lie against imprisonment less than three years. But since 1937 and earlier, a Syiem's Court was empowered to deal only with cases arising within its jurisdiction, between Khasis only, while over non-Khasis, the jurisdiction of the Assistant to the Deputy Commissioner was extended. Concessions, however, were allowed to the Khasi Syiern to deal with such cases when both parties willingly submitted to the arbitration of the Syiem's Court. Appeals were recommended to lie with the Deputy Commissioner in civil cases.

National Conference

The Khasi-Jaintia National Conference; however, was opposed to the continuance of the Federation and came forward with the plan for the Autonomous District Council in the regular set up, agitations of the two parties filled up the constitutional forums although during the last stage.

The said Conference faced adverse reaction from the Khasi States' People Union. During the plebiscite held in 1948, the latter swept the polls and during the Khasi Constitution making durbar, it won the majority of members present that the Federation should continue. However, during the final arrangement, the Sixth Schedule was applied to both states and British Area. The Jaintia Durbar was a principal party in Jaintia Hills. It arranged the sending of a member to the Assam Legislative Assembly in 1937. The Khasi National Durbar was merged into the APHIC

The early History of the Garos, is shrouded in mystery. Most of the traditions locate clearly that Tibet was their home from where their forefathers had been diffused to different places. They recount that they came eastward from the Himalayas and reached Gondulghat, then traversed westward to Amingaon in a circuitous route. They crossed the river Brahmaputra over rafts built of plaintain trunks and came to the south bank in Kamrup District. During the Sojourn, they were connected with Kameikha, Ka makha or Kamakhya.

Garo traditions centre round one of their great Kings, Nokma Abong Chirepu who united and wielded the different tribes in the land under one kingdom and made them a people. The Ambeng, Kotchu, Akawe, Duab, Atong, Megam, all acknowledged his suzerainty whose headquarters was raised on Mongri hill overlooking the Simsong. Historical antecedents now have to be briefly assessed. A popular tradition ascribed that they came migrating from Kamrup to Rongtungbari, Sameguru, Rangshal, Agal, Dileng and Patal and Matiapanshia in Goalpara where at Matiapanshia, Garos, Digils, Megains, the Khasis and Ranga Kutches traded and bartered, the market that was known as Sangkadik Wakmitim and where a loose confederation was instituted. It was there the sons of Siram (or Sirampe), children of Megam-Nongal, Ronga Kutch and Doli tribesmen agreed to confine heirship to daughters and to adopt the cross cousin marriage. This was agreed to during a great feast held in the house of Bonepa, a Rajah of Rangbaldi-Rangbalda at Matia Panshia where delegates from all over were entertained at the feast with meat, pork and fowls and beers brewed of rice, millet and maize.

The consent obtained, the different groups of Garo skirted off through the dense jungles of the wild mountain tract. It is said that the batch led by Aiuk Rajah and Asilik Gitel with Simbe and Sambe their respective wives, of the Lyngngams or Megams, were settled at Godaram Soeram and spread to Dalram Sek Segram on western Khasi. A batch went on to explore the enchanting Simsang valley which soon was inhabited. Buia, Rengwa, Salbong, Suapa, Nengilpa, Nibo and Changbo lead another party which were finally settled at Demik A. Ding and Kimarong-Patal the next batch occupied Chambilgre in the valley of Dareng river. Stories still told are of Joreng. Doreng of great physical prowess who, while exploring the Tura range, killed a monstrous hawk which had killed and carried off both men and cows.

History later on became essentially mingled with the vital relations cultivated among the Garos with their neighbours, the Ahom, Bengalee and Muslim through trade and other contacts. Internally the administration was based on the system of NOK-MASHIP practised through the ages.

British Period

A record history comes with the British advent. The East India Company in 1765 took possession of Gowalpara (Goalpara) following its renunciation by a Mughal Emperor in an agreement concluded with the British Government. Now tension had grown between the Garo and the plain men; but even before that serious conflicts had taken place between the zamindars and the tribesmen. The Moguls to guard their boundaries had entrusted a class of zamindars known as Choudhuries and a militia was placed with them. The Choudhuries enjoyed large autonomy besides collecting rent inside their own estate, arranged trade also with the hills. The Zamindars now imposed levies upon Garo traders. They held the monopoly of the Garo cotton, renowned for its quality. Zamindars which Garos had dealing were Howrahghat, Mechpara, Kalumalupara, Karaibari, Sushong, Sherpore and Bijni (the latter ruled by a Rajah). The Garos being exploited were incited to revolt. Large groups of Garo settled at the plain were also exploited. The earliest raid perpetrated by the tribesmen occurred at Kalumalara. The raid following at Mechpara had caused an exodus of population elsewhere. Troubles would have ensued with Bijni Rajah but for a timely intervention of the sepoys at the disposal of the government from Jogighopa in Goalpara the force being stationed in Goalpara to meet airy eventuality arising of the Garo raids into the Company's dominion. The Garos reacted by suspending their cotton trade. Garo inroads mounted-up.

New Regulations

New administrative regulations were enforced since 1765, when a revenue collector was placed at Rangmati, a new arrangement being made that the Zamindars would pay revenue in cotton to the government in place of other trifling goods and all tribute was now directed to be deposited at Rangmati. Later on, payment in cash than cotton was insisted upon. From 1794, market transit dues were charged upon goods passing through the Zamindaris and the burden fell heavily upon Garo traders in the plain.

Garo head-hunters were then actively engaged in carrying off enemy heads motivated by the religious demand during the cremation of their chiefs; skulls were also valued as village trophies. Many persons were carried off from the plains as slaves. The loss of cotton markets also caused other difficulties. Clan vendatta and inter-tribal feuds also filled in the pages of history. Moreover, Garo landlords fought with other Garo chiefs while Garo Zamindars waged war also with the non-Garo landlords.

Government, on the other hand, was seriously concerned with the state of affairs. It led to the appointment of a Commission to assess the situation. The Commission examined the affairs elaborately and brought over their report. They recommended that all hat levies hitherto imposed upon the Garos be abolished and the Zamindars be paid compensation for their renunciation of rights. This measure was devised to pacify the Garos. But it brought about a confrontation from the Zamindars. The Rajah of Karaibari took his stand and challenged the measure up-till 1815, the date he was subdued. To rectify his claim he had taken steps to reduce the neighbouring Garos to complete subjection.

Irrespective of these measures, Garo raids still increased from 1795 to 1807 which had brought about large tolls. Within 10 years before 1816, Garos ravaged a number of villages and caused loss of 178 lives. Karai-bari was exposed to large-scale raids in 1806 alone. Head-hunters in considerable swarms lurked the plain and during each visit, came back home with a large number of skulls which attained eminence at village dances and festivals. The next move of the government was the deputation of Mr. Thomas Sisson, Joint Magistrate, Rangpur to study the situation in 1815. Sisson undertook the task and came out finally with a recommendation in which Mr. David Scott was proposed to be appointed as Commissioner and on whom devolved the task to assess the relations.

The subjugation of Karaibari Rajah in 1815 no doubt, had relieved a section of Garos from the Zamindaris' exploitation, but Garos settled at the Zamindaris' located in the plains were still subject to the Zamindaris' control. Mr. Scott submitted an elaborate report which led to the promulgation Regulation, X of 1822 which bifurcated the Thanahs of Goalpara, Dhubri and Karaibari from the jurisdiction of the Rangpur District and consolidated into District, northeast of Rangpur called Garo Hills, the District of Goalpara, included. The Commissioner was in charge of the District vested with judicial, police and collectorate powers, he was to work under the direct order of the Governor-General-in-Council, has had full power to conclude terms with other Garo Chiefs.

Mr. Scott, Civil Commissioner in 1816 to the charge of Goalpara thanahs, started to negotiate with the various Garo Chiefs and later on concluded terms with them who wished to accept British protection and submit to the jurisdiction of the British courts and police stations and abstain from head-hunting. They were allowed to carry trade on the plains except Garos in the interior hills who, in exchange for passage, were conditioned to pay duties. The Garo area, under a new arrangement, was divided into two divisions — Nazarana mahals and Zamindari mahals. The former applied to the highlanders who without being actually subject to the British laws were, tributary to the British authority. Zamindari mahals returned the revenues and deposited them to the government, out of which the Zamindars were paid compensation. Besides, there was a group of Independent villages excluded; it was they who protracted the annexation and consolidation of the entire tract for several decades. It was up-till 1873 that the annexation was accomplished. The Garo Sarbarakar was appointed to deposit the revenue collected by the laskars and the Sirdars; they with their Sarbarakar were to receive compensation in the form of remuneration in addition to the official costume. The new Commissioner's jurisdiction was geographically to extend over the Garo Hills but the true administrative control was exercised in the hills not until the formal annexation in 1866. The system had not removed the Garos totally from the hold of Zamindars in a considerable measure in which Garos had many obligations to perform.

Many stories told are of David Scott, the first white man who was acquainted with the Garos and received at their homes. He attended many council sittings with the Nokmas. His adventures in the face of oppositions and plots in the unfriendly circles are told but he escaped all the perils by the dint of his strong wits. Scott was versatile and creative. He urged the government to set up, a school for the dissemination of education to Garos. Mr. Fermie, a school teacher, was appointed to a first school in Singimari but the educational project received its death-blow in the sudden death of Fermie and the project was revived not until 1847 when another Garo school at Goalpara was set up, supported by Captain Jenkins, Commissioner. According to a tradition, three Garo boys were sent to, a Serampore for study during Scotts' time. David Scott was later on associated with the Khasis from 1826 up-till his death in August 1831.

The new settlement had produced better results. The territory claimed by the Garos and that claimed by the Zamindars were transferred to Government. Rent to be returned from mahals in the transferred territory called Garo mahals was regularised and the area was assessed to house tax. Within a short time between 100 and 200 Garo chieftains, west of the Simsang river, came to negotiate with Scott. The settlement brought about a temporary pacification.

When Mr. Scott was appointed Agent to the Governor General for the Northeastern frontier in November, 1823, resulting from the Burmese invasion, his place was taken by the Principal Assistant to the Commissioner assisted by a Garo Sarbarakar. In 1826, the Goalpara District which comprised Garo Hills was attached to Assam.

The Uprising

The peaceful state was soon broken up by an uprising when 700 Garos rose against their landlord at Sherpore. The Government, at times, closed down the markets to the Garos for preventing the further recurrences of raids but it bore little effect.

Many more difficulties were encountered in dealing with the Garos. The tribute due from them was not punctually paid. Mr. Robertson, successor to David Scott adopted several punitive measures to bring them to terms. In 1833, the expedition despatched from Goalpara came into conflict with Garos at Cherangiri and of course many chiefs had pressed, were forced to accept conditions. In 1834-35, Government brought some of their chiefs to their senses who paid now the arrear due to Scott. The British officials visited the most sensitive areas such as Rissogiri where incidents had taken place.

The Ambeng Garos grouped in the Desani mahal were the most contumacious who withheld payment of the revenue for numerous years although in 1834-35, (chiefs of this group) after having been reduced, came to an Agreement with the government in which they promised to refrain from killing each other, to abandon the practice of hanging human skulls in their houses, to seek Government assistance for the adjudication of sentences for cases which they could not settle themselves and to contribute materials and labourers required for road-constructions, to turn up when called for by the government officers at Bangalkatta and abide with other conditions so stipulated. The situation was getting worse so that an expedition was sent in 1837, which collected the arrear of tribute and stopped waging of wars among the tribes. The Garos were against the payment of revenue and felt that all that was agreed with the government was done by the previous generation in which they were not a party to.

In 1847, an expedition marched to Kissogiri to investigate matters in connection with the murder of one Nokma. But a handful of sepoys dispatched in the expedition was found inadequate. Another expedition was sent, but the warriors fell upon the sepoys and wounded some of them. This matter dragging on, the government at last adopted measures with a view to subdue the whole tribe than merely punishing a few villages involved. The expedition placed in the charge of Capt. Reynolds was urged to do all that it could within its power, to make its impact strongly felt.

At Bhoogamara, Reynolds bore upon the neighbouring village chiefs to aid in the road-construction while at Bangalkatta where he next reached, the local people provided him guides to accompany him. Kissogiri, the village implicated in these undesired activities, was deserted and so Ripugiri, the next village, was found abandoned. At Rangtupara where he halted, many chiefs came and expressed their desire to remain allegiant, the events which followed showed that the Garos were as hostile as before. In 1852, seven raids are recorded in which 44 persons were killed. Again from 1856 to 1859, many raids were perpetrated. Now it was found that the enforcement of the blockade of the hills did not bring about the desired result. The blockade, in fact, hit hard the loyal subjects in the plain.

The Viceroy, Lord Dalhousie, advocated the policy of non-intervention, as the most effective means to deal with the tribes, while recommending some conciliatory measures to pacify them. In 1861, non-intervention in the wake of troubles was found to hardly suit with the situation.

Worsened Relations

Relations were worsened when the Rajah Sushong sought to exert his claims upon the hill and collect revenue at the highlands which led to the outburst of the revolts but an expedition soon went up the hills to stamp out the uprising. But the villages overlooking Mymensing were causing frequent raids into the plain in protest against the Rajah's continued exaction of tribute. In March 1866, two columns of police visited the area and inflicted punishment.

Attempts were made just before the consolidation of the administration to entrust police powers to the laskars and the Garo Zamindars with police functions were created and effective steps were taken to reduce the powers of the Zamindars. Other means were envisaged to counteract raids from the hills. However, all these did not bring about any lasting solution to the problem.

The Government finally abandoned non-intervention and adopted a forward policy and the process of consolidation was worked out from July, 1866 in which date, Lt. W. G. Williamson took over as the Deputy Commissioner for the Garo Hills, he was responsible to the Commissioner of Coach Bihar. Advance for Tura was made which was, selected as the new headquarters. All the neighbouring villages were called upon to join the new administration. Since 1868, the Deputy Commissioner exercised jurisdiction over the Garo Hills on behalf of the Chief Commissioner. Yet when Tura was occupied, a big mountain tract, still classed Independent, was excluded. The active administration was commenced at least in Tura.

A final adjustment was necessitated with the Zamindars whose claims extended to the hills. Adjustment with Mymensing was earlier made, but the pretensions of the Sushong Rajah right up to the middle region, were now to be considered. In 1862 the government enunciated their decision to exclude the tract north of Mymensing from the territorial jurisdiction of the Zamindars and the merger of that area, in the portion of the Goalpara district which comprised Garo Hills. It was also felt desirable to extend the administration to cover all the places so adjusted.

The Government, however, persisted on the need to alter the boundary and by the Act XXII of 1868, that portion of the area hitherto defined, was merged into the Garo Hills and placed under the direct administration of the Deputy Commissioner. A boundary settlement was worked out with Zamindars and those who forfeited their claims for good, were pai compensation.

Rapid Steps

Rapid steps were adopted to evolve the administrative control. Government was hard pressed with conflicts between the dependent and the independent villages in which Mandalgiri, an independent village assaulted, the villages of Mandalgiri and Chandeegiri. Government was due now to interfere but Williamson's intervention in July, 1868 was foiled owing to the inhospitable means of communication and the inadequate number of men to cope with the situation. Moreover, summons sent to the headmen of the independent villages were not complied with and raids inflicted on dependent villages went unabated till October 1868. In these circumstances, Williamson at the head of a larger expedition marched to Mandalgiri to apprehend the ring leader. He was on the way joined by the loyal village headmen; during their march, a few village chiefs who had joined Mandalgiri came to terms with the government but when Mandalgiri was reached, it was found deserted while the whole village population had been taking shelter on the other side of the hill. After some negotiation, a meeting was arranged with Sanja Nokma, a veteran who reported to Captain Williamson that the feuds not of recent origin centered round the question of possession of land. But Sanja Nokma did not report to Williamson for the second time when, the latter was compelled to set fire to the portion of the village where Sanja's residence was situated. Other villages which failed to cooperate were also punished. This incident took place in January 1898.

The topographical conditions, the different patterns of village life and other factors necessitated the carrying out of a survey operation. The boundary with the Khasi and the southern region needed a proper adjustment. In 1870, the survey expedition headed by Major Austen aid accompanied by Williamson went to explore the entire tract in which many villages came to acknowledge the British authority although two villages showed sway of resistance; obstruction was also faced with from other smaller villages. Although they were suppressed, the surveying party had encountered great difficulties and had taken long time to deal with the resistance. Also it was known that many belligerent villages would not lot other dependent villages remain in peace but the latter were subjected to many punitive measures taken by the former. The surveying party had come to learn that the Garos had been bent upon staging their final liberation war and called upon the western Khasi Syiems to provide them assistance.

Vigorous Operation

Government now was finally prone to take over the whole tract by enforcing a vigorous operation in order to demonstrate their power fully and compel all independent villages to enter administration. Towards the close of 1872, a joint operation under three columns from Mymensing, Nibari Swar in Goalpara and Tura itself were directed to march into the interior hills. The columns from Tura and Mymensing were successful which opened contacts with many new villages, the two columns met somewhere and coordinated their march to Rongrengiri; the third column met resistance on the way but the offending villages were subdued. This joint operation regularised the establishment of the administration and by the beginning of 1873, the whole district was consolidated. All the villages covered in these tripartite operations had come to profess their allegiance to Government, promise to pay tax, agree to submit to British courts and entertain police operations as and when necessary. Laskars were appointed over the newly administered villages.

From 1873 onward no more uprising had taken place except in 1882 when some village people showed sway of resistance and against the road construction but it was suppressed before it could fan out into a movement. However, the five year resistance shows that the love of their land ran deep in their veins.

The administration became largely organised when the hills were pacified finally. In 1874, the District was attached to Assam over which the jurisdiction of the Chief Commissioner of Assam was extended. Not only was it that the area of the new District had finally been demarcated from Goalpara, Khasi and Mymensing but vital administrative arrangements were worked out. The consolidation was not easy at the mountain tract in which physical hindrances were so formidable, the land covered for its greater portion with dense jungle, infested with wild animals. The earliest British administrators exerted tremendous pressure to establish administration with the help of Garo dependents and allies. The hard labour paid well its dividend. The removal of claim of Sherpore and Sushang had helped to mitigate the complications and produce repercussions at a uniform level with a common system of taxation and revenue assessed though at little variance from place to place. While the mouzalidars were responsible for revenue collection in the plain, in the hill it was a task performed by laskars. The appointment of laskars to the charge of village administration in secular assignment was an important measure.

The Deputy Commissioner held almost unlimited powers. He was overall in charge and was responsible to the Chief Commissioner of Assam from 1874, the year that Shillong became the capital of Assam. All civil and criminal cases beyond his power lay with the Chief Commissioner who exercised highest police powers. The Deputy Commissioner was provided a police force and played vital role in extending the spheres of the government through other departments such as public health, agriculture, veterinary and animal husbandry, census, PWD which gradually were set up as small units. All appeals from the village councils lay with him. By the Government of India Act, 1935 the Deputy Commissioner was directly responsible to the, Governor of Assam in all matters. The District secured representation in the Assam Legislative Assembly since then.

Laskars conducted the village administration, settled cases, collected revenue and conveyed the administrative decisions. They acted on behalf of the Deputy Commissioner. They furnished labourers and building materials as and when necessary in course of road-construction and other building works. In respect of police, a rural police acted as and when directed by the Deputy Commissioner. Most of the powers of the Deputy Commissioner have now been taken over by the District Council by virtue of the Sixth Schedule of the Constitution of India.

The administration had entailed an enormous expenditure consolidate the District. No doubt the previous punitive expeditions had taxed enormously upon their resources. When the district was consolidated, income to the government was obtained from house tax, elephant mahals, forest levies in reserved forests. By the Act of 1869 the district was excluded from the jurisdiction of the civil, criminal and revenue courts and office establishments under the general regulations and Acts which imbibed a distinct pattern for the district. The Regulation of 1876 banned the entry of the outsiders into the district for trading purpose without obtaining the government special permission with a view to extend protection to the indigenous people. The Inner Line Regulation, however, was barred. The Chief Commissioner by the Regulation II of 1890 was entitled with the concurrence of Governor-General-in-Council, to rescind operation of any law in force in the District which enabled since 1884 the exclusion of the Civil and Criminal Procedure Code, court fees, stamps, transfer of property and registration to be held in abeyance although some of them were introduced in which the indigenous people were not directly related. The Code of Civil Procedure had not been extended to the district.

Before the departure of the British Government, the political elites were concerned with new arrangement to be made in the new set up of the Dominion, Indian. The Garo National Council which had emerged, pivoted public opinion and negotiated in 1946-47 with the highest authorities that all powers of Government including taxation and administration be vested in the Legal Council and the only link proposed with the Provincial Government was in respect of a few subjects like higher education, medical aid, etc., other than the subjects of Defence, External Affairs, etc., which were not provincial subjects.

To assess the conditions in Assam hills, a Sub-Committee of the Constituent Assembly was constituted with the Assam's Chief Minister, Mr. G. Bordoloi, as Chairman. One of its members was Mr. J. J. M. Nichols-Roy, a member of the Assam Cabinet who was returned from the Shillong constituency in the elections of 1946. He did the drafting of the Sixth Schedule which finally was approved by the Constituent Assembly. It was intended to provide District autonomy to Mizo Hills, Naga Hills, N. Cachar Hills, Mikir Hills, Garo Hills and UKJ Hills. In the last named district, it replaced the Khasi States Federation which acceded to the Dominion of India during the Interim period.

New Epoch

The Independence ushered in a new epoch and many transitory events took place. They culminated in the upheaval of the movement staged and directed towards attaining a separate state. The Independence and other developments, consequent to the enforcement of the present Constitution, were the new landmarks. Fortunately the hills consolidated in Meghalaya in contrast to the then other Hill Districts were entitled earlier to secure representation in the Provincial Legislature through the elections held in 1937 and 1946. Moreover, election to Shillong Municipality held earlier must have provided public incentives and given the chairman and members concerned vast experience in the administration. The principle of universal suffrage introduced by the Republican Constitution had entitled all the Districts to secure the representation in the Parliament, the Assembly and the Hill District Councils newly constituted.

Delimitation of the constituencies accordingly was worked out for holding the first General Election in 1952. The Khasi States Federation now lapsed and was replaced by the United Khasi and Jaintia Hills District Council and a Garo District Council was also instituted. The provision with regard to the framework for the administration by District Council are spelt out in the Sixth Schedule. One thing was clear, the District Council would be entitled to maintain the relations with the State Government in the affairs concerned besides cultivating similar relations with the large and small States and evidently with the Elakaships known as laskarships or Daloiships, as would be defined. The Executive would pivot the administration and frame suitable policies. The experimentation of a tier system of administration with all its burden and obligations affecting the States and the Local units would be indispensable. The Deputy Commissioner would conduct the administration from the other levels defined.

We find shortly after the States Reorganisation Commission completed their rounds, receiving on memoranda from parties in 1954-55 that the concept of tribal solidarity held its ground. Rev. J. J. M. Nichols-Roy, the eminent leader who had served as Minister of Assam on the earlier occasions, on quitting the Congress and retaining his seat as Independent in 1957 election, during his last days championed the cause of Hill State to be bifurcated from Assam and constituted separately. The antecedents were worked by the then parties, the Hills Union, National Durbar, United Mizo Freedom Organisation which presented their memoranda in favour of Hill State.

Even the conference in which the Autonomous District Ex Councils were represented at Tura in 1954 wanted to carve a Hill State to preserve the racial, linguistic and cultural identity of the Hill people while other parties favoured the amendment and the Sixth Schedule. Parleys, negotiations and exchanges of views had taken place actively among the then leaders, Khasi, Mizo, Garo, North Cachar and other tribes. The Tribal Union which symbolised this concept of Tribal Solidarity had gathered strength and in the election held in 1957, captured several seats in the Assembly and District Councils. The Union renamed Eastern Tribal Union which conceived a compact organisation having its wider jurisdiction became subsequently formidable.

This led to the birth of All Party Hill Leaders Conference (APHLC) which was an alliance of Eastern Tribal Union, Khasi-Jaintia Conference, Garo National Council, Mizo Union, People's Democratic Party (North Cachar) and other minor organisations. The formation of APHLC was consequent to the proposal offered by the Assam Leaders to introduce Assamese as State Official Language. It was planned to carry out the Hill State movement effectively and intensively. The central organisation, the Council of Action, the chief organisers of Volunteers' Wings, the formation and appointment of these bodies was directed to that end. They had rejected the move to enforce Assamese as state language; even the then eminent Congress leaders joined the conference.

The first conference was held at Shillong in 1960. The second conference laid down the plan for Hill State. The Centre sought to intervene by endorsing a bilingual language plan known as Part Formula recommending the use of Hindi and Assamese but it fell short for acceptance. At an Assembly session which passed the original Assamese Language Bill on 24th October, 1960, that very date was fixed as Hill State Demand Day when massive hartals, processions and demonstrations were held at the District Headquarters in which business, trade and traffic were brought to a standstill and piquet were performed.

The third APHLC held at Hatlong (November 1960) made a radical demand for the formation of Eastern Frontier State (as its new name) to comprise the autonomous Districts, NEFA and Tribal areas in Goalpara, Kamrup, Nowgong, Manipur and Tripura. The constitutional provisions accordingly were envisaged.

In redressing their grievances, Mr. Nehru now spelt out another proposal known as Scottish Pattern to ensure them certain safeguards in language and enabling them to have the fullest control over the educational and cultural matters. A tribal regional Committee formed with the elected MLAs accordingly would be responsible to the Assam Assembly for any proposal with power even to veto such Bills. A Cabinet Minister in-charge assisted by a Minister of State and one or two Deputy Ministers would deal with a few allotted subjects with power over expenditure control in them. Besides, the provisions in the sixth Schedule were thought to be liberalised.

At a conference held at Shillong on April 5-7, 1961, the Hill Leaders, however, disagreed as a veritable control over their own affairs was not practical in a proposed pattern. Consequently the District Congress Committees, Garo, North Cachar and Khasi quitted the APHIC. To make their point clear, non-cooperation movement was proposed to be staged now. The APHIC, however, resolved to contest in the 1962 General Election in which APHIC polled 11 out of 15 Assembly seats whereas the MP for Khasi and Jaintia, Mikir and Cachar Hills defeated his Congress rival. The APHIC decided to withdraw henceforth the Assembly members from Assam Assembly on the 24th October 1962 as the first step to launch the non-cooperation movement.

In 1962 at the Lok Sabha Session, Prof. G. G. Swell, APHIC MP; convinced Parliament that an ultimate solution lay with the conferring of a Hill State. The Eight Conference (August 2325, 1962) resolved to stage a non-violent Direct Action before March 31, 1963 as a means to intensify Hill State Demand. On October 24, 1962, the Hill State Demand organised through the hartals, picquets and processions was successful. On that memorable day, 7 MLAs resigned from the Assembly. But owing to the serious menace arising out of the foreign aggression, the APHIC dropped the entire direct action programme and joined hands with the government in intensifying defence efforts in the Hills. They truly joined the rank and file of Government to strengthen the defence.

And as because the Direct Action programme was dropped, the APHIC again came to participate during the by-elections for filling up the vacancies caused by the erstwhile resignations of party's MLAs when 4 candidates were returned in the Khasi and 1 in the Garo Hills. But in Mizo Hills, a more radical party, the Mizo National Front was born;

since then the APHIC's influence became mitigated and the Front followed the new programme. This led Mizo Union to quit APHIC in 1966.

The APHIC held at Shillong on June 4-6, 1963 accordingly informed Nehru that it was due to the foreign aggression that the Direct Action plan was dropped.

Post-independence Era

Nehru Plan

Nehru, realising the implication of the move, came out with another offer known as the Nehru Plan in which the APHIC held at Shillong in October 1963, opined to accepting the Nehru Plan on trial basis but while accepting it, the leaders insisted on the establishment of a full-fledged Secretariat enlarging the powers conferred in the Sixth Schedule and the inclusion of Shillong within the Autonomous Khasi Hills. An increase in the Assembly and Parliamentary seats was also pressed to a total of 30 members in the State Assembly. The Pataskar Commission thus was formed to suggest constitutional remedies in context of the Nehru Plan. While envisaging no separate legislature for the hills, the Commission recommended to institute a Hill Area Committee to screen matters for legislation under a separate Hills Minister with jurisdiction over the subjects to be transferred to the Hill Areas Department. The Minister would be mainly consultant with regard to District Council and special Development Programmes affecting the state in general and the Hills in particular and especially in the effective functioning of District Councils.

Moreover, the office of a Commissioner was proposed to be instituted for expediting administrative and developmental measures. The Additional or joint or Deputy Heads of Departments were recommended to the charge of the administration of subjects in the Hill areas. The joint cadres of services for the whole State were to continue. There should be a separate Area Budget in respect of the transferred subjects. The Hill Area Committee would formulate its view in matters relating to the budget. Nothing came out as the proposal was unacceptable, even a six-Member Cabinet Committee headed by Shri G. L. Nanda, who during the middle of 1966, evolved a Sub-State Plan which sought to confer on the Hills a separate legislature and Cabinet, could not bring about a satisfactory solution.

The APHIC had resolved to go for a non-violent direct action as the effective steps. The leaders had decided to boycott the general election scheduled in 1967. At this juncture the Prime Minister, Indira Gandhi, came to Shillong in December, 1966 to explore the possibility of a workable solution; she offered a plan towards the Reorganisation of Assam resting on a federal structure where both the Valley and the Hills were to attain an equal status, failing which they were due to be separated and the latter carved into a State. On this assurance, the APHIC reverted their previous decision and came out to contest during the elections scheduled in 1967. The rose was selected as the election symbol of the

Conference. During the election, all the five candidates from the United Khasi and Jaintia Hills were returned, two of whom who came out uncontested.

But opposition against the newly enunciated Federal structure was also organised at the Assam valley where hartals and processions at many places were held.

The Deadlock

In this state of deadlock, Government deputed a Committee headed by Ashok Mehta to examine the problem and thrash out a finally agreed formula. The Committee was scheduled to consist of two APHIC and seven leaders from the valley belonging to different parties. The APHIC, however, boycotted the proceedings and insisted on a full fledged State; irrespective of that fractions, the Committee held discussions with the leaders from the valley.

All the proposal enunciated under the new schemes were unacceptable to the APHIC. As a long delay had hitherto been caused to the announcement of the government on January 13, 1967 relating to the Reorganisation of Assam, the 9 APHIC, MLAs resigned from the Assembly.

The 18th Conference held at Tura from 25th to 30th June, 1968 expressed great resentment at the continued delay caused and reiterated that "any form of Reorganisation of Assam must confer on the Hill Area requisite dignity and equal status with the rest of the present State". The Conference further reiterated its resolve to launching a non-violent Direct Action.

Critical Hour

At this critical hour, the Government of India upheld to change this issue from local to national level. The Autonomous State plan was ultimately offered.

The 20th Session of the APHIC was held on the 14th and 15th October, 1968 decided to give the plan a fair trial; The 20th Session of the APHIC held at Tura has received comprehensive reports of the meetings held in this connection in the various parts of the Hill area.

Now, therefore, having fully considered the public opinion in the Hill areas, the political realities in the country and the larger interests of the country as a whole, this Conference resolved to give the Autonomous Hill State Plan a fair trial with the clear understanding that the APHIC will continue all efforts to achieve a fully separate State comprising all the Hill areas of the present State of Assam". The 20th Conference issued direction for keeping in abeyance the launching of a non-violent direct action. But to Hill State People's Democratic Party just born, the acceptance was a hasty decision. The party was opposed to the limited powers while the APHIC contended that their acceptance was to give the plan a fair trial.

The Constitution Amendment Bill was necessitated for review and passage for constituting a Hill State in Assam to be called Meghalaya. The Constitution Amendment Bill (22nd Amendment Bill) was introduced and passed in Parliament in April 1969, then circulated to the states for their ratification. This facilitated the tabling of the actual Bill on 15 December, 1969 envisaging the formation of Meghalaya. The Bill so introduced was passed by Lok Sabha on 24 December 1969.

The same day it was passed by Rajya Sabha. It was sometime called the Christmas gift which meaning we could no longer grasp now. Actually it got passed itself on the auspicious Christmas Eve. Meghalaya would originally be confined to Khasi and Garo Hills but the option to joining it would be opened to the Mikir and North Cachar Hills. In February 1970 the two District Councils voted by an overwhelming majority to be excluded from the Autonomous State. Inauguration of the said State occurred on April 2, 1970. The Assembly would be constituted by an Electoral College formed with the Members of the then existing District Councils. The said Provincial Legislative Assembly as a show off was inaugurated soon at Tura but its permanent headquarter was fixed at Shillong.

The said Provincial Assembly had a very brief existence. This was due to the defects inherent in the constitutional framework itself. This had made the legislative and administrative machinery cumbrous and complicated. This was because the Sub State exercised its powers over 61 against 65 subjects, whereas the parent Assam Government and the Sub State would exercise their concurrent of power of administration over certain select subjects. The Assam Government retained their power over the most fundamental subjects. The fourth schedule of the Act provided some amendments in the Sixth Schedule of the Constitution. To complicate matters, Meghalaya, was limited to raise the town and village police within the limits of Shillong Municipality. Moreover, the joint cadre of services in the most essential subjects was retained. There were many constraints worthy of attention.

Formation of New State

The formidable events leading to the attainment of full State can be reiterated below:

On 10th September, a youth gathering at Durbar Hall, Shillong, adopted a resolution to include Shillong in the administrative jurisdiction of Meghalaya. The 22nd APHIC session held on 19th and 21st-22nd September, 1970 adopted the following resolution in favour of a clear cut full State. Whereas in its 20th session held at Tura in 1968, this Conference, while recognising certain inherent defects of the Autonomous Hill State plan, decided to give it a fair trial with the clear understanding that the APHIC would continue all efforts for the creation of a fully separate State; and whereas from the difficulties already faced by the Meghalaya Government in working out the plan and from indications also, this Conference is now convinced that the autonomous Hill State Plan will not succeed, now therefore this Conference strongly urges the Government of India to take immediate steps for the constitution of Meghalaya into a fully separate State".

Similarly the Meghalaya Assembly Session on September 30, adopted a resolution thus: Having regard to the difficulties which have already arisen to the surface and which are bound to confront the government in increasing manner in the implementation of the complicated scheme embodied in the Assam Reorganisation (Meghalaya) Act, 1969, this House resolves that the Government of India be moved to take immediate steps to bring Meghalaya on a par with the other sister State of the Union by converting this autonomous State into a full fledged State. Mrs. Indira Gandhi addressed in the Parliament thus: 'As the House is aware, sometime ago we reorganised the state of Assam and constituted the Garo Hills and Khasi and Jaintia Hills Districts into the autonomous State of Meghalaya within Assam. This arrangement took into account the need to provide adequate scope for the political aspirations of the people of this area while preserving the overall unity of the state of Assam. The decision to grant Statehood to Manipur and Tripura however necessitated a fresh look at the status of Meghalaya.'

Towards the close of October 1971, the Northeastern Areas (Reorganisation) Bill was almost ready which besides endorsing the formation of the Northeastern Council provided for the establishment of the state of Manipur and Tripura, the formation of the state of Meghalaya and of the Union Territories of Mizoram and Arunachal Pradesh (a new name for NEFA). The Northeastern Council would exist as a high level advisory body and seek to integrate and coordinate policy matters on regional balanced development and security.

In the final arrangement with regard to Shillong, the Bill provided that Meghalaya State shall comprise:

- "the territories which immediately before that day were comprised in the Autonomous State of Meghalaya formed under section 3 of the Assam Reorganisation (Meghalaya) Act, 1969; and

- so much of the territories comprised within the cantonment and municipality of Shillong as did not form part of that autonomous State and thereupon the said territories shall cease to form part of the existing State of Assam".

Thus a composite State of Meghalaya came to existence on January 21, 1972 marking the inauguration of a new State in India. This subsequently facilitated the shifting of the Assam Government establishments to their new capital under construction at a site in Dispur.

$$\boxed{4}$$

Geography

- -

Meghalaya has an exciting nomenclature, Meghalaya a Sanskrit word means the abode of the cloud. It has become the title of the state since it was born between 1969 and 1972. The indigenous tribes of the state mainly are the Khasi and the Garo.

Physical Features

The Garo landscape, broken up by rising precipices and ravines; has a number of waterfalls. The most famous are the falls of Khanchrurisik, Mokma, Rongbang, Chibok, etc. They are of sheer beauty, located in picturesque spots which evoke smoke phenomena as being the favourite abodes of nymphs and fairies. Most as the eminent ones are located on the southern region. The most famous of them are Mrig, Warima, Redingsa. There are many awe-looking pools of certain depth and expanse. Garo Hills are rock in minerals; the resources so far traceable are Coal, Felspars, Glass sands, Gypsum, Iron ore, Limestone, Pyrites, Phosphates and Clay. Coal admixed with the sand stone lies scattered near Tura, Rongrenggiri, Daranggiri and Siju. The deposits are found scattered on Simsang river valley, but the seam from here extends eastward into the gorges of the Nongstoin State. Rongrenggiri has also a thin seam of coal.

Felspars for industrial use are located near Tura, Anogiri, Jengjalgiri, Senthagiri, Chisakgiri and certain other places. There are deposits of glass-sand near Siju and other places.

Gypsum located at Tarapara, Meringgipara and Mogopara is found in small crystals lying in the shale beds. Limestone lies along the southern flank of Tura range from Athambing, running through Siju, Dapsi, Darugiri and advancing Damalgiri. The Simsang valley is said to contain thin isolated deposits of limestone. Much smaller deposits occur around Darang Era Aning. There are phosphatic nodules occurring in Bandarigiri obtained from the dark grey shales. The nodules vary from light grey to dark with different ingredients.

The local tradition recounts that valuable minerals such as mica, gold, silver, rubbies, and oil lying scattered about their land, were once actively exploited. This is about the Khasis in the past. There was during the pre-British period, the practice of gold washing actively conducted on the reverine sands and inside the caves. As a rule many Syiems of Kings possessed gold mines of their own. This made a few Kings very rich who had in their possession a number of gold mehurs and ornaments. There was an active excavation of copper largely used for the manufacture of urns, cups and utensils. It is well known that iron smelting was in vogue and that manufactures from the blacksmiths in the shape of tools, implements, instruments, the ancient arms, ammunitions and explosives were circulated near and far. A chemical system of melting metals from quartz, gneissose, carbonaceous elements and other constituents for procuring lead, brass and others was resorted to, Coins and state discs from the various metals were brought out in the prominent states.

The geological survey has classified the minerals as follows:

- *Clay:* White clay located at three places near Sohrarim on Shillong Cherra road: smaller pockets near Sutnga and Shangpung are also traced.

- *Fire Clay:* Near Jowai whereas good plastic clays are recorded around Larnai.

On Chinese clay:

- *Kaolin:* Applicable for ceramics clays representing the fine, pure and white types reported in and around Sutnga, mostly a type of Felspars or Gneisses while that reported from near Laitkseh is Iron stained. Deposits near Mawphlang are interspersed with weathered granite and pegmatites high percentage of silica.

- *Lithomarge:* Recorded between Nongryngkoh and Myntrang and near Kupli-Khar-Kor junction.

On Bauxite: M Beauxitic: in a thin deposit reported near Bapung on the Jowai Badarpur road.

Coal deposits are located at Umrilang area, Mawbeh Lakhar, Sohrarim Shyrmang, Bapung, Jarain, Rymbai, Sutnga, Kynden Tuber, Lakasein, Umte, Garampani-Kharkor, Mawsynram, Shella-Mawlong, Cherrapunje, Laitryngew, Pynursla, Lakadong, Lumshnong, Tenglah, East Darrangiri and Langrin or Umblei area.

On the coal mines, a slim analysis can be reiterated below:

The Umrilang has a considerable reserve but Mawbah Lakhar seam is small having a poor quality of coal. The Shyrmang-Bapung-Jarain-Rymbai-Kynden Tuber seams which extend to Jarain, Rymbai-Sutnga-Tuber and with gaps as far as Umte and Garapani-Kharkor has so large its reserve capacity where an intensive coal mining is now taking place and the daily coal traffic from here to other places is immense. This area previously desolate has now become overpopulated. The local people think that coal deposits stretch in an enormous belt, hundreds of kilometres away and touch several places known as Mawstem, Pyrma, Pamra, Sutnga, Nongkhlieh as far as Lakadong eastward. The coal deposits in fact are diffused over several places and several seams proportionately large and small exist at Mawsynram-Mawdon, Shella Mawlong, Lakadong, Tenglah while the more minor seams can be traceable at some interior places. Minor seams now include Sohra, Laitryngew, Langkyrdem coal mines, the bulk of coal (being now almost) already replenished after many long years of extraction.

Natural Location

The State occupies a mid-western position in North-East India, its southern and western border being situated couterminous to Bangladesh. It is bounded by Coalpara, Kamrup and Nowgong districts of Assam on the north, by the Mikir Hills, the North Cachar Hills and Cachar districts of Assam on the east and by Bangladesh on the south and west. It occupies the total area of 22,429 sq km with a total population of 10,11,699 persons in the census of 1971. The total population returned in 1981 is 13.36 lakhs.

The undulating terrain of the land basically characterise itself; hill spurs after spurs rise and roll before the eyes, presenting their intensive craggy formation in the most steepish part of the terrain is noticed. Therefore, several saddles dominate the central highlands which form a great plateau. The most steepish hill chains make the narrow gorges and ravines at their bases adjoining between the mountains. The precipitous formation at places amid the central ridges is formidable.

The uniform steepish character in all cases is not warranted as the hills open out into flat lands, lower valleys and shorter level lands which are more congenial for passage, transport and traffic. Such open places like meadows, valleys, dales, alleys, flat river basins are seen within the terminus of Shillong city, the State Headquarter itself, the other District Towns and dominant Trade centres. Experience has shown that at the lower level and spacious flat lands, agriculture and other enterprises can be conveniently pursued. Some of precipices evidently are barren of such activities. The Shillong Peak encircled by lower river basins and valleys is the highest in the state (1,966 m).

Some of the southern slopes mostly steepish and precipitous, due to the presence of rich soils have been, on the contrary, the cradle of various kinds of farming and mining. The southern mountains indeed make an abrupt end before merging themselves with the Surma and Barak valleys in Bangladesh whereas, on the north, the outlying hills open out into the Assam Valley losing their heights gradually.

Major Rivers

The principal rivers be bouching the hills, increase on and become large when tributaries join them. At certain places, they are navigable in which rafts, canoes and boats are used. The drainage on the south has greater discharges owing to the heavy downpours. On the hills, rivers introvert between the softer landscape and take zig-zig and angular bends when facing the higher cliffs. Lakes and pools are many owing to the heavy rains.

The land abounds in streams and rivers. The rivers which rise from the Shillong Peak are Umiam Mawphlang or Wah Shella or Rupa Tylli (known in Bangladesh as Bogapani) and Umngot both flowing southward to Bangladesh. Mynkhen also rises from the same peak, flows northeastward into Jaintia where on its eastward edge bebouches the hills for the Brahmaputra valley. Kynshi, a western river, rises near Sohiong and flows westward where it receives the larger tributaries such as Umblei and Rilang and from the junctions, flows southeastward to Bangladesh where it changes its name into Jadukata. Wahummawpa, its tributary, rises near Sohiong, contiguous to Shillong plateau.

Another river, Umiam Khwan flows eastward, then northward to bebouch the mountain for Assam. The western river is Khri. Synnia which rises, from the Kyllang peak whose tributary is Khri with its headwater near Laitdom. The Umtrew river flowing past Byrni on Shillong-Guwahati road rises from Sohpetbneng, a peak of renown; from a watershed in Jaintia emerge the eastern rivers which fall into the Kupli. The Kupli rising near the eastern boundary flows northward, joined by Umiurem, Myntang and Mynriang, thereby becoming a large river finally becoming emptied in the Brahmaputra in Lower Assam. The other southern rivers such as Rew, Myntdu, Prang and Lukha which do not flow for a great distance. The northern rivers flow northward to Kamrup and Nowgong and are finally mingled into the Brahmaputra.

The rivers, as a rule are torrential. The follow the direction of ridges. They form waterfalls along the precipitous edge of sheer beauty, the waters ejecting out with great velocity. At places they are navigable, boats laden with fruits, crops and timber are seen and used. Extensive sandbanks along these rivers lie interspersed, with quartz, pebbles, shilgles and perhaps fossiliferous matter. The swollen rivers carrying eroded matter, rush with great speed during the rainy season. The water turn blueish clear near the southern extremity but some rivers on the north carry less discharges.

There is a number of waterfalls. Tourists and travellers into the state are aware of the falls in and around Shillong and the falls at Shillong are Bishop's falls, Elephant falls, Spread Eagle falls, Crinoline falls, Beadon falls, and the Sweet falls. Near Cherrapunji are the Dainthlen, Nohsngithiang, Risaw-Mawtyngkong, LJmsaw and Urmasi, Nohkalikai, Wahkaba, Lapkhnai and Latara. The Lale, Myntriang, Turshi and Ryngki are famous falls in Jaintia Hills. Some of the waterfalls hitherto unmentioned have been noted. One is kshaid Mawklor, situated near Mawsynram on the Mawdon Bazar road where two rivers converge at that fall. Weisyntai is another fall near Tyngnger village cloved by a crag into two channels and the waters joined below dig out a deep and big pool. The Umrem fall near Mawong on Shella Bazar Road flows down the cliff, its waters also clove and again-joined near the bottom of the fall.

Numerous rock-caves are obtained from various places especially on the southern region.

Caves in Khasi-Jaintia Hills are Lumlawbah, Mawsynram and Syndai. They are many miles long, full of water splashes. There are many images such as household furnitures, racks, cods, tables and platforms all in stone. The Garo rock caves on the right bank of Chibe, Dobakkol, Derang Era Aaing, Durokma are also wonderful and provide a panoramic view of mysteries which lay half concealed in nature. The rock caves of bats near Siju village where a great number of bats dwell is one of the wonderfully know caves. Stone structures inside the caves in their natural form are thrilling in which one would imagine to have seen large halls, stages, corridors, utensils and large lanes of water scattered inside.

Natural Wealth

Geologically the presence of some minerals indicates that a variety of rock and soil formations are in existence. The rocks evidently vary from the archaen to the lower tertiary sediments; quartz, sandstones, carbonaceous shales, limestone, sillimanite elements, schists, shales, slates, granite veins, basalt, crataceous composition, ferruginous, iron stone and a rich variety of these constituents widespread at places, show their special phenomenon. This has given thought to the possibility of tapping the mineral wealth perspectively some time in the future. The species of the vegetation are also as much varied characterising themselves with the surface and sub-soil condition based on the system of stratification.

Not to speak of the administrative division, the three physical division in the state are Garo (Western), Khasi (Central) and jaintia (Eastern) hill divisions. The state has a narrow corridor of the plain area at places on the north towards Assam Valley and southeast on the Barak Valley and slightly little towards Bangladesh.

In the Garo Hills, the Tura range occupies dominantly a middle position running west to east where the Nokrek peak is located. The other parallel range in the north is Arbella. The Someswari is a range which with Kylas, lie towards the southeast. Flanks of other ranges bisect each other in the country. According to the Gazetteer of India, "the Tura range and the Simsang Valley are the two most important physiographic units of this region. The Tura range extends from Tura to Siju, a distance of 50 km and contains the highest peaks of the Garo Hills, Nokrek (1,412 m), Megongiri (1,283 m), Meiminram (1,196 m) and Gowangdara (1,011 m). It is a typical horst bounded by two fault lines. Along the northern fault line flows the Simsang river eastward for about 45 km before turning the Tura range from the Kylas; range, and ultimately coming down to the plains near

Baghmara. In the plain the river is called *Someswari"*. The Tura peak lies east of Tura but Nokrek is located south from the town.

Among other hills, there is Pindengru located contiguous from the southeastern portion; another peak Chandedengga, lies in the south of Jaksongram hill. Chitmang in the southeast appears to be next to Nokrek in altitude. There is Aratacha Ronggira peak on the northeast.

In Khasi-Jaintia Hills, ranges are interwined with curved alignment, the east-west direction which the gentle spurs throw being distinct on the central uplands. Gentle spurs from the middle region are imposing, the flat valleys lying athwart their bases add to the charm of the country side. Some central table lands, viz. Smit, Swer and Mawphlang break through the spurs in a great chaos to become themselves entangled with the Cherra, Langkyrdem and Mawsynram platforms which impress themselves as the imposing mountain scenery. The highest plateau extends from Mawphlang to the Rableng hill. Spurs of ranges in Jaintia Hills are shorter in height than the Shillong plateau; hill bases lie side by side with flat lands, valleys and meadows which have for a great portion, converted themselves into wet-rice terraced and flat rice fields. Unlike the southern portion of Garo Hills dominated by gentle slopes, the southern part of the Khasi-Jaintia Hills is precipitous.

The Shillong peak and the Nokrek peak are the great water partings of rivers flowing northward and southward. Damring (Krishnai), Simsang (Someswari), Dudhnai (Manda), Ringgi, Bugi and Nitai are the principal rivers. Damring rises south of the Tura range, flows northward and is finally mingled with the Brahmaputra in Goalpara District. It is joined by Dudhnai, an eastward parallel stream which converges it below the foothills, Ringgi another long river, rises northeast of Tura and flows north-westward across the terrain; till it leaves the hills for the plain.

The Ildek (Deosila) is a river of northeastern side. Bugi or Bhugai emerges from the Tura range, flows south and de-bouches the hills for the plain near Dalu in a southern extremity. Dareng (Nitai) also rises from the Tura range and flows southward, it leaves the hills for the plains West of Baghmara. The Simsang is a river which carries tributaries such as Rompa, Chima and Rongdik. The other southern rivers lying west are Bahdra, Sanda and Darong of inconsiderable length which emerge from a central range, many of which are mingled in the plain. The other two southern rivers are Mahadeo and Moheskali, the former rises from Balpakram and leaves the hills near Warima where the source of the latter is also located and on flowing on leaves the hills near Moheskhala.

The great earthquake of 1897 with its epicentre in the Khasi Hills, caused a dislocation in certain feature of physiography especially on the western and southern places. Many old rivers dug out new channels as a result of the convulsions in the earth's surface. This also occurred in the Garo Hills, when the old bed of the Damring turned itself into a big lake.

Coal Mining

The intensive coal mining now actively conducted in Jaintia Hills and more appropriately at Bapung, Tuber, Rymbai, Dy-khiah, Mynti Hati, Khliehriat, Deien Shynrum, Mawsaing Lamare, Molamanu, Thangskai, Lum Shnong, Sutnga almost at random and without any perspective planning, has brought about so large the environmental pollution injurious both to the landscape and society. Coal mining has hit hard agriculture and forestry pursuits and during the five years past, has caused great congestions with the overlapping coal stations on roadside due to the absence of proper depots. It has overburdened highways, State and District roads with heavy coal truck loads passing on causing innumerable traffic jams, heightening the liability of frequent accidents and does not keep motorists and pedestrians safe; roads easily are dumped out quite injurious to the problems of road maintenance and in passing through Jowai, District headquarter of Jaintia and Shillong, cause the heavy traffic congestion.

It has increased congested campings for thousands and thousands of labourers and caused a large number of unplanned markets to appear just on road sides lying adjacent to the coal mines. It is reported that 1,44,000 tonnes of coal was extracted in Meghalaya in the year 1987. This highlights the over concentration of coal mining for the rapid exhaustion of this mineral so actively pursued for the quickest accumulation of wealth without keeping in mind for a long-term reserve and steady extraction. The essence of a long-term planning would have been most feasible with a view to maintain the ecological balance and protecting the society from the undue hazards.

It is found that heavy coal mining is injurious to the continuity of forest lands in the vicinity of coal mines. To aggravate the danger, "Wildlife and disappear in the process. Water gets polluted caused firstly through the discharge of acid mine into streams and secondly through release of toxic sometimes radioactive substances to the water bodies. 'At times lowering of the water table has also been observed. Mining operations also cause air pollution through the release of coal dust and pollutant like carbon monoxide, sulphur dioxide, etc. to the atmosphere. Open cast type of mining practised in some areas also leads to the rapid erosion of land, land de-spoilation also occurs in the course of mining activities resulting in the problem of solid waste disposal. Coal mining in the state has led to a number of undesirable socio-economic changes like sky rocketing of prices, influx of labour from outside, rise of anti-socials, etc.

The problem to the injury caused can be solved by implementing land reclamation both by mechanical and biological reclamation that is restoring the ingredients of the soil and enforcing the congenial plantation in term of the fitting species to the maximum possible. Coal mines in the state are privately owned; all the works in mining are privately conducted. It appears that the demand from outside is increasing on; it has benefited, therefore, considerably the coal mine owners, the coal traders and trafficking parties as well.

Besides, mention may be made of the following:

Corundum: This occurs simultaneously in the sillimanite bearing rocks lying at Sunapahar, there are traces of dumortierite lying near Mawshynrut also; we find that Pathar Knang reveals the trace of sapphirine and other valuable gem stones. Traces of iron ores in slim quantities are seen at various places. As regards copper, lead and zinc, traces of these elements admixed ox separately are seen at Umpyrtha, Umsohryngkew and near Langrin. Glass stones the most valued mineral for manufacture of both glass and sheet glasses are reported near Lait-ryng-ew. Moreover smell-oil seepages have been discovered at Narpuh as well as Tekcherra, Khasimara, Dholai, Dhamalia, and Someswari. Limestone are diffused widely on the southern belt occurring heavily at Langrin, Therria, Shella and Mawsynram; there is a considerable limestone reserve between Shella and Bhologanj.

A smaller reserve exists at Sohra and yet smaller are the deposits lying at Pynursla, Langkyrdem and Nongtalang. A concentration of a highly developed limestone bed occurs between the Prang and Lubha rivers and between the Hari and prang rivers in Lakadong. The other beds exist near Syndai, Nonkhlieh and Sutnga. Phosphates are the other minor minerals known. Above all Nongstoin has its reputation for sillimanite and Sonapahar comprised in Nongstion state has a big reserve of the high grade silliminite combined with the corrundumores.

Forest Resources

The land has the rich forest resources. The vegetation is diverse ranging from, tropical to temperate; the different timber species are seen beside other plants in which the hard and the soft wood are comprised. The vegetation accordingly may be classified into tropical in the plain and outlying, hills, semi-tropical in the lower hills and temperate or near temperate in the highlands. Sal is a valuable timber exploited on the north but becomes limited on the northeast where sal saplings become more limited.

Teak in combination with birches, nahor, cham and many others are at places profuse. The indigenous pine (pinus insularis) dominates the upper highlands. The pine groves are profuse at the elevation of 3,000 to 5,000 feet. Another impressions is the prevalence of the bamboo distributed in both the hot and cold places, there being many species. Cane as a rule is limited more to moist and sometimes warm places. The upper region is dominated by a variegated vegetation which among others, consist of chestnut, oaks, nutmegs, firs and some berries. Among the Khasi temperate forest, some of them are seen scattered near the water courses, but others, are fairly distributed at other places. It is believed that the constant practice of iron-smelting conducted on the hill sides till the British advent, have left them barren forever. Vegetation evidently varies according to the topographies formation. It is found also that some, eroded or precipitous sites are barren and devoid of vegetation. Consequently afforestation at a few places has been rendered difficult as the forests upturned once are transformed into small grasslands with a thin under growth.

The Garo climate being hot, as a contrast we see that the temperate vegetation is restricted to some of the highest hill tops and some places in the valley. Medicinal plants in a large number have good scope to thrive. Already a variety of them are available. Shrubs, palms, long and short grasses are as much variegated. Also trees of enormous length with large top canopies are profuse towards the plain. Bulk of the wood species in Garo Hills are admixed with a larger proportion of the sub-tropical species.

A variegated flora available in the state have made their great attraction. To quote Sir Joseph Hooker: "The flora of the Khasi Hills in number and variety of fine plants is the richest in India and probably in Asia". The land has a rich collection of flora resources in such a small sphere; moreover ferns, mushrooms and other species of undergrowth have their added importance. But even the Garo Hills are also rich in flora; a variety of about 200 orchids are reported from Balpakram hill side, Simsang valley, Baghmara and the Nokrek range.

The wanton destruction of forests has proved disadvantageous in many ways. Shifting cultivation coupled with timber exploitation for daily domestic use has displaced a number of forests. Deforestation has occurred because of the shifting cultivation practiced since the past. Moreover resumption of road constructions and buildings, hydel projects and other installations have displaced some of the forests. The wanton destruction of forests has caused shortages of arable lands and has been in the stage of replenishing the valuable timber. This becomes most vital to us because forest is a source of fuel and timber, because it is a nuclear of wildlife because it is a soothing green and a giver of rain.

Basic Figures of Forestry in Meghalaya

(in sq km)

1. Total Forest Area Under State Government	= 993.02
(a) Reserved Forests	= 713.12
(b) Government Protected Forests	= 12.39
(c) Wind Life Sanctuary	= 34.21
(d) National Parks	= 267.83
2. Total Forest area under District Councils	= 7,791.83
Grand Total Forest area	= 8,784.85
Geographical area of the state	= 22,429
Percentage of forest area in the state	= 39.17%

Different levels of exploitation should and ought to be determined consistently for construction, industrial installation, supply of fuel and charcoal, cabinet making and other concerns. There is the need to secure the more purposeful tree plantation in wastelands, house gardens and house compounds. The timber exploited or displaced should be made up and replaced by a proportionate tree plantation.

A Collection of Famous Forestry Quotations: 5th of June is internationally recognised as the World Environment Day. On this day people of all nations are lending their mite in whatever possible means towards restoring the greenery and Forest tree cover over the earth.

Though there is no better means than by practically raising trees till they attain maturity authors, scribes and agencies that contribute to the cause through publicity, etc. serve it equally well. In our own way, we too would like to contribute to this cause bringing to the readers a range of Famous Forestry Quotations collected from famous speech and/or composed personally.

1. Trees existed long before man. Man won't exist long after the trees vanish.

2. He who destroys forests is a fool — shun him. He who protects forests is a wise man — find him.

3. Just as the knowledge of forestry has no beginning. The benefits from forests have no end.

4. Forest precede man. Deserts follow him.

5. Trees mean water.

    Water means bread.

    Bread is life.

    Preserve forests. (Anon)

6. When a man is borne into the forest

    You may take him out of it

    But you can never take the forest out of him (Anon)

7. When you enter a forest

    You enter the unknown

    Fear it not

    For this is where we truly belong

8. A genuine hunter is one

    Who when he awakens

    Realises the need to preserve forests.

The typical species of wildlife are fast disappearing. Indiscriminate killing of the wild animals has driven to extinction some of the finest species. This is due to the fact that games were essential not only for the purpose of meat but also hide and skin, horns, tusks and plumages which man's instinctive faculties put them various uses. Wildlife has immensely suffered due to the tempo of constructions and extension of inhabitations into the hitherto isolated places. Hunting and shikari still provide the very good games to the modern generation.

Flora and Fauna

Meghalaya is a nature lover's paradise. An exotic treasure trove of orchids graces the land. It is a botanists delight to catch a glimpse of the carnivorous pitcher plant. Bird watches specially throng to the dense forests of Meghalaya to enjoy the rare species.

This beautiful land of abundant natural beauty has immense tourist attraction. The ethnic tribes, their habitat, arts and handicrafts that form their culture attract many. A glimpse of Meghalaya will set make of you packing your rucksacks for your next trip to the mountainous terrains of Meghalaya.

Meghalaya, the land infested with waterfalls, embedded with abundant natural beauty; rare species of colourful birds and blooming orchids attract many to this enchanting land.

Important Animals

Among the animals found close to human inhabitation, mention may be made to elephants, apes and monkeys, deers and sambar, elephants also come migrating to the outlying hills during the winter time. Monkeys stay on fringes of the grove but not in the interior jungle areas. Different deer tribes, sambar and hare are located at different altitudes. True wildlife in the jungle comprises the tigers, leopards, wild pigs, wild buffaloes, wolves, mithuns, bears, etc. and varieties squirrels, musk rats, pangolins, antelopes and others.

The major tribes take up their respective lairs and come around the jungle in search of the meat of smaller prey but a few of them live on fruits, herbs and vegetables. Rhinoceroes appears now to have been extinct of rare. Birds and wern are plenty. Peasants, jungle fowls, wood cocks, cotton teal geese, lower snipes, quails, spot bills, whistling teals are common. Peacocks, Partridges, pigeons, horn bills mynas and parrots are also found.

They take up their spheres in thickets, shrubs and bushes. Besides there are other uncountable number of birds and fowls. Some of them use to migrate in a flock from one place to another and some choose their permanent abodes. Crows are not too many as in the neighbouring plains. Herds of animals such as leopards and tigers used earlier to migrate *en route* the state from Bengal.

The State has exhibited itself as a meeting place of some types of Bengal, Assam and Himalayan fauna. Some animals, pigeons, woodcocks and other birds, are seen in the government reserved forests where hunting is prohibited, but the most vigorous ones are confined in jungle clad hills and mountain summits. The Government has taken steps to educate the public about preservation of wildlife and forests. More animals are found in Garo Hills.

Owing to the range in elevation, climate varies from place to place. The climatic conditions range from subtropical to semi-temperate. The Shillong plateau being higher than Tura, the former's climate is more pleasant. The Garo Hills District has hot summers and pleasant winters. The climate of Tura is like that of the northern Khasi Hills. The temperature goes down upon the higher altitudes.

The Simsang valley in Garo Hills, as an exception, has the most pleasant climate. The uplands of the Khasi-Jaintia Hills have a salubrious climate characterised by warm summers and cold winters. Foothills of the state on the north and south share the tropical climate of the neighbouring plains. Climatic variations are shown as follows:

Place	*Average Maximum in April*	*Average Minimum in January*
Garo Hills	34°C	4°C
Khasi-Jaintia Hills	240C	120C

The wettest places in the globe are located in Meghalaya, Sohra (Cherrapunjee) and Mawsynram being the rainiest places. The highest precipitation would have totalled 10,415 mm or even more in either of the two places.

Syndai and Mo-te-le-knup known to be the wettest places in Jaintia Hills have not shown any rainfall record. Southern Garo Hills lie in the same rain belt and should have received the high precipitation. The rainy season starts from April and middle of October. Heavy downpours sometimes at Cherra or Mawsynram continue at a stretch for 14 days without break. The gales occur during the spring time. The sky is overcast during the downpours and fog envelops the shadowed rain areas.

5

Society

Meghalaya mostly is a Hill tract, it is a land of eternal charm. The Khasi and the Garo are the people with a cultural heritage inhabiting this charming land of folklore and mythology, rich historical events, rich democratic and other pristine institutions. The matrilineal organisation which exhibits itself is unique. It is an context of this observation that a review of the social and ethnic traits, necessary for discussion, is highlighted.

We will endeavour to highlight the social and ethnic characteristics mainly. This is because Meghalaya survives uniformly as the island of matrilineal societies distinct from the patriarchal societies which surround it: Yet Meghalaya with its distinct matrilineal family and social organisation has found enough room to adjust itself to all the situations which have affected the state. Most of the Bodic or Sino-Tibetan speaking people at one time exhibited strongly the matrilineal traits, who at the laps of the long ages, switched over to a patrilineal society. This is proved by the Garo Society which still retains its matrilineal customs of succession and inheritance.

Typical Society

Matrilineal Social Fabric

The society is matrilineal, children adopt their respective mother clans. The Garos by ascription recognise an heiress to family property from a daughter obedient and most loved in the household who is called *Nokna* and her husband is Nokrom in which the girl's father generally succeeds to get her married to one of his nephews, this kind of cross-cousin marriage being known as A-Kim by which this avuncular relationship is given continuity. If no nearest nephew is found, a distant man in the father's clan is taken or an heiress is married to a man outside her father's clan. Burling says, 'if a boy is taken as an heir, he will move into the household of his wife's parents. He will be expected to make free use of all the possessions of the family, to participate in the work in the family's fields and to share in the responsibility and in the rewards of the family labour'.

The Nokrom shoulders more responsibilities since she looks after the affairs of the whole household whereas his sisters-in-law have less responsibility. Yet females are only titular as the real management for household and estate devolves upon the father and consequently his son-in-law. The bulk of the family property, ancestral or parental house, cattle, tools, utensils, furniture, clothing and ornaments, buildings, other forms of movable and immovable property is bequeathed upon the heiress and into which the self-acquired property of her husband is merged. Other sisters receive fragments but are entitled to use plots of land for cultivation and other purposes. The son-in-law steps up to the position of the father in the house after his death or becoming invalid. 'The material goods owned by a couple are essentially family property, though some of them are of course used more by the husband and some more by the wife'. The chrra or maternal uncles exert influence over the conduct of their nieces and nephews while assuming the position of fathers in their children's place. So they have intimate relations with their respective wives' relations and inheritance is confined to the same clan.

Some variance is noted. There has been a tendency at certain places to make the youngest daughter the custodian of the property. Should the Nokna be disqualified through misbehaviour, another daughter is chosen to take her place. Should she be childless, one of her sisters or a daughter of the latter is to succeed her who is to discharge responsibilities temporal and spiritual under the guidance of selected persons from the mahari. If she has misbehaved leading to a divorce with her husband, she forfeits her right while he is free to marry another lady from her mahari (family) or machong (clan). If a man divorced her, he has no claim over the property which subsequently will pass on to her next husband. The male person, however, is compensated to take a concubine if the first wife is barren or physically unfit. In case his wife expires, he may marry into the same house, provided a living survivor is a widow or spinster in case of unmarried girl. The lady, in the event of being childless, is entitled to marry to her husband's lineage which probably means that she has been separated from hire. Polygamy existed in the past, restricted to rich men who required many helping hands to cope with some business undertakings in which case, the concubines from the same house were preferred but the wealth reverted to females of their clan rather than his. The kinship terms are Machong (a clan), Cliatchi (a group of clan) and Mahari (family). They are prohibited to marry within the same clan or a group of the clan.

The father-in-law imparts incentives to his son-in-law. The latter works on a separate field in the same family plots. Unmarried sons cultivate at their respective plots of land, they eat from the same hearth and live with their parents. They produce from their fields is integrated into the family barns from which they take some sale-proceeds to meet their personal expenditure.

Vast estates of family lands are known as Aking over which, the Aking Nokma supervises but proprietary rights may have been held by a Nokna his wife who has no right to exclude members of her Mahari from cultivating in the plots of land. Spokesmen of the Mahari meet to decide issues relating to the sale of lands or renting out plots, the sale-proceeds being divided, leaving the largest share to the custodian. The Mela-Salbonga is a traditional panchayat system which deals with inter-village disputes, but a simpler way of settling disputes is by referring such cases to spokesmen of groups concerned who explore ways and means for reaching a mutually agreed decision. Some plots of the Aking are parted of to other groups of maharis in which donors hold proprietary rights and titles.

In Garo customs it is the girls who propose a match to boys.

Approach directly or indirectly has been a new tendency that has grown in the town's circles. The match may have developed when they make acquaintance and then report to their respective parents and if both sides are willing, the marriage is arranged. If the situation has got out of control, the two settle as husband and wife as a case of concubinage without any formal marriage being made when of the two maharis meet and confirm the matter.

A marriage other than by seizure exists. Such marriage comes out of the consent among the groom's and bride's parents as a premarital condition. It is a simple ceremony conditioned by a bath which the bride takes at the village well; the next salient feature is taking the bride in a procession to a groom's place. No ceremony is held but the intention is to bring him to his in-laws' place in which a marriage will be conducted. The bride in the procession is attended by her close kith and kin from her mother's mahari. At the groom's place, the groom is called out and persuaded to join them as the time has been due and not to tarry. The groom may try to obstruct going with them but the clansmen of the bride force him out. His parents insist on the company not to take him but being unable to resist on the company not to take him but being unable to resist, they let him go sometimes amidst sobs since they are to lose him. The couple are brought to the bride's house. The sacrifice of a hen and a cock is performed. The party partake at the feast. The groom is guarded lest he absconds and comes back not again.

The ceremony is simple. A priest performs the ceremony. No elaborate marriage contracts or interchanges are taken.

The priest thrusts a cock at the backside of a boy and a hen at the backside of the girl, decapitates the necks of the fowls, looks into the entrails and reads the omens. The groom is then given a meal with a chicken curry prepared. After sunset the groom is taken round the village in company of his attendants. He may have visited the Nokpanle (village hall) and a few houses. All present partake in a feast at the bride's house. In another case, the marriage is performed at the bride's uncle's. This is different, the girl having stayed with her finance at her maternal uncle's place for sometime past. It is something of girl's briefing. After acquaintance has become mature, the couple leave for the bride's parents' place where they are to settle down. Just before their departure, a ceremony is performed when a priest strikes the girl with a chicken at her backside first and then at the boy's and beheads it. He takes out another live chicken but now he hits it upon the boy first and the girl finally. This chicken is cut. The party partake at a sumptuous feast. The couple do not take curry from the beheaded fowls. They relish a soup prepared from another fowl. The betrothal earlier held centres on the bringing of a girl to her uncle. She is accompanied by her father. They had brought with them bundles of meat placed inside the baskets or wrapped in leaves. A feast was served at which the groom also joined. The father of the girl took leave of them and the girl stayed with the groom until they shifted to bride's place.

Unique Custom

The marriage by seizure is their original custom which appears to have no parallel. It is not so much practised now as it was three or four decades back. In this they make a surprise seizure of a would-be-groom. Suppose if any girl has fascination of any young man, a few nearest clans-men are engaged to get that person caught and brought to their home. Such a capture of a would-be-groom is common. The seizures take time to study his movements and arrange a convenient capture of him which might have taken place on the road or market or field or grove whichever if that gives them an opportune occasion after a careful contrivance among themselves as to the simplest and easiest means. It comes upon a victim like a surprise, he being caught and led into the house of his would-be-fiancee where he is confined.

The girl develops acquaintance and woes him. The guards keeps proper watch of him. The man may manage to escape for which a second seizure will be made and he is brought again. Even if he escapes for which if he absconds, he is set free. On the night during the third surprise catch, the couple are left alone. The groom still has freedom to leave her provided he returns a sort of compensation to the elders in their household, even after he is forcibly married to her. In other cases he is just to announce that he is unwilling to be her lifelong partner and set free.

The couple in course of time have become properly acquainted and settled. The marriage having been confirmed, the couple after a few days go to visit the husband's mother and give her some presents. The husband brings some of his personal belongings consisted as his acquired property to his wife's plan.

Garos burr, the dead. Normally the corpse is retained for two or three days just to have time for relatives to assemble and pay their last respect. They have elaborate rituals of sacrifice and care of the corpse. Batch after batch of relatives pour in, whose coming and arrival is indicated by the beat of gongs which they carry. The nearest relations contribute various offerings to the household of the demise. The village folk may arrange firewood for the cremation. Rich persons keep several gongs near the corpse and wash it with large quantity of special liquors. The corpse is laid at an open machine in the rear of the house and cremated at the compound of the house in which the bier is placed at the elevated pyre.

Cremation usually occurs at the evening, sometimes extended to midnight. The pyre is supported by uplong poles. Rich persons keep engraved figures and decorations over the poles. The corpse is burnt till finally consumed. The charred bones are collected inside an earthen ware and buried inside the ground over which a small wooden shed is constructed which marks that usuary. Elsewhere, the bones immediately after collection, are thrown in the river and not interned. Sometimes the charred bones not immediately buried when collected, are wrapped in a place of cloth and kept in the house. Burial of these bones in a pit takes place later and the usuary will be marked by a shed which has receptables over the edges of the wooden or bamboo pillars in which some grains of paddy are laid. Moreover a deceased's effigy planted in the form of a carved post, the clothes and some belongings of the deceased used in his lifetime being suspended from its side. The effigy stands erect near the cremation side. A tradition points out that sometimes the bones of the deceased are taken to his mother's place, his mother being incumbent to perform the internment of his remains. The shed marking it will be destroyed after six months. It is post-funeral, in which a cow or any animal is sacrificed and dance and feasts are held. After cremation, the household offer food to the deceased for a number of days on the usuary where the bones are laid. Funerary feasts among them is common.

Traditions say, Garo chiefs were once given pompous cremation but it was the custom that such dignitary was burnt with one of the skulls being considered to be a hard-won trophy the deceased had obtained during lifetime. Garos in the past not only brought human skulls for display in village hall and houses but with such skulls they made the rite complete. An influential man was cremated for which at the time of cremation, two bulls were sacrificed, one near the pyre and other at some distance simultaneously whereas drummers beaten their gongs vigorously. Sometimes a funeral procession following the cortege went out into the village in which drummers beat their gongs all along before the corpse is finally disposed of.

The household survivors, after an interval, perform certain allegiances to the close relatives of the deceased. To a mother is given a gong by her deceased son's children. Were he a Nokrom, his mother would have received more, even if the demise was a woman to her family were sent some presents.

The people believe in the existence of the world hereafter. It is located on the famous peaks, one of which is Balpakram and the other is Chitmang; it is only a temporary haltage before the spirits embark on a longer journey yet into a permanent abode, guided by other guardian spirits in their journey against fiends and evil spirits which obstruct and in which the demise, still needs sustaining and spiritual support from the living counterparts for which it is constantly offered with food and beers. Accidental deaths, made dead persons to meet more hindrances than those dying of normal deaths. The Garos seek to appease the Ogre by wearing heavy earrings; he helps the spirits of their dead in their onward march.

The Garos believe in the theory of rebirth of the soul. They do not explain how it performs its cycle. They believe in the state of eternal reward and punishment. Those who live a virtuous life will attain bliss or reborn into higher stages. Those who have not conformed to moral standards are to become beasts or ghosts.

Their philosophy of religion is a clear-cut perception of both theistic and animistic beliefs. They believe in Rabuga Tatara or Ranka Taka, a name for their Supreme Being held in great awe and reverence as the author of creation, dispenser of time, architect of the universe, the source of life and strength and the disposer of human destiny. But he is more removed from the people's affairs. Talkame Kalga, another god, is omnipresent; he guides the individuals and empowers minor spirits to torture human beings for their acts of omitment and commitment. Some think that this spirit has the female attribute. Nuring or Muring or Nuring is a supreme goddess and the executive instrument of the universe, she is the source of light (Kalgra) who moulds the firmament into its form and gives to the heavenly bodies their radiance, beauty and light. She controls the myriad phenomenon of nature through her different agencies. Saljong is identified with the sun; he exercises control over the animate beings. He is assisted by his wife, Minim. Yet many speak of him as the lord the crops.

The mother of the human race, sister of Mining Muja was married to a son of Dongjongma and when the nuptials was over, the tradition has it that Saljong and his wife retreated to heaven. The Bhutias and the Garos claim descent from this parentage. Goera is a god of thunder and lightning. Susime is a moon god. Garos claim a divine origin to their race and consider themselves the descendants of gods. Mogma god, son of Asni Dingsni, was their progenitor.

Nature, vegetation, and waters come under the spheres of different spirits. Nastu originated all waters and transformed and gave the landscapes their vegetation and wildlife. Raga Gauda Abek is a god of fountains. Durokma is a Queen over tigers and tigresses. Horaman is an earth deity. Rengram is a malevolent spirit; chual chiggal is a bad spirit which destroys the crops. Fairies and denisens cause insanity to animals, men and women. There are spirits which seek fun by obstructing prayers and sacrifices to Saljong.

Abodes of Deities

Many of the peaks are the abodes of their deities. Sacred places and groves haunted by the spirits are marked. Head-hunting renowned in the past was a religious institution connected with fertility rites. Other deities of hunting, fertility, wealth and wisdom receive appropriate offerings.

The philosophic conception is rich about nativity of their race. They have a story how their deities came incarnate and sacrifices are offered to undo the action of bad spirits. But bulls are a potential form of sacrifice in which belong posts are raised. Normally the bull is cut with a single stroke of the blade. The blood is collected in a pan and placed with the head and a lighted lamp under a sort of canopy near the altar. All present bow themselves to the ground. A white cloth is then drawn over the arch and all is left undisturbed for an hour that the demon may come and take to what he desires. When the veil is lifted, cooking begins for the feast.

Normally the office of priest is not hereditary. Priesthood is guided by an understanding of some recondite mysteries, conduct of sorcery and the experience gained in the performance of sacrifices rites. Some have power to heal illnesses. Divination is restored to by mean of egg breaking in which the auguries are read from the falling and location of shells. In examining the entrails of animals, they consult the omen from the cohesion in the intestines in which a cohesion is a good sign and the gap is a bad sign. In marriages, sickness and fertility rites, they kill the chicken, cow or pig and look into the omens. Purgatory rite is performed to clear the household or person of any contagion, violation of taboo or any immoral action. Counter-enquiries conducted to get a clear answer involve a larger investment in eggs and animals and entail time and expenditure. All these rites an beliefs resemble the Khasi exactly and to some extent the practice of the other tribesmen.

The Garo practice sacrificial rites for appeasing or invoking the spirits. The spirits are appeased during sickness by sacrificing fowls and other animals. By divination they find out the cause of any mishap befalling them. The spirit who is the cause of trouble is appeased. The sacrifice centres round the altar, a mound of earth with four sticks or pillars or oak tree leaves in which various offerings are laid and in which several dosages of festival beer are poured. The priest or sacrificer raises invocations and cuts down a fowl on the neck, besmears the sticks or pillars with its blood and throws some entrails upon the altar. It is followed by the sacrifice of a goat in which if its neck is severed in one stroke, it indicates to be a good sign. All join in feasts and drinks are served.

The Garos observe some fertility rites. Felling and burning of jhums, weeding of plants and reaping of crops are inaugurated by their performances. They seek to invoke the spirits to save their grains from being devoured by wild animals, to procure sufficient rain and bless them with good harvest. The rites are enlivening with colourful dances, musical relays and jovial sports. The village Nokma holds an important portfolio in inaugurating the agricultural seasons.

Calendar Year

The calendar year starts with the performance of Agalriiaka, which finalises the burning of jhums. It is winter time, conditions are good for burning in which flames, rise up from all over the fields and consume all combustible matters. The fires last until the late night hours. The next day is a festive occasion. Various families now perform egg sacrifices at the sacrificial sites in their respective fields. The altar contains a single oblong bamboo planted and offerings of rice and curries are laid at its base; to make the rite complete, libations are also poured. Family feast follows in the evening at all households. Meals and beers are taken. The ceremony lasts for a few days and intervenes between burning and the first sowing of the seed. At Denbilsia which precedes the ceremony, a goat is sacrificed at the Nokma's house. The night resounds with beats of gongs and a colourful dance is held. In one of the sowing seasons, the village folk sacrifice a cow at the community level and then various households undertake sacrifice of eggs or fowls at respective fields. When rice plant has sprouted, the Nokma sacrifices a pig at his field and invocations are offered on behalf of the village. It is weeding rite. There is no dance but music of the gongs, wind pipes and hones is vigorously played. The other festivals are the following:

Rongchugala in which the first plucking of paddy from the old field and millets at the new fields is performed associated with men's war dance against the background of gong beats played in different arts. The sacrifice is located near the field. It contains some offerings of food and sprinkling of liquors. Dances occur in respective houses.

Ahaia which inaugurates the plucking of paddy. It is autumn time and the plant has ripened. Several digging sticks are accumulated near the farm house at the field. Household members at the field take these sticks and make ceremonial representation of some phases of cultivation after which the grains are neatly plucked and bounded in sheraves. Food with meals land fish is offered to the spirits. The households partake in the light, feast. At night households perform, dancing and singing in their respective places. The households observe some taboos: no fruits are taken and sale of yam is prohibited. The greetings A-ho-ho, A-ho-hop are raised towards the end of ceremony.

The richest and most original festival is *Wangala* and the final of all fertility observances during the year. Every village looks gayish and wears a new festive look as the season of the festival has approached on. All persons now take out new dresses. Repairs of all houses are actively engaged; cane and bamboo are brought from the grove; other timber and creeper plants are heaped up. Men are seen at work in fastening the thatch in the roof, replacing parts of the cracked wells and fixing parts of the machine village roads, wells and water points approach roads; lanes are also cleaned. The final funeral ceremony of the deceased in the year past is performed simultaneously in which the sheds covering the usuaries are done away with once for all. The living household is no longer disturbed by the memory of the deceased. In some such ceremonies, cows are slain and dances are conducted.

Wangala lasts for many days. Some variance may be found from one village to another as regards the details in the performance. Lots of animals are kept in family stock, best grains are stored and beer is brewed in large vessels. Women do most of this work. The central sacrificial rite is an offering of food wrapped in a plantain leaf. The festive dance is all the more colourful and performed in varied arts.

Beats of gongs resound from all corners, each household has much to partake in feast and much music to make. While music on the ear, the colourful and pompous dance rolls before the eye in the elegant dance of maidens in their fashions with gentle bends and turns; while make drummers and pipers attend them beating up their gongs bending low and hopping up to keep the art and make the mood of maindens more expressive and conveying it with some meaning.

It seems the dance which girls display conforms in moods and gestures to digging the earth or falling the bough of tree or plucking of fruits. It is not meditative. On this occasion boys and girls court friendship and acquaintance. In each of the houses there is the burning of incense from a scented wood or leaf. People decorate their houses with rice gums. The folk dance is first held at the Nokma's residence is illumined with rich decorations and lights. With this festival performed, culture glows at its best and it reminiscent of the rich heritage, philosophy and folk traditions of the people. It is called now a hundred drum festival.

Major Tribes

The state of Meghalaya is a small state and is one of the seven sister states of North-East India. It is surrounded by Assam on North and East and by Bangladesh on South and West side. It acquired statehood on January 21, 1972 and consists of the former Garo Hills district and United Khasi and Jaintia Hills district of Assam. Its capital is located in Shillong and has seven districts with a population of about 17 lakhs. The state has the word's wettest, place Mawsynram located 58 km from Shillong with an annual average of 12,163 mm or 486.5 inches. This is caused by orographic lifting (1,872.97). Dr. Hooker has collected more than 2,000 flowering plant species within ten miles of Cherrapunjee.

Agriculture is the main occupation of over 80 per cent people of the state. Main crops are paddy, maize, potato, cotton, tejpatta, cabbage, cauliflower, pineapple and oranges. Coal and limestone mining are also sources of income for the people.

The state has a very rich floral diversity. The Khasi flora, according to Dr. Hooker, is of Malayan character, which is characterised by the prevalence of brilliant glossy leaved evergreen forest tree elements. There occur over 20 varieties of palms. Other predominant plants include cultivated betel-vine and arecanut, figs of different types, oaks, oranges, Diospyros, jacks, plantains and screwpines. Laurels, wild nutmegs, Pinus Khasia are abundant in forests. There are several beautiful orchids, fems, mistletoe, mosses and Lycopodiums occurring as ground flora. Bamboos of many kinds and several grass species are also found. These forests shelter several kinds of wild animals such as the wild buffalo, wild boar, tiger, etc.

The state with abundance of rain and rich vegetation host three major tribes as described below:

The Khasis

There are conflicting views about their exact origin. The four groups of Khasis have generally been recognised as 'Bhoi' who live in northern part of Khasi Hills, the 'Lyngngam' who live in western part; the 'Wars' living in southern part and the 'Khynriam' who inhabit the central plateau. Khasi people are generally short-statured (1 m to 1.5 m tall) with Mongoloid facial features. In earlier days males used to wear 'dhoti' and 'turban' but now they prefer European dress. Females wear a long piece of cloth tied on the shoulders hanging down to little above ankles called 'Ka Jainsem'. Khasi women are fond of gold. The Khasis use swords, spears, bows and arrows as weapons and carry shields for their defence. Children and adults are also very fond of catapult (Culel) (a stone throwing device). Marriage within the clan is not permitted. The ceremony consists of mixing of liquor from two different pots (gourds) and eating by the bride and bridegroom from the same plate. The youngest girl remains in her parents' house and inherits property. The Bridegroom has to shift there with his small belongings such as clothes, etc. Divorce is common and is effected by the public declaration. The Khasis relish pork, beef and dry as well as fresh fish. They also eat fermented soya bean as chutney with dry fish. Their other typical favourites include Soh-phlang (Moghania vestita, a leguminous tuber eaten raw after deskinning), Nei-lieh (Perilla frutescence eaten as chutney), Sohriew (Coix lachryma jobi, a kind of maize), Digitaria cruciata var, esculenta (a small millet), Soh-ngang (bitter brinjals Solanum gilo, Solanum Khasianum, and Solanum torvum), Jaiur (zanthoxylum acanthopodium), tree tomato (Cyphomandra batacea), ricebean or Rymbai ja (Vigna umbellata) and Soya bean (Rymbaiktung). The chewing of 'kwai' (betel leaf, lime and raw arecanut) is very common, be it day or night, except when asleep. It also generates heat in the body and because of its protein and calcium content as well as chlorophyll, increases body resistance. In winter, "Kwai" keeps the body warm. In ancient times Khasis never used to take milk as such, but now take it with tea which they like strong. Khasi houses are built upon stone pillars or wooden (or bamboo) pillars, due to the hilly and seismic terrain. The non-Christian Khasis used to believe in a God or Creator and there was a ladder or a communication between Hynniewtrep and the Heaven. Some also worship cobras of a species called *"thlen"* but this is prevalent only in very remote areas and the sect is now rare.

In general, people are very conservative in moving out and treat other as 'dkhars' (foreigners). The typical Khasi dance 'Nongkrem' is unique in that the girls wear lot of solid gold jewellery, slowly inch their feet only without any jerks or move up the ground and young Khasi boys holding "chamars" or fans in hands make a circular motion. Only virgins are allowed to take part in the dance before the 'SYIEM' or the Chief of the particular area.

The Garos

The Garos are believed to belong to the Bodo group having Tibeto-Burman lineage and trace their origin to a place known as 'Tarua' in Tibet. There are two major groups-hill Garos and plain Garos. Unlike the Khasis, Garos are polygamous subject to a maximum of three wives, and marriages generally are contracted outside a specific group. The major groups among the Garos are Marak, Sangma, Momin and the Machong (Maharis).

Garo men traditionally wear 'Gando', a blue cotton loongi with red stripes. The women wear 'Riking' which is fastened on shoulders with two strings and leaves the knees bare. They are slightly darker with Mongoloid features and have sturdy physique.

The major occupation is agriculture which is largely practised on "jhum" (slash and burn) lands. The sole agricultural implements are a dao (a kind of broad sword) used to clear the jungle and a small hoe. The principal jhum crops are rice, maize, cotton, yams, Aroids (Colocasia, Alocasia and Xanthosoma), ginger, turmeric, sweet potato, millets (Foxtail and Finger), etc. The seeds are dibbled into holes dug up at some intervals at the onset of rains. The men remain in field houses during crop season in order to protect their crops from wild beasts. These are built high upon big trees to ensure safety from rampaging wild animals. They use bamboo ladders for climbing into these houses.

The Garos will inter-marry with any person except Jugis or Sweepers. The marriage proposal is generally from girl's side, though groom's parents' consent must be obtained. In the Abengs it was customary for the youth selected to run away when asked to marry a girl. Divorce is recognised and, widows are allowed to remarry but they must do so in their husband's family. A Garo, like a Khasi, leaves his native village and settles down with his wife. Normally they set up their own house after marriage. The property is inherited through the female to the daughter and through her to the son-in-law.

The non-Christian Garos believe in the Supreme God and in evil spirits. The evil spirits are pleased by animal sacrifices to save themselves from misfortunes.

The staple food of the Garos is rice. In addition, they eat all kinds of meat whether of dead or killed wild and domesticated animals. They eat meat of snakes, lizards, white ants, elephants, buffaloes, cows, pigs, goats, fowls, etc. Dried fish and beef are relished much. Other eatables include yams, Colocasia (Kachu), Alocasia (Mankachu), Xanthosoma (Dudh Kachu), beans, millets (Finger and Foxtail), maize, chillis, bitter brinjals, etc. Milk and butter are not on the menu, in villages.

The village headman or Nokma is considered to have authority on jhum lands. All members of the village are allowed to cultivate land rent-free and a newcomer to the village is required to pay a nominal rent. The village councils used to decide most of the disputes through the laskars who were the Honorary Magistrates.

The Jaintias

The Jaintias are also a Mongoloid tribe. However, not much has been written about them in the historical accounts. They are also known as 'Pnars' or 'Syntengs'. The dress of Jaintia women is distinct as they wear a sort of dhoti black in colour having a white strip on the side and over that the 'Jainisem' like Khasis. The religion of Jaintia people closely resembles Hinduism. They never take beef and worship the cow on certain occasions. They used to be averse to milk and butter or ghee. Rice is the staple food. Pork, mutton, fowls and dried fish are also their main dietary items. Pnars generally marry within their own tribe. In Pnars, however, there is a striking difference in respect of married life. The Pnar husband, after marriage visits his wife's house only at night as in rural Kerala. Generally he remains in his mother's or sister's house. The property is inherited from the mother to the eldest daughter known as 'Ka Mai'. The Pnars can have more than one wife but never from the same village. The Jaintias believe in one God whom they call 'U Blei', the Creator of this universe.

Typical Culture

Megaliths most of them serve as memorials of the dead. They are comprised in sets of upright and flat stones. The funerary importance of these stones matters most. Menhirs or pillars stand upright, their base being dumped inside the vault while dolmens lie flat infront. They are called *Mawlynti* or *Mawkjat* laid during the cremation of a deceased or disposal of bones of demised members of the house (No. 3 pillars and 1 flat stone). Mawknii maw pyrsa commemorating the senior and junior uncles vary from 3 tall pillars (in an uneven number) to 11 or more associated with 2 or more dolments. Mawkyrteng have 5 menhirs and 2 dolmens commemorating the clan ancestress. Maw Kait and Mawksing in each case have stones, 3 × 1 and Maw uniko! symbolising a purgatory rite range from 3 to 9 × 2 dolsmens. Mawpird lying in the central highlands marking the demarcation of sites or boundaries are pillars of considerable height.

Megalithic erection common in some great markets mark their-beginning; they mark some auspicious events or acts of feats flat stones scattered around, serve as seats when chieftains and people assemble at Darbars or when the elders sit to discuss the market revenue collections or administration.

It is in these hills that Megalithic culture has made its eminence, the land of the typical stonehenges accumulating with their own form of complex and solidarity and throwing their variegated manifestation in shapes, styles and structures. Some look like the great tombstones with their unique height, some of them being pillars and dolmens conjuring to the length of 26 to 30 feet as we found specimens of these at Nartiang and Laitlyngkoi.

The technical device, used to establish these curious architectural forms and the arrangements of the components in the form of stone block, slabs, titles and other grated materials must have been more impressive, they depict the shapes of huge and sometimes herculean constructions. Few of the standing menhirs have the figures scooped out in them as those we see at Mawsmai (a stone wearing a disc or crown on the top) and Mawsngi having a plate with the carving of the sun beaming with his rays showing soiree concentric circles and some spotted figures.

Megalithic remains show also the degree of great physical prowess which this ancient race of people possessed in carving out, chiselling and transporting the huge boulders and crags and permanently laying them as the collasol pillars, pavilions and platforms. Evidently some technological skills were used in this system of masonry. This is also evident in the structures forming the megalithic bridges spanned by immense slabs two or three to five resting over the pillars. This is similar to the Jarain bridge. But a single span of stone forming the bridge is a common sight especially at rainy places.

The Umia-knieh bridge displays a peculiar architectural pattern dumped inside its culvert than on the outer surface of the bridge. There are steps cut in its exits down to a pavement. The culvert down underneath forms a wall by the plastered stones and its top is enfolded into an arch. The culvert on the opposite side is a wall enfolding a pillar frame and these support it at the two ends in and between them, three great clusters triangularly framed like pillars dumped in a river bed, support and join the spans forming the pavement. Below the arch projecting from the side of the river bed, and on the wall, there are sculptural marks of a horse with wings (gardada) and a disc. Two great slabs form the pavement. The bridge highlights the great engineering skill and architectural dexterity of its makers.

The architectural styles are still seen such as Kpep or funerary maunds (or pyres) rectangularly constructed resting on the stone walls, the crater being dumped with gravels and top surface overlaid with earth or stone rows where the cremation of Syiems was performed such as Sohra Kpeps. They form small platforms.

There are Kors, these are stone benches, secured inside the stone walls rectangularly built providing a corridor for stepping inside and from the inside walls, benches are flanked which serve as seats. They are small rectangular structures, the heights of the walls being considerably dwarfed. They are intended to perpetuate the memory of the dead. We also see structures like stone stools resting on uprights scattered out at places. Palong these are huge bed-steads.

They are massive structures, their length varying from 25 to 30 and width 10 to 15 feet. The head and foot position are secured by elongate, narrow blocks and extended upward by innumerable titles making a crescent shape. The narrow, up long blocks are fitted to secure the top and base on the side of the lengths and these also helm the principal blocks. Most of them lying on Shillong - Shella road side have in part, crumbled to ruins and only one or two retaining their solid structure.

Citadel — as seen near Sohrarim — is wall overlaid with small narrow slabs, and the roof fitted with a similar layer overlaid with slabs. The side of a door forming the entrance is seen. The citadel we saw at Syndai is more elaboration ending in a dome attaining a considerable height, a cluster made of red, light bricks.

As a corollary houses laid out in solid stone or lower walls made of stone and upper walls of wood, stone stilts or structures supporting the dwelling houses, stone walls demarcating house compounds and roads made with stone pavements are seen. Even till quite recently, skills in masonry and architecture both traditional and modern are maintained. Now the essence of continuing these skills has arisen.

The Mawmluh Sarcophagus where the bones of the dead are treasured are walled, roofed and sealed with stone blocks of regular size, their surfaces smoothened out. They are made fiat and the flat topped block which conveniently roofs it. Crave possession in the shape of gold and silver cones, quivers, vessels, ornaments and lime pots were kept with bones, the practice which persisted among the rich families mostly. Sculptural remains of a wide range are confined to the eastern hills and valleys lying on ways and outskirts of the ancient State centres. There are found a rock engraving of the elephants in pair one facing sunrise and the other sunset at Ritiang besides the carving of bull and elephant is combat at Mawryntung; foot prints of a tiger and rhino have been found near Namdong. There are the rock engravings of a pig at Jowai and Khon Skhnong, an elephant at Rapuson, a frog at Syndai, a rhinoceros at Moteshroi, a pair of bullocks carrying a yoke near Barato. In 1977, we unearthed a sculpture near Umroi bearing the clear cut figures of a goat, elephant, a baby and a sword or dagger in a concentrated surface of an oval hard sandstone which evidently reflect the mark of the sacrificial rite; this piece of sculpture is now kept at State Museum, Shillong. Engravings of human figures lie scattered about such as U Khawang Myllep lying near Tkloh Ksi, U Sajar Nangli's foot print at Mawbakhon and among others, marks of human skulls and footprints found at the other interior places. These are some of the highlights.

New findings in brief highlights consist of pictorial drawing of a human figure of a man lying flat on the surface of the rock where the marks of the head, ears, arms, and feet come out clear at Barato. Another slab lying close carries the portrait of an elephant of a robust size, the trunk, feet, body, tail, still eligible clearly for the purpose of deciphering, the rock's surface being eroded at places where nearby is a carving of some ambique inscription lying flat on the stone and close by there is another rock caring of a figure of a ploughshare secured to the ends of two supporting poles and also the portrait of a human figure which according to Dr. H. W. Sten is a figure of a lady, Queen Latympang after she defeated King Slein, her rival in a bet. There are marks of several small holes bored down the great strata of a rock and penetrating the great length of distance downhill which had served the purpose of flag hoisting for ages. Bulk of these marks are concentrated in the arsenal and capital of a once great Kingdom ruled by Queen Latympang, the great historical figure which have lasted for 800 to 1,000 years. The place is called Sieh Lama commemorating the great event of falt hoisting against those small appertures bored down the rocks, marking the existence of a great kingdom, in a survey which we conducted on 13 February, 1987 at the spot and in which the use of photographic and sketch drawing aids have been found exceedingly useful for the purpose of deciphering. Marks of finger and footprints lie about nearby.

Sculptural relics found in a survey conducted on July 17 and September 9,1978 at Raitong, the great ancient headquarter show a variance from the usual figure carvings. The bulk of the stone at the sites being eroded, the difficulty in deciphering has became enhanced. Fortunate Dr. Kynsai Warjri then a very young, promising artist and Cajee, a young architect rendered considerable assistance in measurement, assessment and sketch drawing and by using means of carbon drawing, a cardiogram was finally prepared. The cardiogram reveals the figure of a waistcoat, the kilt and the belt with a kind of fine embroidery running through characterised by the familiar floral, twig, stem cutting designs familiar in the oriental world. Most probably they are connected with the old burial practices in which the dead were highly revered.

The stone where the portrait lay imprinted is oval. Its corner side even eroded reveals the marks of certain inscriptions, resembling the ancient pictorial writing for which, we have almost been prone to consider that due to their ancient migration and the other relations maintained with the distant eastern lands, the ancient folk may have been acquainted to using the oriental alphabet for reading and writing as they had been used to using Bengali or Arabic for keeping correspondences prior to the British advent. Close by on the surface of a stone in a semicircle, we discovered the marks of the inscription which are represented at the plate in this volume. On its presentation by Kynsai Warjri, and on careful analysis, we have reasons to believe that the ancient Bhoi Skyiems had hitherto used their own form of lettering and the inscriptions apparently were the ancient Khasi alphabetic symbols used for keeping correspondence and for maintaining embassies. This original script must have preserved the common features with the inscriptions found at Barato and elsewhere. How far the people had been influenced by the oriental script, this question cannot be answered. Another perplexed notion arises, how and why this script was abandoned after the Bhoi Kingdoms were integrated with the Central Kingdom? They are the letters marked on stone (ki dak ba la thoh ha a maw).

Historic Corroboration

The Khasis screened by several kingdoms and having established a far-flung sovereignty, had definitely established relation with East. The corroboration from the other sources has been amply testified.

Dr. Warjri also deciphered other figure carvings of stones located at Mawlieng, the valley lying down hill Raitong and the centre of a fertile wet rice farming. The figure carvings reveal the portrait of a sailing boat and a rising sun lying very close to the rude stone tables scooped in the shape of a saddle, boat, safe and other things, for which the pictorial sketches have been provided in a plate contained in this volume. The other ruins seen at Mawlieng, now a deserted place testify to the greatness of a great, ancient capital. The findings mark the ancient historical coincidence and reveal the ultimate importance of Raitong as the once great meeting place of the Khasi and oriental culture.

Familial Relationship

Mother kinship among the Khasi groups is dominant. The tribe is a conglomerate of clans. The mother is the custodian of family rites and property always to be succeeded by her youngest sister who attains the position of the next custodial entrusted with the post of trust and responsibility. Being instrumental to perform the host of family rites and celebrations and affecting the family gatherings and assemblies, and being caretaker of her parents and other unprotected members of the family. She secures the lion's share of the family including the ancestral residence which she cannot part off, her elder sister(s) also getting the share of property in the shape of lands, jewelleries, ornaments, vessels and articles of household furniture and goods. The elder sisters generally move with their respective husbands, but the youngest stays in her residence, the custom being matrilocal.

The system in keeping with its original pattern and moral efficacy has been nowadays largely distorted especially when the female custodian is habituated to neglecting her duty and even disposes of the ancestral property and fails to deliver the goods she ought to do so. The avuncular power of the meals has been adversely affected leading sometimes to the deprivation of the youngest daughter by the avaricious manipulation or hatching a plan by her uncles with her to dispose of the ancestral property. The couple on the other hand by virtue of Meghalaya succession Bill 1984 enacted as an Act are eligible to dispose of their self acquired property to sons or daughters and provide education or in the event, the wife is poor, this is usually the husband's entire responsibility. There are exceptions. The sons may have secured other kinds of relief or investment from their mothers to establish themselves in which case, the earnings increased out of it is to be bequeathed to their wives' children although normally sons otherwise get only small gifts with personal belongings when they are married. Nowadays, if a man shares with his mother any business, he gets a dividend. The father has the right to transmit his self-acquired property to his children. He, has the right to conduct his children's affairs; if he earns jointly with his wife, both will manage the house. If through his self-acquired property (kamai khun) he has made provisions for his children by constructing houses or purchasing plots of lands or groves or fields, they remain until he has made a formal division unto them. But if he has started business with capital supplied by his wife, they latter apparently has a greater voice, if she possesses ancestral or self acquired property in greater proportion, he becomes the adviser or assistant in the management.

A great portion of the bachelor's earning (Kamai Khynraw) goes to his mother before marriage but he is not prevented from transferring it on marriage to his wife nor his wife after marriage, can prevent him from transferring a portion of his earning (Kamai iing khun) to his mother if she deserves assistance. A man exercises a dual function as U Knii, i.e. maternal uncle (counsellor) for his mother's kin and U Kpa (the father) at his wife's home. In the war (southern) areas, the father has got more authority at his home since his children are eligible to obtain shares of property from him, it might be the one that has been inherited from his mother. The youngest daughter, in Christian families still exercises her moral duties and obtains the biggest portion of ancestral property today. She is bound to take care of her unmarried brothers and sisters. She is the guardian of the parentless and homeless members; the mother acts are a moral force to unite the family as the spiritual head.

In the Jaintia Hills, the form obtained is not conjugal originally like Garo and Khasi, but the Pnar or Jaintia form is more due local as the father is titular, leaving total family responsibilities to his wife, all his earning being integrated with that of his mother's and to his wife he renders a normal provision (bai kait) only.

Daughters do not inherit to their father's property but get it from their maternal uncle and brothers. But today, the growth of conjugal system as of Khasi pattern and the development of nuclear families is a social trend of noticeable growth among Christians leading to the corporate living and supervisory care of both husband and wife over their children.

The war system of inheritance (in the southern Khasi Hills) offers a contrast to the main matrilineal system in which both men and women inherit property which is divided amongst brothers and sisters. In many places, the youngest daughter acts as the keeper of the house, and an elder brother acts as manager of family lands and for this, he is allotted a plot of land called *Ri Nongsaid* for his family's use'.

Betrothal as premarital condition is performed at the girl's house in which the avuncular personages representing the two houses cite solemn exchanges of address; handing over of a ring to the girl or exchange of rings also occurs. All taboos or social constraints affecting the sanctity of clanship must be averted.

Traditional Marriage

The marriage is performed at the bride's place. At both houses, feasts are held but larger they are at the bride's place being more illuminated with decorations and orchids. On the morn of that auspicious day, the bride's party send daities with meat, pulao and others to the groom's mother. The groom in a retinue which comprises his maternal uncles, father and his brothers, the groom's brothers, nephews and other relations and his friends, march to the house of the bride. Half way the party are met by representatives from the girl's side where an exchange of betel-nuts takes place.

The marriage centres round the citations of contracts between the Ksian or spokesmen, the pouring of beers from two respective vessels follows and the priest then holds three pieces of dried fish as a token of solemnisation and the ceremony is over by their placing over the roof of the house. All present partake in a grounded rice which serve as a wedding bread. Female kurs, i.e., mother, aunts, sisters and nieces of the groom never go with him on the wedding day but are in their house to entertain other friends and relations.

At jowai, the marriage occurs after dusk, the groom is brought to the bride in a company bearing woodpine torches along the way. There are exchanges of marriage contracts and pouring of libations. The dress is different from both ordinary and dancing in which the wedding white raiments are used, the bride apart from wearing a jainsem, etc., may keep a white wrapper tied on the body and bunch of flower tied on her head. Divorce cases are not absent; conditions are not rigid to obtain a divorce.

There are rules relating to the division of property and disposal of other things at a formal divorce. There are concubinages which lead to a settled life of the couple, but they fix their dwelling only after such constraints are cleared with their parents.

Three days after marriage, the couple visit the groom's parents handing over to them some fruits, bananas and rice cakes. The groom now takes overall his possessions from his parents to his in law's place.

Christian weddings are solemnised at churches. The ordained and recognised pastor or clergy conducts. Then the party are entertained at the bride's residence or an appointed venue. The boy stays at the girl's place permanently if she is youngest, he is united to her family interest; if she is the elder, it is just an *ad hoc* arrangement before they shift to their separate residence. The invalidated or unmarried is represented by her next elder sister and the ancestral property consequently will descend to her daughters.

A historical retrospective can be condensed as follows:

"women acted as custodians of family property and rituals. The change thus affected the household organisation since warfare was over, women took more liberty whereas the avuncular authority of the uncles was broken down. The old usage insisted on women to adhere strictly to their position as dare-takers of the house and custodians of the religion whose task carried much sanctity. Women were always under the supervision of their uncles and never moved out without an escort of males. Subsequently with the progress of Christian conversion, women stepped down from their position whereas they maintained their rights as inheritors to family property". This distortion caused has provided a nucleus for the more effective review and orientation of family institution which should be viable and responsive to the modern needs.

The monotheistic conception originally underlined the religious thought. It was once all pervading, carrying its impact strongly, it highlights itself on the concept of creation and the nativity of mankind. The Supreme God, is U Blei Trai Kynrad, a Nongbuh Nongthaw or God, the Lord Creator and omnipotent. The personality of God held in sacred is combined with Ka Blei Nonghukum, the Goddess, the giver of the law, the ordinance and the covenant. There is Ka Blei Syiishar, goddess the ruler and sovereign.

There is ka ktien, the word which regulates the order and creation. There is Durbar Blei the heavenly council over which God himself is its Head; God and the durbar is one in its purpose, object and goal. The religion based on the covenant sought to keep alive the links between God and Hynniew Trep, the first children of man. The first covenant evidently reflects the concept of nativity and the second which developed later oil man's seeking of reconciliation with god after he was fallen to sin. Man's fallen cause, according H. O. Mawrie, is espoused before god on the basis of Ka Ryngiezcs equivalent to conscientiousness, Ka Dazu a sense of conviction and Ka Nia (the law) which provide a consistent framework of rationality.

At the beginning of time ka Hukum created ram-ew an equivalent of the underworld and from it, the sun, the moon, the wind, the fire and water emerged. Ram-ew (a feminine nomenclature) was given in marriage to Ryngkew (the earth spirit) and from their union, was born two children which were a maw, the stone and khyndew (the soil). Then Ka ram-ew conceived and gave birth to the myriad plants, animals, insects, birds and other animate beings. Hukum always stayed in heaven with her children, the sixteen huts, ka ram-ew then cried out to Hukum to send ruler over the creation over which the goodness in council agreed to send the seven households or seven huts to colonise the world while the nine celestial households would make occasional visits to the world through a ladder of gold. The seven huts led by a Syiem Lakiar and in company with the ministers and a host of followers including the goldsmiths, blacksmiths, craftsmen, weavers and other grades came down to reside permanently on the earth.

Ka sotti juk the age of nativity marking the celestial origin of the tribe is aptly demonstrated. It had survived and lasted through a great length of time till it gave way to mied synnia or the dark ages symbolising a chaotic situation due to man's falling to sin in which a long intercession for reconciliation with the heavenly power was sought and the reconciliation obtained, it brought about the emergence of juk Ksiar, the golden age or the age of enlightenment which centered round Pah syntiew, the ever loved Queen of the land, hence a glorious history started to gain momentum in all respects. Evidently the sacred covenant obscured or darkened during the dark ages gave way to a consecration of animal sacrifices. Religious customs and practices by and large evidently had their positive role at a later stage. Animal sacrifices in the shape of goats (mostly used during the state ceremonies), bulls chickens are intended to bridge up the last communion and affecting search of the golden path. Prayers, divination and sacrificial rites and a chain of these performances rotate themselves round the family, society and the state in a process in which the priests, sacrificers and diviners are involved. Finding out the cause, intersessionally and rectifying by the sacerdotal means are the characteristic features.

Characteristic Features

The characteristic features which dominate the religious belief and ritual can now be deduced. The theistic elements as such are admixed evidently with the monotheistic principles but to many, the former are subsidiary to the latter. For instance thanks giving to the spirits known as Phan longkur (who gives increase to the clan). Phan Longrngiew (who enhances the concept of the manly dignity or who adds strength to the human nerves), Phan Longbriew (identified with a sound moral) are believed to represent to goddess as her agents.

These and other spirits are propitiated only when through divination, her permission is obtained. Thanks giving to the Supreme Being or the Goddess representing Him is signalised by casting 9 or 7 or 5 pieces of the entrails of the animals slain at the altar, a small lump of red earth where the leaves of an oak are planted. Therefore, the concept of blei iing or deities of the house who guard and defend them is followed. For instance at Shangpung, Blei Sngi, the sun goddess, Blei synshar, Tholang (a male progenitor), Thaw Niawbi (ancestress), Lukhimi (spirit of the fire place) are all embodied to be the manifestations of the power of the supreme god.

The cult of the dead represented by Lawbei (the ancestress), a Thawlang (the paternal patriarch), U Suitnia (the uncle, brother of the mother) which means the intercessor or advocate are held in reverance. Megalithic culture is intimately connected with the cult of the dead for preserving their reverent memory but this culture not funerary entirely, has created also the other manifestations in architecture. The three persons symbolising the intrinsic house hold are glorified. The cremation of the dead is a series of the observancy of prayer, intercession, sacrifices and purgatory rite. The post-cremation on a grand scale becomes extended to a festival full of colours, symbolic exchanges and demonstrations. Similarly, agricultural fertility is sustained by the performances of sacrificial rites, dances action songs and feasts.

U Blei Lyngdoh and Ka Blei Lyngdoh, the deities in their male and female character embodying the Supreme Being are worshipped among the priestly classes. Priests are sacerdotal assisted by priestesses in their family and in the state set up. In the Khyrim State annual festival, God is acknowledged as the preserver of the race and giver of the convenient and religion. All prayers open with a notion of God.

The priestess assisting in the conduct of the solemn ceremony attains the title of Lyngdoh Soh Blei Sarn Sla, the custodian of the ceremony pursued in the performance for recovering the communion. The ornamental beads flashed with gold Mokor Kyndur and Mohor Paila displayed at State ceremonies symbolise man's search to discover the path of gold which link up heaven and earth. U Soh Blei designates the sacred person of a priest U Syiem performing the sacerdotal and secular duties as the Head of the State and acting as official priest in the few allotted ceremonies, he is the father, guardian and benefactor of his people. The female royal inmate is Ka syiem Sad acting as the state priestess. Sylem Blei are Syiems of divine origin and Sysiembrew, the Syiems of some other titular ancestry. These indicate the vast and variegated culture matching with a grandeur of its own.

Sacrificial Rites

Most of sacrificial rites related to family, society and state are held indoor, outdoor and at appointed sites according to usages followed. Omens are read through the processes of divination in which at egg breaking or other sacrificial rites, examination of entrails of egg shells or animals slained are minutely followed and in which intercessions of diviners characterise themselves at finding out the root causes which concern many things. The causes of spiritual or material prosperity or misfortune are traced to observe punctually the family taboos enshrining the moral cause, or daw lum or entagling with the evil forces of nature due to man's falling short in doing wrong things which violate the prescribed ethical norms or daze shnong owing to a contagion caused into a society, civics and citizenship. The Khasis place great faith in enlivening the cause of the household, the state and society, for enhancing their prestige. Ka rasong means scoring of victories, spiritual, socio-economic, cultural or otherwise. Monetheism as a concept and usage is a compound structure. Legality and infallibility are as such the consistently combined concepts philosophically, ethically and socially.

The theistic elements also dominate according to the situations affecting the families and social organisations. Evidently, in spite of the monotheistic background, the people are haunted by the fear of malevolent spirits in the form of ghosts, friends, witches and other wicked spirits who cause torments also to human beings. Appeasement of malignant spirits must have characterise itself in the religions practices depending upon the situations. Evidently these spirits must have been empowered to punish and torment the human beings. But nervousness and superstition are thought always to be tantamount to the lack of strong nerves or balanced consciousness. They are tantamount again to causing personal or social disasters at the different angles.

The great post-funerary festival occurs during the assemblage of bones of the deceased of a clan of its branch thereof from different cairns and their internment inside, the common cromlech or sarcophagus. It is a scene of celebrations highlighted with dances and ceremonial salutation to the mother sponsoring the festival by her sons' children and grated children. The releasing of a bull or oxen laden in to horn with a pair of cups of silver or gold is a great impression. Processions in batches especially for taking away the bundles containing the bones finally to the sepulchre climaxes the occasion.

As regards mortuary customs, we find that a good deal of time and attention is given by wealthy families in giving pompous cremation to their deceased. If the funeral ceremonies take the form of thang shyngoid or siar knit, decorations on lavish scale attend the performance of the ceremonies, shyngoid is a luxurious bier, a sort of a well and elaborate constructed bier with a cover made of good timber, otherwise for a poor, the bier is made of bamboo for its floor then lifted up to a sort of a semi-circle elaborately covered with bamboo splits and tied with strings. Many decorations in gold and silver may have been given. Siar Kait is a decoration made on the pyre. The corpse especially the deceased of a royal house receives full honours. Guns are fired, drums are beaten and flutes are blasted out in accompaniment to the lamentations of women sometime amid the scenes of dances. Funereally assemblage and feast are properly arranged.

Patterns of Housing

The other physical and material characteristics are now essential to our consideration. As regards house models, an indigenous house pattern is oval in shape. This pattern generally has timber as uprights, posts, pillars, cross beams, rafters, etc. Some houses are stilt with oblong stone pillars, floored with planks or logs and timber again is used for fencing. This is the model usually followed in the uplands. The climatic conditions evidently characterise the house structural patterns. Therefore, houses made of bamboo are prevalent on the north, south and west. The house has the following compartments. The first in Ka Kyndur used as a porch where agricultural and other implements are kept. Ka Nympei is a family hall which is levelled with stones or planks and reached from the porch by a staircase.

It serves multifarious purposes-cooking, eating, sitting and is congested with household articles. On its centre, there is a hearth with three stones. On the two sides of Nympei, there are four small apartments called *Kyrdin* and *Inq Kyndong* the two apartments the same name facing each other, in which one of Kyrdeins serve as store room of water and the other as barn where crops are placed. The two Inq Kyndongs are sleeping apartments. Behind the hall, another room called *Rympei* is provided as another sleeping place, Kyndur or shyngkup on the front lies side way of the main door into the house or it is a porch through which the house is entered. Firewood is kept in it.

Walls are either planks or stones or the lower half with stone while the upper with wood, a feature noticeable at rainy places. The roof is thatched. The leaves of grass are lowered down the sides of the walls and sometimes loop down to reach the ground. Bhoi houses on the north are mostly made of bamboo; the roof is thatched and the house is a pile dwelling with a platform and balcony but designs differ from place to place. So also in the War areas, some houses are mechang raised with a balcony. Whatever deviations caused, the system of the same compartmentalisation follows in Bhoi (north), Synteng (east), War (south) and the uplands (Nongphlang or Nonglum).

Palaces are large buildings. The roof is thatched, the walls made of stone and planks and floors of timbers. There are many apartments somewhat more collosal than the ordinary. The shlur in the centre is large in which sacrifices and prayers are offered. The posts are sacred, erected by various units with some ceremonial performance. The threshold is a pavement in which religious dances or Assemblies are held.

Style of Living

Dress and Ornaments

A skirt is used for women called jympien which is either a cotton or endi type over which an apron (Kyrshah) is suspended from the left shoulder and loops down to the legs. In outdoor use, however, a jainsem is applied suspended from over both shoulders and looping down to the knee. A head cover is tapmoh the upper ends of which keeps the head enfolds and the two end fastened behind the neck, it loops below to cover the upper part of the body.

A mantle is draped from over the shoulders, its two ends being tightened at the chest. It covers the lower end of the tapmoh and hangs down to the knee. There may be an inner garment worn beneath the Kyrshah which is a loose sort of shirting. The dress differs from place to place and those whose climate is warmer use loose garments. In Shella the jainsem is not suspended from over the shoulders but it is used as a baldric towered from over the shoulders to stretch sideway below. Phars rarely use Jainkup except on occasions.

Among men's dress, a, sleeveless coat was worn until the close of the last centre, it was cotton cloth of thick texture having a fringe below. A waist girdle of cotton was worn beneath. Over the sleeveless coat of jymphong, a wrapper (silk or errandi product) was suspended. Later on a dhoti (silk or cotton) was replaced for the waist girdle. A triangular or oval cap and a woollen head gear were worn. Ordinary men wear mostly cotton clothes while Syiems and other dignitaries prefer silk patterns.

Dancing costume and jewelleries comprise the following:

Female

- Kyrshah dhara or Nara a valuable jainsem pattern tied from both ends of the shoulder and looping down to the legs.
- Mukmor a velvet cloth of fine texture which covers the sleeves.
- Jainpien a sort of loongi tied from the waist and loops downward, its upper end being covered with jainsem while its lower ends are visible.
- Coronet — Ka pangsngiat a crown in pure gold or silver with a flattened top which varies in shape between oval and round.

- Wahdong — round earrings of pure gold which are like chains, the topmost ends converging with the upper portions of the ear.
- 'Siar Kynthei — earrings bedecked in the ear-lobes and looping down. It must be of pure gold.
- Lakyrdeng — for ear-lobes, of gold.
- Ki tad ki mahu — wristlets of gold.
- Khadu syngkha — bracelets of gold, very thick and heavy.
- Shah ryndand — necklace of gold tightened at the neck.
- Kynjri tabah —bands of silver worn down from the neck.
- Kanupad — coral beads and water pearls of reddish radiance but half of them being modelled in pure gold.

Male

- Pagri a multi colour red and yellow turban of pure silk.
- Sleeveless coat for the body.
- Bor Khor or Khaila — silk dhoti with multifarious colours or plain cotton dhoti for boh Khaila.
- Kynjri — silver chains.
- Coral heeds — half of which in the band are of pure gold.
- Wristlets in pure gold.
- Siar shynrang — earrings of gold to distinguish from siar kynthei of women.
- A sword belt and scabbard in pure or plaited of silver on which the sword is hung.
- Quiver — of silver on which three arrows are placed.

Dancers at state festivals wear a profusion of ornaments in gold and silver. Kynpham Singh a noted critic specified them as follows:

- Pansngiat in silver or gold.
- Langkyrteng.
- SiarKynthei.
- Siar shaba dohkha, these are ear pendants, ear tops, ear bracelets, drops, earrings and chains all in gold.
- Namte.
- Mokor Kyndur, these are ear ornaments like circlets of gold.

- Mahu.
- Syngkha.
- Tad.
- Bajubon, these are wristlets, bracelets(thick and heavy), bracelets (also lumpy) and armlets, all of gold except tad made of silver and syngkha of gold or silver, neck ornaments consist mostly of these.
- Rupa Tylli, a necklet of silver.
- Kanupad a neck band of solid gold.
- Kpieng Ksiar bad Paila, these are strings of coral and gold leaf shaped beads.
- Kynjri Ksiar bad rupa, these are the gold and silver necklets, chains, toques.
- Mynjli, Kpieng Ksiar bad pailaintroverting with gold and coral beads. The shoulder ornaments basically are made up of gold.
- Kynjri deng, chains or torques of pure gold.
- Kynjri tabah, a sash of silver link.
- Kynjri syngkai a waist chain of silver.

Besides there are:

- Shan ryndang or gold necklace.
- Khaila ksiar or the drop earrings.
- Kynjri rupa or a silver necklace.
- Kynjri saipan or a silver waistbelt.
- Siar shrong or the gold ear pendant.
- Kynjri lyngkniap, a silver necklace suspended with chain bands.
- Sai Khyllong, a head ornament composed of a string, falling in a pendant inserted with three plugs.
- Khan, ksiar and rupa — simple bracelets of silver or gold.
- Khadu Khi or men's bracelet.
- Sahti rupa and Kslar or silver and gold finger rings.
- Kynjri tympong — which is like kynjri saipan, simple earings known as rila.
- Sahshkor ordinary gold earrings.
- Shanam is a vessel having a lid in brass or copper or silver held by a chain and used as a lime pot.

Among others, a silver quiver (ryngkab) with three arrows of silver tucked inside its cone is suspended from the waist the dancer wears on, and Waist mastieh tapered in steel armed by a dancers are the other attractions.

Evidently the items turned out from the richest metals reveal the intricate system of folk jewelleries in the state. Metallurgy apparently was practised extensively; the system of excavation of gold, silver, brass and copper, was once extant. The long continued excavation, however, led to the exhaustion of the precious metals carried out till the dawn of the British regime, when mining and metallurgy had already become dwindled. Work in goldsmithery in catering to these cultural needs had become enhanced and till quite recently, the goldsmiths at centres like Jowai were intensively occupied in making and providing ornaments, traditional and non-traditional not only in Meghalaya, but also neighbouring places such as Mikir, Dulfla and others Hill areas. Work in goldsmithery at present has also dwindled but if offers a prospective undertaking in the near future if not now.

Food

Meats relished are pork, beef, fowls and fishes. Meat boiled with or without vegetables furnish good soup dishes. Meat and fish smoked, dried and broiled are taken. Therefore, broiled, fried, dried and smoked fish is greatly relished. Fish dried in red-hot stones (kha kynthah waw) or baked near a chimney by piercing the fish lengthwise and holding it with a stick or Kharang are the favourite indigenous items. It is baked also over the red hot charcoals.

In winter time everywhere fish is basked in the sun to make it preservable for a long time. Now meat and fish fried with oils, onion, ginger, garlics, pepper, turmeric is very common. These things as well as tez pat are available locally. They prepare fried rice with pork and chicken called *ja-doh* which is different from ja-snam, rice cooked with blood and selected entrails such as liver, kidneys, etc. of animals. The real delicacy is a pig's head which in the first instance is thoroughly boiled, the brain and the tongue portion being boiled separately having them wrapped in a leaf. The meat ready is rendered into fine cuts, when the tiny fractions are besmeared with tongue and brain and proportionately mixed with onion flakes, ginger, chillies and salt. The boiled water inhaled from the meat serves as gravy. Meat of wild animals relished extends to wild pigs, some horned animals, pigeons, jungle fowls and rhinos, pheasants, partridges, but does not include snakes, frogs, tigers, bears, monkeys, elephants, etc.

Dried fish is prepared by various ways. They take a boiled dried fish boiled with potato, tomato or wild herbs; it is as well fried with spices or without them: a smoked one rendered into a paste with onion, ginger and chillies serves as a pickle. However, it is prepared into various dishes according to one's choice.

Condiments from seeds (called *Nei Lieh*) are quite tasty. The seeds are baked and then grounded till they get moistened added with little salt grains. Turungbai, a paste prepared from the beans melted specially and then fried with onion, ginger, pepper, dhonias seeds and cinnamom, is very much relished as a condiment.

Now, curries boiled, fish and meat fried and intensively and less intensively spice curries obtain themselves. To whatever curry made dishes of meat mixed with selected vegetables proportionately are served or vegetables cooked, boiled or fried separately are delivered. They get several vegetable herbs with a few grown species serving as salads. They arrange regular meat, fish, vegetable stalls out of their own resources or with supplies brought from outside through the regularly weekly, by-weekly and daily markets.

Rice cakes are many in which a different type of paddy are planted for rice cakes. The common cakes are pu jer, pu syep, pu doh, pu maloi, pu nei, pu khlein, pu niang half, pu saw, pu tyndong, pu lum, etc. Pu jer is a fine powdered rice eaten at the important ceremonies. In all the stages of preparation for these different rice cakes, rice has first to be pounded. In case of pu tharo, the cake has to be processed in a sarow, an earthen basin and then baked. In case of pu syep, the rice pounded minutely is strained, then wrapped in a piece of cloth and boiled, but the lid of the ware has pores through which the steam is discharged.

In the preparation of pu saw, a little bit of soda and baking powder is added, otherwise the preparation is not so different from that of pu tharo, pu doh is like a pork patty, well baked. Pu maloi is very much boiled like idli common in southern India. Pu nei is added with local jhiras and fried. In preparing pu khlein, powdered rice with little water and molasses mixed is fried. Pu niang hali is something like a jaintia fried biscuit (salted). Pu tyndong is a moistened grounded rice packed inside a chungnga (bamboo tube) and baked over a fire.

Pu lum is a plain rice cake like pu maloi but drier than the Litter. In preparing them all, powdered rice is carefully strained in the process and a refined paste only is used. They prepare various fruit salads by mixing sour and sweet fruits with proportionate quantities of leaf mustard and leaf of local yams specially meant for salad with salt and chillies either green or pounded. They relish milk separately or with beverages and with or without snacks. A special species of rice grown, somewhat good smelling, is taken as a snack but not as regular meal known as Khaw jashulia and such special species of paddy are grown for making those rice cakes, breads and biscuits.

Lad um, common beer, is brewed from rice mainly but sometimes a leguminous plant or millet or maize is used. The preparation consists of a fermentation in which yeast is applied into a rice; in the case of iad hiar a liquor, it is twice boiled but in the case of iad um, it is boiled only once. Beer is important at ceremonies and sacrifices. It is refreshing and vitalising. But drinking and drunkenness have definitely spoiled the moral character of many young persons while, in the past, it was taken with restrictions. They use a sort of a local earthen kettle and may be a sort of saucer for staining. The by-product (jyndem) is used to feed the pigs.

Drinks

In the preparation of beer, rice first is boiled when at the next stage, over it is sprinkled some yeast. The preparation is laid in a ware, the mouth being covered with a plantain leaf. The ware is kept as it is for a few weeks until it is ready. Beer is also prepared from sticky millet and tapioca. The fermented rice by-product is used by people both as fodder for pigs and sacrificial offering. Wanti is a specially prepared beer fermented of rice and sprinkled with a special medicinal plant in which the ground rice besmeared with that ingredient is laid in a ware, the mouth of which is wrapped with a leaf. Some Garos plant their own tobacco leaves which are used for smoking after they are powdered and rolled. Beer is considered as nutritive enough and is taken to repair physical strength. But drinking is bad in that it imbibes habits and addictions especially -at festivals when beers are taken without any bar made.

A cake called *Minik* is prepared from a sticky rice specially planted. It is pounded, admixed with either salt or sugar and cinnamon and moisted in water. It is wrapped in a leaf and boiled in a ware having a lid with pores and obtained from the result of steaming. It is like pu-syep.

In some dances, Garo men dance with their weapons. The weapons comprise a melam, a sword, blunt point, oblong, straightened with a light bend on a middle joint. Garo spears (Selu) are elongate with wooden shafts and iron-heads. The spear was used in all attacks. The shield generally is wooden or bamboo plaited, oblong and rectangular. Warfare being a story of the past, these weapons now-stand as decorations.

Garos as head-hunters were renowned in the past. It mattered little whether the skull was of a man, woman or child and whether it was actually chopped in consequence of a fair fight or surprise attack. The skulls were buried and later on disinterned and kept in a Nokpante or distributed among the actual head-hunters. Head-hunters-became glorified. Definitely head-hunting was associated with religious obligation that all rites would be incomplete without it. Garos used their weapons according to the emergency of the situation. The sword was used in duels, face to face, the spear was used as a thrust. Villages were built on the spur of the range so that the approach of the enemy from below the base would be pushed back by a counter repulse. They entrenched themselves in their mountain fastness and kept the slope down with many pitfalls in which sharpened bamboo spikes were laid upward and hidden by bare covering. They had various modes of warfare.

They have old war haunts, harvest, partners' and fertility dances besides the other group dances which depict different moods and gestures and reflect the cultural emblems.

The war dance (Gyika) belongs to men, while women from the corners just cheer up. Males hold in their hands a sword (on the right) and a shield on the left representing combats but it is also warding off the evil spirits. The harvest dance is Wangala which we have discussed. In partners' or elopement dance (jikseka), girls and boys appear inappropriate gestures as if they were suitors' approaching and advancing while girls expressed either decline or acceptance.

The boys turn rivals to one another. The dance is held as if it were against the background of the blossoming boughs of trees. They represent plucking of fruits (chamdilroa) in which a boy with a tail tied behind his waist and looping down is surrounded by 3 to 5 girls performing plucking as the boy skips or hops to turn round and round his tail. Fertility is indicated by the striking of digging sticks as if the group was performing tilling or digging or actual plucking of crops. In a group dance (chroka), a line of dancer, strike with their feet one inverted in turn by the other and women moving in and out their hands around. In the past, head-hunters demonstrated their accomplishment by drums in the uproarious festive dance held. Gariroa is a merry-go-round, boys taking side on the left row and performing blowing of pipes and trumpets, beating gongs and drums in an orchestra while girls on the right row dance and hop forward and both go round and round the circle. The highly accentuated dance form is noticed.

Gongs called rang when resounded mark certain auspicious occasions like meeting of councils, opening of markets, resumption of community works and location of festival dates. In the past, war men were sent off on expeditions with the hoary beats of drums. Similarly they were welcomed from their victorious campaigns, with drum-beats. Nokmas had drummers whose different beats conveyed different meanings either as summon or warning or anything auspicious. Members of Nokpantes were trained in the arts of dance through drumbeats and music. Garos recognise more than a dozen kinds of gongs measuring anywhere from perhaps a yard in diameter to more than a few inches and variously made of iron, brass or bell-metal. Some of the first gongs are decorated with engraved outlines of elephants, tigers, snakes and other animals. We should note the Garos assign the gongs for use on different occasions. Kram is a drum played by a Nokma, its left side more reduced than the right. Natik is a very small drum. Chingring is a drum made from the reeds.

Besides, there are drums (dama) with heads of animals' skin commonly used by male dancers beating them and dancing at the same time. They are beaten as accompaniment to the music of flutes and pipes. They are played by clapping upon the skin with the arm and not by clubs and sticks. They use cymbals also.

Other pipes are played on the mouth in which the notes are produced by hissing or sibilance in various fashions. One of them is a buffalo horn (Adil) with a bend which when played, produces a coarse note. It is a must in festive dance and music. This pattern seems to be indigenous to many races of the Himalayas. Others comprise bamboo flutes and pipes of different lengths. Bangsi is one instance of such pipes. They are hissed and the notes are changed by fingering on the hallows of the flute. One mouth instrument is known as gongmina made out of bamboo and steel.

Performing Arts

Dance and Music

Dance is held at an open ground or premises of royal residence or public place. In a group dance, women confined to the inner court dance in diversion of smaller groups dance in which crawling of toes and the balanced movement of the body (in which the hands are hardly moved in and out) characterises itself. The occasional lifting of the heel almost escapes unnoticeable. The dance is a snailish move. They dance with steadfast gesture and countenance.

Male dancers dance in groups at the outer court around the women; they dance with a fly-flap or brush known as symphiah in their hand, the dance being featured with stepping up forward and backward, occasional hopping also vibrating when in their inclined position hold aloft a symphiah and while reclined, bending down their bodies, lowering symphiah waving softy, sometimes flanking in and out in pacing directions. They do not take out, for reasons not known, a sword at general dance as it is in mastieh, shad wait, shad thma, those types or rounding up and combating dances matching with the manly dignity of dancers. It is not known again whether the discipline of dance good in harmony with the orchestra characterised by the shrieks in high octavings and the ever fat hanging tunes of the flute and loud echoes of drums and cymbals or has gone loose nowadays, if any flaws, dances lose their matching grandeur. The dancing ground furnishes a sea of apparels and ornaments in gold and silver, the brilliant radiance of crowns which women wear being largely symbolic, shining forth with their resplendent dresses. Women dancers are all virgins and children. Male dancers, old, young and children dance in the ground.

A sword dance (shad wait) is a typical combat dance in which males only participate holding a sword and a shield and showing signs as if they were assaulting, thrusting and duelling. A mastieh in which male dancers use a sword and fly-flap consists of stepping forward and receding, starting three steps forward, then bowing down their heads and process is repeated. Dancers in groups face each other charging forward and receding in the above style.

One of the fertility dances is Longhai in which both men and women stand face to face in two groups, in one hand they hold a hoe. The dancing consists of descending a hoe to the ground with one hand and raising it up with another in alternate succession with melody hummed and music played at the background. We saw Bhoi girls dancing at Mawrong wore white cloth caps, aprons suspended from one side of their shoulders, green loongis or blouses and red stocking wrapped to their legs. Men also wear their traditional dresses blended either to the old pastoral or the traditional peasantry character. Some of them are just like folk recitals or action songs.

We can reproduce dances briefly as follows:

> Laho a Jowai dance, this is a kind of a ballet, a girl conducted among two men stretching hands each other on the position of backside dance characterised by flapping of feet on the ground, pulling on and off in slow, soft pacing direction mainly. The three make a row and the several rows participating add also to the gaiety of dance. The costumes, the chequered black and white pattern, the wearing of colourful nara or dhara, a double tied apron from the shoulder, another jainsem fitting in as a colourful waist band or sash, the distinct sets of earrings, paila and elongate gold lockets make the presentation highly colourful. There is no orchestra band. The dance is danced to a song of singer to the accompaniment of a flute and drum. Lukhmi in Bhoi is like a Laho but a row is made of several persons including two or three women, mid the male dancers passing on their feet, embracing hands over shoulders among themselves and expressing their bodily and rhythmic motions against songs sung or music played. Female dancers do not wear crowns but tuck themselves with bunches of flowers on their heads. Mastieh is danced in many styles according to the local diversions. Dancers are many, the above being the most exemplary.

Folk Music

The reconstruction of folk music has been constrained in the state first by the increasing popularity of western music (music by ear predominating while music by discipline through prescribed standards confined to a few) while codification and reformalisation of folk music is rendered extremely difficult owing to high octaves along with the quick changing notations and quick super-session of notes, this is about the music blasted on a principal flute called tangmuri played together with drums and cymbals at dances. The manipulation of this orchestral music and marches devolves mostly on veterans who still continue the great and small traditions. Folk music besides is appropriately the form of mistresly (strumming and fingering on string) or by siat, sibilance with a form of nasalisation on flutes and pipes or jingput and rhythmic beat of drums or ksing. The flute called *sharati* is used for expressing sad tunes like dirges; tangled is similar to sharati not always confined to dirges; besh a very simple pipe has its multifarious use in giving typical tunes to songs and music belonging to different backgrounds; mieng, a jew's harp is played mostly to match with peasantry, pastoral and hunting music; minsterlsy leas its different philosophic and social connotation and used as a medium for reciting allegories, parables, epics, lyrics and ballads.

The art of drumming is padiah conveyed to the different rhythmic and accented stresses, connotative in their mild form to domestic tunes and in their loud form to public performances. Pitches with slurs at short bars and accented form at long bars characterise the folk music. Drums mainly are nakra, tasar, padiah, naila, katasa and kynphong. In all cases, heads of drums are surfaced by skin plates or sheets supported on wooden frames howled out from the selected tree saplings and would in and round their oval bodies by small skin straps. Nakra is a big drum resembling a half end mortar and beaten on its main head by sticks.

Tasar looks also like nakra. Padiah is a small drum looking like a flat bowl. Katasa is very small in the size of cymbal. Naila is beaten very fast and give great speed to fast dance like Darrang, women's dance which does not go slow like Shillong highlander's dance. Kynphong beaten on both heads with hands, looks like a cucumber. It is used mainly at women's dance sometimes in accompaniment with other instruments. The task of drummers is varied in being proficient in beats characterising their places. Therefore, minstrelsy is manipulated body harpists and minstrels with power to recite, sing and interpret themes and contents profuse in folk poetry and music Sing diengphong made of soft cane and reeds is a medium played for mild tunes. The popular harps are maryngod, sarong, marynthing and duitara. They are scooped from wood species. The crader or round back is a lump of wood like a half cut bowl or ball. It has either a small head or few cavities. A wooden bar adjoining to the pegs excepting duitara is thick where strumming and fingering are essential. Sarong is a violin swayed on its string by a bow made from the hairs of a horse's tail. Strings are modelled from the silk or muga threads, marynthing carrying 8 strings, duitara 3 to 4 and others 2 to 4.

Tangmuri is made from a special wood spanned like a cup having on its bar, 7 holes; it uses a reed and a suckler; sharati and tanglod almost similar in structure also carry holes, sharati having 8; besli is a thin bamboo pipe its upper surface like chuwiang carrying 6 to 8 holes. Bhoi Tawla is a larger bamboo made flat carrying larger holes on the corner and one hole on another corner, the former used for fingering, the latter for hissing. Ronsing once was a great horn, a buffalo's horn sounded like a trumpet, Turoi, a trumpet made of brass, elongate, spanned upward then passed in a curved direction. They use brass and copper cymbals looking like lids of bowls known as kynshaw and maira.

Now it appears that minstrelsy, piping and percussional beats in slow fetching and moderate beats can be formalised and even reduced to a prescribed formula. Drums being largely connotative to State events council sittings, public demonstrations are helpful to conditioning or orienting key notation in company with other instruments. The state, social and religious concepts of music and dance can now be understood. A variegated form of tunes, intonations, key notations still existing can provide resources for orientation and reconstruction.

Because western and church music both formal and informal proponderate the present social scene (the formal music being meagre and compared to the proportionately larger informal Music), the advisability of combining the western and indigenous instruments for traditional songs, instrumental or vocal can be thought of and some efforts at reviving the Khasi music, perhaps now are gaining ground conforming to the real disciplines music pays better with training.

We believe strongly, that music helps to build the mind and all senses perceptory and receptory to the medium of art. Music by imitation has brought about a large number of pop bands and rock concerts. Current Khasi music falls into the following divisions: (1) Fertility songs with actions, (2) Vocal solo in which the duitara is used, it serves for citing stories or parables to the accompaniment of its notes, (3) Debates in which two or three minstrels sing and play on their respective duitaras, citing, reciting and arguing on the tune of duitara, (4) Phawar citation of couplets with a choral ejeculation, (5) Dancing troupes in which loud piping and drummings from the stage are resounded during the holding of folk dances, (6) Anthems with drums during the public processions and meetings, (7) Criers-making announcements in accompaniment of drum beats, (8) Solemn music at prayers and festivals, (9) Cowherds; pipes with Ka besli, Ka mieng, played to the pastoral tunes, (10) Lamentation-common in the Khasi folklore conveyed in musical terms.

Drums and pipes boom high at public celebrations. Mild drums make the solemn tones in the domestic circle. The matter of updating voice training on these grounds has become essential now, insisting itself upon the improved techniques of harmonisation, unison and rhythmisation, training in local dance and music in keeping with their standard and decorum is necessary. Programmes of the colourful music and dance have to be regularly demonstrated. Songs presented as truly traditional focusing the rich local themes as new compositions have their foremost importance since the bulk of songs included in some recreation programmes and video cassette tapes are evidently modernistic or neo-modernistic and cannot be largely thought evoking and heart throbbing on the real traditional themes.

The styles of percussion which have bearing on important themes may be briefly reviewed below:

Ksing Lynghai: drums beaten for sending out the state message.

Ksing March: a fast vibration by runs up and down, a march.

Iam Meikha: drums beaten to offer a salutation to a living ancestral mother during a household ceremony.

Ksing Theb Mawab: beaten in salutation to the deceased members of the clan or family during the collection and disposition of bones at the cromlech.

Ksing Nongwei: a march in moderate timing.

Ksing Shadwait: a sword dance, drum beaten in regular beats.

Ksing Mastieh: a combination of regular and faster irregular beats matching with fast steppings.

Ksing Lynti: a slow march.

Ksing Rong: a type of demonstrative beats.

Ksing Khrup: beaten in alternate light and heavy scales and slurring indication.

Ksirig Khot: drums sounded as an invocation.

Ksing Paid: beaten at the opening of state Assemblies and demonstrations.

Ksing Pyllun: beaten with flutes and cymbals at general dances.

Ksing Kynthei: small drums beaten for slower paces to suit with the female dance.

Mastieh Khla: drums beaten to exalt a victorious killer of a tiger.

There are Ksing Naila, dum dum and Ksing Mang beaten at dance rehearsals or actual dancings.

Shiphew Ksing ha ki arphew hynview skit is the great state band presented by drummers at the sacred State assemblies. The most sacred is Ksing Blei offered as invocation to God. Ksing Maw among others perpetuates the revered memory of their dead. Drums that climax state ceremonies are shongkoob which presents the mutual salutation between the great clans or nobles; Ksing risa announces the celebrated dance of men; Ksing risa ba-khraw symbolises the dance of the nobles. Risa bah implies the celebrated dance of the King and nobles; Shad tyngkoh consists of vibrating steps where the King and his nobles dance. Shad Bakhraw is the dance of the great clans, where the chosen delegates along with King and his Prince consort present a mastieh. These performances are observed at the annual festival of khyrim State held at the Syiems residence in Smit.

The main groups of the Garos are: (1) Ambeng who inhabit the western area which includes Tura, (2) Atong confined in the Lower Simsang valley, (3) Akawe who reside on the northeastern area of the district and extend into Goalparea and Kamrup districts, (4) Matchi who settle on the central highlands, on the upper reaches of Somang river, (5) Chibok on the Upper Bhuri valley, (6) Rugh at the Lower Bhuri valley, (7) Dual close to Matchi on the upper reaches of Simsang, (8) Chisak north of the Matchi and Dual, (9) Gara-Ganching who dwell on the mid-south-eastern portion, west of Atong, (10) Kotchu on the mid-eastern part, (11) Koch on the southwest.

Besides, there are Megams, an admixed Garo-Khasi group on mid-western Khasi Hills and Digils. Digil is equivalent of Diko a tribe known in Khasi. The Duals are found in Mymensing District. Attempts are made to examine the various aspects of Garo society and culture.

Significant Festivals

Drum Festival

The people in the past were barely dressed. Moreover during the summer season, heavy clothing was not necessary. Diversifications in dress pattern are due to the climatic conditions. Those who live in Bangladesh and Assam prefer light and thin textures while people on the hills, need clothing with coarse and heavy texture. Garos have cotton ginning as cotton is the principal cash crop of the District. Today weaving of yarn has occupied woman in urban areas who turn out sashes, shawls, bags and provide themselves for their needs from their own weaving. And yet it is practised on a limited scale.

Women use a body cloth; it is black. Sometimes it is red against white or blue stripes. This pattern is used as shirting. Besides, women use an indigenous skirt known as Dakmanda (in Ambeng). Men, besides the body both, use an apron covering the waist and passed in and between the thighs, the front-side in it being a patch of ornamented brass seals, stones and cowries. They wear a turban on the head but women use headbands only in dance but men on all occasions manage to keep their heads fully covered. Women are embellished with heavy ornaments in which necklaces and earrings which keep the ear-lobes distend and are weighed heavily. They use heavy necklaces both corals and metals. Males nowadays conveniently use shirts and pants as items of modern dress in advanced places. Women have adopted improved patterns of shawls, blouses and other accessories for their full dress. At dances, men wear special costume, make themselves resplendent with ornaments and over their turbans, affix a feather of bird or cocks. Over the lower fringe of the turban, they affix a few beads. Clothes as modern innovation have embroidery, vertical and geometrical patterns. In the past, men carried large haversacks and bags. They were held by neatly woven threads and have decorations of cane slips.

Dress becomes more colourful during the Wangala festival. It is winter time in which people can easily wear their tribal costume and rich robes. The sight is like a sea turbans decked over with by long feathers in which dancers dance to their hearts content in many transitions against the interludes of gong beats and pipings. Body sashes were also worn.

Houses are machine models especially the, rear portion which an elevated height. The house is elongate and has four or three compartments. Posts, pillars, cross-beams and fences mostly bamboo are used. Rich men of course use sal trees Community halls sex habit their own pattern. To a few are attached barns and woodsheds. Field houses are laid over tree trunks and branches as those we see in the northern Khasi and jaintia. The latter are guard houses against wild animals.

The house entered, we meet a porch along the level of the ground or slightly elevated which provides a shed in which paddy husking, ginning of cotton and other wicker works are done. Behind a family hall exists and contains the household equipments such as a fireplace, racks, shelves, baskets, containers and others. The fireplace is an earthen hearth.

Next comes the sleeping appartment. On the rear most, a latrine is provided for the family. An open portico lies along the side of the house fenced with bamboo railings. The roof is thatched in which the gable end receives intensive cover from where the grass is stretched upon the entire roof but the eaves are not so lowered down. Fence is by bamboo slips plaited like mat.

Some families have pens for chickens outside, some shut them in a porch. Some keep pigsties, others keep them below the machine.

The central hall is congested with important articles of furniture, foodstuffs, utensils, earthen wares, etc. Meat and fish laid over the racks suspended from over the fireplace becomes dried through smoke congestly on the hearth. Bamboo vessels serve as containers. In the gourds are stored the beers.

Horns, tusks, hide are kept as exhibits of trophy. Gongs are the valuable art treasure. Wooden and bamboo motifs skillfully carved over the house posts or walls are decorative.

The important items of wealth are the gongs. Their possessions comprise houses and buildings, digging and agricultural tools, weapons and ornaments, furniture and other household goods.

Some Aking lands comprise valuable groves, stones and boulders, lime stones and coal quarries, orange and lemon plantations. Wet rice farming exist in the river valleys and foothills. Minerals have been worked out just from scratch.

The Nokpante (Village dormitory) where bachelors stay in to pass the night, plays an important part during the village festivals and meetings. Here village boys receive training under the guidance of veterans. They learn here their traditions and acquire knowledge in the arts and facets of community. Boys learn here their games and sports. Teams of traders and war men from here planned and conducted in the past. Headhunters on return celebrated their victories in it, before being showered honours from other home, where they were confined to assist their parents in their home, at the grove and field, become integrated into it at night. Its impact as a club is obvious. Its importance has diminished at many places owing to the increase of schools.

Engravings and motifs over the front and wooden pillars in this building survive as architectural and artistic relics. They have them in wood. Such motifs are common in Garo Nokpantes. Some gongs used at the festivals and Assemblies and markets are kept. The Nokpante has a stage and a fireplace. It has a dormitory where all boys sleep together. In the past a number of human heads were kept. They were the heads of the enemy. The Nokmas kept at their homes some skulls and Government prohibited the keeping of skulls. So these warfare and religious symbols were exterminated. Gone were the days of brave acts and deeds of chivalry. The Nokpante is a machine, one portion of the portico being open while the rest is properly housed fenced with the plaited bamboo mats. The pillar is wood. The straw along the roof is neatly polished and made uniform.

Rice, maize, millet and tapioca are the food cereals. Pop corns and sugarcane are delicacies to children. Arun plant and bamboo shoots are important items in a family menu. They are prepared into curries. Sweet potatoes are relished. There are the varied and edible mushroom and tuberous roots. They like wild vegetables taken as salads. Nowadays modern vegetables have been used largely.

Meat is their delicacy. They take cooked, dried and smoked meat and fish. Meats prepared as soups are common dishes. They preserve meat by drying it over the kitchen racks which lasts long. Sometimes meat is salted and packed up inside a bamboo chunga with other ingredients to keep it longer. Fish is caught from the stream. Those with crabs, frogs and tiny species are available from the hill streams. They are prepared as delicious curries or smoked or boiled. At lower altitudes where rivers bebouch the hills for the plains, big fishes are obtained some as large as masheers or the same as those in the plains. In the large catches, fish is preserved after it is sunned or dried. Dried fish is relished. Fish is also dried from over the fire where the bones or sharks are cast away and the fish is suspended from a stick. People from Simsang use to distribute dried fish all over the hills, but imports from the plains are not small. Dried fish is used also for making local chutneys mixed with onion, ginger, chillies.

Animal meat is cut into slices. Sometimes they just roast the full size and distribute the meat from it. Crabs and frogs are considered as having food value as fish itself. Meat of elephants and snakes is a delicacy. However, these items may have been restricted as not all take them. They relish on occasions the rice boiled in a Chungaa bamboo tube, having been wrapped in a leaf. They take dried bamboo shoots cooked with meat and fish.

Some Garos are acquainted with chewing of areca-nuts with betel-vines. The bark of the nut instead of the real nut is chewed when the fruit is out of season. It is chewed with a piece of betel-vine besmeared with lime.

Festival of Music

Festival music uproarious and melodious, forms a background to the art of dance. Dances are held to the sound of an orchestral music. Balladists have several folk tunes which preserve their legends and history. Some are meditative and invocative. One folk tune, reminds the migration of their forefathers long ago from the north bank and their crossing of Brahmaputra when thousands of people were flown on rafts of plantain trees into modern Amigoan. Oral poetry emerges from hills and rivers, the beauty spots and the charming scenery. Love songs are melodious and penetrating.

Meghalaya societies in a span of a century has been largely transformed. The material aspects of the change can briefly be reiterated below:

Social change, norms and needs have come with the proper adjustment to modern life. The British administration with its uniform pattern at the district level, enforcement of the uniform code of laws and exposure of the districts to the outside world, have made these repercussions. With the advent of Christianity, education and administration, transformation in social life is inevitable. Christians have largely departed from their indigenous beliefs, sacrifices and ceremonies. A reversal in cultural and traditional way of life has since the last century gathered momentum. Marriage, birth and death customs have been affected. In Christian localities, the megalithic constructions and the Herculean art forms, have disappeared very fast. Some great religious festivals and State performances have also been adversely affected. The law of inheritance has been misinterpreted so that the strong avuncular influences have suffered great strains and stresses and the family custodian was relieved of performing the sacred rites. Many old industries have suffered and new trade structures emerged. The improved house models, better dress patterns, new sports, games and trades have come to stay. The old system of community education is replaced by modern education. The non-Christians on the contrary are still preserving their folk and traditional Characteristics. The indigenous culture among the Khasi and Garo, owing to the revivalist measures, initiated by the organisations and clubs, and supported intensively by the public can still find room to make its manifestation and expression. It has become essential to impart new incentives for creating bases to the development of the socio-economic and cultural consciousness and creating a pattern of viable and consistent leadership in all these issues.

Up till now some of the change is innovative. It has given us the benefits of modern democracy, improved standard of living and new patterns of consciousness. Better housings, builders, constructions have produced their repercussions in which our generation should develop these skills. Education with all its merit and demerit has caused the pattern of consciousness and some of which would have been relevant to our present world situation. The patterns of socio-economic and cultural consciousness have their foremost importance for vouching a future to which these activities will have by all means to be consistently managed.

Sports

Tourists love the majestic Meghalaya lakes offering them opportunities of water sports. Archery is another sport that is very popular in Meghalaya.

6

Education

It was the Welsh Presbyterian Mission that came first to educate the people that happened in 1841 when the first Welsh missionary entered the District and resided at Sohra (Cherra). The indefagitable labour of that Missionary (Thomas Jones I) and his successors paid its dividend. The first missionaries stood alone with hardly any official patronage extended to them. And it was after long decades of their continuity in the field that Government came forward and assisted them. However, the beginning of education is traced to the days of William Carey. A tradition recounts that a few students went to several places in the near and far of plains to prosecute school and college studies. It is not known if any Hill Student even went to study in Fort William College in the Bengal Presidency. The historical antecedents to the growth of Education are important for our review.

Traditional Educational System

The ancient literate section of the community having no script of their own, used Assamese and Bengali and even Persian and Arabic to preserve some State records and documents. They used tutors from the plain; they also used these scripts for maintaining missionary relations with their neighbours. The literate section beyond doubt was meagre, literacy being confined to a few royal and trading families. The Khasis residing in the plain read and wrote more fluently.

Even prior to the arrival of the Welsh Mission, a few students (Khasi and Garo) had studied in the colleges of Bengal including the Serampore college. This is referred to by William Carey who said that among the students belonging to different communities, Muslim; Bengalee and others there were two Khasis, three Garos (the latter sent by Scott then Commissioner of Coach Behar) that was in 1819; the Serampore College then being started in which William Carey was its founder. Evidently Scott had not contacted the Khasis yet. The first Khasi Students known were Ram Ringh and B Tham, sons of rich persons. Again in 1831-34, the record says that there were "Nine Garos and three Khasi princes under Christian instruction" reading in that college. Among the three, two were heirs of the Rajahs of Khasi States and the other was brother to him who killed the three gentlemen.

Glimpses can also be had from the first Bible translation into Khasi in Bengalee script which according to a letter in 1817 from Serampore says "a few Khasi St Mathews had been distributed to those Khasis living nearest to Bengal and who could read and write the Bengali alphabet". Evidently a large portion of the population of the tribe settled in Bengal or Sylhet plain, were able to read and write. The printed gospel in 1816-17 was revised later on by A. Lish, a missionary of Serampore, who resided at Sohra in 1833-38.

Elated by the success of Krishna Chandra Pal, one of the first Indian Missionaries who worked under Carey and who in 1813, at the southern foot of the Khasi Hills baptised seven men, including two Khasis, an Assamese and seven sepoys in a river in the presence of 600 Khasis and two native (Khasi) princes, Carey thought it right to start the Bible translation into Khasi and a for Khasi pundits was made. Carey rejoiced in December 1813 when "he secured one for Khasi, he said he believed he was the only in that nation who could read and" write". It is admitted that the first two converts of Pal "included the most literate Khasis among the residents of Shella". Yet a letter of May 20, 1815 from a Sylhet official to Serampore reads that "Five or six boys, sons of rich persons and people of consequence in the tribe may be obtained through the different Rajahs to undertake the translation". The first gospel could have been a one man's work but the Khashee New Testament in full which came out in print in 1831 was the work of a team of these boys or young persons. This New Testament was full of faults; it lacks clarity, full of ambique words and unsuitable phrases. Evidently there was no common medium; the translation seems to have been conveyed in a near obsolete dialect. It suffers tremendously because it was translated direct from a Bengali and not the English version.

The branch of this Mission was established at Sohra in 1833 in the person of A. Lish. He opened the first three schools in the Sohra localities. He was popular among the local people. He started writing books in the Bengali script. But in 1839, due to some mishaps, the Mission was-forever withdrawn the hills. In 1841, came here the Welsh Mission.

Basic Form of Intelligence

Now we endorse fully that education is devised "to acquire the basic form of intelligence as also the shaping and coordinating of its inherent forms and faculties and evoking rights patterns of consciousness in some inherent affairs of society, statesmanship, culture, civics, sciences, religion and other issues which affect us. The motto is to make intelligence more and more implicated. The solution of human problems cannot all be devised its framework alone. Therefore, other Departments and Agencies have been devised to cater with these problems. Misuse of Education may either bring a collapse or stagnation of civilization and culture".

The Welsh Mission started the work mostly from scratch. This switched over to the use of Roman alphabet for translations and writing the school books. Dr. J. Fortis Jyrwa attributes that to a certain extent, the indifference of the natives including some Rajahs who favoured the Bengali script instead of the Roman script, contributed towards the slow progress of Education. In the early sixties, schools however, had appeared among other places at the Mylliem and the Khyrim States, the other places offing Jowai Subdivision and in many southern Sirdarships. The Mission made their sustained efforts to spread Education. The station Middle School and later on the Normal School had commenced not unite 25 years post, the first schools were ever started at Sohra, the government acknowledged the Mission's enterprises and generous grants were made over. Government inspection was regularised. Education solely was manipulated by the Mission in which Government was bound to exercise their administrative control. The situation soon changed for the emergence of the local educationalists.

No Schools

Even when Shillong became the Provincial Capital neither Government not the Mission had started High Schools. Serious complaints raged over the long delay to provide secondary education. It was U Jeebon Roy, the first eminent local educationalist who strove hard to explore the possibilities of starting High School which enrolled a number of students and which ran for many years. It was started evidently in 1876-77 as Sib Charan Roy his son passed the Entrance Examination from Shillong Zillah High School and sat for his exam at Sylhet. Jeebon Roy steered the High School single handed providing the greatest part of funds from his own pocket. Simultaneously a Mission Minor School under the aegis of T. Jarman Jones, Shillong resident Missionary was established and a batch of passed out pupils from that Middle School flocked to Shillong Zillah High School for their higher education.

Jeebon Roy insisted on Government in complying with public aspirations to provide good High Schools: The consensus of opinion was reached after many years of Roy's lone services in the field. The Government, however, made positive response much more later. The new Government decision was affected and the Zillah School was amalgamated into Government Boy's High School started in 1888. Consequently this brought an end to Zillah School. Government Boy's School became a well equipped school with hostel accommodation and providing the minimum school requirements. The Zillah School recognised in a decade pioneered High School education in our State. A consensus of opinion was reached that a Missionary educationist deputed from the Mission was to serve as its Headmaster.

Later on the Mission accepted the plan to start a Girl's High School with an attached Boarding. The Welsh Missions Girl's High School was started in 1892-93, a Welsh Lady Missionary serving as its principal. The two schools were among the Province's premier schools and enjoyed the reputation of their excellence at least for five decades. To them students from near and far flocked. The Normal School of the Mission now called Training School was shifted to Shillong from the erstwhile District Headquarter.

By the beginning of a century 6 middle schools of the Mission with hostel accommodation had already functioned in the towns and the other villages. Government later on set up a European school for girls with an attached boarding. This was Pine Mount School.

Jeeban Roy besides, founding the first ever high schools had also invested a huge amount of Rs. 3,000 to establish the Mawkhar Bengali School in 1899. Jeebon Roy was an illustrious personage. He was the seasoned educationalist, administrator, litterateur, philanthrophist; he had introduced some new economic measures and started a good press.

Considerable Boost

The entry of the Roman Catholic and Ram Krishna Missions gave considerable boost to the increase of schools. A school of the first Catholic Mission St Anthony's School starting in 1908 or so was recognised as high school (Sohra) were recognised. The entry of other Catholic denominations led to the beginning of Loreto and St Edmund's both being the girls and boys English schools respectively (catering however, with the Cambridge course like Pine Mount). Government high schools at Jowai on the local persistent demand was started in the forties and among others, were Government, Jail girls and boy's Government high schools established at Shillong.

U Joel Gatphoh was another noted educationalist. He advocated quantitative increases and urged upon the Presbyterian church to raise a handful of rice collection (Khaw Khan) from every Christian family to be collected by the church seasonally in a month. The plan was accepted and as early of 1900-01 the sale-proceeds of rice so collected more than Rs. 10,000; half of this amount was utilised for supporting schools and raising new ones. The other half was given to the Home Mission.

Oliver Thomas, the Headmaster of Government School introduced the laudable methods of teaching known as Dalton method in the Shillong Training School which imported Teachers' Training to deputed teachers housed in it. The record of his service was published in a book entitled Some Experiments in Indian Education about the first world war time. The Government School over which he was Headmaster enrolled- 800 students and these, the record says, were drawn from every part of the Province.

U Nissor Singh, Deputy Inspector from 1913 stroved hard to cater to the needs for English and Science education and produced some of the first books on the subject. He had seen to the problem of teaching and study and made considerable efforts to elevate their standard and update school disciplines in towns and villages. From 1914 he was Deputy Inspector in Tura and was mainly responsible for taking over the Baptist Schools to Government. He died in Tura in 1918. MacDonald Kharkongor also served as Superintendent of Teachers' Training School Tura and had his reputation in raising the standard of teaching.

Another illustrious personage was U Mondon Bareh. He had up to 1930, 30 years' experience in educational work and served in various capacities as a Primary School Teacher, Headmaster M. E. School, Theological College Professor, S. I., Assistant Headmaster Government High School and Deputy Inspector. Simultaneously the notable increase of schools Presbyterian-Mission and of the new Roman Catholic denominations had expanded the work of the Department to multifarious issues. He held that Education is a living seed; and whatever changes the economic or social fabric might undergo, education will always be at the helm of affairs to guide mankind to its destiny. This system of cultural enlightenment has always to be disseminated and its impact felt in the near and distant villages.

Mondon Bareh envisaged that a pattern of felt-governing education should be strove at and that the educational aspirations of the people be directed towards reaching that goal. In spite of difficulties caused by the difficult terrain, lack of roads, and economic depressions, the task of the department, for administrative organisation and reconstruction against the various hazards was undertaken inspection work which is the core of educational management was boosted. Some basic criteria for the concept of school integration was laid down. Evidently, the Department headed by the D. P. I. with two Inspectorates carved out, for the Assam Valley as Surma Valley + Hill Divisions, the District Level Inspectorate under the D. I. in each District, had extended its jurisdiction over the vast region. The highlights on the Departmental activities can be briefly enunciated on the basis of progress of Education in the District entitled the Quinquinneal Review of Education for 1926-27 to 1931-32, laid down by U Mondon Bareh.

First and foremost, statistics reveal the increase of scholars from 12,200 in 1926-27 to 16,786 in 1930-31 and the public expenditure involved for the tatter totalled Rs. 1,13,327. There was the increase of aided M. E. Schools which amounted for the increase of expenditure.

The allocation of sources worked out as follows:

> Year 1931-32 Government funds Rs. 1,07,882, Municipal funds Rs. 5,445, Fees 27,648 other sources Rs. 1,57,555 Total of Rs. 2,98,530. While 30 Primary Welsh Mission Schools were closed by the Mission for want of funds, the opening of 60 venture schools was made recently by the existing Missions, hence an expenditure gap was caused.

The recognised school and their enrolment strength in 1931-32 stood as follows:

Against the government funds and school fees of Rs. 4,311 and Rs. 3,753 respectively, the amount of Rs. 8,064 was incurred on building, furniture and apparatus for all grades of schools including special schools.

Diversified Interests

Committees of Shillong Aided Schools represented the diversified elements and interests in views of the fact also that Shillong as Headquarter of the Province is the centre of Government Departments and forms a resort of the choicest brain of Assam. The task to setting down the District Inspectorate and their staff was formidable.

Schools which were awaiting recognition were Ram Krishna Mission Middle English Shella and a Proceeding High School of that Mission, at Sohra. The District Inspectorate was indeed encumbered with difficulties owing to the fact that the Managing the recurring grant for Girls High Schools was Rs. 6,905, M.E. for boys Rs. 652, M.E. for girls 2,880 and Primary Schools Rs. 2,24,49 for 1931-32.

The report also reviews the up hill task evolved at the Conferences towards establishing Education on sound footing. Several District and local conferences were held to assess educational defects and suggest remedies arising from defective enrolment and wastage, slow methods of teaching, inadequate number of the Inspecting Officers, low morals of teachers and poor staffing of Primary Schools. The following remedies were offered - "Improvement of the teaching staff by securing a large number of teachers under training; use of rapid methods of teaching, holding refreshers' courses in the Jaiaw Normal School once or twice a year, selection of schools every year for special improvement; securing the sympathy and support of villagers by holding frequent meetings with them" (1926-27).

In October 1930, Mr. S. C. Roy Inspector of Schools chaired the conference of Inspecting Staff and Jaiaw Normal Schools Staff. That Shillong conference laid special importance on 1) Physical Culture, 2) the necessity for framing a log — book scheme for five year concentration of few selected schools every year, and 3) envisaging suitable measures to update moral welfare, corporate life and discipline in the schools.

Adopted Subjects

The subjects at issue adopted vitally at such conferences related to grouping of schools with centres; proper methods of teaching Arithmetic, Handwriting, Geography, self-supporting education: School Buildings. Physicals Exercises Development of Night Schools. As a follow up, it was reported that the teaching of General Arithmetic was improving, good improvement in some cases had been made in schools building, some villagers actually helped in contributing towards the pay of teachers. Interior District conferences were held alike. The aim of Scout Movement was explained. Over 58 schools due to the interest taken by the Inspector and Deputy Inspector were selected for improvement.

Moreover "the Log -Book sheet which was monthly submitted shows the efforts made in every school for the general improvement in teaching, cleanliness and tidiness, in securing the sympathy and support of villagers and the schools authority in their efforts ". To remove certain gaps, "actions taken in these weak and closed schools, were consulting the missionaries incharge in regard to the appointment and pay of teachers, appointment of headmen in each school to cooperate with teachers, urging parents in each village to send their children to schools and provide them with books and slates, instructing teachers in the weak subject and showing them how to teach geography". We find that the Departmental activities were extended to many issues.

Therefore, other favourable responses were noticed. Night teaching had started in a few villages; standard in improvement of cleanliness was noticed; a provisional Scout Committee was held; the Mawlong R. K. School reported: "Some of the friends contributed something irregularly, the total of the irregular income being Rs. 3 or 4 a month ". A troop of Rover Scouts was started at Bhoi Lymbong; at Nongkrem the report says, 'the villagers have started an independent school of their own by collecting a monthly subscription of Rs. 2 per house every month from those who want to send their children to this school up to March 1932, they have collected Rs. 197. There is a committee which manages this school. Bulk of the village population were non-Christian and "the Syiem of Khyrim has served a Purwana to the village to build a bigger house".

Among other subjects, Agricultural Education in a very limited measure was adopted at Normal School in vegetable farming but little success was achieved owing to unavailability of land. In music, tonic solfa was taught only in Government and Mawkhar M.E. School (earlier known as Minor School and now Mawkhar Christian High School). This discipline had suffered enormously being neglected.

As regards condition of service, in the case of non-aided M.E. Schools, "rules are framed by different Managing Committees for services of teachers and these rules are subject to the Departmental rules and orders". With regard to the Mission schools both aided and unaided, matter of appointment, pay and control and dismissal of teachers, rest entirely with the Mission Bodies".

Wonderful Transmission

Despite the short comings, a wonderful transformation was noted in the habits of life, food, dress houses of villages even in far interior. "Education has also effected improvements in matters of community and social life". Notable efforts were made to spread mass education through publication of readers and story books and despite "want of knowledge of dramatic art as well as dearth of suitable plays, the thing is going on" that was the staging of plays or playlets had been taking place in towns and villages.

As regards High Schools, St Anthony's was raised to the full standard of High School and High School classes were added to jail Road Boys' M.E. and Islamic Madrassa. A

High School was proposed to be started at Jowai but the D.P.I. thought that the number of pupils in the top class of M.E. Schools being 14 in at Subivision that could not justify its establishment for a time being. Few of the schools were being elevated to High Schools. The persistent demand for Jowai High School went on and the school started to function only in the early forties.

"Decrease in the fee receipts in the case of unaided M.E. Schools is accounted for partly by the fact that the Rai Bahadur Anuchand Hindi M.E. School was returned as unaided school in the previous period and partly by the addition to two unaided Welsh Mission Schools, viz Shangpung and Mawphlang with very low fee rates."

On Teacher Education, 'the incredible decline in the number of trained teachers was due to the amalgamation of Jaiaw Guru Training School and the Normal School attached to Shillong Government High School which resulted in the abolition of Guru Training classes'.

As regards the class room coverage of the subjects for M.E. exam, it is stated that the cloud of weakness gathered itself around one subject — Arithmetic; it has shifted its centre also to the new correlated subjects, viz., History and Geography. Under Oliver Thomas move, Geography was attached to a map drawing system to begin within the Conference of teachers at Jowai and in another Conference at Jaiaw. These two conferences were big gatherings. The outline was worked out as follows:

"Correlation of History and Geography. No geographical name or term should be passed without having it located by the pupils on the map, such as scenes of battles, rivers, cities, plains and the homes and scenes of nations of greatmen...."

Visual Memory

In the teaching of Geography, the use of maps was always insisted upon intelligent direction of visual memory should replace parrot like repetition of names of place... memorising should be based on the visual presentation of the subject framed by pupils themselves through map drawing exercises....

But improvement in one subject was achieved at the cost of some other subjects as a natural outcome of reaction on concentration unwisely directed. And as improvement in Arithmetic was achieved at the cost of Geography and History, so the strained efforts made in improving the later subjects reacted on the subject of English". There led the Conferences held, to consider minutely as how the teaching of English would improve the remedial measures as such were taken. "A habit of committing to memory English sentences should be formed in the children. After one sentence is committed to memory, new words may be introduced and different combinations of words may be formed with sentences, based on the similarity of ideas. Every interesting lesson and every new mental development based upon it, is a result of the proper idea of what is known as the law of the association of ideas. The defects in English are the outcome of defects in vernacular teaching. If pupils are properly drilled in the grammatical elements of their own mother tongue, many of the difficulties they are finding in learning the English grammar will disappear. The order of thought and the modes of expression of thought are essentially the same in every language."

It is reported that "out of 564 teachers in Primary Schools, 123 are returned as trained . . . consideration has to be made for increasing the number of trained teachers in some such shape as the reorganisation of the Jaiaw Normal School". On women's education encouragement had been given to the Welsh Mission Girls High School, another M.E. School at Jowai and St Mary's School at Shillong. "These schools are classed as secondary institutions". Pressed by the dearth of training, the report elucidates the problem as heretofore quoted below:

> "If the Mission Bodies want to have their teachers trained and if the Agreement signed by the students under training is to be of any value, a better kind of cooperation should exist between the government and Mission authorities. If the teachers trained at Jaiaw are intended to serve as Mission teachers, the Mission should have a share in the cost of running the institution: this will give them a real claim over trained teachers and save the Jaiaw Normal School from being an anomaly of an institution."

In vocational education, mention is made of the Shillong Weaving School for girls, the Fuller Industrial School and Industrial School of the Catholic Mission.

Textbook committee consisted of D. P. I. (Mr. J. C. Cunningham, later on Mr. G. A. small), D. I. Member *ex officio*, one Missionary, Reverent S. Evans and Rai Bahadur D. Ropmay: proposed to include Rev. L. Gatphoh (Head of Anglican Church). Proposed to compile Advanced Khasi Reader for High and Middle Schools. A committee with D. P. I. as Chairman, Rev. Evans, Rev T. E. Pugh (Headmaster), Miss H. M. Jones (Principal) and D. Ropmay was constituted and proposed that biographical, Geographical, Scientific, Poetical, Biblical and folklore pieces be included.

As regards P.T., some schools were yet to be organised into some models for carrying out physical and mental instructions. Drills has beef started in some Primary Schools under trained teachers.

As regards, Scouts and Guides, the beginning was made, "but the Scout movement started and carried on during the years '28, '29 and '30 had been affected by the complete lack of help from Government and private sources . . . There are three troops; one troop of 40 Scouts and two troops of 48 Cubs each'. Simultaneously there was a general awakening of interest in games. At Cricket, Badminton, Hockey and Football, our team rendered a good account of themselves. They carried off for the 2nd year the Arbuthnot Hockey challenge cup and secured brilliancy in all the other tournaments. A class of athletes is being started with a gymnastic Apparatus'.

One Shillong School had raised 4 scout troops with 32 scouts and 2 non-warranted officers. A remarkable feature in the opening of scout work in Primary School is the publication of a Khasi Scout Manual. Some teachers "gave already introduced scout drills and games of their own accord ". . . 'A most important event was the opening of the Branch Scout Association in Shillong with Mr. S. G. Nalle as Secretary. "He writes it as follows:

"On the 1st July 1931 a public meeting was held at the YMCA Hall, Mawkhar, for the purpose of starting a Local Association of Boys' Scouts in Shillong. Mr. G. A. Small, the present Provincial Commissioner of Scouts, Rai Bahadur N. N. Choudhury H.L.C., the Asstt. Provincial Commissioner, Mr. T. E. Pugh, M.A., Secretary of the Assam Provincial Boys' Scouts Association, and other prominent persons, were present. It was then decided that a Local Association be formed and a provincial (District) Committee was appointed to give effect to the resolution. The provincial Committee met on the 25th July 1931 and the Local Association was organised under the name of the Shillong Boys Scouts Association. Office bearers and members of the executive committee were elected. On the 6th August 1931 a meeting of the executive committee was held to consider the draft by-laws of the Association. The by-laws were duly passed and approved by the Provincial Committee. On the 9th October 1931, the Secretary of the Local Association arranged a concert patronised by Mr. K. Cantlie the Deputy Commissioner of the Khasi and Jaintia Hills District and a sum of Rs. 140 was realised and credited to the accounts of the Association fund. The Secretary submitted a report of the concert in a meeting of the executive committee held on the 7th November 1931.

Organised Administration

Since the Local Association was organised, two troops of scouts and rovers scouts were registered. At the fete held in December 1931 in aid of Dr. Roberts Hospital where the Late Governor of Assam, H. E. Sir Laurie Hammond and Lady Hammond attended, the Khasi scouts did excellent work, that the Private Secretary to his Excellency sent a letter of appreciation for the splendid work done by them.

At the meeting of the executive committee held on the 7th November 1931, the Secretary was authorised to raise money for the Association fund and Secretary is now arranging another concert which it is hoped will be a great success.

The D.P.I. assisted by two Inspector pivoted the work of the Department. There was also an Inspectors or Lady Inspector of Schools who looked after the interest of girls education in the Province.

As regards Examinations and Scholarships, there was a Board of Khasi M.E. Schools Exam whose President was nominated by Government and the D.I. was its Secretary which conducted the Annual M.E. Examination. There was also the M.E. Exam . . . . Board for qualifying pupils for the purpose of awarding annual scholarships to brilliant students. A total of 12 M.E. Scholarships was awarded to meritorious students, the scholarships called Provincial and Municipality Scholarships. An enactment into this system reads: "the distribution of Scholarships for the students located in the Shillong Municipality has resulted in a ruling from the Directorate of Public Institution that the Provincial Scholarships for those schools with an advantageous position should be limited to two, leaving ten Scholarships for the backward schools outside the Municipality ". (Mondon Supplement to Quinquinneal Report).

As regards the transfer of schools from the Mission to the local Church Assembly and with a view to establishing self - governing education, these views were reiterated time and again in the Quinquennial Report. Expressions in that behalf were many of which the exemplary one is quoted below:

> "The authorities of the Welsh Mission have shown themselves to be such self contained body that they could not brook the slightest interference from outside in regard to the administration of their own affairs and the dispensation of their own Rupees. One of them has said in so many words that he was responsible for his own action to his Missionary Council. Well, let us wait to see how long our friends can carry on their work in this spirit and how far they can assume this self contained attitude of mind in their dealing with the changing Governments . . . . on the one hand and the tottering Khasi Presbyterian Church on the other. I am not a Prophet or a son of Prophet and do not like to Prophecy. But let us wait and see".

In these circumstances, the Foreign Mission of Wales worked out the modalities for the transfer of Education to the local church while retaining with their Missionary Council, Khasi Hills issues such, Theology, hospital management and other institutions.

Review of the Work

Reviewing the work of the Department during those decades in affecting the utilitarian system is Education, and in giving coverage to all the issues involved, we find that important bases were laid down to establishing education which would make such responses to the needs of the age. This had fostered the birth and growth of the first colleges oily 5 years after 1932. Education made a notable progress also in Garo Hills within a few decades. The antecendents to its growth are also necessary for review.

Scott started the first Garo school in the twenties. The school and as we notice was short lived. We also find reference to a small number of students deputed to prosecute higher education at Serampore College. Education, however, was sought to be stabilised in the following decades. A landmark was caused when in 1847, Captain K. Jenkins, an English Commissioner started a school at Goalpara.

The outcome was successful. That school had in its enrolment a few Garo brilliant students who were to become the first distinguished educationalists working hand in hand with a team of the seasoned American baptists who had been exploring on to establish a Mission in that District.

The baptists made their first contact in the Kamrup-Goalpara plain. The initial success drove them to establish the first churches and schools in the plain. There were good responses to education and Ramkha (one of the first converts) became the founder Principal of a Mission Normal school at Drama about 1864. He kept liaison with the first missionaries in the field. The other educationist was Sonaram. He is known to have started a few schools in Garo area in the plain under the Missionary scheme.

The earliest Garo centres of education were born and showed the healthy signs of growth, success was due to the fact that Government had rendered full support to the Baptists educational and literary projects. The Normal School later was shifted to Goalpara; this school which apparently played its vital role in education was again removed to Tura coinciding with its beginning as a Christian centre, and after the missionaries moved to this new born District in the seventies. M. C. Mason and E. G. Phillips among the missionaries deserve mention, later on the joining of Rupsingh Sangma greatly contributed to the cause of education.

The difficulties encountered by the Educationists appear mainly to have centred themselves in the framework of curriculum; partly the difficulties were due to the adoption of Assamese or Bengali script in which many school books were written and translations alike conducted and also certain educational wastage; initially experienced. In spite of these, Education made notable successes. Bengali or Assamese orthography after being used for three decades for printing school books and scriptures proved to be unfit; it involved difficulties in printing; it taxed pupils to learning three languages at a time. Later on it was abandoned and Romanisation in active scale was undertaken during the first decades of a century. The transliteration provided an epoch of a grant transition in the field of writing. Years of transliteration finally consumated in regularising, all books hitherto printed on school subjects, scriptures, church book, etc. to be finally evolved in Roman characters about the first world war time.

Garo like Khasi in these circumstances became a District Medium and English became an overall medium. Then again, apart from the schools established in the plain, village schools also started to appear in the District; Government also started schools; this was the nucleus in which other private non-Mission schools were to be started. To the Station School at Tura was added a Girls' school whereas 9 other Mission Primary School existed in 1890.

The girls and boys schools again were amalgamated attached to with boardings. The schools had produced learned persons placed in different positions. Intellectuals, writers, teachers, medical personnel and other grades came out. A few students including J. D.

Marak an educationist of repute went to USA on his own cost for study. Writing, spelling, arithmetic, scriptures, grammar of primary level were taught. Cotton ginning as a vocational subject was undertaken. Subjects also included debating and other co-curricular activities. Vocal music was taught. Drills and P.T. were resumed. New contents to the course were added from time to time. The High School was started comparatively at later years. In.. 1940 when the High School had initially started, over 250 schools or more classed as upper primary existed, 30 per cent of which were private schools.

The Complications

Certain complications had arisen with regard to educational management. The matter of improving education later was not taken by the District authority alone. It was taken up by Sir Bamfield Fuller, Chief Commissioner and the matter of implementing suitable policy decision was entrusted to Archdale Earle, D.P.I. The then administrators thought that actually no improvement in school structure and implementation of good course was seen during the late years. Most of the schools were old fashioned and bulk of the curriculum centered on religious institutions. It was J. C. Cunningham on taking over the Department from Fuller who was instrumental in giving effect to the policy of the Administration for the taking over of schools. The Departmental take over was implemented by Unissor Singh and to a great extent by Jobang D. Marak, Deputy Inspector.

Under the Government of India Act, 1935 Garo Hills sent two elected members while the Khasi (British) or administered areas and the Jaintia Hills Subdivision excluding the Native States sent three elected members. They included a lady legislator elected from the Shillong Women's Constituency.

Mavis Dunn the first woman MLA and later on Minister raised in 1937 a question in Assam legislative Assembly an extract of which is quoted below:

"We have heard the urge to Government to take up primary education and to make it compulsory in the Province. I am sure we would all like nothing better than to see the whole of Assam educated, yet would not the schools be failing in their objects if the subjects taught will have no bearing on the future of the pupils". A highly utilitarian system of education spoke for itself. This also signifies that the elite wanted to raise the standard of education and promote higher education in the first instance.

Similarly Benjamin Ch. Momin in 1940 dwelt on the matter relating to the award of Government Scholarships quoted below:

"There are about 300 Lower Primary Schools and 7 M.E. Schools within the District, but there are only 2 M.E. and 16 Primary Scholarships for the Garo Boys and Girls for three Districts, viz, Kamrup, Goalpara and Garo Hills which is too inadequate, in view of the large area for which the competition is open. Therefore, I submit, Sir, that at least 7 M.E. Scholarships and 25 L.P. Scholarships should be allowed for the Garo Hills District."

Jobang D. Marak said, "whatever we want is good results and this can be only achieved with a smaller number of schools with better qualified and adequately paid teachers".

Mavis Dunn in seeking to improve the teachers conditions presented her maiden speech in 1937 as follows:

> "I wish to refer to the Lower Primary Teacher who gets a ridiculous sum of Rs. 12 per month which is hardly sufficient for a menial. Though . . . . we are crying for the observance of economy in every Department, yet I feel very strongly that it would be a false economy to extend this principle to the hard worked teacher who practically slaves in and outside school hours for the development of the moral, physical and mental welfare of his or her pupils".

On the bifurcation of school inspectorate she addressed thus:

> "It is an extraordinary fact that in spite of the growing number of girls' schools there is only one lady who lead to do all the Inspection work in the Whole Province. Consequently our Assistant Inspectress has not the time either to see -11 the Girls' Schools or to make adequate inspection and give advice. I would earnestly request the Education Minister, to pay heed to the repeated demands of the Director of Public Instruction with regard to the Inspectorate of Girls' Schools".

In 1932, Miss Dunn advocated active methods to improve the Women's education. Within two years past, three private colleges sponsored by the Catholic Mission denominations had already functioned, they were St Anthony's College recognised in 1935, St Edmund's College recognised in 1936 and a Women's College — St Mary's College opened in 1937, Lady Keane Girl's College founded and patronised by Lady Keane, wife of the Governor was also opened in 1936. Therefore, on providing adequate assistance to the Women's Colleges, Miss Dunn said:

> "With regard to the expenditure between Men's and Women's Colleges I shall do better here to quote of the words of our Governor Siar Michael Keane, last year in the figures for educational expenditure on Colleges, Government provided and spent op Boys' Colleges Rs. 7,05,000 and against this sum was able to provide the Women's College, Rs. 2,100". "The first charge on the surplus funds", she said, "should be for the education of the future mothers of the nation".

In 1939, Mavis Dunn was enlisted to the Cabinet and became Minister. She held the portfolios of Registration, Cooperation and Industries. Subsequently she was solely in charge of the Department of Public Health and Medical. She was the first ever Woman Minister in any Province in Eastern India and was second to none except to Miss Vijaya Lakshmi Pandit Minister in UP from 1937 to 1939 in the whole of India. But Miss Dunn was Minister for a longer period from 1939 to 1946.

Jobang D. Marak likewise in October 1939 opined, "all the school teachers in Government Primary Schools are getting the maximum pay of Rs. 151-20, and there is a Selection Grade of Rs. 20-1-25 and a further Grade of Rs. 25-1-30". He was referring most probably to the case in Garo Hills. As regards increasing the schools to more areas, Marak argued, "the question before Government is not of possibility or impossibility. It is a question of funds. The village school teacher is to teach various gasses and various subjects". The original resolution was implemented in which the Selection Committee recommended to increase the salary of school teachers with an enhanced D.A. which took effect from 1942.

With a view to secure all-round development in education, Miss Dunn on the other occasion said: "I would recommend here a radical change in the system of education and would advocate a system of suitable education — cultural, vocational, sanitary to make us good assets in the country".

Certain Lapses

As regards certain lapses, Miss Mavis Dunn in 1941 remarked, "it has been a sad experience that our people may be due to insufficient education, have been unable to manage their own affairs and therefore, it has been found necessary to exercise a good deal of official control, supervision and advice".

In 1937, she was elected as MLA. In 1939 she stepped up to the Cabinet rank and was Minister in-charge of Cooperative Department, Industries and parcel of the sanitary education. Some hospitals evidently were entrusted to impart a system of training to nurses apart from maintaining their own staff. This led also simultaneously to the institution of a degree of nursing for the province in the medical institutions. The member of hospitals, health centres and dispensaries was increasing and projects for their construction owing to the ravages caused by the war were implemented at the distant eastern Hill Districts excluded and non-excluded. The matter for training Medical and Nursing personnel was taken. Simultaneously the Assam Medical College was started. Miss Dunn, however, regretted in the Assembly in 1946 the government inability to implement the project for the construction of a Medical School at Sylhet owing to the supply and transport problems caused by the war, that the firms could not supply immediately equipments and storages necessary for its installation. Moreover the Indian Medical Council addressed for the abolition of licenciate Medical Schools or elevating them to a Medical Colleges. The project for a time being was abandoned.

A message from Debes War Sarmah, the colleague of Mavis Dunn and a previous Cabinet Minister in Saaddulah Ministry and Ex-MP which was read at the Mavis Dunn 27th Death Anniversary Celebration held on 10 and 11 October 1989 reads as follows:

"I consider it an honour to be asked to write a few lines about my one time colleague, late lamented Miss Mavis Dunn. I knew her when she was a member of the Assam Legislative Assembly in 1937-38.

She was a well educated lady member in the Assembly and was much appreciated by other members as she took keen interest in education and, also in the matter of health, for the sick anal the poor. If I remember a right she was the first member in the Assembly to take up the cause of the poor students and poorer elementary school teachers. She pointed out the poor state of equipment and condition of L. P. Schools and teachers as well as the nurses of all Assam (including the Khasi and Jaintia Hills).

At that time few members took up the two subjects of primary school teachers and nurses of the state of Assam.

She pleaded whenever any opportunity occurred that the pay of the teachers both of L. P. Schools and the conditions of the schools were miserable. Education was of a very poor order. It has much improved now. In fact, she was the first person in drawing attention of the public and the government to the miserable condition of L. P. Schools teachers and also nurses in medical and health services, which were few in 1937.

She was a brilliant student. She passed Matric, I.A. and B.A. with distinction from Calcutta University. She qualified also for B.T. and B.L. In 1930 and 1933 from the Calcutta University and was the first ever woman graduate in law from the whole of the province.

The proceedings of the Assam Legislative Assembly held on the 19th November 1942 on Assam Primary Education Amendment Bill, 1942, reveals Jobang's role in this context."

Arguing its clauses, J. D. Marak said, "Now, Sir, regarding the policy of education in the Garo Hills, we had several conferences with Sir Bamfield Fuller; the Chief Commissioner of Assam and Sir Archdale Earle to decide which sort of educational policy should be there in the Garo Hills. I was strongly opposing the policy of education of that time. The educational institutions in the Garo Hills at that time were in the hands of the American Baptist Mission and I was strongly against that policy and I explained why I was against that. The Chief Commissioner after hearing my points and of the then Deputy Inspector of Schools remarked like this in conclusion of the conference that it was unsafe to leave education entirely in the hands of the foreigners. Then my another point was to have a High School in the Garo Hills, if there will be a High School at all, must be a Government one. Sir, Now there is a good number of Government Primary Schools in the Garo Hills due to my attempt, they are pure Government schools and their number is not less than 300.

"I am against Compulsory Primary Education for the time being, only for this reason that all over the world in civilized countries Primary Education is free. No compulsion is there".

Jobang D. Marak's role as a seasoned educationist is clearly elucidated. He set himself to establishing Departmental control over the schools.

Challenging Office

That was even a very challenging office of trust and responsibility. Taking over the schools had taken more than a decade. He was also a distinguished legislator and on various occasions, made effective speeches which were enlightening and which contributing also to the standard of debates. Many of them provided insights for the clear-cut policy decisions. Definitely he played also his role the establishing higher education in the District.

We can also mention here the work of Wilson K. Marak, Deputy Inspector of Schools; he was a brilliant student; he passed B.A. Exam of Calcutta University in 1930 and B.T. In 1935 and became probably the first Bachelor of teaching in the District. He is one of the eminent literatures and educationlists.

The Assembly was divided on passing the Assam Primary Education Bill, 1942, Ayes totalling 12 and Noes occupying 14 votes.

The Bill initially had solicited support from some of the distinguished legislators in the Assam and Surma Valleys and even the noted educationists such as O' Leary the Principal of St Edmund's College appreciated its proposed framework. Mavis Dunn from the beginning had certain reservations on the Bill which sought to provide compulsory education as otherwise the prospects of building suitable careers in the truly utilitarian sense might suffer. J. D. Marak however was vehement in opposing some of the clauses although it was a public move which had received also a considerable Government support.

The administration were shifting themselves between policies with regard to Education. At first they fully supported and championed the cause of the Baptist Mission Schools but after 50 years or so (the, approximate date of the beginning of education was 1864), they reverted their policy to taking over the schools. However, the Mission had laid the system of education in Garo Hills and the earliest missionaries compatibly assisted by the local educationists were so dedicated to its cause.

The development of education in a condensed than detailed narrative is preferred. The progress in a century was not considerable. Based on historical antecedants, we find that one of the best, brilliant products was Annamon than who passed the entrance in 1902; At Bethune College, Calcutta, she stood first in Arts Examination from the whole of Assam and was awarded Scholarship(s) for her B.A. However, she fell sick and discontinued study. Hari Charan was the first who passed the Matriculation Exam of Calcutta University. Dohory Ropmay, topped the candidates from Assam in the Matriculation Exam of Calcutta University i 1994. He was continuously a scholarship holder and passed B.A. Honour with flying colours in 1898. He had brilliant career and later on held the post of Deputy Commissioner and Vice - Chairman, Shillong Municipality.

The number of graduates steadily increased, "Khasi Female Graduates are being recruited as Mistresses of High Schools for girls in the Province and a number of our girls are giving their services as nurses and lady doctors not only in Assam but also in other parts of India". (M.Bareh) several men who graduated in Arts and Science came in. On some occasions only Khasi Students topped others from the Province in Matriculation Exam of the Calcutta University and may have secured up to 5th, 4th positive in Bengal and Assam.

The next landmark was the bifurcation of education from the Mission and its transfer to the local church. A Commission on enquiry consisting of the three most distinguished personages, representing the Mission of Wales came to Assam. The decision was arrived at to hand over education to the church. Thus the Mission withdrew their control over education. The new policy was accepted by the Local Assembly held at Wahjajer in 1937. In 1947-48 there were altogether 428 schools, 14,777 pupils and 557 teachers belonging to the Presbyterian church.

It was most probably due to the wisdom of the Foreign Mission that the change - over was affected. The Mission here made their suitable responses to the local aspirations. The work done by this Mission to build e the system of education for almost a century will forever be cherished with grateful thanks and appreciation by the Khasi Church Community.

Traditional Patterns

The traditional patterns of economy have these basic importance in which masonry, carpentry and basketry are our important consideration. The masons show considerable skills in making stone foundations, walls, chimneys, linings, pavements, stone hollowed blocks and buildings. There are carpenters working in wood, timber and corrugated sheets. The variegate items of work can now-be enumerated which consist panniers and cones (khoh), oval boxes (trop or japi), Khoh kit, briew (a mobile bamboo chair), Knup (rain and sun caps), Stools (mula), and other articles. Various mats are turned out from palms and bamboo species.

Baskets in a variegated number exist while are long and short polo or bamboo screens knetted or having hallowed fences (used for stocking cotton, areca-nuts, tez pat, vegetables, fruits), various cages (ruh) for keeping live pigglings, poultry, birds, fish traps of various kinds, bamboo tubes and chungas, trap or straps, kriah or trays, winnowing fans (known as pdung and prate) and various kinds of baskets (shang) modelled into different shapes. There is a strap called star used for fastening loads to the backside of the body and carrying them across. Knup and star are patches of some typical leaf bounded outside by neat strips or strings of bamboo in a crosswise direction. Bow, arrow, quivers are in their body made mostly from bamboo. Bulk of the baskets and other items are used mainly for storing and transaction items of merchandise consisting also of grains, crops and other kinds of merchandise. They are used also for other domestic purposes. They use some typical canes for the purpose etching and notching in some baskets and mostly in handlings of knives and choppers.

The head of the hoe is triangularly modelled and is not a shouldered celts commonly noticed elsewhere. Its body is clumped into a small thin and sharp hook on the other side and is projected and fastened into a socket which is connected into a sharp rising tube serving as its handle, formed of a span of bamboo, wood or iron. A host of iron tools and implements in the shape of tongues, hammers pokers, bores, jumpers, daos, knives, choppers, axes, urns, locks and keys, sickles and others are the out-turns of the village blacksmiths specialised themselves in these trades. The blacksmiths use cowhides and the goldsmiths use goat skin to serve them as bellows and not the wooden or bamboo pipes. Choppers of meat or fish are different from those used for wood cutting or the others used for household purposes. These implements serve well for the purpose of agriculture in following the different farming purposes and the several kinds of construction and building.

The people in the past reared great herds of cattle, pigs and poultry not only for the purpose of consumption but also 'for sacrifices and divination which were so numerous in a year.

Because of these reasons, blacksmithery and basketry still have their important roles to play in the economy.

The process of cotton ginning and weaving has been there in which a hand operated roller (dieng tylliat), carding instrument, instrument looking like a bow (ryntieh), a pulley or pynshi and a spinning wheel or gynter are used. A bamboo reel is used to roll the yarn. As regards eri, cocoons first boiled and beaten up to pulp then woven into threads. They use various- dyes out of bark, turmeric, amla (mylleng) or a wild fruit, raw lae, betel-vine for processing their colour clothes. Steaming up the dyes and the yarn placed in a utensil on the fire in all cases is of absolute importance. The loom, a throw - shuttle ground operated or lifted up held by three pegs is just a simple appliance used for weaving. Weaving is dwindling on. But cotton farming and cocoons' domestication in respect of muga and eri still exist in a limited scale. They are also the trades practised since the ancient times. Bhoi weavers have now been used to produce just a limited number of the festival costumes. Other weavers are prone to cater to a limited number of mantles (ryndia) mostly and other items like the chequered cloth patterns, plain girdles and sashes on a small scale. As cotton is a main crop, the purpose of weaving ban be served better in the Garo Hills and the weavers are prone to weave a larger number of their garments.

On these trends, Jobang D. Marak spoke at the Legislature Assembly in 1942 as follows:

"There are thousands of mounds of cotton collected in left colonies for instance Tura, Baghmara, Garobadha, Dainadubi, Rome Agar, Bajeydoba, etc., ginning machinery should be set up in those places. At present, the profit is being taken by the Marwaris and the cultivators are not benefited in any way at all. Now sir with regard to the sericulture industry, I have visited the Upper Shillong Farm. I have seen that very small and very unhealthy muga trees are planted and a big amount of money is being spent on these trees. If you go to the Garo Hills, Sir, you will find healthy and beautiful trees fit for muga rearing. Thousands of such trees are available without any cost. But somebody would introduce the method of rearing of muga and endi there". On weaving, Marak said, "There was one weaving institution in the Garo Hills, and that institution was established as a token of good services rendered by the Garo people during the last world war. The late Sir Beatson Bell said thus: "I do recognise that it will require money to improve education and industries in the Garo Hills, but I do not grudge money because the Garos played well in the last great war weaving institution was closed down on account of the activities of the Deputy Commissioner, who was against industrialisation. He clearly said to me, "I am wholly against Industries ......"

The prospects of sericulture till 1977-78 were bleak as time were only three sericultural farms, 2 Eri seed grainages, 38 collective Mulberry farms, 24 Eri concentration farms and loak Tassar Plantation Farm in all, (1) the volume of production being 383,000 kgm. mulberry, 2,218,000 kgm eri, 65,811,000 kgm muga and 1,730,000 kgm Tassar. The centres where farms are located are muga farm at Resubelpara, eri seed grainages at Nongpoh and Shillong. Therefore, Oak Tasssar plantations have been set-up at Iohksi, Iapngar and Barato. The number of collective Mulberry and Eri, concentration centres has recently been increased. The Department has already implemented projects to disseminate training to trainees in sericulture and assist cocoon farmers in some other ways. Bulk of threads produced in traditional ways is sold by farmers to parties outside the state then utilised for local weaving. The qualitative types of cocoons and the good host plants have to be specified.

Weaving, however, cannot flourish on small scale as is being practised now in Bhoi and Jaintia. It has become a tiny household occupation not catering itself with commercial propriety. The traditional dress otherwise is rich in texture, designs, colours used at dances. As such, modern dress designs can be created also. As such, winter garments and shawls with improved designs can be created also. As such, the valued nara, muga, ryndia, sarn, khor, khyrawang shella can be made up locally. Various types of garments can also be initiated. Healthy signs of weaving in several items of produce are noticeable in Garo Hills. Yet, the more improved patterns among them will sooner or later be wanting.

In the weaving schools, the use of fly shuttle has become prevalent. The school caters in a limited degree to produce the number of aprons, bed sheets, curtains, table cloths and towels. They are mostly of supplementary and not basic needs. No orientation so far has taken place for reorienting weaving suitably to produce the move valued and colourful patterns, traditional or otherwise; there are trainees attached to the schools or centres and they are small stipendiaries. It has become so necessary to increase their production strength. The Department has taken steps further to arrange for the distribution of weaving looms to the aspiring weavers, and furthering the training of suitable persons in various weaving modes including textile designs. The weaving classes now are operating in Shillong, Jowai, Tura, Resublepara." The cooperative sector in weaving holds a very limited capacity.

Art Specimens

Some specimens of the art and craft items have been seen in the Museums and the collections made at District Industries Centre, Shillong. Therefore, some distinct styles of basketry, weapons, wood carving, dress, wood, crafts, painting, dolls, plagues and furniture items have been noted. At present, arts and crafts properly conserved for trade have great scope for development and for contributing to the economic production. Styles and designs definitely merit arts and crafts. Craftsmen and artisans indeed are the creators of designs. Arts and crafts can be developed into the innumerable things of utility not withstanding the fact that the traditioning form of basketry is still very important for both household and commercial purposes. The local blacksmith is also contribute still to the importance of the constructional and agricultural tools and implements. Garo craftsmen skilled in woodcarving and basketry have created some new arts and craft patterns. Some of these arts and crafts have been given encouragement by industries Department through exhibition, training and assessments for Natural Award. Tribe can be conveniently conserved on emporium basis and open markets as well, publicity, propaganda, and frequent demonstrative media have their considerable importance to boosting sales and popularsing the local textile products, crafts and utilitarian articles, training, employment and conservation media are most essential to create production centres concerned in boosting sales and services. At present, baskets, handicrafts, blacksmithy products traditionally operated command market and take care of their own. Other arts and crafts with improved designs can also be developed which should and ought to be commercially feasible and fetch good incomes. After all, talents in arts and crafts are not wanting. Arts and crafts have their variegated meaning and contain both the old and new patterns.

Pottery was till recently a flourishing industry at Larnai and Tyrshiang villages. In 1984, we found that the potters were catering to bringing out daily items known as sara tmoh kshoo or a dish, kshoo khyndew or a cooking pot, kum, a large jar, bhot a kettle used at distilleries, khiew-dot for storing milk cream, flower vases, ash tays and others. They went in circulation to Guwahati, Shillong and village markets. It wk's a paradox that immediately after a survey was conducted that pottery which survived for ages all on sudden went to extinction. The potters were since then prohibited to use the black loomy and fire clay available locally. And no such soils are available any where nearby, unless these soils are given back to the potters for use, this industry is doomed to extinction forever.

As an epilogue and with regard to the beginning of any schemes set forth for the economic reconstruction, we feel that the extracts quoted from the Assembly Speeches 50 years will help us to gain some historical insights to the problem.

The Founders

Pugh evidently was one of the first scientists who pioneered Agricultural Sciences in India. He pioneered also in the field of Educational Administration and took over charge of the office as Principal of four colleges.

Miss Silverine Swer, among others, was a noted Educationist. She had served the World order of Guides' movement since about 1937-38; she had served first as local Adviser-cum-Treasurer, later on as District Adviser and finally as State Commissioner. She travelled to several centres and the movement was intensified in Assam, the Surma Valley and the hills as well. Updating services of Scouts and Guides was considered essential to Education. It would help to discipline the mind and body and ensure good habits; community services have their relevance in the field of education. For some time during the war, her service was transferred to the Department of supply and Government awarded her the title of Kaiser-e-Hind Medal. She was also the recipient of Padma Shri; this was in acknowledging her services and more recently the State Government awarded her, the P.A. Togan Sangma Award.

She served in North East Frontier Agency as Chief Social Assistant Education Officer from 1952 to 1957. Then she served as Chief Social Education Officer in the Agency with headquarter first located at Margherita then shifted to Changlang and was the first Principal of Buniadi Shiksha, the Teachers Training Institute which notably conducted the important experiments in Basic Education and in which the course of training was intensively updated. The Agency itself then held great potentials for intensifying the basic education true to its course and principles. It had grown into one of the craft centres besides giving training to teachers in many facets of teaching. She also advocated Vocational Education, that education which is mingled with a system of craft or enterprise based centres which should open avenues for the growth of village industries and growth of entrepreneurships in which in the North - East, these things are lagging far behind.

There has been little in the field of medicines. The field however, has been covered by Dr. Orlando Lyngdoh and Dr. Erasmas Lyngdoh, Dr. O. Lyngdoh having specialised himself in Anatomy had earlier served in jowai Presbyterian Hospital as Assistant Surgeon I. He served there on deputation by government. He had served also in Assam Medical College as Assistant Professor of Anatomy from 1951 and later an Professor till 1960. From that year he was one of the pioneers in the establishment of Medical College Guwahati having served in that college as Professor and Head Department of Anatomy till 1968 then transferred back to Assam Medical college as Vice -Principal besides holding the Department of Anatomy as Professor Head Serving till 1970; his services were Shifted to Meghalaya on which he served as its first Director of Health Services and from 1978 to 1981,. served as Principal of Regional Medical college, Imphal. He had served earlier on various capacities as Member, Medical Faculty of Guwahati University. Health consultant North - Eastern Council, Member, Indian Medical Council, Member, Indian Nursing Council.

Dean of Science in newly established Manipur University, Chairman Meghalaya Public Service Commission Member, Meghalaya School Board of Education.

Dr. Erasmus Lyngdoh, qualified himself in M.B.B.S.; he also qualified for D.T. and M.H. from London University in 1957 and M.R.C.P. and F.R.C.P. from Edinburg. He had some of his works published in the eminent journals of Indian Medical Science Associations. P. T. Marwein writes that some of his books were published by Government of India. Served as Registrar of Medicines, London in 1957-58; then served as Assistant Professor of Medicines in Assam Medical College, Dibrugarh and became Professor. Later he served as Adviser, Health in the State Government. Because of his competence, he became the Honorary physician of the President of India. He was Professor in Medicines for some time and most probably the first Professor of Social Preventive Medicine.

Nursing hitherto has become hitherto essential as the very vital branch of medical profession. In Reference Asia Vol IV Asia's who's who of Men and Women of Achievement, we find reference to Miss I. Lyngdoh; BA, RN. RM Hons, PHN and FB Dip NSG Administration, Sr. Hospital Admn (ND) who was trainer of Health workers under WHO Thailand, she had since served as PHN Instructor and State Examiner. In capacity of Matron of G. D. Hospital, she is Life Member and Secretary, Trained Nurses Association of India, Shillong and Treasurer, Meghalaya State Branch: She is also Chairman Nursing Service, North-East Zone. Updating this profession has received considerable attention recently. This is about the essence of Education in Health Services, Sanitation and Medicines.

Post-matriculate students till Independence had to go to distant places for Higher and University Education. The opening of Guwahati University and Northeastern Hill University recently has greatly helped students to prosecute post-graduate and other kinds of science education. The number of schools, colleges of higher institutions of education has increased by leaps and bounds. Yet, bulk of students in prosecuting studies in Engineering, Medicines, Computation, Technology, Mass-communications, Radiology, Veterinary Sciences, Fine Arts, Forestry, Agriculture, some Social Sciences where facilities are not available still go outside according to the allotted seats that can be procured. The formation of Meghalaya and the establishment of NEHU beyond doubt has given great boost, to the spread of education involving as it does the concepts of specialisation. The inflationary and quantitative trends have obviously raised new points for orientation of education and making its varied sectors qualitative as well.

Obviously there have been some signs of population explosion in the size of students communities and other sectors as well. Signs of commercialisation in education have become more and more perceptible here and elsewhere. At the same time effective measures are now necessary to curtail these inflationary trends and the educational wastages, signs of educational progress in other respects are seen to go side by side with these trends. These things remind also of our immense need now to develop the different business, professional, social, economic and other sectors to divert students to these sectors in their future careers. Brilliant and weak students are also to make their marks not only in their present classrooms but should find rooms also to make tangible contribution to society in future. A condensed analyses of the present state of education seems to be indispensable.

Basic Education

For so long Primary Education was taken care of by the Department. Circumstances in accordance with the constitutional provision, necessitated the transfer of education to the new constituted District Council (Khasi-Jaintia Hills and Garo Hills District Council and jowai District Council later on). The modalities for the transfer were worked out which later on led to the handing over of Primary Education to the District Councils. Schools lying within the Municipality and Cantonment, however, were excluded. These schools set up their respective Inspectorate manned by their own staff and Inspecting personnel a few deputed by Government. As regards funds, part of them was given by State Government as grants and part of them provided from their resources. The experimentation over long years proved a failure. During those years, these problems came to highlight in the press owing to Primary Teachers' agitations which have seriously affected the educational machinery. These educational crises looming large, the handing back of Primary Education to Government had become necessary. First, the Garo Hills District Council surrendered Primary Education in 1980, the Khasi Hills followed in 1984 and Jaintia Hills District Council also gave way in those years. Now the Department has inherited the problem in which the smooth functioning has become by and large constrained in many cases. This most probably must have seriously disturbed the proportionate balance as Middle Schools besides coping with their own work were bound to offer rectification to batches of primary passed out pupils since many village Primary Schools have largely remained neglected. The energies of the State Government have considerably been taxed. The competence of handing back Primary Education to District Council seems to be now under consideration and public opinion with largely be decisive to settle the issue.

Inflationary increases against the statistical enumeration can now be reviewed as briefly as possible. A provisional estimate in 1977 shows the over-lapping increase of institutions as follows: (a) Pre-primary and Basic — 379; (b) Primary and Basic — 3,445; (c) Middle and Sr. Basic — 387; (d) High and Higher Secondary — 155; (e) Teachers

Training; (f) Basic, Non-basic including U.G. standard — 110; (g) Schools for vocational, professional, special and other education — 125; (h) Colleges — 12.

Number of institutions estimated in 1980: 8,113; High Schools — 150, Middle or Sr. Basic — 400, Primary — 3,500, High Schools distributed District wise were: East Khasi — 97, Jaintia — 19, West Khasi — 25, West Garo — 80, East Garo — 33.

The increase is based also on the development of communications, growth of urbanisation, and formation of new Districts and Administrative Subdivisions. There has been in particular the over concentration of High Schools in Shillong and the growth of innumerable mushroom institutions. There were two Higher Secondary Schools previously but were in course of time reduced to High School standard in keeping with the uniform conditions. Bulk of these schools had developed from the old M.E. and Primary Schools. New village venture schools have quickly sprung; the elevation of these schools to their still higher level involving their recognition have become indispensable. Some of the old Christian Missions have also contributed to building schools and other sister institutions in the Shillong

As a rule Government Schools are few located mostly in the District headquarters. The number of schools have been rapidly increasing during the last one decade. The schools in respect of Departmental coordination are grouped into Government, deficit and private aided schools. There is also the *ad hoc* system in which the weaker schools are administered.

Besides the four colleges (three of them are Mission Colleges) established in the thirties, the addition, steadily was made as follows — Union Christian College which was commenced in 1952, Shankradeva College (founded in 1962), Shillong College (founded in 1956) Synod College (founded in 1965), Sengkhasi College (commencing about 1974), Tura Government College (initially starting in the fifties as Private Evening College (started as Private Evening College) and Jowai Government College (started as Private College). The number of colleges has recently shot; to cite, they are Mendipathar College (founded in 1971), Ashengrangmanpa College at Mahendraganj (founded in 1983), Tirot Singh College at Mairang (1981), Sohra College (founded in 1982), Sngap Singh Memorial College was also statrted recently at Mawkyrwat. There is Ri Bhoi College at Nongpoh. There is Raid Labal College at Shillong. The Commerce College in Shillong was initially a private college but recently has been taken over by Government, Law College in Shillong was started in 1964. The upgradation considered a few years ago. Most of colleges especially those situated in towns offer subjects in Arts, Sciences and Commerce in accordance with the syllabus followed.

Competent Management

Competent management of the schools and colleges counts essentially for creating the brilliant school and college products. The distribution does not seem to be equitable as brilliant students usually flock to the reputed centres of learning in spite of the facilities, provisions, amenities that may be provided in other institutions. As such other institutions housing the weaker students suffer from this disadvantage. In fact the improvement of study patterns, as also the frequent conduct of classroom pattern with regard to accelerating the evaluation and reinforcement schedules as frequently as possible seems to be so indispensable to raise the standard of education. Formulation of other responsive media to the creative instructional patterns on the media of frequent tests and diagnostic programmes seems to be highly necessary. A competent management and an intense system of teaching suitably oriented and reinforced has been accepted all over the world to be the best medium for elevating the necessary standards and norms. But unless the responsive habits and attitudes of students are alerted and states of mind are fully channelled in these patterns, it is regrettable to say that the learned and seasoned educators we have mentioned and the continuity in the system of improved instructions seems yet today to be so indispensable.

The utilitarian concept can further be quoted below:

"The inherent problems of providing a highly utilitarian system and equipping the students under instructions have been pointed out. That the aims and purpose of education to provide the necessary critical and even mechanical devices, to shape the mental faculties fully and consistently, this fact is ever accepted in educational circles: The need to reinforcing these facilities is felt everywhere. It is not known how far the system of teacher training has been feasible to all these issues. In the absence of facilities and resources compatible to these needs, teacher training has been accepted as the most valuable asset to give teaching its requisite functioning. Therefore, education as the system of reinforcement of programme suited to the diagnostic search of the inherent draw backs and deficiencies of this issue is necessary for our consideration in the present world situation. It provides certain devices and remedies to rectify them. Tapping the mental faculties with the reinforcement of critical acumen, evolutionary tastes, analytical approaches and the power of education seems to be the most essential thing despite the inflationary trends which education is subject to."

The Advantages

The advantages of utilising teachers training for giving the required impetus to education has been accepted by all States in the region. More recently those institutions have been updated in the Hill States within the confines of North Eastern Hill University. The services of State councils for educational research and training in these states are in demand for helping students in the subjects including science and mathematics. The task to updating teacher training is looked to from many angles. Theory and criticism in the bulk of subjects oriented to Teacher Training lay emphasis on educational methods, technique, experimentation, psychology and practical subjects such as educational administration and organisation. Science laboratories are also essential to the system of training. The coordination of different units of education has become a variegated and expensive affair in which the institutional management, effective teaching and scrutinisation, course orientation, realistic screening at examinations and boosting students to activities and verbal expositions, etc. as would be helpful to the Department through its various branches is also essential to the task of Inspection to the minute issues of school management and performance to produce their efficacious results.

Teachers' training has by and large been integrated into its continuous process. It dates back to the middle of the last century coinciding with the establishment of the Mission Normal School. It was given proper impetus after Government schools was set up in Shillong, training later on was no longer confined to Middle Standard. Under the. Affiliation granted by Calcutta University. L.T. and B.T. classes were started in St Mary's College in 1937. One boys' college is learnt to have conducted B.T. classes but for a short while. These colleges give combined instructions in various subjects ranging to Graduate and Intermediate level. The need to conduct Teachers training more conveniently seems to have been envisaged.

The situation impelled the reorganising of teachers training from infrastructional level. One private B.T. College in these circumstances was started in the mid sixties. At its meagre and infrastructions the college was housed in a temporary building. The college under S. C. Majumdar, its Founder Principal made sustained efforts to grow. After a decade or so, the college moved to, its permanent building. It is retitled Post-graduate Training College. The B.T. or B.Ed., colleges take both students and deputed teachers from various institutions and extend to then the requisite facilities for training: The course normally does not extend beyond one year. They are entitled to choose subjects of their interest. The usual subjects of Educational Philosophy, Doctrines, Expositions have their relevance; also the Sociological structure with regard to teacher and society, problems of the North-East, Educational Psychology, Methodology, some inter-disciplinary processes may also have their importance. Teaching specialisations in the school subjects have obviously their special importance. Teaching experimentations, demonstrations, scrutinisations and rectifications have their prior importance in this functional system of education. Micro teaching evidently forms part and parcel of training. The training qualifies teachers at high schools.

The Government Normal Training School, Sohra runs a two year course, it qualifies teachers at the Middle level. There is another Normal School at Tura. They function under the Directorate of Public Instruction.

Training for Primary School Teachers is given at the Basic 'Training Centres and Teachers' Training Centres both Government and private. There is a Teachers' Training at Sohra which functions under the K. J. P. Synod. Under the department, there are the

Basic Teachers' Training which function at Malki, Resubelpara, Rangkhong under the charge of their respective Deputy Inspector of Schools. There is Government Teachers' Training Centre at Tura placed under the Inspector of Schools. They are Lum jingshai Training at Marbisu and St Mazerello Training Centre, Jowai which exist as Private Centres. These centres house deputed teachers from several places. The management of the Training Centres rest with the Principals of their attached staff. They seek to update teaching of school subjects; school organisation, social studies, nature study, teaching programmes and evidently the methods have their important bearing.

SCERT (State Council of Educational Research and Training) definitely has made important contributions in the field of Training Research and Survey. The Council is conducting multifarious programmes. It seeks in general to identify the area of educational wastages and weaknesses and offer remedies to remove these problems. The council appears to have boosted programmes to strengthen the teaching of science and mathematics in which the students are weak. Coaching classes are held to help High School Students in Science, Mathematics and English and this advantage is extended to Pre-university, students in Mathematics and Science. In service training to science teachers through short courses is also held. Enrichment materials for teachers are circulated. The council through UNICEF programmes seeks to update fruitful studies in environmental sciences. The council is carrying school mapping with regard to parity or disparity of educational institutions. These are the highlights of its most important services.

Shillong Polytechnic caters to Technical Education. There is no College of Engineering of Technology yet established. The Polytechnics offers a three year course which extends mainly to workshop, laboratorical and theoretical management. The elementary course is concerned with work shop management in various trades. Workshop Management at infrastructural level is connected with welding, carpentry, smithery, fitting, mansonary, machinery, furniture, painting, etc. Laboratorical management extends to preliminary components in physical, chemical, mechanical, engineering science, etc. Theory classes mainly relate to management, economics and English. The course is conducted in four terms in which the combination of subjects pertaining to each term is aptly followed. Some departments offer scholarships or stipends to students in which these recipients are bound to execute the Bond of Agreement. It is a diploma course and passed out students can prepare and sit at exams conducted by the All India Council of Technical Education which can offer them certificates equivalent of Bachelor (Engineering), Master (Technical) and Doctorate Degrees. Admission is opened to HSLC passed. A hostel, school and workshop are attached. The Polytechnics was started in 1965. It accommodates a good number of students.

The Industrial Training Institute also caters at infrastructural level to Industrial Training. It started initially in 1965 housed at Guwahati then shifted to Shillong housed in a temporary building. The Institute moved to its permanent premises in the city till 1985.

It offers course of training to Electricians, Mechanic (Radio and Television), Civil Droughtsmen, Wire men, Mechanic (MV), Fitters, Carpenters and even Stenographers. It functions under the Directorate of Crafts men's Training and Employment. The entry qualification is Class VIII or HSLC passed (the latter confined apparently to Electrician, Radio and Television Mechanic, Civil Droughtsmen and Stenographers). The IT women's branch started only two years ago, caters training in dress making. Subjects offered for Engineering towards trade include Theory, Engineering Drawing, Workshop, Laboratory, Practical and Social study. Simple subjects are not loaded with Laboratory and Engineering in their distinct patterns ITI Tura offers courses for Electrician, Mechanic, Plumber; Carpenter, Welder and Stenographer. Most of the trainees are stipendiaries. They enjoy the benefit of free tuitions and using the libraries. Hostel facilities exist only in Tura. The annual out-turn of trainees is on mild scale. ITI is understood to have qualified trainees for using their experiences consistently.

Recently the State Forest Services College was opened at Byrni. The college has a hostel. It trains Foresters to the level of Forest Guard Training for Forester Training in conformity with the procedure adopted by other States. Usually the subject offered in Forestry are Botany, Forest etymology, Forest Pathology, Mensuration, Forest Engineering and Surveying, Silvicultu, reforest laws, Forest utilisation and Forest Economics. During the few years, Industries Department have contributed to Industrial Training in a few trades and have set up the following units.

At Nongrim Hills, black/tin smithy/iron-steel fabrication have been installed in their training-cum-production centre. In that complex there are the leather works. Hand made paper making and machine knitting units. There are the mechanised carpentry/ furniture and cabinet courses imparts at Umsning, Mawsynram and Nongrim Hills. These cater to the Departmental Works just at infrastructural level in East Khasi. In the west Khasi, there are cane and bamboo training centres at Mairang and Nongstoin. There are hostels attached to them. There is also a cane and bamboo training centre (without hostels) at Nongstoin.

Various Training Facilities

At Tura, there are the cane and bamboo training, carpentry training, carpet weaving training and blacksmithy and fabrication units now functioning. The knitting training centre is now functioning in Tura. It is anticipated that the centre would move soon to Asanagiri with hostel facilities in the terms now being chalked out. There are the carpentry and Blacksmithy Training now at Dalu and Tailoring and Knitting centre at Baghmara and these centres provide hostels accommodation to trainees. In Jaintia Hills, the centres which have hostel facilities are the knitting and tailoring training at Maulsei (Saipung) and the Tailoring, Knitting and Embroidery centre at Khliehriat. Training in Jowai is confined to knitting, turning, fitting and tractor servicing, and carpentry training.

The Industries centre, East Khasi Hills besides has arranged the *ad hoc* service of Master Craftsmen and Craftmen for imparting training in trades/crafts comprising cane and bamboo, artistic sheet metal works, woollen weaving, hand prints and embroidery, stone glass, ceramic engraving, art metal works, architecture, painting, steel and other crafts. Trainees most of them are small stipendiaries.

Education should be so devised that it will produce effect not only in elevating the moral and cultural standards but using dynamic means to build a sound economic structure towards increasing the national wealth.

Secondary and Higher Education

Although the state of Meghalaya does not occupy a mammoth portion of the Indian turf but it is developing into one of the most advanced and technically sound states. Meghalaya education has played a major role in this metamorphosis. In fact, according to the data collected in the 2001 census, approximately 63.31 per cent of the occupants of the state of Meghalaya are literate. This is a humongous achievement in itself despite of the limited number of resources that are provided to it.

The central university that coordinates the actions of all the smaller educational institutions of the state of Meghalaya is located in its functional capital of Shillong. To add that touch of modernisation and sophistication toeducation in Meghalaya, quite a few number of colleges are being put up to provide a platform to the youth of the state. These colleges are equipped with the latest state of the art facilities to procure assistance to the students in all the various fields. They include 'Shillong Engineering and Management College' which is positioned at a venue known as Mawlai.

To keep up with the other neighbouring states of India, the policy of free and compulsory education for all the children under the age group of 14 years has also been espoused by the state of Meghalaya in the sphere of education of Meghalaya. The 10+2 system of education that exists in all the other states of India has also penetrated into the state of Meghalaya. A list of the various educational institutions of Meghalaya are mentioned below as counted in 2005:

- Primary and Junior Basic — 5,851.
- Colleges for Arts, Science and Commerce — 54.
- Basic and Non-basic Training Schools — 7.
- Middle and Senior Basic — 1,759.
- Universities — 1.
- Polytechnics — 1.
- High and Higher Secondary — 711.
- Teacher's Training Colleges — 2.

Schools

If you happen to be perplexed regarding your child's future, then just close your eyes and seek admission in any one of the reputed Meghalaya schools. Indeed the schools in Meghalaya provide apt guidelines for your child's proper mental as well as academic development.

The experienced panels of teachers who execute all the various proceedings of the schools of Meghalaya have taken it to their responsibility to procure the best possible means of education to your child. The method of teaching that is followed in the schools of Meghalaya truly deserves acknowledgment as their pupils really find it very interesting and at the same time can extract loads of fun from it as well.

There are also ample scope for various types of games as the teachers encourage the students to participate in them and experience the jollier side of life. They also teach that participation is much more important than winning.

The Meghalaya schools conduct regular examinations to keep the students up to date with the syllabus. Special attention is given to the fact that no extra stress should be applied to the students as it might have a detrimental effect on them.

The most important schools at Meghalaya are mentioned below:

- Assam Rifles Public School Laitkor, Shillong.
- Kendriya Vidyalaya has three branches across Meghalaya. They are situated at the following places — Upper Shillong, Laitkor Peak, Shillong and Happy Valley, Shillong.
- St. Edmund's School, Shillong.
- Laban Bengali Boys' High School, Shillong.
- Pine Mount, Shillong.
- St. Edmund's High School, Shillong.
- Jail Road Government Boys High School, Shillong.
- Mawkhar Christian High School, Shillong.
- St. Peter School, Shillong.
- Gorkha High School, Shillong.

Colleges

Meghalaya Colleges have made their mark in terms of providing quality education to the various aspiring doctors, engineers and businessmen who desire to make their mark. The colleges in Meghalaya procure all various sorts of courses that aids them to choose between different options. They can also seek the advise of elite professors in these colleges to choose the correct and most suitable stream for them.

The different colleges of Meghalaya are enlisted below:

Engineering Colleges: The state of Meghalaya only houses a sole college dedicated to the engineering students known by the name of Shillong Engineering and Management College. The AICTE or All India Council of Technical Education has also approved all the courses offered by this college.

Management Institutes: Shillong Engineering and Management College that is located at Mawlai.

Nursing Colleges: Repsbun School of Nursing is the sole nursing school in the state of Meghalaya. It is located in East Khasi Hills.

Polytechnic Institutes: There three polytechnic institutes including Jowai Polytechnic, Shillong Polytechnic and Tura Polytechnic. All these colleges at Meghalaya are AICTE approved.

Law Colleges: Department of Law, Northeastern Hill University, Khad-Ar-Doloi Law College, Tura College and Shillong Law College.

Biotechnology Colleges: St. Anthony's College and Department of Biotechnology.

Hotel Management: Institute of Hotel Management in Shillong is the only college that offers a course in Hotel Management.

Computer Institutes: St. Edmund's College and St Anthony's College at Shillong.

Mass Communications: Department of Mass Communications in St Anthony's College in the venue of Shillong provide courses in Mass Communication.

Universities

The two major Meghalaya universities are the North Eastern Hill University and the Indira Gandhi National Open University. The North Eastern Hill University is one of the leading universities in Meghalaya established on 19th July, 1973. The Shillong regional centre of Indira Gandhi National Open University is as old as 1998. Currently, the Shillong regional centre manages and controls all the curricular activities across entire Meghalaya. Some information about these two major universities at Meghalaya is given below:

The North Eastern Hill University is counted among the most renowned universities of Meghalaya, as its main campus is located in the capital city of Shillong. An additional campus was set up at Tura in February 1996.

The university offers courses in almost all the major branches of education. The university is divided into seven schools and all the departments of the university come under these schools. There are as many as fifty-three undergraduate colleges that are affiliated to this renowned university. There are 8 colleges under the university that provide professional courses.

Indira Gandhi National Open University is one of the most popular Meghalaya universities. The courses offered here are varied – diploma, certificate and degree courses. The educational activities of the Indira Gandhi National Open University at Meghalaya spans to various training programmes, research oriented work and extension education.

Education is offered at the Indira Gandhi National Open University of Meghalaya in two different ways - open learning and distance education. Both these modes of education have become very popular among the young professionals of the state.

Distance Education

Meghalaya distance education is gradually gaining in popularity after initial circumspections following their introduction within the academic structure of the state. The inhabitants of Meghalaya have slowly but surely awoke to the fact, that pursuing higher education with some other vocation is almost always a wonderful option. Apart from the major universities, there are many institutions for distance education in Meghalaya that specialise in distance learning.

State of Distance Education

Like everywhere else in India, distance education at Meghalaya was not greeted with great enthusiasm at its inception. Students were doubtful about its worth. Most preferred a regular education system to distance education in Meghalaya and often left for universities outside the state, to be enable to pursue some job alongside their education. However, soon a change in the mindset was noticed, as the inhabitants of the state realised the fact that the same facilities could be availed from within the state. The distance education of Meghalaya opened up the possibilities of education for all interested students who were not able to take up education as a full time engagement because of various constraints.

Indira Gandhi Open University and NEHU

Indira Gandhi National Open University and the distant programme of the North Eastern Hill University (NEHU) are the most popular of all Meghalaya distance education programmes. While IGNOU offers a wide range of courses for the students to choose from, the NEHU course offer degrees and diplomas more on the lines of the university curricula. Most universities of India have been presently forced to offer distance learning courses as a part of the diversification programmes of their operations. NEHU is also a great attraction for the research scholars because of their M.Phil. and Ph.D. Programmes.

Vocational Education

Meghalaya Vocational Education is extremely popular because it opens up plenty of placement opportunities for its students. The rapid growth of industrialisation in Meghalaya has increased the demand for skilled and semi-skilled labours to a great degree, consequently making Meghalaya Vocational Education all the more lucrative. Meghalaya vocational education is greatly encouraged by the government. The state directorate for employment and craftsman training is committed towards the optimisation of the human resources of the state through the distance education facilities offered by the various institutions of the state.

Vocational Education Facilities in the Polytechnic Colleges

The polytechnic colleges take a major role in imparting Meghalaya Vocational Education, apart from the various degree courses. The students of these colleges are equipped in various technical capacities, which help them to play an important part in the many industries of the state, as well as to explore possibilities of self-employment. The polytechnic colleges which offer vocational education at Meghalaya are:

- Jowai Polytechnic in the Jaintia Hills.
- Shillong Polytechnic in Shillong.
- Tura Polytechnic in the Garo Hills.

Other Vocational Courses

Apart from the semi-professional and Vocational Education in Meghalaya as offered by the various polytechnic colleges, there are various other vocational courses on offer by other institutes as well. Vocational education of Meghalaya play a very important role in the economic empowerment of the womenfolk of the state. They are trained in various skills of the technical as well as the craftsmanship to secure jobs in the big as well as small scale industries of the state, which are fundamental to the state's economy.

7

Language and Literature

Language

Meghalaya language is a reflection of the rich culture of Meghalaya. Although the state language is English; but the principal languages of Meghalaya are Khasi, Garo and Jaintia. To begin with the Meghalaya language, it can be said that Khasi is one of the chief languages of Meghalaya. Khasi, which is also spelled Khasia, Khassee, Cossyah and Kyi, is a branch of the Mon-Khmer family of the Austroasiatic stock; and is spoken by about 900,000 people residing in Meghalaya.

It is interesting to know that many words in the Khasi language have been borrowed from Indo-Aryan languages, the most important being Hindi and Bengali languages. Moreover, the Khasi language had no script of its own in its onset. But, it is said that William Carey was the first person to pen the language in Eastern Nagari script in the 18th century.

Garo also deserves a special mention in the languages of Meghalaya. In fact, it is noteworthy that Garo, like Khasi, is also the official language of Meghalaya. However, the language has a close affinity with the Bodo language, the official language of Assam.

Garo, spoken by the majority of the population, is spoken in many dialects such as A'we, Chisak, A'beng, Ganching, Kamrup, A'chick, Dacca and Matchi.

Another language at Meghalaya, which deserves special mention among the languages of Meghalaya, is the language spoken by the people of the Jaintia Hills. This language, as matter of fact, is a variation of the standard Khasi language. The Jaintia language is spoken, along with the Khasi language, by the tribal groups, viz. Khynriam, Bhoi, Pnar and War.

Thus, we find that the languages in Meghalaya shares the characteristic traits of the social-cultural pattern of the different regions of Meghalaya.

Khasi Language

Khasi is an Austro-Asiatic language spoken primarily in Meghalaya state in India by the Khasi people. Khasi is part of the Khasi-Khmuic group of languages, and is distantly related to the Munda branch of the Austroasiatic family, which is found in east-central India. Although most of the 865,000 Khasi speakers are found in Meghalaya state, the language is also spoken by a number of people in the hill districts of Assam bordering with Meghalaya and by a sizable population of people living in Bangladesh, close to the Indian border.

Khasi is rich in folklore and folktale, and behind most of the names of hills, mountains, rivers, waterfalls, birds, flowers, and animals there is a story.

Script: In the past, the Khasi language had no script of its own. William Carey attempted to write the language with the Eastern Nagari script between 1813 and 1838. A large number of Khasi books were written in the Eastern Nagari script, including the famous book *Ka Niyiom Jong Ka Khasi* or *The Rule of the Khasis*, which is an important manuscript of the Seng Khasi religion. The Welsh missionary, Thomas Jones, in 1841 wrote the language in the Roman script. As a result, the orthography of the language in Roman script is quite similar to that of Welsh orthography. As it was more easily adapted to the Khasi language, the Roman script for Khasi was adopted.

Alphabet:

- Capital letters A, B, K, D, E, G, Ng, H, I, Ï, J, L, M, N, Ñ, O, P, R, S, T, U, W, Y.
- Small letters a, b, k, d, e, g, ng, h, i, ï, j, l, m, n, ñ, o, p, r, s, t, u, w, y.

Garo

Garo, besides Khasi, is also the official language of Meghalaya. Garo in Meghalaya has close affinity with the Bodo language, the official language of Assam. Garo is used as the second language in Meghalaya and boasts of a literacy rate of 23 per cent (according to 1971 census). Garo does not have any myth related to the genesis of the language. The ancestors of the Garos hail from different countries, outside their homeland and it is remarkable that the Garo language of Meghalaya has a strong bearing upon their ancestry.

Further, talking about the dialects of Garo in Meghalaya, it can be said that the language follows distinctive patterns in the different areas of Meghalaya. Some of the important dialects that deserve special mention in this context are:

- Matchi,
- Ruga,
- Ambeng,

- Atong,
- Matabengs,
- Akawe (also Awe),
- Chibok,
- Gara-Ganching,
- Duals,
- Chisak Megam (also known as Lyngngam), etc.

Megam, which is known to be a sub-tribe of Garo, is also a dialect of Garo at Meghalaya. Besides, the Achik dialect is said to be a predominant dialect among the other intelligible dialects of Garo.

A snapshot at the Garo language of Meghalaya can be as follows:

- Total number of speakers (Garo population in India) — 575,000 (according to 1997 census).
- Region comprising the Garo speakers (including Meghalaya and the adjoining areas) — Garo Hills District, Goalpara, Karbi Anglong Districts, Kamrup, Kohima District, Jalpaiguri and Cooch Behar districts in West Bengal, the Udaipur subdivisions, and Kamalpur Sadar subdivision in south, north and west Tripura Districts respectively, and Bangladesh.
- Language used — The standard Garo is used in most of the regions in Meghalaya.

Thus, as it is evident, Garo is one of the principal languages spoken by the residents of Meghalaya.

Evolution and Development

Modern Khasi Literature With Special Reference to Post World was Period Till 1979 (As printed in Sarat Bose Academy Institute for National and International affairs 385 Jodhpur Park, Calcutta ...69) Annual Publication — 1885.

Primary Role of Serampore Mission

It was in 1841 that Khasi literature was born. That was after Khasi was reduced to writing in the Roman alphabet. It was the Welsh Calvinistic Methodist Mission (later on Presbyterian) which put down Khasi to writing in that alphabet.

Contribution of the Welsh Mission

The Welsh Mission caused a considerable number of Christian writings and school books to be published. During the last century, a great deal of spade work was done by the Welsh Missionaries with their Khasi collaborators in the production of books. These were the seedlings implanted in the soil, the nurseries for the further growth in, literature. A number of school books and Christian treatises were published. The publication of the full Bible for the first time occurred not until 1899.

Cultural Orientation

The first publication of the full Bible over, a cultural orientation as a new force swept in the literature when the present century opened. This was because several writers proverbialists, folklorists, poets, prosodists, rhetoricians, playwrights, grammarians, religious philosophers, historians and even anthropologists had come out who made manifold contributions to immortalising the glorious heritage of the race of people against the background of multifarious themes and contents.

Although spade works they were, they carry their own originality in thought, style and expression and some were very naive creations of poets and writers. Soso Tham was an outstanding literature whose Ki Sngi barim U Hynniew Trep, 1937 ranks as the ever best Khasi classic, the supreme poetic creation in which the indigenous conception of heaven and hell, righteousness and sin are captivised which centres round the celestial beginning of the race of Khasi. The ethnic and cultural grandeur eulogised in verse are set down below:

> "In time, the mighty tribe was born, With traditions so ripe and but, with one polished language used:
>
> One religion-though offerings diverse were offered
>
> One arts, one dress, one life style exposed:
>
> In time, a unique Constitution was drawn up
>
> That united the country into one".

Cultural orientation subsequently, saw its flowering and this was because the more seasoned and refined writers were coming out whose contributions are acclaimed.

World War Time Development

There was nothing much during the world war time. The whole world war hectic about the war and many catastrophic events flared up. Later on defence preparation plans were chalked on the eastern frontier with a view to resist the invasions of Japan. As such literature was reduced to a stage of neglect.

The advent of Independence kept the people engaged with the constitutional issue and adjustment in a constitutional frame work, arising from the British departure from the northeast. Something that came out took the shape of political pamphleteering. Literary revival became marked out from the fifties onward. Until that time, this literature has drawn inspiration from culture — its form, contents and significance and does not depend simply on social scene or characterisation.

The appearance of a journal entitled Ka Syngkhong Lingtip in 1957 and its fresh edition in 1959 caused a landmark towards the spontaneous growth of revivalism in the field of letters, the sponsoring body being Ka Seng Jingtip, a Society of learned personages which sought to highlight the social, cultural and linguistic grandeur of the tribe. There antecedents led to the publication of an English book entitled: A Short History of Khasi Literature which first print occurred in 1962 and in which its review was brought out in the Calcutta Statesman dated February 3, 1963.

The treatment being so much condensed, we seek, therefore, to focus only on the basic forms and contents of the creative and recreative processes of the growth of literature with special emphasis on cultural renaissance and its rationalised concepts.

Literature

Poetry

The most popular titles in poetry in continuation of the past attainments are enumerated below:

Title	Author	Year
Poetry Khasi	V. G. Bareh	1957
Nala Rympei	B. R. Kharlukhi	1964
Ka Ryngkap	Morkha Joseph	1967
Ka Jutang jong ki sur-Pangnud	Oscar M. Wahlang	1968
NaLum Khasi	D. S. Khongdup	1968
Thombor	B. C. Lyrwa	1973
Ki Saimuka ka Duitara Khongwir	Chosterfield	
Ki Mieng Pynpang Mynsiem	Jerome Diengdoh	1977
Ki sur jingrwai u Hynniew Trep	S. K. Majaw	1977
Ka Ftlakhaj	E. W. Dkhar	1978
Ka Phang Rupa	H. T. Pariat	1979

On V. G. Bareh's work, a critic observed it as follows:

"The poems ...have been intended to suit to the Khasi music composed by
the poet himself. The music is sometimes so sweet and melodious that it
makes the reader forget the sense for the sound...the metro is quite novel as
the accent is stressed at the end of the syllable ....very true to the Khasi genius
and philology". Victor Bareh sought to provide imageries to the thrilling
natural scenes which considerably mould the human sentiments, moods,
temperaments and other philosophic concepts. He follows the traditional
usages to recalling the wonders of the ancient antiquities and indigenous
folktales.

B. R. Kharlukhi provides important dictions to the cultural symbols inherent in
religious beliefs and practices, and casts out appropriate reflection on the intrinsic beauties
of the golden age which brought about great feats and accomplishments and the transition
that led to its collapse resulting from man's fall to the evil things.

Morkha Joseph's work although Western influences permeate, a lyric entitled Sir
Lapalang is largely an elagiac product of indigenous thought, craftsmanship and folk
elements. O. M. Wahlang's work is a poetic representation of the ancient folktales mostly
elagiac echoing like lamentations over the tragic happenings which occurred during the
far off past.

D. S. Khongdup's capacity to set down odes and sonnets is acclaimed besides which,
he sets down constructive practices and pursuits. Khongdup recreats interesting ballads
on the great deeds of heroes, scenes of warfare which brought about both victorious
and disastrous plights and in which the ancient folk shared the bright and dark side
of the event.

B. C. Jyrwa's lyrics preserve its instinctive musical quality; the remarkable poem U
Klew based on a popular folktale provides a highly distinctive cultural model dramatised
in a train of appropriate sequences. Jyrwa's another work, U Ksan bad a Thombor an
appropriate word painting in a blank verse, ranks as - an illustrious epics focusing on
the unique beauty of the ancient traditions and institutions, a heroic verse, equally
indicative of the social disfigurations and tensions which marked the ancient society and
equally demonstrating the validity of popular decisions integrated with the ancient form
of Khasi democracy.

C. Khnogwir, a reputed composer himself, demonstrates some traditional views on
nature, scenes and environs; some verses are equally motivating for greater attainments
in one live's sphere.

Jerome Diengdoh's sonnets are captivating on love themes the love pangs and chagrin
caused by untold hindrances — he creates beautiful sentiments, the outward form and
more so the eternal power of love which ever moves us engraved in different styles. He

discards the traditional and adopts a modern approach. S. K. Majaw's poem sounds more elagiac centring on the departure from the virgin state of nature which simultaneously caused a great moral and spiritual destruction. The disastrous plight arising from the omission of the golden rules and the several moral losses caused which are irreparable are stressed, still the past reminiscences provide glimpses of hope and resurrection and even U Tirot Singh the great hero made a long arduous struggle because he championed the moral cause.

E. W. Dkhar's work, deriving influences from the immortal poet, U Soso Tham, is a subplot on the inherent beauty of the golden age which produced its efficacious role and orderliness and how men fell to the evil, the reason for which, the end of the greatness of a race was caused. This theme is oriented to indigenous form of ethnic philosophy.

H. T. Pariat provides feeds to the mind from the naive forms scattered out in nature, the simplicity of life stored in native huts and cottages.

Drama as an art and literature has received more impetus. The playwrights having made several innovations in which some plays published are connotative of a cultural grandeur. With few exceptions, plot construction, characterisation and style have considerably improved; they are mostly social, traditional and historical dramas. Until the first world war, a few spade sorks came out, mostly translations and a few originals.

B. C. Bareh, the first modern play wright in drama entitled U Tirot Singh published it 1957 presented Tirot Singh the great hero and illustrious personage. He made use of historical tradition to freedom struggle championed by Tirot and great leaders and the great split displayed to keep intact the socio-economic, civic and cultural system inherited from the past and preventing the Khasi territories from being disintegrated. Not only U Tirot but other stalwart figures: U Monohut, U Bor Manik and even women personages like Ka Phan Nonglait played the illustrious role which enchanted the war and other social scenes.

Mondon Bareh's play U. Mihsngi (1966), a social drama serves like a satire upon domineering, self centered and vulgar women whereas the appearance of hen-pecked and clownish husbands has caused special distortions and moral degradations. The play is a typical representation of social conditions in the twenties and thirties.

F. M. Pugh brought out Ka Sawangka a Ki saw ngut ba lap myn- saw in 1966, a historical play which ascribes social tensions and confusions to the neglect of family taboos and moral values which upset the smooth maintenance of civic system bringing about acts of violence and unnecessary bloodshed.

In Ka Sawangka is ki Saw ngut ba lap (1967), F. M. Pugh through proper characterisation exposed some bad habits and vices and demonstrates the bad effects of juvenile delinquency which cause explosion of social ills, distortion of families and societies and destruction of the best careers of bright promising youths.

A play, an adaptation of one of the finest folktales U Baieit Donshkor appeared in 1968; D. S. Khongdup is the playwright. Characterisation which abounds in contrasts and diversifications to innumerable subplots makes the play a successful undertaking. The hero U Donshkor is profusely represented, his creativeness, shrewdness and witty mind, use of exact stratagems, his flashing and infallible mind has created miracles and wonders and fishing tactfully from the trouble waters, he was immensely rewarded finally becoming a sovereign to two great kingdom.

S. J. Duncan, Ka Tiew Larun obtains itself as a traditional play based on a famous folktale but the appropriate characterisation, clever manipulation of plots, presence of cultural symbols, have largely enhanced the themes making use of such diversifications to uphold the moral and ethnic cause of the ancient tale. The characters, weak, feeble and short sighted are easily prone to make immature decisions but strong, far sighted and stable personages exploit such situations to save the world on the verge of its extinction.

O. Lamare caused an original and superb play entitled Ka Kut Iapnagar to come out in 1974, an adaptation of a charming folktale centering round Queen Ka long Saring, a historical personage which gives coverage to the multifarious themes and social scenes in a train of captivating incidents combining the fertile political and civic creations of the past great men, exposing the landmarks of art and architecture, depicting military strategies and war scenes, illustrating decisions made at councils (in concord with indigenous form of democracy) and combining the finest love stories. Plot construction, style and imageries have been made consistent with the themes.

H. Mylliem Ngap's play Ka Synjat bala shem pat (1979) is an exposure of an indigenous folktale which focuses on a family separation and family reunion mainly due to the mercy of circumstances and not the use of human insight and sagacity.

Novel

W. Tiewsoh has a profilic contribution: he has displayed brilliant wits to locate things correctly in which the social and civic potentials have been consistently tapped in his novel, Ka Kam Kalbut which appeared in 1979 and in which characterisation has been tactfully reflected. As a novel, it is the best because it abounds with the indigenous conception,' craftsmanship and production, making a series of competent observation upon the social conditions obtained at Shella near Bangladesh border the scenes shifting themselves to Laitryngew and Shillong during the second world war and post-independence times.

Story

Stories as products of fictions are treated of as modern stories in which D. S. Khongdup and S. J. Duncan rank as competent writers and in which several episodes created and represented are entertaining and some yet very thrilling. D. S. Khongdup in his Ha ki sngi U Syier" (1968) depicts different motifs and in which his creation of different characters, princes, ballad singers, cow-herds, simpletons, jesters has become elaborated. Personification of animals their attributes, instinctive features, contrivances, creation of moral lessons and reflections on Social Sciences out or the themes have been intensively sketched than what we see the picture in other animal fables. The presentation in enlivening.

S. T. Duncan: Phuit Ka Sabuit Bad Kiwei Ki Khana 1978: a collection of writings in prose and poetry has emerged as realistic pattern of story writing which throws vivid reflections on social situations-tense, panicky and hectic scenes occurring from certain omitments, making misleading conceptions whereas freedom from fear is connotative of the best social norm. Superficialism breeds social confusion and infests many crimes. Detective traits are present in a few stories.

U Pyrkhat by B. C. Jyrwa, which appeared in 1976 is a narrative upon tensions caused by social ills and contagions. Jyrwa's capacity to create strong and serious characters, elucidation of Social Sciences and presenting some forms of human struggle after a suitable characterisation and well contrived plot is remarkable.

K. W. Nongrum's work, Ka Pung Ka Jingieit is a modern love story whereas, U Shanbor bad U Wadhor, which saw its light in 1976, his other work is more of singular presentation and plot.

Kharkongor's Ka Biria U Peh Sylli which came out in 1973 is a booklet of riddles and comical sketches. With these, several comics, stories by artists in pictures have came out.

Essay

R. T. Rymbai's essay Ban pynieng is ka Rasong bad kiwei de ki Ese, a collection of literary and historical criticisms came out in 1979. It is acclaimed to be a standard contribution in the hitherto neglected field. An exposition of literary and historical conception, it seeks to review the confused historical sources and make them consistently framed up. The integration system and the oneness Khasi Pnar War Bhoi tribe, along with the creative processes of its formation maintained at different levels since times immemorial have been laid intensive emphasis.

Other works of national genius and greatness and the roles played by the civic, social and religious principles towards its formation have been treated of systematically. The wrong sources of information resulting from the British arrangement and the concept of divide and rule have to be discarded as should have been suitably rectified. The pages dazzle with the wonder and grandeur about the illustrious creations of our forefathers in the field of socio-economic and cultural undertaking. The work has a captivating style carrying its lucidity and directness. The Essays seek to thwart divisive elements and social fragmentations revealing the formation of historically great kingdoms. Gone that grandeur to oblivion is, yet presently all available resources have to be suitably tapped towards obtaining a solution of our present problem, Rymbai acknowledges the power of youth that performs its duty, displays its glory, scores a victory.

Literary criticism is an exposition and interpretation of literary landmarks: sharpening of the methods of critical analysis are deemed essential besides which writings in prose have been surveyed in one Essay. The work seeks to evolve appropriate styles and methods. The sequences evaluationary and historical been followed up consistently.

Garo Literature

The potentiality of Garo was noticed by the English officials even before the Garo Hills District was constituted. As early as 1849, W. Robinson mentioned Garo in an article entitled "Notes on the language spoken by various tribes inhabiting the Assam valley and its confines" published in the Journal of the Royal Asiatic Society of Bengal, Vol. XVIII, 1849. There was great need for grammars and books on the language. W. J. Williamson, the first Deputy Commissioner of Garo Hills Districts, realising this need, wrote an article on "A vocabulary of the Garo and Koch dialects" published in the journal of the Royal Asiatic Society of Bengal, Vol. XXXVIII, 1869.

The first baptism of the Garos occurred in 1863. The first pioneers to examine the need for opening a mission were Dr. Stoddard, Revs. Comfort and Bronson. Rev. E. G. Phillips, then briefing in a neighbouring Baptist Mission, went to take up his residence at Tura, in 1876 with his family. After a short while, he was joined by Rev. M. C. Mason with his family.

The first converts were Omed and Ramkhe, inmates from the same house, who were baptised in 1863 at Guwahati. T. J. Keith did the outstanding work in the development of the language. His works on the language entitled Dictionary of the Garo Language-Garo and the Bengali-English (Jalpaiguri, 1873) and An Outline Grammar of Garo Language (Sibsagar, 1874) were considered as authoritative. They were spade-works which helped to develop written characters in Garo. The language was put down to writing iii the Bengali alphabet. The translation of the Gospels was taken up, followed by the publication of the Gospel of St Matthew. This Gospel published in 1875 and a primer by T. J. Stoddard were first books to appear in print. The records how that the second edition of the primer of Stoddard appeared in 1887.

The Awe dialect spoken on the north and the adjacent plain in course of time became the medium of instruction. The missionaries took up the project with the active association of the local collaborators in the field. The missionaries were fortunate enough to have the cooperation of Ramkhe and Omed. Ramkhe, known as M. Ramkhe Momin, had to his credit other contributions to literature.

With his active cooperation, the mission now made considerable progress in the field. Fortunately, the administration, at the initial stage, had already extended full support to the missionaries, and advanced other kinds of help. In acknowledging their contributions, the government entrusted to the Mission, the manipulation of education and placed adequate financial assistance at their disposal, T. J. Keith had acquired a good knowledge of Garo. A dictionary and a Grammar published in 1873-74 were the pioneering works which opened the field to further contributions from the future writers. Keith sought to promote other publications in this language.

The Bengali alphabet continued to be in use as the medium in the schools and churches for a little more than thirty years. The missionaries later on switched over to the Roman alphabet owing to the inconvenience faced in continuing the Bengali alphabet. The records indicate that the Gospel of St Mathew was one of the first books ever published in Garo. Then followed a catechism and four Gospels published in 1876, the works of T. J. Keith and his Garo Pandits or collaborators. The latter should have been Ramkhle Omed and Thangkhan Sangma who came first in the picture.

These publications, in the Bengali alphabet, were used in the early village churches. T. L. Keith, by virtue of his contributions, howsoever these might appear, became the father of Garo written word. E.G. Phillips, on coming into the field, continued Keith's noble task to building up this literature. The early missionaries were determined to continue translating the Bible with a view to propagating Christianity. There was the need now to prepare the primers and school lessons. For these reasons, cultural orientation in letters was so insignificant at the beginning.

The retrospective publications in respect of the Bible during the first quarter were the following:

- Acts of Apostles, 1890 by M. C. Mason.
- Mondoli Palokhi Kitab, 1891 (a Pastor's handbook).
- Matthew (1893).
- First Catecheism (perhaps a reprint), 1893.
- Genesis with explanatory notes, 1893.
- Torornko Skichengami (relating to religious instructions), 1893.

A landmark in the first quarter of its growth was the completion of the translation of the New Testament. It was published in 1897. It was preceded by a hymn book entitled Achikni Ringani containing 161 pages in its published form. In these were enshrined the new lights, concepts and values of Christian teachings. All these were in the Bengali alphabet. A pamphlet entitled Mission Kama Miksongata by Rev. Thangkhan Sangma was published in 1895. A Christian treatise entitled Jisu Kritoni Gimin Bi Sarangni Katarang containing 110 pages was also published. However, the Bible Society, other literary societies and institutions had also contributed enormously in accelerating the earliest Garo publications.

We have now to examine the contemporary growth of literature in respect of textbooks, journalism and grammars. Stoddard's primer had hitherto been in use for the beginners. In course of time the need for more school books was felt.

During the first stage of the growth of this literature we find certain contributions in respect of this literature published and circulated among the people by the Mission and the churches. E.G. Phillips, did a great deal of spade work; he had published immense literature for the Garos, while Keith gave this language an alphabet. The new alphabet has aroused the people's interest in reading and writing. As a result more and more students came out to prosecute study for higher classes.

Most of the first school books had an attractive get-up provided with appropriate illustrations. Phillips assisted by his wife and other local collaborators, improved upon the designs from time to time, to make them appealing to school pupils under instructions.

A grammar entitled Grammar Part III by the missionaries as a third edition, came out in 1892. Besides the readers prescribed in the curriculum, there were efforts made to produce arithmetical lessons such as Practical Arithmetic in Garo which appeared in two editions in 1890 and 1897, while the Mental Arithmetic, the work of Mrs. E. G. Phillips was edited in 1890 and 1899, in separate editions. The Mission had produced important books for the use of schools for several years which have been revised from time to time. Besides Phillips and Mason, the local collaborators and writers had a share in the production of lexicons and grammars.

Among them, M. Ramkhe Momin did a laborious work in compiling an exhaustive Bengali Garo Dictionary containing 884 pages. It appeared in 1887 giving a pride of place to the Garos as it remains the bulkiest volume of all the books so far published. It was widely used during those days when Bengali was used as the medium in the schools. Rupsing Sangma similarly produced a sort of lexicon entitled An Introduction to Bengali for Garo Pupils in 1900; it was one of the last books to be written in the Bengali characters. In the same year came out the A'chik Grammar by E. C. Phillips. Almost all of these publications were brought out in Bengali alphabet. The switch-over to the Roman alphabet was later contemplated owing to certain difficulties to continue with in the Bengali alphabet.

As we can make out, certain archaic spellings used in the old publications presented a difficulty in correctly reading the titles as well as their contents. There were certain deficiencies in technical terms and vocabularies which necessitated the missionaries to make them up by entries of loan-words from the neighbouring languages. Some technical words for adaptation, it appears have not been sufficiently explored by the missionaries and the early philologists. These difficulties have been expressed also in the adaptations of arithmetic lessons. They ought to have made much more effort to rediscover such technical words for the benefit of students and general readers.

Circumstances made it necessary to switch over to the Roman alphabet missionaries decided upon Romansing the then existing publications. The task, however, was expedited within two decades (1890-1910). The task had entailed extra-responsibility but it proved worthwhile in the long run. So in line with the need for a simple orthography, the Mission took to themselves to the Romanisation of all the publications as already come to light. Its results were good as it brought about a more favourable response from the people and led to a further increase in literacy. The earliest publication in the Roman alphabet was Anchingni Kam by, E.G. Phillips in 1902, third edition.

Another early publication in the Roman alphabet, entitled Ka tobgni Janera (Mirror of the Heart), was published in 1896 with thirty eight illustrations compiled by M. G. Momin. A few others included the book of Genesis, Nama Katarango sea ....Japang Kata (inductive course for gospel history) and a trilingual catechism — a reprint of English and Hindustani with the addition of Garo by Rev. Bangal Singh, A. Momin in 1899. The missionaries were not alone, being assisted by Rev. M. Ramkhe, Thyangkhan Sangma, Modhunath G. Momin in the early phase of Bible translation. A number of persons were connected with the translation hymns. A hymn book (second edition) in the Roman alphabet came out in print in 1900.

A landmark in the transliteration was also the Romanisation of the New Testament, Niam Kitab, containing 464 pages published in 1912. It was, however, preceded by the Romanised Four Gospels of 218 pages which came out in 1904. The rest of the New Testament (in the Roman alphabet), in continuation of the Gospels, published in 1912, contained 219 to 414 pages. Bengali as the additional medium was dropped and Garo pupils were facilitated in receiving instructions direct in their mother tongue and English. The use of Bengali, however, was important because it helped to incorporate entries and loan-words from Bengali, Assamese and Sanskrit to make up for certain inadequacies in Garo vocabulary.

Grammars provide the basic need for the growth of the language. Almost all the previous grammars, incorporated entries from Bengali and the use of the latter had been necessary during the first stage of its growth. The missionaries had become more and more acquainted with the language, usage and other characteristics and sought to depict them consistently and systematically. The need of grammars was obvious with the increase in the use of English. The Government had too encouraged the publication of more dictionaries and grammars. A dictionary and grammar by T. J. Keith, we have mentioned, came out in the 'seventies. We have also referred to a Bengali-Garo Dictionary of M. Ramkhe, published in 1884. Rupsing Sangma followed in by producing a lexicon entitled An Introduction to Bengali for Garo Pupils which appeared in 1900 in the Bengali characters.

The switching over the Roman alphabet necessitated the building a suitable lexicon and orthography side by side with English. E. G. Phillips and M. C. Mason were the chief figures who engaged themselves in this task. The former's work entitled A'chik Grammar came out in 1900. He followed it up by the publication An Outline Grammar of the Garo language in 1904. Both are still of a remarkable importance on the subject. The wider use of English was recognised by M. C. Mason whose work entitled Introduction to English for School Pupils was published by the Baptist Missionary Union which replaced Rupsing Sangma's Introduction to Bengali for School Puplis. Mason's English-Garo Dictionary came out in 1905. Three of them printed at the Government Press, Shillong were designed to provide instructions to Garos for the learning of English although they might have been lacking certain equivalent words in Garo. Phillip's A'chick Grammar came out in a second edition. Its third edition appeared in 1972, which was published by the Tura Book Room.

During this period, a few more Christian treatises came out. In 1924, the Bible was published, but prior to it, some selected Garo excerpts from the old Testament had already been republished. Until 1940, the themes were obtained from Sengbe (the peep of the day) which had its fourth edition in 1919 (published by Christian Literature Society for India), Graded Bible Lessons (1927), Immanuel (1929), Gisik Raatani (1932), Kandikgipa Nama Kata Biagranga (stories derived from the gospels), 1933, Bible stories for children, An'chichi Bregimin by Miss L. M. Holbrook (1936), Sunday School Course (1935), Mondoli Mong Aro Bipekrang Maikai Nangrimgri Kanichi, Madoliko Bilakatrotoani onggens by F. W. Harding in 1937, I'bri Manderang (1938) by Miss L. M. Holbrook and others. They centred on religious themes and expressions with the intension of building up the day-to-day Christian concepts.

There was considerable progress in Bible translation. The retrospective excepts from the Old Testament were Exodus (1918), Chronicles (1921), Ezra, Nehemaiah, Esther, job (1921), Deuteronomy and Samuel (I and II) in 1923. These publications in parts of the Bible led ultimately to the publication of the entire Old Testament in 1924 and thus the work was completed. The Old Testament (Sastro Gitchamni Bak II) of 803 pages was publicised in 1924 leading to the publication of the Bible in one volume in 1934 acknowledged to be the second edition of this holy Scripture. The Bible has been a source for creative literature as authors had sought from its light the carving of models both in prose and poetry. An important treatise entitled Mondoli Ong'chenga Ba Watatarangni Kamrangko Skiani concerning the growth of the first church, containing 208 pages was brought out by M. C. Mason in 1912 and was good contribution to the study of a Bible. The double work of evolving the Garo Bible first in Bengali or Assamese and then switching over to Romanisation was undertaken by the white and the local missionaries alike. The task indeed was stupendous undertaken against the severe odds and hazards.

The Baptist hymn book became enlarged in the subsequent edition. All these works sowed the seeds of new spiritual concepts which had struck new roots in the soil. In 1949, the hymnal underwent the 15th edition. Also the song books with solfa notations had appeared from time to time. One of them was A'chikni Ringaniang Aro Olakiani Kitap which totalled 451 hymns and was retitled Ring'Ani Kitabni Sulrang in a following edition, which came out in 1966. There was a separate issue of A'chik Bi Sarangni Ringanirang, an anthology of songs with solfa notes for the use of children.

A new series of school books appeared in a larger number. The Chanani Kitap Bak II, Rev. Phillips work published in 1908 underwent its next edition in 1916. In 1902 come, the editions of Gisiko Chanani Kitap in two parts Bak I and Bak II. The earlier editions of these two books was published in 1904 for Bak I and 1906 for Bak II. The works gave a model to school readers and arithmetical lessons in currency and revised from time to time. The other additions were Skichengani Kitab Primary by the missionaries of the American Baptish Mission Union, 1915, Skichengani Bak II by M. C. Mason, 1920, and the Garo School Reader by members of the Mission in 1922. To these, may be added the publication of Toding Marak in 1913, entitled Maharani Victorian Kata which was a leaf from history relating to the reformative tendency of the British Empire. A Mackonald, a Khasi stationed in Normal School, wrote a Teachers Manual in Garo published in 1916. It was designed to provide improved instructions in different subjects. It contains 112 pages. A similar work entitled Skie jari Ksoami (90 pages) was also about providing instructions to training of children published in 1916.

More of primers and readers were also coming out. They included the Wetherbee Readers published in 1931 by the Women's American Baptist Foreign Missionary Society. The school series included Rikki Tikki (mangoes), Aro Gipin Golparang Sunni Rani (Queen of the snow). In 1920, Katongni Janera (Looking Glass), Sonuni Chongipa Baari (A Small Garden) by Miss C. A. Wright, 1932, Daknangiagipa Do'gep (Ugly Duckling) 1929, Chongipa Milgipa Css, (1) Velgipa Jellabi, which served as model primers for small school beginners and although they were in good rendering, they contained no indigenous stuff, (2) Mention may be made of Miss L. M. Holbrook's An'chichi Breginin which came out in 1936, and Aesophi Goplorang, an adaptation from the Aesop's fables, although it was a flimsy work. Readers in circulation were Poraiani Kitap (Parts I, II, III and IV) (3) and Skichengani Kitap or Primers I and II. The most important publication of this period, perhaps, was Itihasni Katarang which contained lessons from the great characters and personages which Miss C. A. Wright edited in associated with Modhunath G. Momin, Jakme D. Shira, Solomon Raja, Do'bipa contributed to it but a bulk came from the pen of Miss Holbrook and Mrs. Aron N. Sangma. (4). It was published in 1934. A Garo School Reader was published in 1922 and its second edition in 1927. So also Miss C. A. Wright's Sonuni Chonggipa Bari (primer) was published in 1932. A reader, School Poraini (reader) by M. C. Mason was published in 1920. Another reader, Poraini Gitam (Reader NO appeared in 1930.

The missionaries occupy a predominant position in the early stage. Missionary contributions, however, started to dwindle from 1950. Still in the forties came out the publications such as Kristoni Sonani Niam (The Golden Rules) by Miss L. M. Holbrook the publications which followed were Baptist Manual in Garo by F. W. Harding, Paulni Langgitangani (Life of St Paul), An Chingni Bible by James Wood, etc.

We have also to examine similar the works of Garo writers. Most of these contributions came from Wilson K. Marak. One of his illustrious works was the translation of the Pilgrim's Progress (published around forties).

He had translated Sadhii Sunder Singh from an original work and presented a story of a Greek captive boy who became Christian through strong convictions in a series Ka'donge Baltigipak (1986). His original work titled Iisu Rebapilgen came out in 1972 which offers notes on the eschatological theme and power of resurrection.

The Garo educationists felt the need to imparting instructions in their own medium, Education was designed so that it could perform its functions significantly on the imparting of instructions, as also meeting the basic socio-economic needs, and providing training in fields like citizenship and leadership. D. S. Nengminza and H. W. Marak made some laudable contributions, Mengminza being much concerned about this literature, wrote the following:

- The School Dictionary (1944).
- Second book of English Grammar and Translation, 1972.
- A Primer of English Translation.
- Hindustani Nengrae Agangrikani Chol, 1973.
- English-Garo Dictionary.
- Boy's own translation Garo to English.
- Second Book of English Grammar and Translation, etc.

R. G. Momin similarly had his contributions in a book entitled English Grammar Composition in Garo (first published about works in the study of language are N. M. Marak's English-Garo-Hindustani Kusiko Altuai Agangrikani, which saw the light in 1927, and Kenneth Momin's A'chik Composition designed to Help Students for Learning Grammar. The bulk of similar works-models for lexicons-are from H. W. Marak contained in the following:

- Gital English Composition;
- Hindi Gachal;
- Garo-English-Assamese Dictionary;
- Assamese for Garos;
- Garo Primer.

A series of helpbooks for teachers were in the making. Wilson K. Marak, who had long been connected with the growth of education, wrote a scout aid book entitled Wolf-cub-ko-skiani-Dewal published in 1942, and a book concerning physical training and activities was published in 1957. Besides a Primary School Skiani Kata as also Notes on Teaching Primary Schools (Primary Schools Skiani Kata) by Jobang D. Marak, and a Garo primary Skulo Skiani Bewalrang Ba Niamrang, a helpbook for primary school teachers by Marnesh R. Marak also appeared in print.

Different subject-matter in respect of education have been dealt with appropriately-but not so exhaustively.

MacDonald besides a Teachers Manual, wrote also a Garo Geography which probably was the first of its kind.

The Garo History (Part I) by Jobang D. Marak in 1930, although an outline, contained the seed for the future growth of history.

To the above may be added the publications in geometry and adult education. A book on the latter subject was an adaptation of A'chik Dalgimin Manderangna Skianai Kitab by Levison Sangma published in 1957. On Garo folklore, the first compilation by Jobang D. Marak and Samson came out in print in 1927. Mrs. Bimolin C. Momin wrote a book on such tales, but her compilation was only an adaptation from a few Greek mythological stories, Arabian Nights and Cinderella which came out in a book entitled Mingisggipa Golporang, published quite recently and has 193 pages. An anthology under aegis of the Women's Baptist Missionary Society which came out, similarly had no indigenous material and cultural traits. This anthology entitled Golporang A'chik Bisarangna contains the tales for children, all adaptations from the foreign countries in which the Aesop's fables, Hans Anderson, fairy stories, Treasure Chest found place. A few were adapted from the Ramayana. Modhunath G. Momin compiled some of them which in a revised edition came out in 1952. A modern theme is obtained from Jawaharlal Nehru (Bisarangi Ripeng) by Mrs. H. B. Sangma, which gives a glimpse of some of his works as are readable for the children.

These contributions considerably stabilised the growth of education. There had been no secondary school, institution until the 'forties, yet those books provided constructive lessons through the initiative of the Missionary Union and these of the local educationists themselves. Many of the books were adequately illustrated with beautiful jackets and attractive cover designs. The Garos have produced educators and social workers who have given incentives for providing good books towards inculcating formative habits and behaviour patterns, disciplinary norms and thirst for wisdom. These books had large circulations. We have now to see to the growth of poetry, prose, drama and novel.

For a long time past, most of the creations in prose were adaptations from the other literatures. Wilson Marak in envisaging the need of more publications, had the adaptations from renowned classics such as the Arabian Nights (Published in 1970), Tales from Shakespeare (1971), Burning of Rome, published in 1966 and others. One of the most important contributions in this respect is Ka-Donggipa Matgrik, an adaptation of Benhur, by Kenneth Momin which contains about 300 pages. As the case was with the other modern Indian literatures, English literature and the western classics had greatly influenced the growth of the early literature of the Garos. Until Independence or so, seedings into this nursery were transplanted from the outside literature in both poetry and prose. These infused life into the first series of writings.

More recently, the indigenous tales echods and told through the ages have become equally significant, invoking, stirring, and providing a constant source of power to poetry, drama and novel. The earliest work was Garo Folklore Part I by Jobang D. Marak and Samson R. Sangma with only 20 lessons, published in 1927. They bore their enchanting thrills and significant moral lessons, from which the Garo folkorists derive incentives to work upon a system of orientation by breaking away from the tradition followed by the missionaries. The writers sought new lights, concepts and vistas from the vast store of folktales which are still in circulation. Although positivist, some of the Garo tales are sentimental. In their folklore emerge different ballads, epics and wise sayings which recount many of their wonders in their past. Love stories are innumerable, voice which of love's effects as inspiring, healing and harmonising. Love is the architect of human virtue, the moulder of the qualities of head and heart. The wonder is about its mysticism. Some tales are elegiac, others are jest and comedy but all leave an impact of moral lessons. They attribute a living philosophy to the myraid images of nature.

In the faultless are enshrined the activities, adventures and achievements of their forefathers. They preserve the life of their ancient heroes, their style of living, chivalry and their combat with the forces of nature. Garo knights and gigantic frame of mind and unconquerable spirit. According to Dewan Singh Rongmuthu, "the Garos possess extensive traditional accounts, mythology, fables and other forms of oral literature". He observed the processes, tragedies and beauties of nature that form the of innumerable stories. Garo nature myths seek to explain different phenomenon and bear a marked resemblance to the tables of Greece and Rome.

The A'chik Goloporang or real stories as told by the Garos by Samson R. Sangma was another publication with that theme. It is sketchy as it contains only 63 pages but it is reckoned itself to be a good spade work Publications carrying more elaborate treatment followed. There are Goloporangs in two volumes in which Dhoronsing K. Sangma has sought to collate and glean the different tales which are still told totalling to more than 300 pages. A fifth addition of the A'chik golporang Part I was issued in 1970 whereas part II of this little came out in the fourth edition in the same year. Another great contribution is Apasong Agana (A'chik Katta Gitcham) by Dewan Singh Rongmuthu with its English equivalent Our Forefathers Spoke, a volume of 330 pages with 84 chapters. The totality and unity of the entire race comprising different groups, Akawe, Abong, Atong, Chisak, Kotchu, Megan, Digil and other-speaks in it in the most eloquent terms without losing the dim and obscure past, and yet giving the glimpses of men moving out to fulfil their duties, obligations, struggle and aspirations in dynamic scale so much so that the unity accomplished could not be wrecked down, nor the splendour that was their land. Besides, he has to his credit the A'chik Golporang, not the inconsequent narrative. A detailed work on folklore in English is obtained also from Dewan Singh Rongmuthu, Faultless of the Garos (Department of Publications, University of Guwahati)

Published in 1960, which provides a mass of the indigenous Garo Tales and which is acknowledged to be the most valuable work on the Garos, totalling about 400 pages.

Drama is gradually evolving, Kenneth Momin was one of the Pioneers through his work Nokdang (Dakmesokani) which came to light in 1969. It is brief and focuses attention on the social processes working on and the form of social reconstruction obtained from the role of ideal families. A drama Kartcni Bite by Arjison G. Momin may be classed as a modern type of social drama in which five characters are represented, two males and three females. It enshrines with its beauty through the interludes and naive dialogues. The Khalsiri Aro Sotratchi (part I and II) is regarded as a more elaborate work by Redin Momin centering round Khalsin the hero and Sonatchi the heroine which exudes from love pursuits and adventure among them, interspersing with the thrills of travel, climax of love and the pathetic pangs of separation which finally culminate into the lasting joy of a marital union presented in a Bengali style.

Some of the wise sayings are in circulation. Samson Sangma's A'chik Poraiani (1970) contains moral lessons and ethical values current in the tradition and society. The work seeks to keep them intact, not to be lost away in the new social upsurges. It has 119 pages. A typical novel, although an adaptation from Bengali, is Sotiabal Mechik by Samson R. Sangma, 265 pages published in 1968. The characters are in Garo names.

There have been more contributions in poetry. Several persons wrote verses and rhymes but only a few of them possessed a calibre to carve out models in compositions have appeared in a journal entitled A'chik Kurarlg, in which poets and bards communicated their ethos and sentiments. The A'chik Kurang had, therefore, provided models of writing and composition and has been a source of power and inspiration. A'chik Kitrang was what the Spectator had been to the contemporary age in Britain. A'chik Kurang with its equivalent in English "the Voice of the A'chik" has since its inception, pursued its real objective. The earliest hymns and translations were the precursor to the birth of modern poetry. In several of these works we find considerable influence of English and western poetry but there are compositions which fit in with their, traditional system of expression as the people were in possession of their own indigenous oral poetry. Some of the gits (traditional verses) are recited, hummed and sung at the festivals to the accompaniment of music from the gongs and drums, the pipes and trumpets. The bulk of the compositions, as appeared in the issues of the above journal, seem to have been made with the help of the western metre and usage. But some compositions are reminiscent of the achievements of their forefathers.

In poetry the names are too many, but perhaps the names of Tuniram R. Marak, Kosan G. Momin, Gelo Sangma and H. D. Momin stand eminent. There were anthologies which contain excerpts from-the A'chik Kurang as selections designed to meet the needs of school community and the literates as well. The earliest anthology seemed to be A'chik Sunh Gil 1941, which serves as hymns and sacred songs compiled by Khcong A. Sangma from Ranighat, Hahim, Kamrup in Assam. The verses recaptured the religious concepts and meditations on Christian light and only a few ethos fell in with the traditional pattern. The contributions were by Rev. Rikman Sangma, Geecham I. Sangma, Rango Singh, R. Marak, N. A. Sangma, Regan B. Marak, Tochang Pundit, Gabindra R. Marak, Uting Singh J. Sangma, K.O. Sangma, Rornang D. Sangma and Nomal Singh A. Sangma. The renowned musicologists and composers are Mitaram Momin, Purno Sangma, Atting Sangma, Rev. Tillok Chon Momin, Palicarp Momin, Benison Momin, Tuniram Marak, Jackson Momin, Reidson, Millick K. Marak, Santoha Momin, Sorongsing D Shira, Suchindra Marak, and Mrs. J. S. Momin. In respect of the traditional poetry, the Garo metre appears to have been derived from the indigenous art of drumming and beating upon the bell metal gongs which conform to the various phases of dance at the Wangala, the triumphant harvest festival, and as performed at the other ceremonies. These arts in turn gave to poetry a scope for forming a shape and accent in a measure. Most of the songs used at Christmas and New year season are derived from the original tunes and compositions. A bulk of these Christmas Bits appears in an anthology entitled A'chik Songkritan. Krismas Aro Gipin Gitrang compiled by Rev. Tilokchand Momin, Nishangram which have been intended for singing and dancing during the X'mas season; the gits appear to have been rationalised to fit in with the traditional expression of jubiliance for the simple rural folk. The dance is by forming a ring in which dancers clasp each other's hands and hopping on against the background of music and songs. It is designed to revive the lost heart in the joy of rebirth. Some of the compositions have no bearing on the festival alone. However, there are eulogies on the landscape and the simplicity of life reflecting in it. A song on "Meghalaya" is

> My land, abode of the clouds
>
> Full of charming hills and crescenting heights, of sublime scene around, that is called Meghalaya.
>
> Call on your gods and goddesses With offering of rice and millet,
>
> On the cold breeze up the hill
>
> And around the winding streams.
>
> Pour on your tithes with sacred leaves,
>
> And fruits, roots and yams With fishes and meat
>
> That is my country.
>
> Similarly Sudhindra called his land:
>
> My Garo land, My mother land
>
> Where forefathers died: land of the clouds.
>
> Those villages up the hill
>
> And those scattered near the river banks
>
> My soul finds such a rapture.

Seogkimin poetry rang (selected poems) compiled by D. S. Nengminza (with its third edition in 1966), offers diverse scope of treatment although in the form of naive verses, but all are not nursery rhymes. The theme and keynote centres round the sublimation of aspirations, experience, adventure, joy and sorrow, old recollections, and nature. Some represent ethos such as one's birthplace, Garo country and forefathers, wise sayings and traditional concepts, on those noble themes, shed their radiance and meaningful contents in their own fashion.

Another anthology Chasong Gital A'chik poetry rang appeared in 1970 compiled by Kenneth Momin and edited and published by the Garo Literature Society. Love and nature lyrics of simple characteristics form a bulk of the compositions and although influenced by western literature, the compositions seek to lay stress on the indigenous symbols and motifs. Two of its poems appear to have been obscure and cryptic from the comprehension of a lay man not acquainted with the background in which the composition was brought out on the most indigenous theme. Jorangpang Rongmuthu and Monengsing R. Sangma successfully carve out new models to influence traditional themes with colloquial expressions in two poems entitled "Saijong Tasin" "Me'chik" and "Georani Skialo Man Chengna" which appear to lay a background to the religious thinking of the Garos about their gods and their incarnations in the garb of sublimation. The other poems impart incentives to noble aspirations and glorious victories over one's struggle by dint of persistent labours.

Among others, mention may be made of Chimonggimin (1971) compiled by E. R. Marak. It is a collection of poems as hitherto appeared in the old journals. H. W. Marak did tremendous work to build up these indigenous themes. He complied many poems into a book entitled Kurungma (Poems Old and New) but an epic "Dikki and Sonabal" is his masterpiece based on a well known love story and abounds in the lessons of aspirations anal struggle, defeats and achievements of the ancient folk, enriched by thrills and climaxes. The work retails its very musical character and identity.

These have emerged as original compositions, yet with these, a bulk of adaptations is in the making. Wilson K. Marak translated some poems and stories from Rabindra Nath Tagore under the aegis of the Assam Academy for Cultural Relations which was brought out in a booklet of 100 pages. H. W. Marak produced Gitanjali, as adaptation from the original Bengali which speaks of the overall presence and power of God and which combines several theological aspects from the religious teachings. The Assam Publication Board published it in 1966 and it contains 75 pages. The most remarkable achievement of H.W. Marak was his translation of Umar Khayam into Garo with illustrations. Some other languages are lacking this translation in which love pours out with noblest sentiments, of course barring some of the excesses which are carried out in its name.

Tuniram Marak was one of the best known poets, who died during the 'forties. He received his education first at Goalpara where he became proficient in Bengali. He was a teacher at Nishangram. His poem "Haggar an adaptation of the story from the Bible reproduced in a Garo form, is regarded as a masterpiece. His other remarkable composition was "Do 'kua" (King of the birds). His poems provide inspiration also for retrieving an idealistic patriotism to lift up one's land as the people have become servile to many evil influences.

Kosan G. Momin poured out religious speculations on God from the Christian rather than Garo point of view. His work is an appreciated on the vast nature which ever glows in its radiance, beauty and elegance and in which his creations seem to have derived strength from both the Garo and Western perceptions. He was a teacher at Nishangralm. Gelo Sangma composed poems in appreciation of nature. The most learned was benison Momin, son of Jobang D. Marak, a noted educationist. He was a brilliant student and did his M.A. and later became Professor of English in the Cotton College, Guwahati during the 'forties. He wrote both prose and poetry, which have their themes on the paramount need of social upliftment as appeared from his articles published through the different issues of A'Chick Kurang.

Journalism till 1975 has been in existence in Garo for over more than 75 years. Of the journals and newspapers in circulation the first was A'Chikni Ripeng started in 1880 which still survives. The earliest educators contributed several articles to this Christian monthly. The A'chik Kurang (Voice of the Garo), a social and educational quarterly had been in circulation for many years. Its potentiality as a source of power and inspiration to several models of literary creations has been pinpointed. Another social quarterly Nok Dangni Ripneng edited by B. K. Sangma has been in circulation. A political weekly A'chik Sangbad is being, ably edited by N. Marak. A monthly of the Catholic Mission Seng'ba has been in circulation for many years. And then there was a monthly Do'arnek published under the aegis of the District Information Relations Officer, Tura.

Philosophy

H. O. Mawrie is an exponent of philosophy in which the profundity of relation and its rational and consistent setting is treated of in his Work U Khasi bad la ka Niam published in 1973. It preserves the ritualistic observances and prayers of the ancient Khasis and because of its rational outlook, it is a considerable improvement upon the philosophic concepts propounded by the erstwhile philosophers namely, U Jeebon Roy, U Sib Charan Roy, U Rabon Singh, G. Costa, Dr. H. Lyngdoh and others. Conscientiousness and the consistent performances of religious obligations and one's attainment of manly personality, these and other issues have been propounded and interpreted. The inadequacies largely are caused because of the omitments and commitments which mortals are apt to be involved.

In Ka Pyrkhat U Khasi (1973) Mawrie seeks to propound the purity of religion centering on the sanctity of the covenant which established the wholeness of the religion.

The three tenets in which the religion seeks to establish itself are Ka Daw (law of causes and effects), Ka Nia (a communion attained after the instinctive reasoning) and Ka Jutang (convenient). Man's fall, the Man's obtaining of reunion with God evidently are the basic tenets of Khasi religion. All religious obligations are, therefore, decisive upon all spheres of life. Hei !Nga bat ho la, ka nia in 1974, Mawrie seeks to make a rational approach to the consistency of religious principles and practices, man's image having been enhanced by virtue of his rationality, strength of his conscientiousness and his knowing the art of reasoning and man from his fallen state was assured of his reunion with God: the efficacy of man's moral background, therefore, is testified.

D. T. Lalo's work Ka Rongbiria U Hynniew Trep 1978 is a rational search of the profoundity of Khasi cultural heritage and religious philosophy; it demonstrates a captivating style and lucidity of its own. It treats of the diverse themes which consistently framed, provide strong clues to the divine origin of the people. Even sports and games including archery which provide recreational means, are remirscent of a cultural force which carries a stamp of rationality.

Miscellaneous Items

Besides books have appeared in subjects — History, Education and Sociology, which are intended towards securing innovations in economic undertakings, law of inheritance, land tenure and other topics. In history, various flimsy publications have flashed but not elaborately treated of on grand scale as Dr. H. Lyngdoh, Ki Syiem Khasi bad Synteng published in the thirties; added to the existing publications in Education, a book entitled Ka lingpynroi bad jingpynriewspah is ka Jinghikai is ka Khasi, a collection of learned papers published by Northeastern Hill University, in 1977 seeks to rectify the processes of teaching of Khasi and acquiring of learning at different levels in which teaching in poetry, drama, stories, prose were sought to be suitably modified and creation of new constructive models demonstrated.

Language has received treatment through grammars and dictionaries published since the last century. A Dictionary — Ka Dienshon hi by I Kharkongor published in 1968, provides Khasi-to-Khasi meaning obviously focusing the flexibility and richness of idiomatic phrases. Father E. Bars Khasi English Dictionary (1973) is a commendable enterprise which displays English shades of meaning against the glossaries. It is yet another production after U Nissor Singh's English-Khasi and Khasi-English Dictionaries published in 1913 and 1920 respectively. Three important Dictionaries entitled Greek-Khasi, Khasi-Hibru (Hebrew) and Khasi-Armaik (Aramaic) by S. Sngi Lyngdoh published from Jerusalem and Athens in 1975 also stand as supreme creations in the field.

Journalism provides multifarious themes of literary importance in which several weeklies were in circulation, the quantum of news flashed, in each, however was limited. The latest addition in Dong Musa a weekly (Editor, O. L. Marbaniang) which gives more rational and realistic views on events; highlighting editorial concepts and profiles, focusing national or international landmarks; instituting a system of general education. Several magazines and journals were caused to be published by literary Associations.

Birth Centenary Celebrations

Three birth centenary celebrations of reputed literatures were held by literary Societies. Literatures for whom celebrations were held were U Soso Tham (1873-1941), Dr. H. Lyngdoh (1877-1958) and U Mondon Bareh (1878-1932), in which a Souvenir was issued in each case.

The Souvenir on occasion of Tham's centenary celebration reflects immensely on his life, career and contribution. Tham although highly allegiac on the transition which caused the collapse of the Golden Age and the disastrous situation for which his forefathers were faced, he still pinched faith in the emancipation of the future in verses set down below and in which translation was rendered by O. M. Wahlang:

'You blue skies undisturbed shall lay

When evil rain has ceased it spray,

Dark cloud shall wear a colour new

When rainbow spreads his blessed hue,

Then devil when has trampled he

Then man a child of God shall be.

The celebration was held in 1973. A bust was installed to commemorate him as the symbol of Golden Age.

Both Soso Tham and Dr. Lyngdoh were exponents of philosophy and cultural grandeur at the different levels. Soso Tham is an immortal poet whereas Dr. Lyngdoh is noted for his writing in Prose which centres round the history, cultural heritage and religious philosophy. In a celebration held in 1977, it is summed up as follows:

"Many riddles also occupied Lyngdoh's thought but the fact remained true that religion demanded from man a highest conviction which was in the depth of understanding of the mind a covenant pure and sacred: that covenant demanded from man a fulfilment of two things — first it was a comprehension of tenets and secondly a relationship that was ordained by God which enjoined the relative and absolute character and the religion constructed on a sound logical perception."

U Mondon Bareh ranked as playwright, poet and prose writer besides his contributions as educator. He wrote many treatises and poems in English and his souvenir specially issued reflects on his 'attainments in the different subjects. It might be relevant to focus some extracts from his writing. On efficacious roles of English in the system of education he wrote in 1931 as follows:

"Another point which I would like to place before your consideration this afternoon is the importance of English as the medium of instruction for the Khasi boys and girls. The proposal to boycott English and to introduce the vernacular language as the entire medium of instruction may serve good and useful purposes for the people of the plains whose conditions are quite different from ours. For the Khasi and Jaintia people and the other hill tribes living in Assam, the day seems to be yet far distant for the introduction of such an educational scheme. We have made very poor advance in the field of literature. Textbooks in vernacular are not available even in the ordinary school subjects. Our language has not developed sufficiently to become a fit vehicle for the conveyance of scientific ideas. The Khasi children have to rely on English books for their information in the several branches of human knowledge.

They have therefore a double King of work to do in making their way ahead, they have at once to learn English as their only medium of information and to glean their knowledge through this difficult medium. It is therefore our duty to help our growing boys and girls, by putting them on the proper line of self efforts, to find, that kind of charm or enjoyment, which is attached to every form of intellectual ordeal.

The English language is a very complex King of language being a mixture of Saxon, Gaolic, Greek, Latin, Hebrew, Sanskrit... Representing as it does every form of thought, feeling and sensibility of the human mind in its lowest as well as in its in its highest order, it forms the most wonderful and perfect medium of conveying human thought".

On love of work which sometimes is an attribute of greatness he wrote as follows:

"How can work become a blessing? Work becomes to us a blessing only when we can take delight in it and do it now with a view to any ulterior object, but for its own sake.. No one thing exists for its own sake, but for the sake of another thing or beyond itself... two things duty and man are to the adapted the one to the other. Duty is to be the law and guide of my man, for it is inspired upon me by my God through proper authority... and if I am only forced against my will to do it, either through fear of punishment of some tangible reward so far I am but a slave. I am the most pitiable of all beings endowed with reason. But... so far I am true to myself and to my duty; I am master of myself. I am an honest man, and an honest man... is the noblest being of God's creation. He must be first of all a willing man. Every difficulty which comes to upset him, instead of weighing him down, will serve only as an impetus for harder struggle. It only rouses his fighting spirit and directs his nerves to highest activities. He challenges every hardship, surmounts every obstacle, conquers every opposition."

On education orientation he summed up his views in 1930-31 as follows "The political changes which are agitating the educational atmosphere in the plains have not affected our hills in a direct way. But present world unrest and trouble, cannot but bring new political and social elements to shape the future destiny of our race. Hence, education cannot move on the old fashioned and somewhat easy going lines of the past. New efforts have to be made and fresh schemes introduced in the field of education with a view to adapting our educational ideals to the new requirements and new readjustments which to be demanded by the times. The writer is convinced that the Khasis cannot play the part of mere spectator in the present economic and political struggles... if they want to preserve themselves they are bound to revive and utilise every available resource for their educational uplifting. We are to adapt ourselves to the new circumstances and new forces which are moulding our destiny".

This is a very brief survey of Khasi literature during the contemporary set up. A flimsy coverage is given to 1979.

Crisis in Identity: Extracts: Quoted from Hamlet Bareh, Collision with Modernity — a perspective on life and letters Khasi Tribe Published in India International Centre Quarterly winter — 1989.

Journalism since its inception in the region has played an important role in enunciating social, civic, economic and other concerns. The earliest journals focused upon the problem of cultural identity and adjusting to the new religious ideologies imparted mainly by Christianity and its different demonstrations. Some aspects of the indigenous religion were sought to be updated. Journalism has sustained the dialogue on the problem of identity and discussed it from many angles. The issue was also taken up subsequently by the non-Christian and Christian writers alike. For instance U Nongkit Khubor the earliest Presbyterian monthly, 1892-94, apart from throwing light upon the interpretative concepts in religious issues, also contained articles of cultural interest.

Journalistic writing played its role in the cultural awakening to the Khasis. Hormu Rai Diengdoh was the first editor of a monthly called U Khasi Mynta (The Khasi Today) started in 1894. Its contents, which were widely quoted in English and Khasi publications, reflected the rising consciousness of the Khasis' cultural wellsprings. Sib Charan Roy also edited a monthly called U Nongphira (watchman) which was started in 1903 and for several decades launched scathing attacks on social malpractices.

The confrontation of Khasi culture with modernity produced a strange mix of sentiments, searching at once for an old identity and a new relevance. Both the literary and social media have of late agitated for modifying the law of inheritance so as to entrust more family and socio-economic responsibility to sons, without interfering with the rights of daughter who have, since time immemorial, been maintained the custodians of the family property. The search for identity consequently passed on to the principle of self-preservation, self reliance and general advancement. The issue of cultural identity has been superseded by the new issues which, ideally, would combine social and economic reconstruction with the strengthening of the roots. Cultural identity is discussed in its historical and contemporary context in the History and Culture of the Khasi People (second edition 1985). Industrialisation, it expounds, has to be viewed with caution, weighing the good against the evil as they affect the children of the soil. It brings out the problems of dispossession of the tribal people and the influx of people from other cultures who have no regard for local needs and local cultural moves which have grown out of the specific environment over time.

Recently, Ap phira (Risaw 19, Lyngka 1989), an important news paper, reported a meeting on October 13, 1989 held at Upper Shillong where the problems of environmental pollution and the urgent need to preserve the forest were highlighted. It called for urgent protection of the sources of water supply, especially since about 20 small water heads had dried up. The meeting also released S. Khongsit's book entitled Ki Sim Ki Doh bad ki jingbam jong ki ha Lum Shillong (Fauna and their diet, particularly wild fruits and tubers, on the Shillong range). One speaker reminded the meeting that while we are so involved in the race for greater achievements and development, we should also remember our past and the genius of our forefathers who had shaped the identity of the race.

Among the Khasis dramatists, Dino Nath Roy's work takes pride of place. He staged several plays for the Seng Khasi, a premier organisation which has, till day, preserved Khasi dance, art and music. It was started in 1899 and now has a Seng Khasi College besides several schools and institutions under its aegis. Roy's U Tipsngi (Good and Obedient Person) published in 1924, is exemplary for its plot construction and characterisation.

Khasi literature, from its early expression of indigenous traits and characters, progressed to the search for identity. The early endeavours, although still naive and upsophisticated, gave an honest image of the cultural identity of the tribal as well as the non-tribal people of the Khasi Hills. Most of the writers were concerned about maintaining this identity despite religious differences. Their writings guided public opinion to a large extent. The literature of the 1930s, however, reflected the aspirations of the Khasis-their desire to integrate the historical with the contemporary and yet retain their own cultural features.

Dr. H. Lyngdoh, Soso Tham and Mondon Bareh rose to eminence in modern Khasi literature. In Ki Sngi Barim U Hynniew Trep (The Ancient Days of the Seven Huts), Soso Tham wrote of the "golden age" of his forefathers. In this slim volume the poet has used captivating metaphors and with a stringent economy of words, revealed the richness and magnitude of vision in the ethnic conception of heaven and hell.

Dr. Lyngdoha medical practitioner and amateur anthropologist compiled a study of colourful state festivals with detailed descriptions of the laws, customs, traditions, rites and religious belief.

A symposium on literature held in May 1976 best reflected the common thinking and apprehensions in the Khasi world of letters. It expressed its concern over the problem of alienation in which language as it is used and develops plays a dominant role. As the Khasi language progressively takes its own place among others, the symposium felt that the ethical core of folk literature must never be lost sight of by writers and literary researchers. In these lay the framework for tribal unity and the basis of a community which modern ideologies, fashion and life styles threaten to erode.

The unity of the Arts, as well as the unity of art and life were also strongly upheld at the symposium. The values which informed indigenous life are very different from the sophisticated but superficial values of the modern world with its cinematic preoccupations. The past few decades have seen a rise in the tempo of development and modernisation in Meghalaya, a land of forests, not made for heavy industrialisation and competitive existence. In its confrontation with progress there has emerged a deviation from the pattern of life and social order which existed before independence. It touches all aspects of life from politics and administration to the individual's perception of himself or herself as a member of an organic and unique community. The old cumbersome laws of inheritance as well as the new lure of luxuries have created problems on the path of change-problems as serious as the more visible destruction of the forests which covered the hills.

The bulk of Khasi writing and publications have, therefore, voiced sharp anxiety and concern over the crisis in identity and the crisis in the social, economic and cultural institutions of the Khasi people — a tribe that has shown no perceptible increase in population over recent decades. Khasi writers have not evaded the issues which concern the life and unity of their race.

Editorial Sarat Bose Academy 1985 quotes its finding as follows:

"Among the literatures which have been presented here, Khasi literature is distinct and original. It shines in splendid isolation or at least, so it did till yesterday ...Khasi Literature is therefore fed from two sources, the ancient tribal core and the modern winds of change. It has, in spite of its isolation, reacted powerfully to the impact and currents from India and Europe".

8

Economy

The economic necessities are so pressing to us. Therefore, the economic necessities nowadays are generalised into the bare and conventional necessities. The necessities largely are determined by the living conditions of the people at the subsistence and post-subsistence level. Some of our cultural needs are beyond doubt connected with necessities. The concept of wealth largely depends upon our economic necessities. The concept of wealth in the modern age is also interpreted in terms of conventional and cultural necessities. The concept of wealth has been heightened considerably due to the role of sciences, modern equipments, the widespread use of the modern media of mass communications, growth of urbanisation, the developed means of modern transport and traffic and growth of new trades, professions and practices.

The law of inheritance is largely connotative, therefore, to the processes of wealth formation and accumulation, it is also connotative to the division of property created at the level of self-acquired and ancestral wealth. The concept of wealth, therefore, is tantamount to the means of earning and investment which are indispensable to providing the basic and formal needs which we are prone to acknowledge.

Now we can form certain insights to the concept of private, corporate and public wealth at the angles in which these patterns of wealth formation now are working. Therefore, analysis and assessment on the means of economic production is our prior consideration. The means of production are to be reiterated as briefly as possible.

The mercantile character of the Khasis in the light of the historical retrospector seems to have dwindled substantially. In the past, the expansion of the state was vital to the need of building. The National Wealth and State Power, Economic production and channelisation, therefore, under the efficient management, were handled properly that they would serve for the best interest of traders and distributions and that the quality of goods would not decline. To sum up, the Syiems and other leaders exerted pressure to promote industries, mining of metals and excavation of minerals.

Trade facts between the states were pledged for maintaining inter-state communications. In view of the potentials that iron smelting held bright, canons and flight-locks were also produced and circulated and a record has that these things passed from Assam to Pegy and thence China once. The efficient management of markets, chokeys, hats, trade stations, routes, navigation, forest, fisheries was needed to be maintained. Several centres of iron smelting and mining had sprung and important exporting outlets in steel, iron sheets and rods, and other implements of use had taken their prior importance.

These enterprises were equitably shaped and fostered. Circumstances compelled them to be a hard working, adventurous, enterprising and industrious race of people. The historical antecedents projects upon their sheer physical strength and moving against natural hazards in a mountain terrains with lightning speed laden with several articles of merchandise. The people believed in a system of corporate than individual existence. Until the final quarter of the last century, the articles of merchandise, viz. limestones, tez pat, iron implements, sticklac, honey, potatoes, lac, arecanuts, betel-vines, chillies, black pepper, Indian rubber, turmeric, ginger and a host of fruits, constituted the main exports.

Economic Development

Development has its own etymology. It is one of the organs aimed at elevating the standard of living in towns, townships, villages especially among the backward community. The work to evolve developmental progress is distributed through the Blocks, each block following a hierarchal order in staffing and having an allocation of villages with a total population brought under its jurisdiction. The task in up dating Economics, Statistics and Evaluation is shouldered with regard to analysing the minute works in research, registration and statistical enumeration.

Education has both its broad-based and specialised connotation. It is a combination of different facets: technical, general, basic, adult and science education has its foremost importance. The administrative academic and cultural concerns of the Department are very vast; hence a regular hierarchy in staffing at the Directorate, inspectorate and other level is essential to its functioning. The State Museum, State Central Library, Institute of Art and Culture and their respective branches are also connected with Education. The Department maintains the Government Colleges, Schools, the Shillong Polytechnic and updates all the deficit and private institutions. Meghalaya Board of School Education is chaired normally by the DPI There is a Secretary who executes its functioning. Elections are mainly concerned with constituting the Parliament, State Assembly and District Councils.

Although Employment and Craftmen Training is mainly concerned with administering Employment Exchanges located at the headquarters, the Department also runs the Industrial

Training Institutes at Shillong and Tura. Excise manned by a commissioner concerned with production, transport, purchase and sale of spirits; it also collects excise revenue. Its enforcement wing sees to the measures for control of illicit distillation and smuggling of liquor. It maintains prosecution works against excise cases involving the offences. Its narcotic cell sees to the prevention of excise crimes. The Taxation Department also collects taxes on the basis of several Taxation Acts.

The concerns of Forest Department here and elsewhere are in close concord with Wildlife, Forestry, Forest Resources Survey Sericulture, Afforestation, Training and other issues.

The Directorate of Health Services play their important roles in updating the standard of Public Health providing the health facilities, coordinating hospital management as related to equipping indoor and outdoor treatment and coping with all situations, normal and emergency. The expansion of the work necessitates the equitable adjustment with the different standards of generalisation and specialisation. The issues are too many to tackle with especially in the crowded hospitals. The equitable management of dispensaries, health centres, medical institutes and centres counts considerably.

General and plastic surgery, medical specialisation, child specialisation, psychriatistic, paedritic treatment, malaria eradication are just a few issues to name with. The efficiency of training of medical personnel including nurses is upheld. Complaints and cases are too numerous. The hospitals so far known are the Civil Hospital, Shillong; Jowai Civil Hospital, Tura Civil Hospital, Sohra Civil Hospital, Nongstoin Civil Hospital, Civil Hospital Williamnagar, Phulbari Hospital, besides Garobadha State Dispensary, Mendipathar Dispensary, Mahendraganj State Dispensary, B.A.P. Baghmara Restibelpara P.H.C. and others. There are also the Reid Chest (TB) Hospital, and Pasteur Institute at Shillong. There is the Regional Health and Family Welfare Training School and Health Workers Training School at Tura.

P. T. Marwein mentions that there have been 7 Government Hospitals, 22 Primary Health Centres, 92 Primary. Sub-Health Centres, and 42 Subsidiary Health Centres in 1981. Among them are Bright-well X-ray clinic, Ganeshadas Hospital (Children, Women and Maternity Ward) and Lady Kerr Welfare in Shillong. Mentions is made to the old Christian Hospitals also. The figures for 1986 are Hospitals 9, Dispensaries 50, Health Centres 25, Sub-Centres 117, Beds 1,669 all Government institutions. The man power has recently been strengthened. The maintenance of Departmental and Hospital Stores, equipments and instruments is all their responsibility.

The Industries Department, besides coping with the general administration and development programmes has the other establishments. Among them, the District Industries Centres located at the important headquarters play their roles in boosting industrial incentives, coordinating policy decision and implementing some viable plannings. Directorate of Mineral Resources conducts the analytical laboratory and this has necessitated experiments in drilling and mining.

We feel that planning and development being mutually linked up, therefore, the concepts of science and technology have their present relevance in modern planning. Researches with regard to their objective significance and application pertaining to the different projects are the fundamentals of planning and personnel fitting to such performance are posted.

The executive responsibility in Public Health Engineering constituted under the Adviser, is enforced by the Chief Administrative Officer-cum-vigilance officer and a team of his staff; they maintain their Administrative and Technical Staff Stationed at Shillong and outside. In the PWD, the Chief Engineer pivots constructions of roads and buildings; he is assisted by a team of staff stationed at their respective headquarters.

With regards to Sericulture and Weaving, to the Director is attached a team of staff stationed at the headquarters. There are District Handloom Officers and District Weaving officers posted at different places. There are the Government Sericulture Farms, Weaving Schools and institutes located at different places. In Soil Conservation, the Director and a team of Jt. Directors and Soil Conservation Officers stationed at their quarters undertake the work.

In Supply besides the Director, there are the Jt. Director, and Superintendent of Supply placed at the District headquarters. Transport Department is headed by the Commissioner. The team which man the Department consists of Secretary, State Transport Authority and District Transport Officers cum Secretaries RTA posted at the District headquarters.

The Commandant General of Home Guards and Director is in charge of Civil Defence; he is assisted by Deputy Commandant General and Deputy Director. There is a Commandant of the Central Training Institute.

The Meghalaya Civil Task Force is in the charge of a commandant. Among others, the Bharat Scouts and Guides are headed by the State Secretary. The Zila Sainik Board and Meghalaya Rajya Sainik Board are also in the charge of their respective Secretaries.

The important Inspectorates are the Inspector General of Prisons Chief Inspector of Boilers, Senior Electrical Inspector, Chief Inspector of factories and Inspector General of Registration.

Corporations are organised as follows:

In the Meghalaya Mineral Development Corporation, under the Chairman, a team of the Managing. Director and other Directors manage their business. In the Meghalaya Government Construct on Corporation Ltd., besides the Chairman, the Managing Director and staff termed Project Superintendent and Project Engineer man the Corporation. The Mawmluh Cherra Cement Ltd. is manned by the Chairman, Managing Director and a team of other officers. The Meghalaya Cooperative Apex Bank is composed of a Chairman, the Managing Director and Branch Managers posted at several places. The Managing Director and General Manager assisted by Deputy General Manager man the Industrial Development Corporation Ltd. The Meghalaya State Cooperative Marketing and Consumers Federation is constituted of a Chairman, Managing Director, General Manager, Secretary, Deputy Manager (Marketing) and Deputy Manager (consumer). In the Meghalaya Tourism Development Corporation Ltd., the Managing Director and General Manager are assisted by a staff having other designations. Besides the Chairman, the staff concerned in running Meghalaya Transport Corporation are the Managing Director, Deputy General Manager and Assistant General Manager. Similarly, the Forest Development Corporation Ltd. is chaired by the chairman, Managing Director, Production and Marketing Manager. The Public Services Commission is manned conspicuously by the chairman, the Members and Secretary.

Meghalaya State Electricity Board is a very large organisation. There is a Board Chairman. In the administrative set up, the whole organisation is manned by Chief Engineers (civil and electrical). The whole state for administrative convenience is spilt into circles under the Chief Engineers, Superintending Engineers to the rank of Executive Engineers, Assistant Engineers and Subdivisional Officer(s) man the organisation at the State and District level.

Some Departments because of the size and vastness of their organisations, the task in implementing the Departmental Projects has become implicated and their sphere of operation has become largely extended. These are some of the basic or key Departments. They are concerned with implementing some notable project for boosting the cultural, moral and material development at different levels. Most of the posts entrusted to, them are posts of trust and responsibility. Some Departments are concerned with the allocation of resources so that in due course they can create the fields for drawing the potential earnings to the state. The matter to ensuring safety and security and boosting some aspects and concepts of creative citizenship is vital to our present requirements. The task to curtail the unnecessary wastages to the public cause and security is bound to be heavy sooner or later. Steps here and elsewhere need now to be taken to strengthen the State Exchequer as well.

There are 7 Districts and they are: East Garo Hills, West Garo Hills, South Garo Hills, Jaintia Hills, Ri-Bhoi, West Khasi Hills, East Khasi Hills Districts with their respective headquarters located at Williamnagar, Tura, Shillong, Nongstoin and Jowai. In each District there is a Deputy Commissioner assisted by the Additional Deputy Commissioner, Subdivisional Officer, Extra Assistant Commissioner, Deputy Director or Superintendent of Supply, Superintendent Excise and other ranks and files. There are 8 administrative subdivisions. The Deputy Commissioner functions under the secretariat. The responsibilities of the District Administration have expanded due to the location of important administrative branches. The District Administration in Shillong have also their increased responsibility due to the growth of several complexes. The population has shot up incredibly. The State headquarters also houses the Raj Bhawan, Secretariat, Assembly and the Directorates. The headquarters premises of NEC are also located here. She also houses the several Central Government Departments or undertakings. The District Administration of Jowai have their increased responsibility owing to the problem of trade and traffic congestion centering on coal mining conducted at an intense scale over the Jowai's highlands. The difficulties facing the District Administration in Garo can be envisaged likewise.

The Deputy Commissioner is the coordinating, interpretative and executive authority there being no great differences in the functioning of District Administration from other places. He keeps liaison with land regulations, excise, revenue, supply transport and other charges assigned to him. He is the Chief consultant with regard to planning, development and extension programmes. With regard to execution of justice, the District Court has an important role to play. There is a Shillong bench of Guwahati High Court composed of a Deputy Registrar and his staff located at the state headquarters.

Community Development

The significance of Community Development need not to be intensively highlighted as its aims and objects have been reiterated from time to time. The composition of the existing blocks is interesting to note. It is the system of integrating a number of villages in point of convenience of the organisational and administrative coordination; block services, therefore, follow their administrative pattern and in their staffing pattern has been so modelled that the services of these blocks in the public and social framework are reached on the selective or general grades and that the village population will appreciate and utilise them for their cultural or educational advancement. The District Census hand books among other reports contain some information with regard to these blocks. They also give us some statistical indices to the important phases of development. The blocks are Thadlaskein, Laskein, Khliehriat, Amlarem, Bhoi Area, Mawryngkneng, Mawphlang Pynursla, Shella, Mawsynram, Mawkynrew, Mairang, Mawshynrut, Mawkyrwat and Mairang. They range in number from 64 in Mawryngkneng to 243 in Norigstoin C. D. Blocks, even Bhoi Area Block at present contains 256 villages. The blocks distributed in East and West Garo Hills are Betasing, Dadenggiri, Asmanda, Resubelpara East, Resubelpara West, Rongara, Dambouk Aga. Chokpot, Dalu, zigzag, Rongram, Salsella, Songsak and Dambu Rongjeng. In forty years' time or so, these Blocks have come to exist.

The blocks have been instituted to serve as useful assets for developing some core activities which mainly relate to improving the system of farming by providing several kinds of aids and proper upbringing of livestock. The Blocks also provide assistance for the construction of village approach roads. They seek to provide incentives to developing village crafts and enterprises. They look to the needs of village water supply. Some Blocks provide some facilities for promoting adult education. These socio-economic schemes if implemented fully are very helpful to develop the standard of living in the rural sector and interior places. Maximum cooperation as can be devised among the villages is absolutely necessary.

Intensive development of roads has been taking place. The only roads known to have existed before Independence were Shillong-Guahati, Shillong-Sylhet, Shillong-Sohra and Shillong-Mawphlang roads. Even before Independence, a survey was conducted for road constructions linking Shillong-Jowai and some branch roads on the border were proposed. The important addition was Shillong-Jowai Road opened to transport in the fifties. The important road constructions hitherto proposed to link Shillong and Mawsynram-Balat, Sohar and Shella roads and other road lengths across the border were commenced. The roads would also cover village markets which cover possible within their reaches. Cutting, aligning and topping the Shillong-Mawsynram road were found to be the, stupendous tasks against the pressing hazards of the terrain. These difficulties were confronted against Sohra branch roads aligning themselves with a series of ascends and descends across the precipice. Generally matters like road aligning, gravelling, black topping, metalling were needed to be taken up with great care in a mountain terrain. The two National Highways now are Guwahati-Shillong-Dawki and Shillong Silchar roads with their considerable lengths running through the hills. Other roads, therefore, can be informally graded as State, District and Branch roads which usually figure themselves in the Road maps.

Transport is now catered to be Meghalaya Transport Corporation and by several Primary Bus Syndicates. There have been several routes now opened to transport which cover the far-flung areas. Transport facilities have considerably enhanced trade interests where public carriers and trailers also are put to service to cater with the growing traffic. The movement of goods and passengers is also catered to supplementarily by other vehicles including taxis, mini buses and other vehicles. Roads have become the most essential assets to carrying out developmental activities. Roads help to coordinate the administrative interests faster. They provide rooms also for accelerating the educational reconstruction programmes. They help to spread ideal and disseminate the public information media quicker. Roads provide the media for the mobilisation of goods inasmuch easier way and faster and provide the rapid means for their interchanges, these volumes of trade being conducted in the present term of monetary transactions. They have laid down the bases of economic reconstruction to a larger extent. In the remote areas, bridge roads still form the means of communication which entail a longer time to cover the distance.

Some of the Roads known are Shillong-Nongstoin-Sunapahar, Shillong Shella, Shillong-Nongtoin-Tura, Shillong-Haflong; Umsning-Jagi, Shillong-Balat-Moheskhala, Shillong-Mairang-Nongkhlaw, Shillong-Williamnagar and Shillong-Tura both enroute Guahati.

Shillong- Lawbah, Shillong-Mawmluh-Nongwar, Shillong-Mawkyrwat, Shillong-Smit-Laitkroh-Laitlyngkot (now jeepable), SmitJatah-Tynsung, Tura- Baghmar-Rongram, Tura-Baghmara-Rewak, Tura-Rongjeng, Tura-Williamnagar, Tura-Garobadha, Nagalbibra-Dainadubi, Jowai-Naryiang via Barato, Jowai-Nartiang, Jowai-Shillian Myntang-Barao, Jowai-Mynso, Jowai-Nartiang, Jowai-Dawki, Jowai-Sutnga, Umlarem-Muktapur, Jowai-Muktapur and other branch roads. Most of them have been covered by transport. Super buses also ply on some the all-weather roads. Besides the above, road schemes in Garo Hills have been taken up on a large scale. Among others, the roads which cater to transport are Tura-Dalu, Tura-Phulbari, Tura-Mendipathar, Tura-Chokpot, Dalu-Baghmara, Baghmara to Darugiri. Bagmara-Mahadeo, Tura-Mahendraganj, Damra to Rongiregiri, Tura-Rongsengiri, Tura-Bajingdoba, Tura to Mankachar and other roads. Most of them are under PWD.

A few border roads such as Massynram-Moheshkhole road have been attached to the strategic road programmes and Damra-Baghmara Road developed under the Border Road Development. A few road schemes have been taken up by N.E.C. Board. It was in 1976 that Meghalaya State Road Transport Corporation came into existence on being bifurcated from the parent Assam Corporation. On the National Highways, Assam Government is allowed to operate an allocated number of buses but the bulk is run by Meghalaya.

Taxi Services

Taxi services in Shillong have existed for many decades now. The regular city bus services started here about 1940. Now therefore the dimensions of these service operations have been increased beyond doubt owing to the huge commercial and business transactions now going on, road congestions and jammings on increasing scale have featured themselves in Shillong especially on J. J. M. Nichols, Soso Tham, Tirot Singh Syiem and Mavis Dunn Roads. They have posed problems to pedestrians at bazars and shopping centres. Spaces for parking are already tight. Rickshaws are scarce, they have been operated only at Nongpoh and Khanapara side of the state.

On laying proper road infrastructural development, Benjamin ch. Momin the first Garo Legislator addressed to Provincial Legislature 50 years ago as follows:

> "Paucity of communication in our part of the Province is a notorious fact. Constructive of Bajengdoba road was left half finished, and two roads under projects, viz. the Garohada Hilli Lalayganj and Mukhdangra-Rajabala hat roads were not taken up at all. Equally inadequate is the arrangement for medical aid within the District, difficulty in obtaining which has further been enhanced due to the absence of connecting roads, ...I cannot remain without thinking the government for providing some fund for the construction of two bridges on the Tura-Mankachar road for which we are pressing the government

for a long time. The natives of Garo Hills, under the present arrangement do not get any share of the contracts, works of which are executed within the Akhing lands of the Nokmas. Some of the works are construction or annual repairs to (a) Tura-Damra road (b) Tura-Bayengodaba road and (c) Tura-Phulbari road, at the disposal of either the disposal of the Public Work Department, the District Fund or the Tura Fund. It is respectfully prayed that the part of work that falls within an Akhing may be given for execution to the Nokmas for a man of that particular Akhing instead to non-Garoor Garo contractors who have no interest of the welfare of that Akhing. I desire the government to look after the needs of the Garos and fulfil it in no time".

Lack of Facilities

Cooperative Movement has not made advancement sufficiently. Lack of some infrastructure facilities has hindered the progress; moreover training seems to be so indispensable to place the different grades of cooperatives on a sound footing. In the first place the need to enhance the competent services of consumers' cooperatives has arisen from time to time; this matter relates to procurement of stocks, managing the equitable distribution of supplies of the most essential commodities and strengthening the position of buffer stocks. Moreover, the government have also instituted a pilot project for strengthening the services of housing societies at the cooperative level. The Phulbari Cooperative Ginning Mills started many years ago is an exemplary instances of the Processing Cooperatives with regards to updating the system of cotton ginning. The number of these cooperatives till the seventies falls short of the total requirements.

According to Statistical Hand Book, in 1976-77, there was a total of 804 cooperative societies and 548 Agricultural Credit Societies and these included State Level Cooperative Societies. With regard to cooperative societies, the membership shown was 87,855, the share capital shown at Rs. 6,94,29 lakhs. In 1977-78, with regard to Primary Agriculture Credit Societies, their number was fixed at 174 and the share of working capital worked as the ration of 26 lakhs and Rs. 75 lakhs respectively. These laid the seeds for the incipient beginning of State Cooperatives. One oil crushing unit was set up recently, the government having borne a sizeable amount as share capital, besides which rendering a small subsiding for operating the scheme. Some of the cooperatives worked with short-term advances to start with. The number of cooperatives has steadily increased.

The Meghalaya Cooperative Apex Bank was instituted shortly after its bifurcation from its parent Assam Apex Bank. Its working is facilitated by the subscribed and authorised capital. The Government also gave a subsidy termed managerial subsidy to facilitate its operation branches of the Apex Bank now exist and are fairly distributed. It provides short-term loans to the Cooperatives and in particular seeks to meet some basic requirements to farmers. Recovery of loans has been facilitated but the outstanding over due loans have been made difficult for recovery. The important in development is also due to the setting up of Meghalaya State Apex Marketing Federation and the branching of Sub-Area Marketing Cooperative Societies; these work in consonance with Apex Level Consumers' Cooperative Society with regard to stock distribution to cater to the needs in interior places.

There is the Shillong Cooperative Urban Bank located in Shillong, Tura and jowai. In these circumstances, the State Level Housing Cooperative Society was set up which through its agencies, seeks to provide assistance with regard to house constructions.

There are also Industrial Cooperatives which manage to help small industrial and trade units. Owing to the unsatisfactory progress, much work remains yet to be done to reinforce their structural and organisational pattern and system of functioning and make them viable to contribute to the economic development of the state. The Government has already taken steps to strengthen their machinery for updating their functional roles in the matter of raising the necessary depots, in also providing some share capital and granting a managerial subsidy to the cooperatives.

Formation of Meghalaya State Cooperative Marketing and Consumers' Federation has been anticipated to give considerable boost to the role of cooperatives.

The proportion of industrial occupations may now be briefly highlighted. The Assam Cements Ltd. originally established at Sohra (Cherra) in 1955 was taken over by the then State Government in 1964; the name was changed into Mawmluh Cherra Cement Ltd. After Meghalaya was formed from 1978, 250 tonnes production daily has been catered to. There was Assam Sillimanite Ltd. located at Sunapahar; their industry catered to exporting rocks to Guahati, thence to Kolkatta. Later on the refractory plant was integrated with the local industry which greatly facilitates the export of refractory products. The refractory plant was taken over by Hindustan Steel Ltd.

There has been a notable increase in the output of products. A mild pace of industrialisation in fact is congenial now to suit with the requirement of the state. "Meghalaya ecologically and socially provides the good base for small scale industries excepting the areas where larger potentials (with long-term reserves can be conserved)". Meghalaya till now balance is not heavily industrialised and the balance is struck to keep with the tempo of agricultural and veterinary development and conserving the minor forest timber. "Being industrially backward, building the local talents, conserving suitable resources as viably as possible, shaping the industrial competence and norms for small scale industries are the obvious essence suited to economic growth". An increase in the size of company sector is noted a brief mentions being made to the following:

Meghalaya Potteries Private Ltd. — the factory of this company exists at Mendipathar and its establishment at Guahati looks to the administrative transactions engaged in processing and trading with the variety of ceramics, clay refractory items pottery products through analysis of the relevant minerals brought from Nangalbibra in which these potentials are extracted. There is Garo Jute Mills existing as a joint company of Meghalaya Industrial Development Corporation and Air Transport Corporation located at Mendipathar which are exporting the considerable jute products for their final processing at Calcutta. Meghalaya plywood Ltd. located at Byrni, the first of its kind in the Region is engaged in processing plywood panels through chemical treatment. The Associated Beverages a private company are processing the soft cold drinks by conserving the fruit potentials under a franchise procured from Messrs Pearle Exports Company. Komorrah Limestone Mining Company is another venture; they are engaged in extracting limestones as suited to factory uses and exporting them under a separate licence to Bangladesh beyond the border. It exists as a joint Sector of Meghalaya Industrial Development Corporation (MIDC) and Economic and Entrepreneurship Development of Calcutta.

It seems that the company is conducting operation within its specified jurisdiction. There are other private enterprises on local scale hitherto engaged in mining limestones and arranging for their transactions for other uses. Meghalaya Phyto-Chemicals Ltd. with its central refractory unit lying at Barapani conducts analysis of botanical species and sets up farming of them for factory uses, being a joint sector of M.I.D.C. and India Carbon Ltd. Group. Meghalaya Essential Oils and Chemicals Ltd. a joint venture of M.I.D.C. and Camphor and Allied products Ltd. of Bombay is engaged in processing oils out of cinnamon locally available in the Southern Khasi Hills.

In fact, bulk of industries, numbering 2,355 units accounting for almost 90 per cent of the state's total belong to private hands. The ratio works out in the rural area, 1.6 per cent is public, 97.8 per cent private and only 0.6 cooperative sector whereas in urban places the ratio respectively is 1.4 public, 98.2 private and -0.4 cooperative. The proportion of industrial development is very small.

Primary Concern

Industries primarily concerned with processing; production and transaction of goods, and commodities. The trade structure evidently provides communication network for their mobilisation or movement. This governs the transaction mainly from the production to the distribution bases. Trade and industrial sectors if given maximum care have evidently their roles in causing a marked reconstruction or resurgence of the old and new economic framework depending essentially upon the viability of developmental planning and the suitability of launching those most cherished projects. Now, therefore, in view of an infrastructure already laid down and also in view of certain population explosions that so far have become perceptible and also the emergence of youth force, a conclusion almost not unacceptable can be drawn up that some formidable targets of leadership need to be evolved in their consistent and uniform shapes. We can, postulate the fact that the patterns of the suitable economic leadership are now in the making. The correct approach to be adopted towards integrating the forms and facets of leadership can pay in the long run to yield the satisfactory and tangible results in the field of economic reconstruction.

The economic infrastructure that so far has been laid down till a decade ago may not be that promising and richly rewarding, but the present development has also shown some formidable trends. In the evolutionary than the revolutionary concept, these trends produce their mixed results. The statistics occurring till 1974-77 reveal the poor performances. We see the position of industrial units unregistered yet inter factories Act 1948 are as follows:

Number of units in 1974-75, 252 out of which 95 only were using power. These units in all employed only 1,645 persons; only 11 of them had ever received the Banks' assistance and the number of units looking for assistance were 80. In 1977, there were only 54 registered units employing 2,948 persons in all. The State Level Register of Industries shows that only 177 registered units with employees totalling 1.294 existed. It was also estimated that as many as 1,524 were not yet registered and as many as 1,318 of them were located at rural places, some household industries cater to the work of the industrial units. Lack of technical know-how in some of these units in this analysis seems to be lagging behind, in the previous decade.

Dr. P. M. Passah quotes on the basis of statistics a variance in the number of other factories existing within a decade and which commenced in 1971 which returns a decreasing trend. Among them, "the unregistered workshops constitute the second largest group of industrial establishments in the state with a total number of 807 units in all. They form 33.5 per cent of the total number of industrial establishments in the state. As in the case of registered factories (64.5%), the majority of the unregistered units, accounting for more than 55 per cent is located in the urban areas. Again, according to the census of India, an over whelming percentage in both the urban and rural areas account for 96.2 per cent of the total number of unregistered factories in the state."

Another landmark was the constitution of M.I.D.C. Limited. "The Corporation is taking several steps for the orderly growth of industries... It has to provide a multi-national assistance to entrepreneurs in the state. Up to 1976, the corporation has also commissioned several feasibility studies for likely industries be set up in the state and obtained Licences and Letters of Intent, for some of them. In addition; the centre has many schemes for training local talents in various fields to provide a proper indigenous manpower base for the industrial development".

Two Industrial Areas have already been constituted; the first comprising over 116 hectares of land located at Byrni and another area of 150 acres at Dam site Barapani. Besides, two Industrial Estates have been carved out, one at Short Round Road in Shillong and the other at Mendipathar. There are some infrastructural development in respect of Sericulture and Weaving. In this regard, Meghalaya Khadi and Village Industries Board set up is expected to cater to the need of Village Industries Development.

The performances with regard to the contribution to the State Incomes are not encouraging as during 1973-74, the secondary sector in the State Economy "contributed only Rs. 4.61 crores to the Total State Domestic Product of Rs. 61.41 Crores."

Phrangbonsen T. Marwein'z quotes that the only existing large scale industry is Mawmluh-Cherra Cement. The medium scale industries are Meghalaya Plywood Factory, Associated Beverages, Meghalaya Jute Manufacturing Company, Byrni and Meghalaya Phytochemicals. The conspicuously small scale industries are Meghalaya Cements Products, Happy Valley, Shillong, Meghalaya Metals and Minerals Private Ltd. Mawlai, Meghalaya Roller Floor Mills, Mawlai, Meghalaya Steel and Concrete Private Ltd., Byrni. These are also Assam Bone Meal and fertilizers Ltd. and United Fruit Company at Byrni.

In reviewing the economic situation, we find that the new industrial, trade and occupational trends are still largely tagged with the traditional patterns. The trade structures are indispensable towards providing the unifying Concepts in the system of economy.

The hills since time immemorial abound in resources, viable for exploitation and trade transaction. Gold, silver and metals mined locally however were more for domestic use leaving a negligible output for commercial transaction. In course of time, most of these resources gradually were depleting out.

P. Passah quoting from the authority referred to the iron trade for a volume of 20,000 maunds exported from the hills in the shape of hoes to Assam and in lumps of pig-iron to Surma valley in 1853, that time when iron-smelting was becoming nearly extinct. With them, guns and gunpowder were sent outside. Prior to 1950, volumes of iron trade must have been many times bigger. Iron trade saw its collapse towards the close of the last century.

Business and Trade

Trade incentives have considerably dwindled after the British occupation of Assam, more so, after the inception of Shillong as the Provincial headquarters, for since then, the new trade patterns have come to emerge and stay on. Thus the new landmarks were caused which emerged also from a new-work of buildings that came into existence. The principal economic pattern became drastically changed since the bulk of supplies was to be drawn from outside in respect of those not available locally. With these came into picture the new food habits, new styles of buildings, new furniture and household goods, new groceries and utensils, new dress patterns, use of textile products, other things of wide range in which some of the old value became discarded to make room for new ones. A convergence of trade patterns, modern and traditional occurred in which Shillong became intensively exposed and in which this new capital attracted and housed streams of trading communities who were more skilled in operating interdistrict trade whereas a bulk of the local trade survived side by side.

Thus new factors of production and mode of distribution came into picture. The situation was such that some local products *en route* Shillong were transacted outside by a trading, community whereas towards the south, local traders themselves (with a few exceptions) reached a bulk of goods into the plain market. Markets, from Sylhet side still continued to handle the supply of rice, fish, cattle, cloths and other goods directly to the hills and more articles of daily use came via Sylhet and Assam. Station merchants at Shillong made a bulk of transaction for the supply of goods from outside and therefore wielded commercial influence considerably. One adverse effect was that the Khasis had not shown interest to transact supply of goods brought from outside by themselves.

The system as it had come on to stay had not entirely squeezed out the local or traditional modes of production and distributed to a new entrepot at Shillong headquarters came batches of local traders from all nooks and corners of this country to dispose of their products and crops for both District and inter-District trade, in the shape of planks and timber, baskets and village crafts (implements, tools, accessories), fish, meat, turmeric, garlic, rice-cakes, lac, various fruits and vegetables, other several hill products, and drew supply of things such as textile goods, groceries, utensils, foodstuffs, medicines, building materials, stationaries and others from Bara Bazar and Police Bazar, the local products, at the same time being channelled for distribution through the various agencies.

This occurred more on weekly market days than the other bazar days. The local traders reached Shillong by means of roads, tracks and horsetracks. Up-till the first world war, trade incentives had to dwindled in view of the merger of Khasi Jaintia entities into the British India and accession of States (on the basis of a subsidiary alliance) so that until today we see that principal products including potato, broomsticks, tez leaf and timber are daily deposited into the Shillong godowns and the other merchants transact them in turn. These business transactions were accumulating force and reflected the new dimensions also.

Trade and Marketing Intelligence

It is now necessary that trade and marketing intelligence should be tapped so as to prevent undesirable wastage, that the local traders lagging behind be made more and more acquainted with the different processes of stocking goods for timely channelisation as should be adjustable to the modern methods of accountancy and making appropriate investments. Moreover, there is a paramount need to involve them in entrepreneurships, cooperative industries which should and ought to be proportionate with the availability of potentials and resources and making steady (than lumpsum) profits out of the sale-proceeds.

However, there are still bright prospects since the local traders themselves are running trade transactions at markets and hats situated outside Shillong. Thus we see batches of people attending the rural markets spread all over these directions, covering their distance by road transport, horses and on foot providing stocks and distributing them. On account of these trends, the Iewduh pattern of Shillong has become considerably enhanced. "Trade and commerce in most of the hill areas is controlled by outsiders. All the autonomous hill Districts had passed legislation for regulating the trade and commerce by non-tribals

....But it is frequently found that though licences are issued in the name of the local tribals, the financiers are actually Non-Tribals, and the bulk of the profits go to them. They operate in the name of the tribals under cover as salesmen. In some areas they pay fantastic amounts ranging from 1,000 to 2,000 a month for running a shop on their behalf. This indicates the huge amount of profit that they (non-Tribals) earn"

It is relevant also to add here that some new local entrepreneurships have appeared and some new stockists and stores have emerged. Perhaps in respect of mechanical operations the people do not lag behind and can do better provided there is a good or competent leadership which can boost an effective management. New entrepreneurships have come to stay as we see them from a number of new motor and electrical workshops, furniture and cabinet establishments, steel fabrication, hallowed stone block and cement fabrication now being undertaking. Some local men are coping with the distribution of goods while on the erstwhile occasions men were not so much accustomed to these jobs. Besides, mechanised farming has started to appear. But most of these undertakings including processing of soap and candle products, arts of crafts are small scale and it will be the matter of time that industrial technology with sufficient manpower will emerge some modern industries are not purely local concerns. It appears that the people want to have smaller or medium size industries provided they have sufficient resources for some continuous role. The local potentials are such that stone, sands and even clay are quarried and transacted for local supply in respect of building, road making, lining and levelling and some are sold to factories also. Industrialisation entails a great deal of marketing intelligence. Handling of machinery and technical know-how seem to be indispensable and the young persons with regard to providing them with such resources.

In conclusion a good organisation of hats and markets is very important to ensure an effective mode of distribution in the States 16 and Daloiships.

Reinstating the commercial transactions or linkages on advanced lines is allied to the development of the other connected sectors. The land abounds in varied economic potentialities. The situation, however has considerably changed in respect of the forest based industries as at present, people are running short of firewood whereas about 20 years ago the land held bright prospects for the manufacture of wood-pulp, paper, matches and other articles. Such industries can however still be planned on a limited scale where afforestation method can be successfully expedited to make available the raw materials from time to time. A limited number of industries (chemical and pharmaceutical) on those lines can be taken up. We should not forget the other industries where limestones (against their available potentials) can feed them. Conditions are excellent for fruit canning and preservation.

Most of the village industries, sericulture, weaving, crafts and basketry, blacksmithy and others are carried out in primitive methods and therefore, it is most essential that innovations should be applied in those areas, where it is possible, keeping in mind the need to prevent high cost of production, since in the near future, some of the primitive methods can be replaced by the modern ones provided the circumstances are favourable. Besides, prospects for taking up new mining industries will depend on the further discoveries of geologists. Fruit canning will be of much relevance where the facilities of transport exist and other conditions are good. It holds bright prospects, if production can be boosted so that the fruit products will find demand all over this subcontinent and perhaps places beyond her shores. To achieve these objects within a short time, it will require a dynamic and progressive action but this will occur with the further changes in nationalism and in line with the industrial awakenings.

Father wrote: "Where is this wide world will you find such a country, a land of ice and snow, a land of crystal streams and singing brooks, of azure colour peaks and of invigorating air. In such land as microscopic as a coin, as one bard narrates, they have abundant rice lands yielding regular and plentiful harvest, they cultivate extensively the arun plant and potato, the best type of fruits rare on their vicinity are hung on the sloping gardens of the border, weaving arid sericulture thrive, lac and chillies are being produced continuously and in the bosom of their land are stored the precious minerals-lime stone and coal, and metals-silver and gold.

Multifarious cropping will be so important to be introduced on a larger scale for causing larger returns. Khasi forges and iron-smelting works should revive in another form which should adapt themselves to the modern conditions. New industries should be in a position to open further avenues of employment; those industries should be established worked, conducted by the Khasis themselves primarily for their advantages.

In view of the above, the following measures are of foremost importance for pursuance.

First, the manpower requirements should be fully explored and speedy measures taken to shape such resources which also go along with the expeditious disposal of carefully selected schemes of industrial planning. An opinion has already been expressed on the problem of meeting adequate manpower resources for accelerating the pace of development.

We are of opinion too that cooperative training is very important to involve people in various trade and industrial managements and provide resources in those areas where cooperative industry can flourish after drawing up a careful planning to make the operation and transaction have good standard.

In respect of livestock as suggested, tapping of good grasslands into ranches would be very helpful but domestication and farmings on scientific lines should rather be applied on a huge scale both on public and private levels.

New trade habits are so essential to be cultivated on a wide scale. For so long, it appears habits have not been properly imbibed. Sometimes habits, however, are shaped under very difficult circumstances or critical situations. Possibly too much attachment to modern comforts and too easy going have totally spoiled our young people who had refused themselves to be involved in trades with rigours and hazards as one would encounter. That is why a gap was made in which the labour and trade sectors were filled up with persons from outside. Incentives therefore, have to be provided in these very sectors as well as on other trades, callings and professions as related to man - power planning. For so long too, education was channelised to provide assets to white collar jobs and so now, vocational training has to be intensified so much so to meet these inadequacies not only in a few prescribed lines but in so many branches of operation.

We feel that the following areas need immediate attention on the part of our local counterparts: Photography and film-making: printing technique: saloon and restaurant services, dyeing and dry-cleaning: tailoring and shoe making: musical-sales and repair: stone block making, fixture and cabinet making: book binding, umbrella making: modern crafts and orientation of arts:

Other than the above, there may be fair chances to profit from undertakings suggested below: tannery (if climatic condition is good), dairying, meat canning, sauce and condiment refreshers, potato preservation. Manufacturers might relate to stationery, teaching aids, cartography, woollen and garment fabrics, toys and playthings, threads and ropes, ceramics, varnish and paints, cases and containers and a variety of things. There are other designs should be so devised to provide sufficient rooms for improvement. It will be better if the local entrepreneurs or makers engage themselves since in benami practices, the administration would be deprived of good revenue, otherwise this measure is bad since it leads to an undue concentration of wealth.

There is already the problem of accommodation for sites in respect of the above undertakings as already the business centres such as Garikhana, Police Bazar, Bara Bazar have already been heavily occupied by business and trade establishment and as such new enterprises along these lines have recently shifted themselves to Nongthymmai, Mawlai and elsewhere far from those centres, in which therefore, they have to tackle with the problem of transport and marketing their goods. The present situation however is quite encouraging since we hear, during; the last three years, various Banking; and Government agencies have come forward to provide loans and other forms of financial assistance to a number of such enterprises.

But that will not substantially help unless the people acquaint themselves with these problems and exert pressure to solve them and as such would come nearer to the threshold of industrialisation on a mild than heavy scale. The students and young people who are so much to be involved soon would have to take into confidence these problems especially when we hear that in the near future, various problems of unemployment will loom large.

As regards the place of the present exports of agriculture and forest produce comprise jute, cotton, orange, pineapples, lemons, betel leaves, arecanuts, tez pat, potato, mustard, timber and forest products, elephant tusks, bamboo, gar oil and powder, lac, wattle, honey, ranwalfia, serpentina, roots, species of medicinal herbs, they are now the exportable items of the state. Mineral resources include coal, limestone, sillimanite and rira clay." To them we must add agricultural produce natural, turmeric, cinnamon, black pepper, ginger, broomsticks and fruits, plums, apricots, peaches, pears, guava, pumpkins and many other varieties.

Industry

Industrialisation on a modern scale has started from scratch only recently. Mining conducted at several places has occurred over the long decades. Mining referred herein includes among others coal, limestones, sillimanite, mainly. Therefore, the extinction of iron-smelting practised on intense scale which coincided with the coming of the British administration in Assam gave way to coal mining conducted on a small scale since 1841. It provides power to industries and railways mainly it is used at kilns, chimneys and boilers but now, it can also be processed into several manufacturers including the cloth and chemical patterns mainly.

Coal in huge quantity is daily exported, coal being exported in huge quantities daily to several stations, near and far, it will be correct to say that coal is still found useful to provide power to several small and medium factories. Coal in massive quantities mined here is sent to several places of India and till recently, bulk of coal is sent to Bangladesh the trade being handled by the Mineral and Metal Trading Corporation Ltd. Among others, sillimanite mined over the long decades is fairly distributed to other places for the purpose of industrialisation, the centre of mining being located at Sunapahar. Limestone is used for construction, buildings and for feeding industries such as cements, etc. Limestones has ranked as one of the conspicuous exports of these hills since time memorial and found good markets in Assam and Bengal. In the hills it is processed through kilns and chimneys (in which coal or firewood is used for making fires), into shun maw (for constructions), shun kpu (for making house walls) and shun bam (used for consumption). It contains some medicinal propensities and is used as an adhesive. Bulk of its extracted quantities besides being put to trade is also used at the cements factories at Sohra which with corrundum and other clays brought from outside, is processed into cement at the Mawmluh-Cherra Cements Factories started in a couple of decades or so. The industries, private and public at present must have contribute to earning revenues to the state and help also to increase the earning capacities of the working teams attached to them. Hence, their continuous roles have been absured. Hence, a viable and prospective planning with regard to mining and industrialisation is not essential.

Electric power is most essential now to running the industries. The State holds, the enormous hydel potentials. The suitability or otherwise of tapping hydel projects has been envisaged in the previous decades. The electrification of the Shillong Town since the twenties or so has been catered to by one small power house situated below the Sunapani fall in Mawlai, Shillong. Besides the Umtrew and Umiam hydel projects earlier instituted, the survey towards installing Myntdu, Kynshi and Umiam-Umtrew Hydel Projects has been envisaged recently. So far it appears that the state has got these Hydel potentials.

The first landmark in this regard was the construction of the Umtrew Hydroelectric Project which commenced in the fifties and was commissioned in 1957. Developments followed quickly. The banning of river Umiam for the installation of hydel project was expedited since 1960 and activities were resumed and these led to the commissioning of Umiam Hydel Project in 1965. Stages of construction of installation followed in a targeted phase. Now recently this phased development has passed over from. Phase II to Phase IV, the new Khri Division project having been amalgamated with the already Umiam installed capacity. However, the far flung places have been extended the required facilities. Therefore, the generation of Nangwalbibra project (sponsored by NEC) is anticipated to cater to the needs in Garo Hills. The proposed installation of Myntdu Hydel Project is also expected to increase the installed capacity of the state. The installation of Kynshi project is also being envisaged.

Under the Department the sale proceeds can also be effectively regulated so as to provide good sources of revenue to the state.

As regards the capacity loads, the hydel projects are understood to have the installed strength as follow:

Untrew	-	8,400 kW expanded to 11,200 kW
Umiam	-	36,000 kW
Umiam 2nd Stage	-	18,000 kW
Umiam 3rd Stage	-	60,000 kW
Umiam 4th Stage	-	60,00 kW
Garo Hills Thermal	-	5,000 kW

Umiam Stage IV is tagged with Khri Project. It also includes Umiew, Upper Khri, Umiam Stage concentration The Hydel Project schemes also include the Leska Project in Jaintia Hills and Gannol and Ringgi first stage in Garo Hills. To the above Kyrdem Kulai installed recently was supposed to have a capacity of 60,000 kW.

Besides, there is the construction of Kupli Project sponsored by NEC the construction of which is expedited by North Eastern Electric Power Corporation. The catchment area of Assam falls within the Kupli project besides which it will also cover Meghalaya in a very small proportion. The proposed installed strength is estimated of 150 kW. The expansion strength of the establishment of MSEB along with their technical, industrial commercial and administrative branches started initially as early as 1976-77, we find that the transmissions operating under these heads were Umiam Hydel Project, Umtrew

Hydel Project and Nagalbibra Thermal and sales and services were also grouped into domestic, commercial, industrial, public lighting, public water works and sewage pumping patterns, bulk supply (including licences), total sales and transactions with Assam State Electricity Board. The number of villages under electrification has been increasing on.

Industries Identified

The small industries so far identified which have scope to thrive are bandages and cotton (surgical), agro-service/centres, atta-chaki mills, scented supari processing, banana powder and chips, cattle/poultry feeds, cornflakes, fruit canning, essential oils fruit preservations and canning, ginger dehydratation, sauces, barley water, jams, jellies, crop grain threshers and haulers, mushrooms and their processed products, potato chips and starches, tapioca starch and sago, flours, tea, coffee processing (in factory processing)," they all depend upon many factors in which the availability of good packages and containers counts a lot. The private units have, therefore, contributed a great deal to the economy.

For the all round development, stress is laid on: (a) the obvious need to curtail benai practices; (b) to give adequate protection to small scale miners or quarriers, also local entrepreneurships, ownership of mining, metallurgy, etc.; (c) to accelerate the progress of small scale or cottage industries suited to the local resources; (d) essence of modifying the law of inheritance is essential to suit with economic growth and development; (e) socially that more working force both by males and females is availed for production, distribution. Trade, supply, labour and involvement in the actual undertakings; (f) that because normal employment avenues becoming fewer, therefore creation of business management and entrepreneurship at many levels becomes essential, hence more youth force being diverted to tertiary, non-tertiary sectors or otherwise. Any form of population explosion is deemed fit as to have been suitable balanced with the integrated norms of industrial and business creativity, productivity and excellence to our rising generation before emerging to the next century 2000 AD Cements factories, companies and other business patterns being consistently organised; yield stable incomes to the state revenues running themselves with proportionate profits.

Mineral Wealth

Coal was a valuable mineral during the dawn of the British Areas in Khasi. We find that the East India Company stipulated an engagement in a series of Treaties with Kings and State Heads to hand over the portions of limestone and other mineral beds on condition that a royalty be returned arising from their exploitation. Coal mining in Cherra commenced as early as 1841.

Loss of iron trade is now compensated by a widespread cultivation of potato, vegetables and fruits. It seems that proper tapping of other mineral resources would be rendered difficult since the available reserves have become more limited.

Among fruits, the Khasi orange is known since tine immemorial. It was reported in 1828 that the Khasi gardens supplied almost the whole of Bengal with oranges. There was an outreach too of other crops notably tez pat, pepper, turmeric, lac, ginger, pineapples, jack fruit and others. Timber and bamboo were in great demand. Honey, hide and skin, rubber, ivory, errandi and cotton threads were other items of merchandise transacted outside. Other fruits and vegetable were channelised for trade.

The Khasis depended for some of their needs from the plains. Salt was brought in huge quantity for household stocks. Dryfish was another item of import though the people had their own locally sun-dried and smoke dried fish. The southerners, since paddy was not conveniently planted, were compelled to purchase some rice from Sylhet side. Other things such as clothes and clothings, certain crafts and furniture, stitching materials and leather, some herds of cattle, poultry and domesticated animals were purchased and brought up. A lot was obtained through their counterparts who stayed in Khasi plain dominions and in this manner trade dimensions became extended up with the outside world. Even up till the great earthquake occurring in 1897 most of the southerners and other trading families were wealthy whose riches were in gold and silver ornaments and other precious possessions. We cannot, however, say whether this wealthy accumulation was confined uniformly to the whole of the country also. The prospects of this once flourishing trade were dimmed by the partition of India (1947) which brought about a trade closure with the erstwhile East Pakistan.

The trouble was this: The fruit plantations on the southern slopes are situated mostly in precipitous areas, for which reason it had become difficult immediately after the first Republic Day to have direct communications with the market centres on the higher uplands. In fact communication in some places was more accessible to Pakistan. Moreover, staple food crops such as rice which was obtained from Sylhet side were then not available. It was a matter of time to restore normal trade relations with the rest of country by making diversions against the existing means of communication and making new ones. The situation however has considerably improved after the lapse of many years occurring from the road constructions leading to the development of transport and traffic improvement in marketing was also borne upon which came simultaneously.

The Khasi once were adventurous traders. Lindsay in this connection said that they brought a staple of coarse silk from the confines of China to near Bengal and if this was true, it meant that a trade route with China or Trans-Himalaya region existed via the Khasi Hills from Bengal side on one end, entering the hills from Bhologanj (where Lindsay was stationed), thence emerging to Cherra, thence to Shillong and Raitong in Bhoi, thence to Sonapur in Lowere Assam, thence Upper Assam thence into Byrma. The traditions say that they went as far as Byrma and the far-east for trade. They were in close touch to with trade limits located in Bengal and perhaps Upper India as indicated by their use of Muslim and Hindu coins and seals. Barter was conducted among the ordinary people but Kings and high officials used their own coins in making out transactions with their counterparts in the plains. But trade has dwindled and in fact much marketing of broomsticks, potato, tez leaf, and others is now done by the Marwaris for circulating them outside.

Agriculture

The people are acquainted to practising both the permanent and shifting cultivation. However, the methods of cultivation are varied and differ according to climatic conditions. The climate itself ranges from sub-tropical to semi-temperate and thence to temperate. "The soil is lateritic in the foothills and, above 500 metres it is mainly podzolic; while the areas in the southern slopes are in the layer of limestone belts, the northern slopes are mostly podzolic and have red loamy soil".

The Khasi value the settled agriculture more than the shifting. They, therefore, cultivate cereals, vegetables and fruits of a variegated nature. The State is divided into three physical divisions which are the northern valleys and hills (submountain) known as Bhoi, the central highlands located amid 900 and 2,000 metres altitude called *Ri Lum* and the southern precipitous mountain tract bordering Bangladesh, named Ri War. Garo Hills follow the same pattern of this physical division but a distinct temperate climate occurs only at some selected places.

Slash and Burn System

In the rugged terrain we find that the slash and burn system exists. Under slash and burn system, a mixed cropping pattern obtains, the contrast of mono-crop farming. The cultivators have been used to practising a modified system of jhumming since the centuries past. The well known methods of farming are:

- *Rep Sung:* rice irrigated farming in the extensive valley tracts.
- *Rep Half:* rice farming in irrigated valleys.
- *Rep Pynthor:* a terraced cultivation applied in the lower hills and the adjoining valleys.
- *Thang Ram:* or rep shyrti a heavy shift and burn system.
- *Thang Bun:* a turfing system of cultivation.
- *Thang Syllai:* which consists of the extraction of light herbage and utilising it for cultivation.
- *Rep Bra:* which occurs in the south for the cultivation of fruits, banana, tez pat, pepper, betel-vines, arecanuts and others.
- *Rep Lyngkha:* a plot under cultivation, regular, semi-permanent or otherwise.
- *Rep Kper:* a home-stead or kitchen gardening.

- *Rep Rnem:* a system of cultivation by hoeing, applying manuring and putting seeds used for various crops.

Rep sung or hali conforming to wet rice cultivation, this methods prevails in the flat and low level grounds where, at the huge plots we observe that ploughing the soil by a pair of bullocks is essentially followed whereas where, the holdings are small, the soil is just hoed up. The seeds are sown broadcast but in a transplantation, the young roots nurtured at nurseries are removed into the main field. At places, these fields located at spacious grounds having the rich soil ingredients and watered by good streams as few of which we see on the north, form the rich rice lands. Thang ram or rep shyrti, this is followed in respect of dry rice cultivation, it is a slash and burn system of cultivation, also known popularly as jhumming. Cropping pattern under this system varies from place to place. We find also that some of the crops returned under the dry system of cultivation or any of its modified moor serve as some of the best cash crop.

On the north, jhumming mostly is a system of mono rotation; in the first year, the soil holds good for paddy followed in the next year by the cultivation of Kachu and in the third year, if any by errandi (sla ryndia) or cotton plants. In the south millets in rotation is grown with arum (millet seeds mostly sown broadcast, arurii being grown from its barks cut off and sticks laid out with the plant? In the south, after the jhums are bunit, millets followed by Kachu are planted. During the next year, the above are replaced by tapioca or potatoes or both. But elsewhere Kachu and millets may have been admixed or grown in rotation. Dry rice cultivation prevails slightly in the south where rice and job's tears are grown together.

The evils of jhumming have been expressed in several academic forums in that it depletes the fertility of the soil necessitate the constant shifting of the farming communities. As regards the method of cultivation thangram, therefore, is different from thang bun, the latter being a modified system of shift and slash and the arranging of turf drain to prepare the soil. The soil is heed up and turfed and the sods extracted are dried after sunshine and then burnt. Light herbages and shrubs are also conserved; they are extracted, sundried and pile up in beds and burnt with sods. Potato thrives best in buns although sometimes, mixed cropping is also possible.

Crop Calendar

Crop calendar in buns varies from place to place. In the west initially paddy, potato and kachu are admixed, followed by maize in summer and then by vegetables and seeds called neilieh (used for pounding and preparing a paste taken with meals). In upper Shillong soya beans, potato, maize, cucumber, melon, etc. grown simultaneously are followed in July by turnips and radish. At Laitlyngkot, the similar vegetables are grown with phan Hang (or winter potato) in the summers, about the near autumn times.

Buns are operated differently in different conditions. In the west, maize and soya beans initially are grown thereafter, followed by paddy. In central highlands, ginger is initiated then in rotation, admixed with the other vegetables. Bun can accommodate two or three seasonal farming in a year. It suits well for tubers and leafy vegetables. At Nongkrem, this slash and burn pattern continues two to four years in the same soil. It is a system of rotation starting first with potato then gives way to cabbage or cauliflower, sweet potato and maize; the second year of cultivation conforming to potato or paddy or maize or millets and in which during the third year, on the out-turn becomes reduced on. The cycle in the grassland is short but shrubs have a longer cycle extending to eight or ten years.

Another modified system is rep syllai in which the surface grass is uprooted and dibbled inside the ground, then surfaced with earth. The soil after sometimes is scratched and apertures are laid where they plant the potato and maize in them. This is dry potato cultivation which cycle is the shortest one, ranging from four to two years.

There is winter potato (phan Clang) in which the farmers first extract the grass, then turf-drain it and the potato is planted into the grassy packages then covered up with sods. No burning is necessary. A little urea is helpful for manuring. It is grown in August and plucked out in November.

Recently the permanent paddy fields (during the winter post-harvest) which almost are off season phase, have been utilised for potato cultivation in which potatoes are planted in late January or February. It is spring time potato, the soil being prepared and manured properly.

Rice locally grown is both white and red in colour, some admitting them to be rich in vitamins and nutrients. For baking purpose they use jahulia paddy specie in Bhoi and khaw saw rit seeds in the west. Millets and job's tears are used for domestic needs.

For a long time, we see that the supplementary cereals are millets, maize, soya beans, tapioca, job's tears and potato. The latter of course is a principal cash crop. Millets locally available known are raitruh (finger millets), rai soh (fox tail) and rai span (Italian Millets). Rai truh does well in ri war but rai soh and rai span mostly are confined to the central plateau. They have been grown through the ages. Soh riew (job's tears) grows well in ri war but scarce on the upper region.

Mawsing Kharasti out of his great experience in agricultural sciences, opines that in the central plateau potato is the main crop for which an intensive use of fertilizers is made for every year, so as to use the same land for more than one crop by rotation with rice, maize and vegetables". The farmers have been placed in a difficult position for apart from their high prices, their supplies have to be obtained from distant places like Guwahati and even potato cultivation seems to be no longer a profitable cultivation. Production of potato could be increased in the lower regions as a cold weather crop for, there are possibilities of higher yields per acre up to 20 tons instead of 2 tons as at present which is the average villages of the higher regions'.

There are indigenous potatoes and tapioca used as supplementary cereals, named phan dieng, phan rnluh, phan synreh, phan khlaw. Potato cultivation dominates the central highlands, a bulk is the product of bun and syllai but besides them, its adoption into steadfast farms is considerable. At certain places, it is grown and plucked out thrice in a year. The availability of manure and fertilizers, its trade being transacted to outside the hills almost daily. The volume of trade has been as bulky as that of orange during the British regime. Turmeric is grown considerably also.

Cash Crops

Potato now the principal cash crop is considered to be indigenous in these highlands. The credit of introducing sweet potato or Phan karo, beets and carrots may be given to David Scott who brought them here in 1829-32. All the other potatoes are as good as sohlah, the title of the present commercial potato is much indigenous. Scott must have brought sweet potatoes only from the Garo Hills where it was earlier grown.

Another leguminous plant is Langkhud planted during the late summer and harvested usually in the early winter months. It is a tuber. It is after its skin is pealed off and washed in a stream that sohphlang, a very important market item is obtained.

The Ri war or border area is important for fruits like pineapple, banana, papaya, litchi, jack fruits, oranges, limes and lemons, etc. mandarin, lemon; prior to independence it was one of the finest granaries: it still holds good for fruits, spices and other sub-tropical crops. The items may briefly be enumerated below.

Tez pat (sla tyrpad), this is a specie of malabathrum, grown after a transplantation from a nursery; arecanut (Kwai), this is grown from a pad, conducted twice in a transplantation from nurseries as it takes years to grow to a tree height and looks like a tall palm. Thousands and thousands of the pods plucked out are preserved in hallows or pits or trenches and some inside the ponds for keeping them moist and thereafter, circulated on commercial scale. Betel-vines, this is a climber plant, grown from its tree top or leaf, or young stalks; in a plantation, seedlings laid out in beds held with supports of shingles or decayed wood are carefully looked after and when plants have come up, their vines are leaned against the nearby trees. This is what we called *tympew* or pan; Pepper, this is also a vine grown from a small bunch of its wild tree-top or its outer stalk. In fact the above with fruits form the principal cash crops.

Orange, this is mandarin species which dominates Ri War, it has a long stage of growth, grown from its seeds howled out and sun-dried, then dibbled in soft surface soil and covered with the earth and small grasses. When sprouted, it is removed to a regular field where it grows into a tree but not so tall. When grown up to proper height, it is finally taken to a permanent plantation.

Orange of an inferior quality grows also in Bhoi and the upper plateau, but the plateau's fruits are small and sourist and the Bhoi orange is also inferior to Ri War oranges. Next to orange is the pineapple, grown from its crown and requires protection against the attack of pesticides. The terraced plots for a large scale cultivation seem to serve better.

Jack fruits grow well in War, planted from small pods obtained from the fruit, otherwise fruits when fell down becoming decayed, could have scope to germinate, into fresh trees. There are other fruits, sweet and sour grown. There are other innumerable wild fruits edible and cherished for their taste. Busk of these when plucked out are marketed. Other limes and lemons abound, the most common being soh jew and soh myndong besides others named soh mad, soh jyllih, soh sying, soh niang riang and soh khyllung. They thrive both in tropical and temperate zones. Soh myngor (a pomel) is likewise locally available. So hpyrshong (a lime something like a fig) is another useful lime. Some local limes are for the year through are available. The temperate fruit plantations are confined in the Shillong plateau, the valuable fruits planted being plums, apricots, peaches, grapes, pears, william fertility (soh phoh klong) and passion fruit (sob brab). Sohramdieng classed with mango family is also grown and circulated.

The Plantation

Plantain is obtained both as wild and planted product. The most important bananas on which stress is laid as regards their commercial value are joji (dwarf cabandish), kait syiem (cheni champa), kait jrong (long banana), kait mon and kait syiem. They are specially grown and very much circulated.

It is in the central highlands that pear, plum, peach apricot and to some extent pineapples are grown whereas the sub-mountain area adjoining Assam is important for fruits like pineapple, banana, papaya, litchi, mandarin, lemon, etc.

The indigenous vegetables named in the tradition are melon, cucumber, mustard leaf, soya beans, arum, yam, chillies and other uncountable wild vegetables are obtained. However, modern vegetable plantations have become important. Cabbage and cauliflower plantations have become widespread in the Shillong suburbs in which Nongkrem and Upper Shillong take the lead. Cabbage in fact is the principal cash crop, grown both in buns and regular farms. It requires considerable drainage during the spring time and at the stage they young roots are being transplanted from the nursery into the field. The early summer rains help the plant to sprout and are ready soon for plucking.

Among the beans, soya beans is grown widely during the summer where at places, it serves as a supplementary cereal. The flat beans and French beans are the common species. Being stalky, the beans require support where they can spread out. Rymbai ktung is typical bean valued for making an indigenous sauce, turungbai where after plucking the seeds, they are laid inside the earthen pots, their mouths covered up with leaves, and afterwards smoked to dry in the kitchen racks. It is prepared after being frying with certain spices. Sticks planted near the crop help it to grow tall and unlike other beans, it does not require much room to spread. All of them are well circulated in the local markets to meet the domestic requirement.

Among the leafy vegetables, mention should be made of spinach, leaf mustard, lettuce and others which do well in homestead farms. Among the large pods, are the squash, melon, cucumber, gourds commonly white gourds and soh prew (a sort of sponge when dried out and used as vegetable when it is still green).

The tubers mainly are khol knol, beets, carrots, turnips, radish being circulated well in the: local markets. Radish of course is the important cash crop which plantation has spread into the villages. Brinjal is another crop grown.

Tomato of an inferior quality is also obtained besides which the tree tomato recently has been more cultivated. Among, other vegetables we may mention jhingka and hur thhem (which are like cucumber), khoit kait and pashor (a bark and flowering plant of plantain). We may mention other vegetables such as lady's finger (bhindi) or charratis, capsicum and other chillies (black, red and green). Besides onion and garlic are very widely grown.

Wild Vegetables

The wild vegetables well valued are jangew, jathang, jarain and jamyrdoh. Some vegetables do well in buns but a large number are regularly cultivated in farm and gardens where the soil is properly tilled, arranged and manured. A terraced system seems to be so essential in respect of useful vegetables. Vegetables are grown from the respective seeds or pods but recently imported seeds have been used, the cropping varies from place to place, somewhere we find potato and maize are combined together whereas in the west, soya beans and maize are admixed in the same plots.

The real cash crops circulated on large scale transactions are potato (as large as betel-vines was during pre-independence), turmeric, tez pat, sesam areca-nuts, betel-vines, black pepper, ginger, pineapples, oranges and jack fruits and are eminently the products of the Khasi and Jaintia Hills, and almost all the major and the minor cereals, fruits, vegetables, bananas of a variegated nature and all enumerated above, are like the common items noticed universally on district scale. Some vegetables at oft-seasons in these hills are also brought from outside. The local rice fetches higher prices for its market value. Owing to the population inflation, rice supplied from outside at controlled and non-controlled markets is commercially transacted and sold. Bulk of the best local rice is brewed into beer at the country distillaries. The next common market item is mushrooms (u tit) grown or collected wild of many kinds.

In Garo Hills, jhum is the prevalent cropping pattern. It consists of the felling of jungles in which heaps of vegetation are levelled to the ground and basked to sun and air. Jungle clearing occurs in November or December. The debris are to be burnt. So in February the debris are reshuffled to enable the burning to take place soon. The people collect some firewood, bamboos and shrubs which are carried home but the mass is accumulated on the field. Burning of the jhums takes place in March. During the burning process, fire is lit with the help of torches from two or three directions in the field. The unburnt matter is again sunned for final burning. The field thus prepared sustains the crops for a couple of years after which the people shift to another field and repeat this process. Jhum cycle normally intervenes between six and nine years. The output during the second year of cultivation normally decreases from the first year owing perhaps to the applicability of the law of diminishing returns. During the second year, the new field may have become necessary for the cultivation of main crops while the old field is reserved for the supplementary ones. Paddy, maize and millets are the main crops grown. Tapioca, gourds, arum plant, dioscorea, onion, leaf mustard, garlic, brinjals, sweet potatoes, pumpkins, melon and potato also thrive. Cotton renowned from the hills also grows in the jhum. Many of these crops are sown in the months of March and April and precede the plantation of cotton which comes later on. Millets, mainly fox-tail besides job's tears are also grown. The important garden products are lac and indigo. Harvests intervene between July and December although cotton is plucked until the month of February. Some of the seeds are sown broadcast, other just dibbled in little holes in which light scratches only are made. Paddy is sown broadcast. The first broadcasting of the plant is done more neatly in the holes prepared.

Initially it would seen right to say that seeds of millet, chilly, brinjal and other vegetables mixed together are sown. Then varieties of corn, cotton, jute, meesta are planted into holes. Banana, onion, sweet potato; gingers, turmeric are also grown and tapioca generally is planted along the boundary of the jhum plots.

Of their implements, the axe, daos or choppers and some knives or daggers are used for jungle cutting. They also used the iron hoes, choppers, scrappers and rakes of bamboo. Few households use sickles. Some crops are plucked by hands or with the help of daos. But with a handful of these appliances, they undertake digging and chopping with tremendous success in which normally farms and plantations meet their barns sufficiently with crops. They upturn their jungle clad mountains with amazing speed to convert them into the plantation. In the plains they have more of the improved tools and implements. They have several panniers, baskets and trays to receive their grains. In their houses they gather the crops in barns. Some baskets are just woven of cane slips but others are finely polished as of cane fibres. Cotton is stocked in oblong rectangular baskets as tall as twice the height of the carrier tied to his back by a strap and supported on his forehead.

Villages produce sufficiently for their own needs and the surplus thus obtained is transacted for trade. The people have been acquainted to using edibles collected from jungles such as wild roots, tubers and plants. The tribesmen of Meghalaya have been used to relishing herbal plants rich in nutrients as green salads with their meals. They use the indigenous beans for preparing pastes, ashars and sauces taken with food.

The Government presently is trying to, implement village regrouping and make the villages more viable. The programme involved will be more successfully implemented if it is consistent with the pattern of land tenure, existing one and modified. The traditional norms are being envisaged as to what extent the adjustment can be made. Some agricultural grants-in-aid and loans have been utilised by Garo farmers.

New patterns of cultivation which have evolved may be touched briefly. In some of the river valleys and the foothills, vet-rice plantations have been worked out during the last few decades. Permanent cultivation seems to be more fitting in when compared with jhum which entails shifting constantly. Orange and lemons have been cultivated at some places while fruits newly grown have fetched but small incomes to fruit growers. Other crops are arecanuts and betel-vines grown on small-scale basis. Pine apples thrive well. In Tura some of the modern vegetables have been grown. Experiment may prove successful in respect of the introduction of jack-fruits, pumpkins, leech, guava and other varieties.

There are many weekly markets and hats. It is in these centres that agriculture produces such of cotton (this is short staple variety), jute, meesta are sold while bulk of salt, dry fishes, tobacco, cloth, utensils are purchased and sent home. This traditional system still exists side by side with the modern trends.

Noted Crops

Other noted crops in Meghalaya are jute and mesta; excluding Byrni hat in Khasi foothills, bulk of it is grown in Garo Hills; a warm climate and moist places are favourable to their cultivation. Wheat and tea now experimented had shown remarkably promising results. Its cultivation till quite recently has spread to 1,650 hectares and land grown up to the elevation of 1,200 metres in West Garo and nurseries in tea plantation have also started at Umsning in East Khasi Hills.

Natural drainage forms the means of irrigation. Watering flowers, vegetables and a few fruit plants in homestead gardens is universally noticed inside towns at off rain seasons. Owing to the undulating terrain, only small scale irrigation schemes have been introduced through mainly river catchments, lift irrigations and tube well processes. The Rongai valley project and Shella river projects have been included for implementation for covering roughly 5,500 hectares of area under the 6th plan. The PWD so far undertakes the construction and Agriculture Department is allotted minor operations. Approximately 28 per cent to 30 per cent of lands under a settled agriculture is covered. It seems also that damming the river and making use of electric transmission for irrigation is yielding good results. The totalled cropped area stood only at 2,03,017 hectares in 1975-76 against the total 22,48,900 hectares of the geographical of the state. This excluded area for land utilisation statistics, forests, lands not available for cultivation, fallow land; net area was shown at 1,73,824 hectares and area sown more than once at 29,193 hectares. Consumption of fertilizers for 1977-78 (provisional data) was shown nitrogen at 1,020, phosphate (P205) at 411 and potash K20 at 76 all in metric tonnes.

Soil Conservation Department with a view to curtail the bad effects of jhum, has launched projects to distribute lands to farmers and extend to them the better amenities of a settled agriculture. Each family besides being entitled 2 hectares of land, are given several kinds of subsidised assistance in the shapes of fertilizers, implements, seeds for the first term of three years and under the so-called package programme, 50 families can develop into a settlement and communication through link roads is proposed to be extended. At least 9,000 or 10,000 families are scheduled to benefit under the sixth plan target. Hundreds and hundreds of hectares of land have been covered under the schemes known as reclamation, terracing, afforestation and irrigation.

Training and Experimentation

Agriculture can also be envisaged in the light of training and experimentation. The Conservation Training Institute a residential institute at Byrni although involved in silviculture and forestry is also concerned with agricultural utilisation directly or indirectly. It is admitted that fruit experimental station started as early as 1913 by Mr. Holder at Shillong was considerable helpful to initiating horticulture on some lines with regard to modern fruits. It was taken over by Government only in 1930.

There was a small fruit farm at Upper Shillong and most probably, it was converted in 1966 into. Research Station and taken over more recently by ICARU Jeebon Roy, years before Mr. Holder, is known to have taken initiative to introduce modern fruit plantation in Shillong and her suburbs. Demonstration centres on various fruit plantations have recently been set up and horticulture training courses are arranged from time to time to give incentives to fruit growers on various technique, and processes. Indian Council of Agricultural Research has also launched programmes for training' and experimentation. There were only two Government and two private fruit processing factories till 1978. Fruit surpluses are handled by middle men who distribute them to wholesalers and who in turn, transact them to small retailers and prices due to cultivators are considerably squeezed.

Few of the factories are located at Shillong and Dainadubi in Garo Hills. Most of the orchards and groves in the south have been severely affected by pests and the yields have considerably been squeezed. There is a central Potato Research Station in Shillong engaged in giving scientific protection and conserving better processes and standards in identification, selection and obtaining intensive farming operations.

The seminar held in 1987 opines among all problems that Agricultural Marketing is the greatest handicap, trade being the monopoly of private traders centrally located, these have the more advantageous position while the poor farmers labouring so hard are completely deprived of obtaining good prices. Lack of infrastructure facilities to transport, transaction and marketing has affecting adversely upon the poor farming community. Meghalaya does not have the required base and the infrastructural facilities for the organised agricultural marketing.

Over 92 nos. primary market attached to rural places exist and conditions have not been better despite the functioning of MECOFED started in 1975 for offering better prices to surplus agriculture and minor forest produces, distributing some agricultural inputs and extending better facilities to farmers. The need to setting up a Potato Depot at Upper Shillong for protecting the poor potato farmers has been voiced up by the public. The administration now is envisaging on the installation of regulated markets at Mawiong and Garobadha.

Along with these, improving the efficiency of farm managements in Meghalaya in which agricultural holding are small, is urged and insisted upon. The fertilizer nutrients for the time being which assist in the system of crop rotation in the double or multiple cropping and ensuring quantitative yields are also highlighted. Agriculture is the basic occupation occupying 70 or 80 per cent of the population. The simultaneous need to initiate the efficient management of horticulture, wet and dry rice farming, vegetable and admixed plantations, strengthening other plantation bases, intensification of new crops suited to the soils, some of which have been affected and others not yet, has been envisaged. Implementation of schemes on top priority footing with a view to contain the future prosperity or security is heretofore attached with great importance.

Closely connected with agriculture is the importance of livestock and pisiculture. Cattle, pigs, poultry although intensively reared in the past, the value of livestock at present has dwindled beyond doubt. Herds of these at one time had their considerable importance in the sacrificial rites and divination; a great proportion of them was needed at feasts and festivals; they provided the items of family menu, a considerable importance, therefore was also attached to the livestock. A contrast in the situation has become formidable so that herds of cattle, pigs, goats and in massive numbers are now daily brought over from outside for butchering and commercial transactions. Meat markets now depend for the largest supply upon the breeds imported. Frequent epidemics have also caused their great scarcity. The Khasis follow a scientific system of meat utilisation and skin scrapings for keeping meats clean. Cold storages evidently have not been generally, used. However, the traditional and improved system of pig-sites and poultry sheds is now followed and the local breeds have now their great commercial viability; the indigenous breeds highly considered for their nutritious value also supplement the imported stocks.

On the qualitative improvement, it has been felt that "incentives in dairying, improvement of non-descript cows, keeping with other norms in forage production, preservation, utility, curtailing pests and diseases, need their wider adoption. Other

226 Meghalaya

connected schemes such as animals health coverage, artificial insemination, fodder production need to be intensified. Skills in milking, catering and supply are generated. Butter and ghee are the items of dairying necessitating the use of equipages for processing, manufacturing, etc. The pattern of efficient management of dairying activities, coverage projects for assessing best nutrients for care and growth and disease control facilities, have been dwelt upon". Animal hides and hairs when extracted are also valuable items and fetch good income to butchers.

The dairy farming now can be categorised as traditional, improved and scientific. In spite of the vast potentialities and the suitability of establishing ranches at shrub lands, grasslands or otherwise, the statistics as early as 1977 show a poor return in the number of livestock as follows:

		Khasi Hills	Jaintia Hills	Garo Hills
1.	Cattle	1,65,000	82,000	1,82,000
2.	Buffaloes	13,000	1,000	25,000
3.	Sheep	21,000	500 or less	23,000
4.	Goats	69,000	16,000	33,000
5.	Horses and Ponies	7,000	500 or less	500 or less
6.	Pigs	76,000	27,000	42,000
7.	Poultry	4,95,000	1,24,000	4,43,000

It was reported also that over 160 to 175 weekly/daily markets existed. The veterinary staff appears to have been comparatively small as there was only 1 veterinary hospital and 38 dispensaries and doctors or surgeons being reduced only to 70 men strength.

Some of the institutions can as much briefly be located as follows:

There is a central dairy near Mawiong, Shillong which supplies chilled milk to the city. A regional cross breeding and cattle breeding farm exists at Kyrdem Kulai. The other cattle farms are the Indo-Danish project lying at Upper Shillong and livestock farm at Tura. The main sheep and goat farm has been established at Saitsama. The several poultry or pig farms also exist at Tura, Nongstoin, Pynursla and are distributed also at the selected interior places. A scientific system of meat preservation is conspicuous by its absence and very few local persons have taken themselves to milking and improvise dairying enterprises. All patterns of dairying, therefore, have their basic importance in the present situation.

The new to upkeeping and improving the efficient managements of the various units has arisen. These include the intensification of strength in key village blocks, Indo-Danish project, bull calf upgrading, livestock farms, feed mills, fodder farms, sheep farms and extension units, poultry farms and central hatchery, applied nutrition, pig farms and piggery development blocks, veterinary health centres and extension units, veterinary hide centre, clinical laboratory, mobile dispensaries, vaccine depots, disease detection processes, training of staff, students, farmers, milk supply and dairy centres, creamery and ghee making, mode and demonstration centres etc which the state possesses.

Milk ('000 tonnes) - 1979 - '80 - 52.50 against 100.40 total

Meat ('000 tonnes) - 1979 - '80 -18.40 against 36.10 total

Eggs (Million) - 1979 - '80 - 33.25 against 40.20 total

Animal entrails show good commercial value (chart below):

Hides	-	3,200 pieces	-	Rs. 1,28,000
Tongues	-	6,400	-	Rs. 12,000
				(Mawlai slaughter house)
Intestines	-	16,000 kg	-	Rs. 10,000
Livers	-	14,400 kg	-	Rs. 10,000
Hearts	-	1,000 kg	-	Rs. 57,000

(These statistics taken more than a decade ago; prices must have doubled now. Bones are utilised for manufacturing cattle foddes, fertilizers, etc.

Meat shortages can better be understood as the local resources could hardly cater to 60 per cent against the total requirements:

Sericulture

Traditional sericulture and weaving now exist in a limited degree; however, weaving has been constrained by many factors. Eri, cotton and to some extent muga are used for weaving clothes.

Items of traditional dress consist of ryndia lieh or plain white shawl, ryndia stem, a plain shawl, cream colour, ryndia thoh saw thoh stem (chequered yellow, red in squares), Khyrwan (chequered red and white) and thoh saru (a loongi or blouse in black and white).

S. Khongsit mentions the Bhoi pattern as follows: Phali, (a loongi carrying the figures of trees, insects, animals); Pakhar tympha (a girdle or belt), spur, a plain, white or cream colour sheet, jyngki or jymphong or a dark sleeveless coat, D. T. Laloo mentions Pyrthoh Nonfitluh (a white mantle with red stripes leaving soft knotted threads at the two ends as in the case of jainsem or ryndia), jaineeing (a dark mantle cut crosswise by red stripes) and khyndop slory is plain white. Decorations are three-fold; Khmat shrieh designed like thorns, sladieng like rectangular marks, Khmat lyngngoh like crosses.

The decline of weaving is now clearly indicated. It exists barely only in a few families following its tradition.

The typical models are ryndia (appropriately the eri), khor or nare (appropriately the fine silk variety) and the sala (appropriately the cotton). The silk patterns therefore, are sai-pat, a fine silk, sar, a coarse silk and kem khap which is another superior grade. Some of the models are jain — it a sort of strap or sash, thain dop a loin cloth, jain — pein a sort of girdle and tawah or a wrap and various caps are made from cotton. A valued embroidered pattern of loongi is subon matching itself with a typical colour combination. The dominant women's dress is jainsem an apron double wrapped hung from the shoulders and dropped downward to the legs forming a great length, woven from a superior silk and forming a sheet dyed in many hues.

The hems on all borders leave the intricately woven designs in silver and gold threads. They carry the traditional design of a standing lion with its raised tail alternating, with flower designs, the other side shows signs of a diamond lattice designed of silver and gold threads. There are jainsems made of muga cream colour leaving two bands of deep red colour on its border. Men at dances and festivals wear jainsem like a dhoti. About mantles again, there are ryndia lieh or plain white and ryndia or brownish cream colour. Khor a sort of a Chinese brocade multi coloured is worn as a turban by princes and rish dancers. The other dress items consist of banat or cotton satin, velvet and others.

We find that the modern dress has been influenced by new taste, fashion and availability of cheaper mill made garments. The traditional dancing, festival and agricultural uniforms (used at agricultural dances and celebrations particularly in Bhoi and Synteng), count essentially. Dress appropriated for indoor and outdoor use, wedding and auspicious events, cultural functions and state dances and festivals is variegated. Indeed dance (as has been hitherto referred to in some monographs) glows at its best in which dancers wear so rich their colourful festival robes and attires woven out of the best silk, cotton, eri and other constituents, sets of these jewelleries, ornaments and customs have been treasured and are the best among the heirloom and museum pieces.

Pisciculture

Little is heard about progress in pisciculture. The Khasi fisher men and women catch fish through various methods of ankling employing baits with some wild fruits, Kber or insects, grams, plants, worms, etc. Reeling and traditional fashions of fishing exist. They lay down weirs and fish traps of several kinds. Hill fingerlings, prawns and carps greatly relished, are many. In the border on large and swift rivers, fishes are in common variety with those we see in the plain. At Wards' Lake Shillong big fishes looking like black masheers are seen. At farm lake, Laitumkhrah, some carps, of mixed variety are seen.

Some fishes of silver colour are brought from the lake, a water reservoir from dam site within the confines of the Umiam Hydel Project. Fishes have become clever and avoid baits tugged into fishing hooks in rivers we are told. They also use fishing nets and employ various strategies for big catches and horns are made also into knife boards, handles, musical instruments, etc, hides are turned into footwears, straps, bags, etc.

Simple Preservation

A system of simple preservation is followed. Fish cut like small straps is sunned in winter time. Fish lengthwise held by a stick is also bakod at a fire place. Fish is also exposed to kitchen smoke for procuring dry fishes. They turn out dried fish in redhot stones. Besides various means, the Garos also preserve fish in the bamboo chungas. Some families smoke the fish first before boiling, frying or cooking into curry. The exotic fishes of hill and plain variety against the natural lakes, bhils and breeding places in the hill rivers can be properly conserved and intermingled. Therefore, the essence of keeping fisheries at towns and villages against the water reservoirs that can be tapped can be intensified. But perhaps very little has been done. In these circumstances, to start with, a pisciculture Research Centre at Mawpun has been installed and is now developing into a research cum fish seed production and training centre. The project towards a composite fish culture and breathing fish culture can be undertaken now both at the public and private scale.

Forestry

The services of Forestry are very important. Forest since time immemorial provide great resources. Forest wealth in the shape of timber and flora is greatly valued. Bulk of the forests, grazing, buildings, constructions and other installation and communications and have aptly found their place for other purposes. The process now owing to a heavy population explosions caused at present is continuing. In the process of exploitation which has continued through the ages. Some of the forests have been turned to barren lands, many of them have also been converted to thin grasslands and shrub lands. Forests provide us with many of our innumerable species of fauna and flora.

They provide us the recreational games and sports. Forests provide us with different wildlife species which have their great utilitarian uses. Some of the best forests in the state due to the wanton destruction of timber have quickly disappeared. A very viable planning with regard to the issue of displacement and replacement of forest trees has become so indispensible nowadays. Despite the process of elimination of forest lands with their precious species which abound, we still see a number of timber stations existing on the main District roads and it appears that a huge traffic in timber is in process. Export of timber exists by no means in a limited scale.

The grades of forest which exist under the Department are Reserved, Protected and Unclassed. There are the Protected forests under the District Councils. Bulk of the forests, therefore, are privately owned and managed at the individual, family and community levels. Timber species which find relevance are Teak wood, Sal wood, Ply wood and quick growing forest trees. The utilitarian general grades are timber and firewood. Some of the products known are broomstick, match, agar, rosaltia, serpintina, resin, chip, and cane.

The forest products have been reduced obviously in number. The utility of the various medicinal plants has earlier been referred to. Moreover, forests are the homes of various green vegetable and herbous plants. Edible tubers are many. The Department is envisaging a number of utilitarian schemes for the proper maintenance and expansion of forests. The general concept of planning is for elevating tree plantation at the different private levels. This follows the uniform pattern of planning and decision. One of the targets is by disseminating the valuable propaganda to the public to preserving forests and enriching them with frequent plantations. The concept of ecology, environment and social forestry has become indispensible against the present complexes.

Updated Schemes

The Department is seeking to update certain schemes for increasing the plantations and extending their coverages within the framework of their policy of what is known as replacement of poorer strands by a qualitative pattern of richer timber, by strengthening the target of quick growing species, by creating blocks for farm forestry and fuel wood plantation and strengthening the technical and research capability in the different specialised fields. It is anticipated that these steps taken will help to procure better results. Improvement of the qualitative patterns of forest produce is expected to yield good results in the management of forestry. Construction of good forest roads can conveniently cater to these new emerging needs. Approximately only about one twelfth of forests is under the Departmental management. The following quotation may also help us to highlight on the problem of forest based industry on the whole:

> There may be need therefore to restrict timber traffic outside the hills. Different levels of exploitation should and ought to be determined consistently for construction, industrial installation, supply of fuel and charcoal, cabinet making and other concerns. There is need to secure a more purposeful plantation of trees in wastelands, house compounds and gardens. The forests destroyed need replantation.

From the available timber from small reserves, the establishment of small scale pharmaceutical industries, saw mills, furniture and fixtures, match and paper installations and other small scale industries may be kept in mind. A long-term planning is indispensable.

Small wood-crafts both traditional and modern can be developed on emporium basis along both toys, decorative arts and other articles, it will be necessary of course to make the emporia viable and capable of good business. The constitution of Forest Development Corporation is anticipated to accelerate various kinds of development in forestry and in particular determine special resources for the development of the forest industry.

Bamboo grows wild and some are specially grown. Meghalaya is rich in the varied kinds of bamboo. Some species include Ryngngai, a hard stem with thin leaves, Tyr-a, a kind of jungle cane, Siej Shrah, a hard stem with longer spans, Tyrlaw, prevalent in West Khasi Hills, Skong, a thin stem somewhat corky bark, Siej, a small smooth stem, Siej lieh, (a Koka Specie), Ry-ia-n, a thin bamboo with fewer leaves), Nam land, very small tender shoot, Japung, similar to a raddan plant, Kdait, (akra) and Sylli similar to Japung, Lana, a sort of broomstick, siej iong, used as chunga, and tube for carrying water, Shken, this has a smooth skin, Siej bri considered as an inferior bamboo, Rimet and Riphin, these are canes. Ryngngai, this is used for constructions, Try-a, this is used for making fences, barns and walls, Trylaw, this is very good for factorial use and paper making, Ry-ia-in, this is used as a string for moulding and wrapping, Kdait, this is good for making house walls, Bamboo shoots or Lung siej, for making condiments, is seen on the north, Straw or a Sder and Tynriew a palm growing in the south are good for thatching housing.

Garo Hills are rich in bamboo and cane. Some of them include also a few species resembling Khasi bamboo and cane. As bamboo groves occupy a good quantum of forest lands, now steps further can be taken to develop other small scale or supplementary mills.

Rich People

The Garos are also rich in the various forms of bamboo culture. There are many kinds of constructions made from bamboo and various kinds basket and craft and mat making. The semi-tropical climatic conditions characterise the bamboo culture and influence the growth of a rich variety, on difficulties to transact bamboo for trade. J. D. Marak opined in the Assam Assembly thus:" I have learnt that the extraction of bamboos from the Garo Hills is a very difficult one and that a man with the good experience, of the work would be necessary. The next point is the difficulty of transportation to the nearest railway station. If the bamboos are to be, taken in a wet condition, their weight will be very much. The most important difficulty of all is to get the necessary capital to undertake the work. So my point is this; the material is there, the labour is there but only capital is wanting. So I would ask, whether it will be possible for the government also, as the Bengal Government has done to lend a sufficient sum for this purpose, either with or without interest or a small rate of interest.

"Sir, some changes are coming in the Garo Hills. I had a long talk yesterday morning with Mr. Smith, the joint conservator of forests, regarding Garo Hills affairs. He explained in detail what was his programme about cultivation, about Mahaldari system, about royalty, about reserve, etc. He also proposed to increase the number of forest reserved .... I told him this much, I hope you will do this much in concurrence with the India government's order I have read before the House during my budget speech."

The development trends on the structures essential to economic reconstruction in these days of planning and developmental work can be reiterated that the sectors mainly cover Community Development, Transport and Communications, Trade and Industry.

9

Polity

Government and Administration

The administration in Meghalaya, is unique. It is a three tier system; the power of administration, therefore, vests mainly in the State Government, the District Councils and the old States or elakaships still existing. This makes it difficult to coordinate sometimes the power and function of these bodies and at times saps the considerable energy and attention to finding out the correct modalities. Now, the system of local polity in which the indigenous democratic elements, traits, traditions still dominate, will be dealt with.

The indigenous institutions which exist side by side with the present Parliamentary system have survived as the form of the ancient polity. State herein refers to entities which we call Syiemships, Lyngdohsips, Wahdadars. Each has its defined territories jurisdiction; it also applies the population distributed in towns, villages and hamlets located within its territorial boundary and displays the civic organisation of its own. Evidently, Sirdarships, Daloiships, Wadadarships and minor syiemships are in size small but some Kingdoms such Khyrim, Nongkhlaw, Mylliem, Nongstion, Maharam are large occupying the great length and breadth of the districts. The large number of villages comprised in them justify their existence as the veritable states.

The Difficulties

There are difficulties to give a correct interpretation to one of the purest and virile forms of democracy which existed in the past. This is because democracy has suffered stress and strains owing to the changes which have occurred in the present situation in which the concepts and standards of democracy are fast degenerating. And with them, the whole structure of community discipline and public morality essential to it has become distorted. Moreover the tribe since the decades past are acquainted to the system of Parliamentary democracy enshrined in the Constitution.

There are now 25 existing states, 16 of which are Syiemships, 1 is Wahdadarship, 3 are Lyngdohships and 6 Sirdarships. Other Non-states comprise 32 villages in Khasi Hills District and 20 Daloiships in Jaintia Hills District. Daloiships are elakas, each comprised of a group of villages. Sirdars and Dalois in non-states have powers similar to those of Laskars. The recent abolition of privy purses did not effect the Khasi Syiemships.

Among these units, let us treat of Syiemship first.

The Syiem is the head of the state; he runs day-to-day administration, the Cabinet assisting him which functions extend to the administration of the markets, collections of judicial fines, etc. He takes up judicial cases from various units and villages in which he acts as a judge and his council as jury. He has limited powers. He is maintained by levies returned from some of the markets, the market levies sometime being shared with his Myrrtris (Ministers). Judicial fines also constitute the other source of income. He gets income also from imposts levied on distilleries. He has no law-making power, his authority is clearly defined which extends over the departments assigned to him.

The state is known as Hima implying itself (in Pre British times) a sovereign body with organic and ethical unity while the people are called *Ki Khun Ki Hajar* which means children. They are exempted from paying taxes while tributary subjects are obliged to pay taxes.

However, there is a Syiem-Sad, a mother, aunt or sister of syiem who is regarded as the custodian of state ceremonies and title-holder of crown lands. A Syiem-sad is a spiritual head of the state who derives that status from the State Council which delegates the ruling power to LT Syiem and the sacerdotal function to Ka Syiem-Sad.

Dual System

In a few states, a dual system of Syiemship still operates, i.e., two Syiem families carry out jointly the administration in which the two assigned royal houses either share market levies or assign respective portfolios and subjects. In Maharam Syiemship, the old arrangement was that one family furnished the actual Syiem and the other, the Deputy Syiem. In Maharam and Nobosohphon States, the two families ruling jointly are called Syiem-lien and Syiem-iohg. The former are the Dholah Rajahs and the latter are the Kalah Rajah. The Syiems, in these States, however, did not belong to a common origin. Market imports are shared amongst them.

At the background, the existing communities and village organisations known as Basanships or Lyngdohships preceded Syiem-Ship which in course of tune were absorbed, when it was formed which put an end to their sovereign status. The Syiem belonged to the royal house founded in consequence of the contractual allegiance, conventions and covenants in which several village chieftains joined and formed a State and delegated special powers to the royal house. Thus communes, sub-Syiemships and other units became integrated into one kingdom. The history of some great states dates back to thousands of years.

At the state level, the two most important institutions are the Electoral College and the Cabinet, but in a few states the latter performs the functions of the former. The electoral Council consists of hereditary heads of clans or heads of units, the composition of size varying from State to State. This council is responsible for electing and crowning the Syiem with the approval of the people. In the event, other complications arose, the Council refer the matter to the people whose decision was final. In Langrin a direct election exists in which all male adults in that state meet and elect the Syiem themselves. The Khasi States Federation at the interim period adopted the following arrangement in matters relating to the choice of the Syiems.

- In these nine states-Cherra, Khyrim, Nongkhlaw, Mylliem, Nongstoin, Rambrai, Myriaw, Maharam, Malai-Sohmat, the nomination of the Syiems rests with the majority of the small electoral body which is recognised in each State.

- In the case of Nongspung, Mawiang, Nobosohphoh, Bhowal and Mawsynram, nomination in the first instance is with the small electoral bodies in each State, but that in the event of their votes not being unanimous, the decision should, in the first four cases, be by popular suffrage, while in the case of Mawsynram it would rest with the government.

That in the single State of Langrin where no small electoral body is recognised, the Syiem should be chosen by popular suffrage. Besides the electoral body, there is a State Cabinet. It is headed by powerful hereditary chiefs; a few States have chamberlains. States follow the old usage of ascribing portfolios of administration to the State Ministers of different titles such as Basans, Lyngdohs, Dalois, Lyngskors and others. A few of their are heads of communes. With the Syiems, they execute justice, supervise and superintend the administration of markets, collection of market tolls and judicial fines. Some communes are still headed by persons of royal blood called *U Syiem Shnat* or *Syiem Raid*.

Basanships, Lyngdohship or Daloiships are graded as communes following an official title of its head, the commune implying itself a division or a sub-state with a number of village heads each falling under its head. Village heads are elected according to the different usages, some elected by families, some elected by people on the basis of male adult franchise. A Lyngdoh, the head of the state (viz. Lyngdohship representing his priestly family) is elected by all the adult males of his Hima or State.

These elders and officials are assigned land holdings or shares of market levies or dividends accruing from the excavation of minerals and forests and some share grazing tax. As is customary, delegates from their respective units hand over to the Syiem sacrificial animals and other kinds of tithes. All categories of land holdings are never taxed. Local units or communes and villages are autonomous.

In non-Syiemships, for instance in Shella, the four Wahdadars, the heads of Shella Wahdadarship (Confederacy) are elected by the people. In Sirdarship (Non-Syiemships) a similar system is followed, i.e., the Sirdar is elected by the people of his Sirdarship. No family qualification is necessary. A Lyngdoh, like a Jaintia Daloi, is elected from his respective mother's clan or legitimate groups of clans by the people themselves. All male adults above 18 are eligible to vote for the appointment of their rulers.

Owing to the matrilineal set up, a Syiem is succeeded by his nephew or grandnephew or by his own brother as succession is reckoned through the woman. This rule subsists in appointments to all offices in the state.

Features of Democracy

Another feature of Khasi democracy is the participation of the entire population in moulding policies, legislation and judicial decision at their durbars on a principle of decentralisation than centralisation of powers.

Durbars are numerous. The Durbar Hima Pyllun means a full Syiemship Durbar in which the population of the state participate. To it come all the male residents from whatever place but in view of difficulties with regard to organising such a vast gathering, only village delegates, local officials and heads of clans-are returned and is called *Ka Durbar Ki Shonong*, a durbar of villages.

The durbar in the past assumed all the vital matters, determined foreign policy, decided questions of war and peace and solved judicial problems. Today it is still held to approve of or veto proposals laid down by the State Executive Councils. It hears complaints against some illegal actions of Syiems or officials, it hears rival complaints amongst officials. It acts as a Supreme Court and constitutes a real Parliament. It may even veto the appointment of Syiems and officials who on its resolution may be removed. It controls the purse of the states; in the past in times of war it decided lines of strategy, equipments of troops and volunteers and instructed the units to deal with the situation. This durbar, does not meet frequently nowadays.

At the District level there is a Durban Raid (commune), its composition varies from place to place. It is a Durban of a Unit or a commune or any part there of which constitutes a subunit.

The Syiem and his Council does not interfere in subjects within its jurisdiction in matters such as forest, communications, markets and law which belong to it while as a court of justice, settles judicial cases within its jurisdiction. It approves appointment of any official before referring to the State Council.

The Durbar

The Village has its own durbar which holds frequent sessions in which all male adult residents ought to attend. It imparts some training in the art of Self-Government and creative citizenship and guides or directs the standard of public morality. This durbar functions as a court of justice by taking criminal and civil cases and judicial disputes, besides handling law and public administration.

The decisions of State Councils in the distant past, fixed by usage in concurrent matters relating to judiciary, foreign relations and communications and markets could not be overridden by local durbars. A Khasi State therefore, takes the form of a confederation, the federating units owing allegiance to the Syiem only is a common matters, the Syiem's moral duty is to keep alive the unity of the state.

The Syiem is surrounded by a body of messengers whose special duties are to convey messages to nearby and distant places within his realm for holding a durbar at appointed dates. Basans, Sirdars and Lyngdoh also as appropriate officials have their respective messengers and volunteers to relay the message in turn on the village on the durbar's sitting, the inhabitants are forbidden to go anywhere and do their day's job. They are required to cancel their business, stop cutting wood and going to market, stop drawing water and all other engagements. No one can go on leave from the session. Everyone ought to contribute to the deliberation in the durbar in order to ensure success. According to strict usages observed rigidly, absentees are fined or expelled from their habitations.

A Syiem or a Deputy Syiem presides over the durbar; a local Syiem or chieftain presides over the local durbar while village durbars are conducted by respective headmen. The subject for the debate is introduced in a presidential message; other spokesmen are engaged for clarification of some issues which are associated. Deliberations in form of debates then follow and interpellations are raised; trained and eloquent debaters called *Rangsaids* lead as movers for and against the motion. Traditions state that session which would not terminate in a day is adjourned till midnight, fires are served to light up the sittings.

Durbars are usually held in the open and constitute typical open-door councils. The councillors sit in concentric rows. Voting usually is indicated by the counting of heads which is always preferred to raising of hands. Women are excluded from such sessions but in some places they are allowed to listen to the debates as observers.

Strict rules prescribed, should be observed. The durbar is called *Ka Durbar Ki blei*, the durbar of the gods. Attendants should conform to fixed disciplinary rules of conduct in entering the debate which should be systematic and orderly, so as to precluded unseemly shouting or vociferous demonstration, irrelevant expressions and unwise exclamations. Treating the Court of Durbar with contempt amounts to ex-communication from the society in which the victim loses his right of citizenship. Abuses and counter-abuses, personal attacks, disparaging remarks, scathing criticism, insinuations, sarcasm and conspiracies are unlawful and persons using such base means are severely dealt with. Strong rules are imposed to penalise any point of contempt. The judicial durbar sponsored by the Syiem, acts as a Court of justice which irrespective of its powers reduced, is still convened on the occasions when the local authorities fail to dispose of some intricate and technical problems associated with the case.

Nowadays, the Syiem and his Mantris constitute the Court of appeal, and many cases are dealt with by them without referring to durbars of the entire population, as was done in the past. Thus the Syiem's Court is possessed with appellate jurisdiction and authority inside the state. This has resulted from the recognition of Government and District Courts as more powerful than the state courts. The Syiems and heads of small States have been given magisterial powers as defined in the rules. The Courts of Syiems are prescribed to take up the cases within certain limits. The Court of the District Council is now possessed of judicial functions which supersede the State Courts. But village durbars still function as judicial Courts to decide cases and execute justice inside their respective units. Appeals to the Syiem's court are sent only if the village durbar fails to decide cases which are either complicated or lay beyond the scope of their powers.

W. Robinson remarked many years ago that on the day of the sitting of a judicial durbar, villagers stopped to do their work and it was compulsory and binding on their part by law to attend and witnesses raised and the Chief at the close summarised the pronounced judgement. Describing its sitting, he said that the durbar was "something probably after the fashion of the ancient Druids, or as was the custom of the Greeks when the herald spoke, the aged judges sat on squared stone, in circle for debates".

Judicial fines in the pass varied from a few Rupees to Rs. 1,100.00 in the latter cases if crimes were serious. Life imprisonment, expatriation and keeping in stocks (Pyndait diengsong) were the severest forms of penalty. Prisoners were kept inside the cave. Death sentences in the past were not absent, criminals being beaten to death with clubs or by being pushed from over a precipice. Death sentences were served with executions also. Even at present, democratic traits still survive; to quote from a Report of the Committee on Special Multi-purpose Tribal Blocks issued by the Ministry of Home Affairs, New Delhi on the aspects of a Khasi Durbar: "Every village is traditionally governed by a durbar which consists of all the adult male members of village... the durbar chooses its own office bearers.

The durbars have recently been recognised by Government through an Act passed by the District Council and they have powers to inflict fines up to Rs. 50.00 ... There was a case in Mairang itself where a man was fined Rs. 450, and paid up, since otherwise he would have been excommunicated by village community. The durbaris see to everything, they coordinate every aspect of Khasi life, settle disputes and have always looked after the forests, water supply and such community services". Only a few states such as Mylliem and Khyrim now have a formal police force.

Preceding Families

Families which preceded others in settlement are called *Ki Khun Nyngkong* (or literally the first children or group of the first citizens) who have continued to enjoy special privileges of citizenship. The next group which joined them are called *Ki Khun Pdeng* (the second children or citizens) and the last batch are called *Ki Khun Khaduh* (youngest children). These groups paid no tax whatever and were copartners with the Syiem in running the administration, Military clans were entitled to a noble status in recognition of their service in defending their land. Seniority in occupation of the land was, therefore, a criterion which determined citizenship. But contribution of invaluable service in both welfare and warfare were other conditions that qualified settlers to become citizens.

Khasi emigrants are known as *Khun Soh Syiem*; they pay no tax but are bound to recognise the state by paying Ka Pynshok which is graded as protection fee and is not classed as tax or revenue. Another group of citizens is called *Khun Shnat* (tributary). They were the latest group who joined the state and become naturalised citizens. Non-Khasis inside the Syiemships, Wahdadarship and Sirdarships enjoy a large measure of autonomy. Their village units even today are governed by their headman (Gaonburas or Malvis or Gramanis), return small taxes to the Syiems and dignitaries and report cases. In the Bangladesh border, not only land-grants (for the construction of mosques and temples) but fisheries and a small proportion of land called *Khas* land free of cost, for public use leave been assigned.

Land tenure — the original classification of land was two-fold-Ri Kurs and Ri-Raids (Rajs); the former belonged to the whole clan, held in a collective possession; the latter was a village land held in joint ownership by a single village or group of Villages and was managed by either village or State authority. It was meant to be distributed to subsequent new settlers who would be entitled a permanent ownership if they conformed to prescribed rules and usages in exchange for the protection granted to from by the state. They were required to pay a Pynshok, a tributary fee, to the state. Those settlers might be awarded with membership in State Council if their conduct was satisfactory. In its original concept, State constituted a sort of nobody's land kept apart for new settlers. It is important to note that the usages governing free occupation of laid lands and inheritance to them are still in force today. Several plots of Ri-Kurs in the form of ancestral land become inherited and become Ri Kynti or family land as distinct from ancestral land. Another class of land, Ri-Seng, which is prevalent in the South is also a clan's land held in collective ownership and management. Ri-Khein, yet another class, constitutes a land jointly possessed by a particular group. Sacred groves known as Law Lyngdok are prohibited for public use.

State Features

State festivals held annually were equally reinvigorating. Bulk of these were held all over the kingdom approximately till the close of the last century. The only surviving among them are the Khyrim festival at the royal residence in Smit and Sajer Raid Nonglyngdoh in Bhoi. The festivals have been intended to impart the spirit of oneness. They afford the unique a seasons where the appropriate delegations come to State headquarters to join the royal house in offering thanks giving to God. At these festivities, Goat sacrifices, dances and other rituals are highlighted at a week long celebration. In Bhoi Sub-Syiemships many of these age old celebrations still persist.

State festivals combine the inherent features of statehood. The congregation with the different troupes collected from near and far perform their sacred obligations and cope with many activities. They centre on community mindedness, moods, temperaments with their own social and cultural priestess assisted by festive and orchestral music conductors, craftsmen and sacrificers are concerned in these state celebrations, demonstrations, performances. The festival is a chain of prayers, coupled with sacrifices rites combined with processions. The Syiem's representatives look into providing the ceremonial costumes, jewelleries, equipages for the orderliness and consistency of the ceremonies performed one followed by the other, until exhausted in a weekly celebration or so.

There are cases when the Syiem performs these rites jointly with the heads of communes or conducts them separately. Sacrifices of hegoats and animals furnished by the royal house, the other appropriate families or communes or delegates and dances performed community wise or in separate groups are the other attributes. Festival music presented at long stretches highly invocative, dominate the scene besides which verbal recitals and intercessions also feature. The interludes highly symbolic are filled in with other engagements. The festivities breath with the radiance of sets of robes and jewelleries worn on their persons. Definitely it is the system of benevolent form of Kingship upon which, these arts and traditions inculcated, mark it strongly.

The great art tradition of Khyrim state, therefore, still leaves its impression. Drums beaten in so many different styles as matching with their decorum, provide the background to all the rituals in order of the ceremony. They govern the main events in their different transitions connected with the corporal undertaking which the state priestdom, royalty and the delegations entitled to it, are involved to run it from year to year. Dances depict call to and responses from the delegations of state assemblies, mutual salutations and represent the community processes and state formation.

Dances presented as marches, erossed dances, dances into other directions, ceremonies conducts are highly vibrating and symbolic. Dances integrated among the nobles, among them and the King among the nobles and commoners, throw a variegated meaning. Dances in groups and circles are also enlivening, on the last day, the princes dances matching with her royal status in the company of the virgin ladies and men young and old. The system of investiture ceremony also applied to Dalois, Wadadars, Sirdars and Lyngdohs on their being elected to office. State coronations of Kings as rule are pompous and solemn as we see it performed during the coronation of Balajied Singh the present

Syiem of Khyrim which occurred in August 1978. The ceremony started with the performances of purgatory lites held indoor; the reception of delegations who were originally the custodians of the state, even was matching to the occasion. The outdoor celebrations conducted at the house balcony in which the coronation ceremony was performed was both colourful and solemn. It was featured by a series of the public proclamation interspersed with the sounds of gunshots brokens out in the stage of anointment; the formal crowning was symbolised by placing a wound turban over the crowned King's head; this also symbolised the delegation of ruling power to the crowned.

The State rose to ovations when the drummers present their percussional hits. These are just some of the impressions. The Syiem accompanied by the Queen mother the Syiem-Sad and a retinue from the royal house in the actual crowning performed by the State Lyngskor amply indicates the richness of the state heritage of the elaborate system of Kingship which keeps itself in tune with the democratic traditions of the people. Another impression is that the torch fire bearers even at the midday seek ceremonially to illumine the coronation. The ceremonies held in the presence of a great assembly and in the presence of the Government and District Council dignitaries have equally their impact in formulating the concept of the state polity.

The State system of allegiance is symbolised by the distribution of costumes performed by the Queen and handing over them to the nobles. The colourful dances that feature in the last part of the programme added to the rejoicing and ovation of the state over the coronation of a syiem.

At many villages some of these practices are enlivening. In other places democracy tends to become more superficially than functionally complied with the regard to enforcing its rules and tenets. The durbars apparently have become more responsibly observed and their decisions become more seriously pronounced when the community is aroused with the crucial situation and vital matters affecting life and death. The voluntary and welfare norms mostly in urbanised settlements have suffered serious set-backs. The present politics seem to have been disastrous to the public cause and some of them are constructive enough. These degenerating standards are now a matter of grave concern to the serious and conscious citizens. Unless the strong community discipline is now reimposed, the politics as such will fail to pay their dividends. Initiative seriously taken could help to boost public programmes, develop the moral taste and behavioural norms and ensure security to the locality against certain pressing troubles.

Some of the town durbars in Shillong and village durbars outside function themselves in much the traditional fashion or style. There is an executive body which assists the headman or chief and a full durbar is convened annually. Executive durbars as in the case of state highest councils are held indoor but the full locality/ village durbar is held outdoor. This durbar veto or approve the appointment of a headmen and executive members. It initiate programmes in water supply, sanitation, street lighting, road repairs, any other welfare, recreational and cultural activities. The durbar enjoy their magisterial and even the informal police powers to combat with crimes and settle disputes and enforce rules for ensuring good and sound conduct.

Successful Implementation

The success in implementing these decisions depends fully upon the public support and backing up. The services of strong voluntary youth and women's wings in town locality and village durbars has become absolutely necessary. The task of the headman and the Executive Committee Members is purely honorary. They are not paid salaries. Boosting these organisations to greater attainments in the village social legislation, administration, judiciary, social welfare services is a must to the present situation.

Village polity among the old Garos centered round the Nokmas. The person of a Nokma was considered sacred; he was virtually autocratic and wielded power in a village community. Yet in practice he was not all powerful. In performing religious duties, he was advised by the priests and abide by the advice of clansmen.

There were other limitations and restraints imposed by customary laws. In the past, at their confederations, Nakmas used to meet on their council sittings and resolved upon certain issues. Their decisions conveyed, it was for the people to approve or veto them. Nokmas were supposed to be persons of great talents possessed with the sterling qualities of head and heart. The definition given by Rongmuthu on the functions of the Nokmas is embracing. He observes the title has seven meanings:

- A King Nokrna-one who keeps the A-King land of his village on behalf of the chatchi or mahari to which his wife belongs;

- One who is wealthy, possessing immense earthly possessions known as Nokdangi Nokma or Gamni Nokma;

- One who has performed the expensive Gana ceremony known as Mithdeini Nokma;

- One who is hereditary in the position of a chieftain or King or a Bahkapaonin Nokma;

- One who is appointed a village headman by the government so that he helped the government officials in the discharge of their duties; such a Nokma is known as Sorkarini Nokma;

- One, who for visible manifestations of qualities of head and heart in word or deed, is well known and respected known as Chalang Nokma;

- One who, for his deep euridition in the divinities, mythological lore and mysterious profoundly of creation, is generally looked up to as a visible source of spiritual enlightenment by his people called *Kamal Nokrna*.

Irrespective of restriction, Nokmas no doubt had great voice in deciding the village affairs. Nokmas had attendants and followers who had respective functions to carrying out their instructions and enforcing village councils decisions. In the past these councils gave instructions for war and defence, executing administration, concerting action with the other village states, distributing lands to the residents, fixing dates of festivals and programmes, initiating pieces of legislation and looking after other welfare works.

In the past the Garos broke down their village isolation and topographical confrontation by concerting some federations arranged region wise when war and defence became imminent. Villages has trade compacts in which territorial rights were recognised among villages. The titles A Chick and Mande imply the sense of a strong unity loved and cherished dearly by a Garo. The collective and democratic way of living have their own impressions.

The Garo council is known as Mela Solbonga but the arrangement of council sitting otherwise is different. When circumstances necessitated, such a council was convened; some sittings were open door held near a Nokpante; the venue of council was Bandasal especially if reference be had to its judicial character. A small meeting of Nokpante and a few elders could, however, be held inside the Nokpante where dignitaries sat down according to ranks, the Nokma presiding over the meeting. The decorum was perhaps not so advanced as debaters rose one over the other at the top of their voice and speaking simultaneously where women also joined in the deliberations. The assistants of the Nokma were messengers (Dakora) who convened the meeting, Sirdar who acted as a police superintendent and laskar, a judicial officer. At the close the relevant issues only were summed up and a consensus was sought to be arrived at. Now the laskar presides over the village council meetings.

Divergence from the Past

Divergence from the past practice resulted from a series of changes enforced by the British administration in their earliest contact with the Garos. It dates back to 1816-1820, when David Scott created the Nazara and Zamindari Mahals graded as tributary in which laskars and Sordars were appointed revenue collectors from such territories and were paid remunerations for their service. The territories and were paid remunerations for their service. The territory of the Independent Garos was consolidated family in 1873, and the government had taken almost a century or so to complete the annexation and form a District.

The Laskarship in the hills became much more recognised shortly after the formation of the District in 1866. The position of the Nokmas in administrative concerns was largely changed and their place was take by the Laskars. Laskars, under this arrangement, were not only revenue collectors but acted as village magistrates as well, who with their full councils decided civil and criminal cases and could fine up to Rs. 50 in accordance with the Act V of 1861 rectified by the Rules for the Administration of Police and Justice for the Garo Hills District dated March 29, 1937. The Deputy Commissioner was overall in charge and was responsible to the Commissioner of Assam and the Governor later on. Appeals lay to him from the Laskars and their village courts. The laskars received remuneration from the revenue collected on behalf of the government, now it is the District Council. The Nokmas had been surrendering their power to give place to the Laskar.

The British Government recognised a system of indirect election of laskars to office. It was a system in which Nokmas proposed and Government approved. It was combined also with a direct method in which members of the public of a laskar's jurisdiction exercised the right of election. Now the power of the appointment of the laskars had passed to the District Council. It has provided that a full village council be restituted whose members are returned on both methods of election and nomination who shall elect a laskar. While retaining a democratic outlook, matters, on the other hand, might be made difficult, if say a cleavage arises in the council with regard to the issue. The laskar is not a village but an elaka head. The laskar now has been assisted by a sordar. The laskar always decides cases by imposing a fine upon a party at fault. Always cases and decisions are confined to the mahari in which a laskar is not involved as arbitrant but now many of the affairs are gradually passing to the Council.

The supra-structural level in context of the present constitutional provision, may now be envisaged. Meghalaya with regards to its Government is headed by the Governor but the Chief Minister pivots the administration. The powers of the Governor, the Assembly, the State Government and Court have been defined. The Assembly has a total number of 60 MLAs. returned from their respective constituencies. Normally the life of Assembly extends to five years but when the circumstances have arisen that might endanger the situation, one more year may be extended. The Assembly would choose a Speaker and a Deputy Speaker to chair and conduct the Assembly sessions. Rules have been prescribed for the conduct of members and for entitling with rights and privileges due to them.

The State Assembly legislates on matters of State; in the concurrent list and in the event of any misunderstanding with regard to the subjects, the Parliament can intervene and settle the issue. Evidently the Legislature is the ultimate authority. The Assembly theoretically exercises restraints on the executive and frames suitable policies to that end.

The matters relating to the power of the Legislative and Governor are well known. Suffice to say that the Assembly has the power to approve or veto bills and the members can even table the necessary adjournments, motions and even motions of no confidence against the Ministers; they can also suggest alteration or modification in the contents of bills presented. As regards its power over the finances, the allocation of sources and disbursement against Government expenditures, they are the responsibilities of Legislative Assembly determine these priorities, but with regard to the consolidated fund, the Assembly members even when entitled to discuss are not competent to exercise the voting right on it. In case of a unicameral Legislature, the final bills passed are presented to the Governor for his decision. Rules have been framed for the formation of Assembly Committees with all the rights, obligations and privileges attached to them.

The Meghalaya Assembly was to keep itself in conformity with the terms and conditions laid down in the provisions. Practically the Governor performs his status role. He plays decisive roles in all issues of legislation; he plays the dominant role in the crystallisation of legislation. He is the final authority in the system of legislation making. He coordinates actions with the President with regard to the enactment of the proposed bills depending on the nature of their contents, connotation and application. He is the repository and residual authority in law making. Law making because of certain complex factors can be time taking with regard to the screening and scrutiny of bills. In law making with regard to the state subjects, the Governor is responsible to the President. Bills of controversial or extraordinary character which are likely to be one sided or prejudicial have their system of transmittance from the Governor to the President and back to the Governor.

The Governor keeps the vital liasoning with the Centre because he keeps inform them in this issue and several other things. He has the power to issue ordinances in absentia of the Assembly which is deemed to apply to two weeks more after the reassembly of the Session. The Legislature can also advise for its repeal at or after the maturity of its application. Another important thing, the Governor can recommend for the President's rule in the event, certain circumstances have hampered the normal functioning of Government. The state of emergency in view of the conditions peculiar to themselves can warrant the suspension of the Assembly and the assumption of power through his functionaries. In the event of the state of emergency, he can withdraw his concord with the Chief Minister.

Governor's Role

The Governor's assent to the Bill is essential to have its force of an Act. In certain cases he withholds his assent and sends it back to the Assembly for their consideration embodying some of his observations considered as rectifications to it. The said Bill being reconsidered and passed with or without his recommendation at the second stage, the Governor can no longer withhold assent and the Bill automatically becomes an Act. As stated he can reserve the Bills also for the decision of the President.

The term of his office is five years. He is appointed by the President. He is also removable, should the President desire, pending the ending of that term.

The Governor summons, prorogues and dissolves the Legislative Assembly. He may send messages to the Assembly prescribing certain measures for Legislation in the issue which has assumed importance. He is entitled to process the bill to the President for final action if he feels that it will endanger the position of the High Court or derogate the Court's power. He opens the important annual session of the House, broadly emphasising the government programme for the year. He lays before the Assembly the annual financial statement indicating the estimate receipts and expenditures for the year. No demand for a grant or money bill can be introduced. His personal opinion is very vital to deciding Centre-State relations.

The Governor reserves his judicial powers for appointing, transferring and promoting the district judges and other judicial officers. Under the provisions, he is empowered to grant pardons, reprieves and respite of punishment or suspend, remit or commute the sentence of any person who has been convicted for an offence against any law.

The Governor theoretically holds extensive powers but in most cases abides with the advice of the Cabinet; this measure is essential to restrict fractions, to coordinating matters and causing a unified approach. The proclamation of emergency makes his to act in response to the decision and mandate mostly of the President or the Central Government.

In this framework, the Governor responses the Chief Minister's confidence and the Chief Minister commands the confidence of the House being essentially the leader of a dominant party. The Legislature is the arbiter of the final authority and the party in power thus obtains its mandate. The Chief Minister pivots the functioning of the administration of Departments according portfolios. The Ministry is wholly responsible to the Assembly for each and every issue of the administration. The Chief Minister's functions are restricted to non-judicial subjects but holds the real executive and his Cabinet decides the priorities of Legislation.

The concerns of Government are diverted to law and order, normal functioning of Departments and departmental restructuring, social legislation, redresses of public grievances and coping with the other public responsibilities are the issues minutely involved. Practically the Chief Minister is indispensible. With regard to the abnormal situation the view of the Cabinet or Chief Minister would be subject to rectification and in the situation Government is incapable to settle, the Governor will be wholly responsible and act in concord with the Centre. Most of the Departmental initiation with regard to the suitability or otherwise off legislation is censored by the Ministry concerned and by the approval of the Cabinet. A situation has impelled that the Chief Minister, when proving that he commands confidence in the House directly or indirectly maintains his overall influence overall the Departments besides holding a few portfolios to himself. He appoints Ministers from among the dominant parties (monostructural parts or coalition or otherwise) and distribute the portfolios to them who in the most vital issues, are assisted by Deputy and State Ministers from the view point of decorum, convenience and other considerations.

The Assembly establishment or Secretariat performs the manifold duties to chalking out the agenda, coordinating the subjects at issue, preparing the coordinated statements or reports and making arrangements at sessions. The Speaker holds the important post of trust and responsibility for efficient functioning of the Assembly's establishment, conducting the sessions in proper decorum and administering the other issues.

Freedom of expression in the House is guaranteed in conformity with the rules of discipline laid down. The status of the Speaker is considerably elevated.

The Secretariat

The State Government functions mainly at the Secretariat, Directorate and District levels. As regards the Secretariat, the Chief Secretary assisted by the Additional chief Secretary is overall in charge. As of 1986 Special Secretaries, Secretaries, Additional Secretaries besides officers on Special Duty, ran the administration. The Secretariat top personnel exercise the administration over the departments assigned to them. The allocation of Departments is vital to the administration as a whole.

The departments too many to naive are Mining and Geology, Industries, Sericulture and Weaving, Administrative Reforms, Health and Family Welfare, Food and Civil Supplies, Divisions, Revenue, Public Health, Engineering, Election, Planning and Evaluation, Programme Implementation, Agriculture production, Printing and Stationery, Weight and Measures, Hoine (Civil Defence and Home Guard), Passport and Jails, Border Areas Development, Cooperation, Political, Law, Parliamentary Affairs, Finance, Excise, Registration, Taxation and Stamps, Revenue, Trade, Border, Forest, Soil Conservation, Labour, Relief and Rehabilitation, Animal Husbandry and Veterinary, District Council Affairs, Tourism, Information and Public Relations, Transport, Cabinet Affairs, Departmental Enquiries, Education, Youth and Sports, Town and Country Planning, General Administration, Secretariat Administration, Social Welfare, Municipal Administration, Community Development, Fisheries, Agriculture, Social Welfare, Public Works Department, Tourism, Science and Technology Cell, State Level Public Grievances, Personnel, Power, Power (Technical) and state level grievances.

In 1986, the departments were held by 10 Special secretaries, 6 Secretaries, 3 Additional Secretaries, 5 Joint Secretaries, 6 officers on Special Duty, 13 Deputy Secretaries besides holding charge of Departments are also designated State Vigilance Commissioner, Chairman, Administrative Reforms, Chairman, Board of Revenue, Commissioner of Divisions and Commissioners of Agriculture Production being oriented to that term of business. There is a Special Secretary attached to Governor and another Special Secretary attached to Governor and another Special Secretary is attached to the Chief Minister. The Secretary, Planning is also known as Development Commissioner. The Speaker is overall in charge of the Assembly and a Secretary looks after the Assembly Secretariat.

The hierarchy of other Departments may be envisaged briefly:

A Chief Electoral Officer and Special Secretary holds the charge of Elections.
The Chief Conservator is in charge of forest Department; Transport is in the

charge of a Commissioner (assisted by Deputy Commissioner); officers designated commissioners are also in charge of Taxation (assisted by Assistant Commissioner) and Excise (assisted by Deputy Commissioner separately).

As regards, Police, the whole set up is under the Director General and Inspector General assisted by Inspectors General and Deputy Inspectors General. PHE is manned by the Adviser; the Chief Engineer looks after PWD. Directorates are manned by Directors. The Directorates known are Accounts and Treasuries; Agriculture; Animal Husbandry and Veterinary; Community Development; Economics, Statistics, Evaluation; Public Instructions; Employment and Craftmen's Training; Health Services; Fisheries; Housing; Industries; Information and Public Relations; Mineral Resources; Land Records and Survey; Printing and Stationery; Sericulture and Weaving; Social Welfare; Soil Conservation; Supply; Sports and Youth Welfare; Tourism; Town Planning. We find also that chairman theoretically head their respective corporations, Boards, Bodies, they are Meghalaya Mineral Development Corporation; Construction Corporation; Khadi and Village Industries Board; Forest Development Corporation Ltd.; Mawmluh- Cherra Cements; Cooperative Apex Bank; Public Service Commission; State Cooperative Marketing and Consumers' Federation; State Electricity Board; State Housing and Financing Cooperative Society; Transport Cooperation; Shillong Municipality; Tura Municipality. Managing Directors look after the Tourism Development Corporation and Industrial Development Corporation separately, Pine wood Hotel is looked after by a General MaLiager. All these grades are known as Autonomous bodies. Border Areas Development is headed by Officer on Special Duty and Director.

The hierarchy with regard to internal organisation and administration of Directorates can also be viewed. In Agriculture, besides maintaining the tempo of administrative control, the other cells concerned are technical services, engineering, marketing, research, experimentation, information, irrigation, etc. In veterinary, disease investigation, cattle development, dairying, cattle farming, poultry farming, feeds and fodders are the main thrust of development. Department of cooperation is manned by the Registrar but its branches are established at district headquarters also. Community Development among other things is concerned mainly with planning, and carrying out welfare services, for laying down important bases for the educational, material and cultural development of the people.

State Legislature

After colonial annexation, the present State of Meghalaya consisted of the Garo Hills and Jaintia Hills subdivision along with the Khasi states which had semi-independent status in a treaty relationship with the British Crown. In 1964, the district headquarters of the Khasi and Jaintia Hills were shifted to Shillong which also became the headquarters of the new province of Assam in 1874. In 1905, Meghalaya became a part of the new Assam province, when Lord Curzon partitioned Bengal and tagged the area of Meghalaya to the new province of Assam and Eastern Bengal. But in 1912, King George V reversed the Partition of Bengal and the area (now called Meghalaya), became part of the revived province of Assam.

Meghalaya is a new State in an ancient land. The State boasts of a most picturesque and beautiful landscape well-endowed with a wide variety of flora and fauna which inhabit the hill range and intervening valleys which criss-cross the area of the state. In 1970, the new State was given the name "Meghalaya" the abode of the clouds-reviving a name given by a geographer some fifty years back, who coined the name after being impressed by the clouds-which always seem to hover over central plateau.

Shillong being the provincial headquarters had seen the gradual evolution of parliamentary democracy. The Council of the Chief Commissioner set up under the Indian Councils Act, 1861-1909 met in Shillong and so did the first independent Council for Assam set up in 1912. The Council set up under the Government of India Act, 1916 met here for the first time on 6 April, 1916 and again under the Government of India Act, 1919 as the new Assam, Legislative Council. On 3 January, 1921, following the Montagu-Chelmsford Report of 1917 and the Government of India Act of 1919, the Governor-General-in-Council declared the areas, now in Meghalaya, but excluding the Khasi states, as backward tracts under the Act.

Following the Simon Commission Report and the Government of India Act, 1935, the areas, now in Meghalaya excluding the Khasi States, became partially excluded areas within the meaning of the Government of India Act, 1935. These areas were represented in the Assam Legislative Council since 1920 and the later also in the pre-independence Assam Legislative Assembly.

Along with the parliamentary institutions Meghalaya still retains, through the Sixth Schedule to the Constitution, the age-old grass-root system of tribal democracy as practised through traditional rulers, the Syiams, Nokmas and Dolois, who continue to exist side by side with modern parliamentary institutions.

Prior to 2 April, 1970 Meghalaya was a part of the composite State of Assam. After more than a decade of peaceful constitutional agitation for a separate Hill State, the Government of India conceded partially to the demand and the Parliament passed the Assam Reorganisation (Meghalaya) Act, 1969 constituting the Autonomous State of Meghalaya within the existing State of Assam. Smt. Indira Gandhi, the then Prime Minister, came to Shillong to formally inaugurate the Autonomous State on 2 April, 1970. The old Council Chamber was selected as the Chamber for the Legislature of the Autonomous State which constituted of 37 members elected indirectly by the Autonomous District Councils, set up under the Sixth Schedule to the Constitution. The Parliament passed the North Eastern Areas Reorganisation Act, 1971 which conferred full statehood on the Autonomous State of Meghalaya. It became a full-fledged State on 21 January, 1972 and now has a full-fledged Legislature consisting of 60 members.

District Councils

The three District councils, Khasi, Garo and Jaintia Hill are chaired by their respective chairmen. The Chairman guides and conducts the council at session. The executive is headed by the Chief Executive Member and there are executive members with their respective portfolios such as administration, finance, revenue and royalty, civil work, forest, markets and rural development. A judge usually Magistrate first class also serves at their court. As regards the Shillong Municipality, the Syiem of Mylliem in 1913 consented over an application of Bengal Municipality Act 1884 to be extended at the Headquarters and to comprise such villages within the radius of the Court, Shillong. The villages of Mawkhar, Laban; Malki, Laitumkhrah, Jhalukpara, Mawprem were proposed to form the Municipal administration to the villages subject to the maintenance of his other rights and powers as Syiem of Mylliem.... therein and with the reservoir that the rivers Umshyrpi and Wah Umkhrah, as far as they lay within the aforesaid villages, Shillong remain the property of Mylliem State. Most of the members of the Shillong Municipality were elected till quite recently., the election being conducted, on the basis of the delimitation of the Municipality had extended its jurisdiction beyond the villages originally scheduled. The Shillong Municipality and cantonment area combined in 1951 constituted an area only of 12 sq km. The growth of the cantonment can briefly be reiterated below.

"Three areas over which jurisdiction has been ceded to the British Government in the past either fully or partially for the purpose of administration with Shillong. (Rifle range) cantonment and Shillong. Umlong cantonment full jurisdiction has been ceded. It is presumed that the lease now contemplated related only to the Shillong Municipal area". At Present the Only localities excluded from the Municipal's jurisdiction are the cantonment, Mawlai and Nongthymmai and the conglomerate of townships surrounding them. Due to some changes occurring lately, an official chairman is in charge of Shillong Municipality assisted by the Chief Executive Member and their staff in the disposal of administration regarding water supply, health and sanitation, tax collections, drainage and garbages, land allotments, demarcations and other connected issues.

The Elections

In a Parliamentary set up, we note that the election are very decisive in the formation and functioning of Government. The allocation of the Cabinet portfolios also has its basic importance in the working of the Government Departments, the Chief Secretary has his overall role in liaisoning and coordinating the affairs at the Secretariat level. Under this arrangement, almost all the Departments are headed by Special Secretaries to Government and Directorates function under the Departments and the branches of the Directorates function at the state and district level. A Deputy Commissioner keeps the important departmental liaison of the district. The administration of district Councils is conducted by their respective Executive Councils.

10

Tourism

General Aspects

Meghalaya is overwhelmingly beautiful, where everything is impossibly green and alive. The rolling mists in the valleys, the undulating hills, numerous lakes, waterfalls, caves, sacred forests, exotic flora and fauna, together with the unique and interesting destination. Shillong the capital set amidst a picturesque landscape of pine covered hills, rapid streams and captivating water falls provides a perfect getaway from the heat.

Within the city are a number of places to visit, which include Wards Lake, Lady Hydari Park, Sweet Falls, and the Shillong 18 Hole Golf Course, which is one of the oldest in the country. Other Tourist sites around the city are the Crinoline Swimming Pool, Mattilang Park, Airforce Museum, Upper Shillong, Don Bosco Centre of Indigenous Cultures, the Butterfly Museum and Jaya Kalra's Art Gallery.

Besides offering a panoramic view of Bangladesh, the places to visit in Cherrapunjee are Nohsngithiang Falls (Mawsmai Falls), Nohkalikai Falls, Mawsmai Cave, Thankarang Park, Eco Park, Khoh Ramhah, Green Rock Ranch, Sa-I-Mika Park and Kynrem Falls.

Tour of the State

Escaping in the wilderness, enjoying the looming mountains, the fresh air, the cobalt blue firmament, the whispering pines, losing oneself in the never ending mountain terrains, the bubbling brooks that break into cascading waterfalls, you are heading towards the perfect holiday destination, its Meghalaya, of course!! Known as the abode of clouds, Meghalaya consists of the Garo, Khasi and the Jaintia Hills together forming the "Shillog or the Meghalaya Plateau".

Nature

Taking the turpentine roads about 10 km from Shillong you will be enwrapped by the enamouring scenario, the spectacular Elephant Waterfall infested with the blooming Rhododendron and the chirping colourful birds. This mountainous region is invaded with enchanting waterfalls — Nohkalikai at Cherrapunjee, Dain-Thlen, Sweet Spread Eagle, Bidon, Bishop, Krangsuri, Rongbang, Imilchang located at Mawsmai.

Festivals play an important role in the tribal people of Meghalaya. According to the Garo legend, to honour the Sun God Wangala or the 100 Drums festival is held in the Garo Hills. The simple village people for whom nature play a crucial role in their lively hood show their allegiance by performing rituals and participating in dances such as the Doregata dance and the Pomelo dance which are permeated with rhythmic beats. The colourful Nongkrem dance, representing an ancient religious festival of the Khasis is performed with full gusto. Another Khasi dance that displays the entire Khasi finery is a typical thanksgiving dance while the Harvest dance of Southern Meghalaya re-establishes the importance of nature in the lives of the people of the hills. The Jaintia tribe with vibrant decorations celebrates the Behdienkhlam festival accompanied with their rhythmic lahoo dancers.

Tourism Attractions

Living in metropolis one can never gauge the serenity that engulfs the Himalayan states. Enmeshed among the snow covered peaks, pristine clear lakes, cascading waterfalls, hermetic caves, dense forests and verdant woods with an array of exotic flora and fauna, one is amazed at the wealth Meghalaya offers to its visitors. Escaping in the wilderness, enjoying the looming mountains, the fresh air, the cobalt blue firmament, the whispering pines, losing oneself in the never ending mountain terrains, the bubbling brooks that break into cascading waterfalls, you are heading towards the perfect holiday destination, Meghalaya. The Tourists Attractions of Meghalaya begin with the spectacular nature and culminates with the subtleties of the amazing nature. Garo, Khasi and the Jaintia Hills that form the Meghalaya Plateau, is of immense tourist importance attracting tourists' attention. Shillong, capital of Meghalaya is a beautiful city at an altitude of 1,496 metres providing a panoramic view. The Ward's Lake, one of the tourist attractions of Meghalaya is a man made lake pleasantly decorated with aligned flowerbeds and sand stone paths. The Botanical garden has a rare species of exotic birds and endangered species of plants.

The Shillong Peak, about 10 km from Shillong and 1965 metres above sea level offers a breathtaking view of the country below. Shillong Cathedral is another impressive monument that accommodates a huge congregation of worshippers.

Waterfalls

The Plateau of Meghalaya is invaded with waterfalls. Originating from placid streams it collaborates with many to form roaring cascades that offer a breathtaking view. One is often left dazed with the enormous power nature generates that often mocks man's narcissistic achievements. Sweet Falls and Crinoline Falls are the impressive waterfalls of Meghalaya that holds immense tourists importance. Taking the turpentine roads about 10 km from Shillong you will be enwrapped by the enamouring scenario, the spectacular Elephant Waterfall infested with the blooming Rhododendron and the chirping colourful birds. This mountainous region is invaded with enchanting waterfalls — Nohkalikai at Cherrapunjee, Dain-Thlen, Sweet Spread Eagle, Bidon, Bishop, Krangsuri, Rongbang, Imilchang located at Mawsmai.

Caves

The Garo, Khasi and the Jaintia ranges offer Meghalaya with a gamut of unexplored caves. Many like to venture into these spelunk to experience the thrill of encountering the unknown. The most well known caves that attract tourists are Mawsmai Cave, Krem Mawmluh, The Cave of Eocene age, Krem Kotsati, Krem Umshangktat, Siju-Dobkhakol, Tetengkol-Balwakol, etc.

Cherrapunjee

Knap sackers on the trail of beauty, beauty that lies in the vastness of nature, the looming mountains and the poignant silence of the surroundings may find Cherrapunjee a paradise. Though known as the wettest place on earth, Cherrapunjee has the wealth that is not yet explored. While on your way to Cherrapunjee tourist guides may just not venture beyond Noh-sngithiang and Noh-kalikai falls but you must keep in mind that there is much in Cherrapunjee than waterfalls and rains.

With just 90 minutes drive from Shillong on a clear day, Cherrapunjee is ready to shower you with all the magic it treasures. On your way to this spectacular place you may pass Mylliem where you can see the old method of black smithy. You can stop at Duwan Singh or Mawkdok Bridge and drink in the breathtaking beauty of nature, for it is the beginning of Cherrapunjee circuit. It is from this point one can spot an abrupt change in the scenery. The winding mountainous terrain will take you through the spectacles of lush green vegetation until you reach a small hamlet called Sohra-rim, the original Cherrapunjee village or Sohra.

A few kilometres before reaching Cherrapunjee, is the magnificent Dainthlen waterfall. While on your way to this spectacular waterfall you will come across the gentle ruffling grasslands and long stints of rocks that are splendid. The upstream presents some beautiful rock formation until the point where water cascades in amazing force forming froths. Beyond the falls is the Rangjyrthei village, an ancient place with smelting kilns.

Nature lovers should stray for 5 kilometres or so to enjoy the pristine beauty of the ethereal Mother Nature. On approaching Cherrapunjee, the imposing Ram Krishna Mission steals your breath away as in the backdrop of such beauty the educational institution can be incomparable to the other institutions in the world. Don't forget to taste the juicy oranges of Cherrapunjee as well as carry a jar of orange honey.

The most spectacular of waterfalls of Meghalaya, the Nohkalikai falls thunders down creating a deafening sound and the swirling mists covers the area almost blinding you of the near vicinity. If you hold your patience for few more minutes the mists will clear for a moment and you have to hold your breath for the beauty that you would spot for some seconds would remain with you for months to come. These awesome waterfalls of Cherrapunjee are seasonal fed, as it is only in the monsoons can you enjoy their spectacular charisma.

Entering the main Cherrapunjee you will come across an old church of ancient architecture. It is the oldest Presbyterian Church established in 1835. In the heart of the town is the Ka-kpep Syiem or the royal cremation ground. It is here members of the royal family were cremated.

Many frequent the monolithic beauty of the Mawlong peak, popularly known as the David Scott memorial, that offers a birds eye view as well as a lovely picnic spot. Moreover, visiting the Mawlong caves is another thrilling experience. The majestic waterfall of Noh-sngithiang often known as the seven sisters is another of the magnificent waterfalls of Cherrapunjee that cascades into silvery rivulets.

Thangkarang Park laid on the high rocky cliffs overlooks the plains of Bangladesh. You can spot the imposing Kynrem falls cascading down majestically in three stages. The giant Koh-ramhah is also found here; a single rock formation that resembles an upturned koh or basket, which is above 200 ft. in height.

In Laitkynsew, you can trek or take spring baths at the gurgling streams or even go caving. Trekking to the Umnnoi living root bridge should definitely feature in your itinerary. It is 2 km down steep on cobbled stone pathway. Measuring about 53 ft the living root bridge is about 100 years old constructed over a small stream and used by the villagers to reach their betelnut gardens

Located at Tyrna village not far away from Laitkynsew is the unique double decker a feat of bio-engineering wonder. It is a two-tier living Root Bridge measuring 59 ft and 83 ft in length respectively. It is a tough trek that will take almost one and half hours down steep slopes and forest areas crossing bridges hovering above 45 ft above a roaring waterfall. Nevertheless it is exciting adventure definitely not for the weak hearts.

This beautiful land of abundant natural beauty has immense tourist attraction. The ethnic tribes, their habitat, arts and handicrafts that form their culture attract many.

Jaintia Hills

Jaintia Hills of Meghalaya is another spot of tourist attraction. Engulfed in the mesmerising scenic beauty, Jaintia Hills District was created on the 22nd of February in

1972. Homeland of the Jaintia tribes, Jaintia Hills offer you magical surroundings with beautiful streamlets, burbling brooks, cascading waterfalls, winding terrains, splendid valleys, picturesque plateaus and golden sunshine. It is a picturesque little village with the River Myntdu encircling it.

To catch a glimpse of these beautiful hills you can travel by air to Guwahati and then avail the road route to Shillong. Pawan Hans Helicopters Ltd. under the Government of Meghalaya offers regular helicopter services.

While on you way to Jowai from Shillong you will be amazed at the beauty that the Jaintia Hills offer. The grasslands, oak woods, rice terrace lands, burbling brooks and the pine trees serve as great scenic view until you reach the Thadlaskein lake. It is a historical lake about 8 km from Jowai. According to legends it was dug by the bow tips of Jaintia's foremost war leaders, Sajar Nangli. One can spot the amazing cluster of monoliths in the backdrop of the vast openness, a deal delight for a photographer. One of the monoliths is said to the walking stick of Mar Phalyngki 'the Goliath' of Jaintia Hill legend in Nartiang, 24 km from Jowai.

Syntu Ksiar is another remarkable place of Jaintia Hills, a vast pool of calm waters where the Myntdu River that encircles the whole village ends. It offers a remarkable scenic view. Located in the Jowai-Dawki Road, is the Syndai village which has many caves and caverns. This beautiful land of abundant natural beauty has immense tourist attraction. The ethnic tribes, their habitat, arts and handicrafts and the locales attract many.

Mawsynram

The winding roads of the hilly terrain with scenic view of the picturesque snow covered ranges, orchids blooming over treetops and gentle streams rushing out to meet roaring waterfalls, are breathtaking for every wanderlust who make their way to Mawsynram. Another breathtaking, wondrous place of Meghalaya, Mawsynram is a small village in the Khasi Hills about 56 kilometres from Shillong. It is reportedly the wettest place recording the highest rainfall of 11.872 metres but since it has no meteorological department in the area, Cherrapunjee is still officially considered the place recording world's highest rainfall.

Being one of the well known spots of Meghalaya, Mawsynram is frequented by nature lovers enjoying a walk by its steep and down sliding slopes, breathing in the fresh air, loving the clear blue sky, the wind that brushes their face, catching glimpses of the mountain birds and the nearly deafening sound of the roaring waterfalls. The orchids that bloom on the low lands, the thrilling adventure in the unexplored caves that are pathways to many rivers are experiences that remain for ever acting as a balm for the city bred travellers looking for solace in nature's soothing memories.

One of the known caves of Mawsynram is the Mawjymbuin cave. Years of weathering due to dripping of mineralised solutions and deposition of calcium carbonate has given rise to some spectacular stalagmites, which are study of great interest for the geologists. Not only are they the subject of research but its natural formation and the beauty that it embodies, its crystalline surface that glitters in the lights sets one to wonder about nature's benevolence. The stalagmite of the Mawjymbuin cave is shaped into a massive Shivalinga. This cave also has a dome shaped rock with a flat top called the *Symper Rock*.

This beautiful land of abundant natural beauty has immense tourist attraction. The ethnic tribes, their habitat, arts and handicrafts that form their culture attract many.

Tourist Spots

The places of historical interest have their special importance; they highlight the important events which occurred in their own spheres and the sociocultural trends which suit themselves with folk attributes. Some of the sculptural and architecture remains testify to the ancient genius of their makers. They are like the master creations belonging to the different ages of history. They also reveal the very important factors which were decisive to evolving these creations some of them being the massive formations which had created those impacts in the course of history. Evidently the cultural activities in the well-organised patterns on large corporal scales were largely decisive and these brought about the emergence of the age of sculpture and architecture. Some villages had come up the great cultural centres. The political factors on the concept of statesmanship or statehood are also important for our consideration. Therefore, those villages many of which are forgotten had cradled their once virile system of society and polity.

Meghalaya has a rich and charming scenery. Shillong is even called the Scotland of the East. The charming scenery against the mountain scenes has become more confined perhaps to the gentle table lands, hills and valleys. The beauty scenes become scattered out in the vast and variegated panorama of nature itself. The profuse vegetation along with its variegated species of trees, plants, orchids, ferns and other kinds of foliage, the pine trees which dominate the upper terrain and motifs scattered in the natural phenomenon are equally exhilarating and soothing to their close observers. In the country side we also see the various fruits and vegetable plantations which are as good to look at. The hills, valleys and gorges clothed by a thin vegetation or being rendered to grasslands and at times cloved by rivers and streams and on the precipices the waterfalls of sheer beauty (especially during the summers) are also the impressions. At places the mountain scenes mount up themselves to some formidable heights in great chaos. We are seeking to highlight the importance of places which have become the educational and business centres. The places of historical interest have also their importance as follows:

Shillong

Travelling through the hilly state of Meghalaya, you will be taken aback at the natural wealth the state offers. Nestling in the eastern part of the state is the beautiful capital,

Shillong often referred to as the "Scotland of the East". Resembling the Scottish highlands, Shillong's mountainous terrains among the pine conifers and pineapple shrubs is most frequented by the tourists. The city derives its name from "Leishyllong" — the Superpower or God who is believed to reside on the Shillong peak, overlooking the city. From 1874 until 1972, the hill station of Shillong was the capital of British Assam. Shillong has sprawling golf course, polo ground, churches and Victorian bungalows. Shillong today is a typical Indian city still retaining its English charm. It however gets gloomy during the monsoons. Shillong, capital of Meghalaya is a beautiful city at an altitude of 1,496 metres providing a panoramic view. The Shillong Peak, about 10 km from Shillong and 1965 metres above sea level offers a breathtaking view of the country below. Shillong Cathedral is another impressive monument that accommodates a huge congregation of worshippers.

Shillong has beautiful parks to its credit. Ward's Lake, one of the tourist attractions of Meghalaya is a man made lake pleasantly decorated with aligned flowerbeds and sand stone paths. The Botanical garden has a rare species of exotic birds and endangered species of plants. The immaculate Ka Phan Nongliat Park is another popular place to promenade. The William Sangma Museum displays the local flora, fauna, culture and anthropology. The Butterfly Museum is another unique museum of Shillong exhibiting rare species of colourful butterflies. The Lew Duh is one of the most impressive markets of the northeast. It is one of the most bustling and animated places of Shillong where thousands of Khasis flock together. It is a great place to pick up tribal baskets, bows and arrows. This beautiful land of abundant natural beauty has immense tourist attraction. The ethnic tribes, their habitat, arts and handicrafts that form their culture attract many.

Raitong

East of Umsning lying on a knoll, extending to Mawlieng valley situated on its base, this place exhibits some ancient stone remains carved into different shapes; bulk of them designed originally like monoliths, pillars, tables, dolmens and some modelled into some concrete things utility. The ruins are symbolic to the kingdom's greatness. Uphill on the outskirt of the ancient Raitong, the existence of some oriental sculptures and inscriptions has also been discussed. Barring a few hamlets which still survive and some lands under farming, bulk of Mawlieng looks desolate and evidently, it had been hitherto a deserted village. Importance in this context is attached also to some ancient centres notably Syndai, Barato, Nartiang, Nongkseh, Smit, Mawsmai and Sohra.

Syndai

Lying on the mid-southern Jaintia Hills and along the ancient Sylhet-Nowgong road nestling on the mass of cliffs, exhibits a collection of architectural motifs which among others consist of a large frog which appear to have been bounded in chains, a trunkless elephant stooping down a small tank and the rock engraving of the sun and the moon (the latter lying contiguous to each other).

They lie below Syndai at a place called *Rupesor*. An uplong but narrow citadel ending in a dome walled with the red brick tiles in oval shape holding a very limited circle in its inside is noticed. It lies down hill along the part of Syndai-Rupesor road. Closely adjacent to a trunkless elephant, the mark of ancient bridge is seen. The real bridge path or pavement has disappeared but there are some formidable clusters of stone which mount up from the river bed to the level of the bank which evidently are the pillars serving to hold the bridge or its culvert. These leave the impressions that the bridge construction had either been left incomplete or that its upper part was washed away by the angry river. The present village of Syndai must have had provided a haltage to the Jaintia Raja prior to 1835 on his way from Sylhet to Assam for keeping contacts with his plain dominions along the grand trunk road which provided the passage and which was claimed to have been constructed by David Scott. Actually Scott must have only renovated parts of this road which existed for ages and catering itself of to the trade and administrative interest of the once great kingdom.

The relics lying at Barato which formed part of the ancient citadel and headquarters of a renowned kingdom have been mentioned and which among others, the rock engravings reveal the figures of elephants, a person carrying a ploughshare and also the image of a man.

Jarain

This village lies on the central highlands. It served in ages past as a trade holding station on Sylhet Assam road where rows of stone monuments are lying scattered about. There is a circle of small stone pillars which look like stilts for houses and which perpetuate the story of the last Anglo-Jaintia war from 1861 to 1863. The notable models of architecture lying immediately on the village exits are the jarain stone bridge and Umiaknieh bridge. Jarain bridge is made up with broad but shorter pillars and towered on its path with stone spans. One of the stone spans, however, has disappeared which makes the part of the bridge distended and which till recently, the vacuum was made up of by a wooden link to make it passable to traders and travellers. Umiaknieh bridge lying on the opposite village exit exhibits the engineering dexterity of its own but one side of the culvert carrying a wall with an arch or a dome appears to be unique and the wall surface made up with tiles or slabs and so smoothly cohered have a few small sculptural marks the style of pillars supporting and stone spans holding the pavement demonstrate a model of architecture not commonly seen. The concentrated efforts made by the ancient architecture either on the corporate or their own level testifies to the existence of that ancient grand trunk road and the two bridges lying on it demonstrate that the road was ever given great care.

Nartiang

Lies on the mid-northern hills. Its importance has been considerably focused as it was the summer headquarters of the King while jaintiapur now comprised in Bangladesh was his permanent headquarters. There is also a Hindu mandir under a Brahmin whose family has occupied it for several generations and where its residents observe some Hindu rites and poojahs but the tribal rites and celebrations predominate. It is one of the few villages in which Hinduism has struck its roots although the residents have adopted only some of these rites which were convenient in the fixed seasons. Yet this village also exhibits its special phenomenon because it abounds with its typical stonehenges notably in the shape of massive tables, pillars, dolmens, dissolitlis and other kinds. The tallest monolith in the state according to the information till date measuring 36 feet (height) × 2 feet (breadth) × 21/2 feet (thick) exists here in the midst of other collosal pilllars. There is a stone bridge lying in the same direction and it measures 23 feet × 4 feet × 2 feet. They resemble the Lait-lying-kot stonehenge lying in East Khasi Hills, where the most wonderful remain is a great dolmen or table which measures 28 feet × 20 feet surrounded on its side by three great uprights (lait-lyng-kot beyond doubt served once as the headquarters or sub-headquarters of the ancient Shillong Kingdom). Three tanks are also seen at Narting connected with the washing of the human bones being one of the funerary or post-funerary rites performed. Some of the dolmens serve as stone seats to the Daloi and other chiefs when resuming the market inspections. Market rites admixed with the concepts of fertility have their priority in Nartiang and its counterparts, viz. Sutnga, Shangpung and Raliang Daloiships, they have their precedence because they were the first sister communes which formed the state. The King himself in the distant past founded many markets in course of a State inspection and in which among others were Narpuh, Khaddum and Muktapur bazars. The ancient scuptural relics are highly symbolic and respond entirely to the economic and cultural activities and some are like the dominant art patterns. The whole country once was breathed with a series of these activities. Nartiang historically was one of the dominant centres of the kingdom.

Nongkseh

This place lies on upper Shillong where immediately on its vicinity there is another stonehenge full of collosal monolithic structures evidently the elongate pillars and large-sized dolmens resting on their sides. Marks of the ancient trenches which structured the old palisades are seen. The Nongkseh outskirt now desolate once housed the Shillong Kingdom's headquarters; its importance was enhanced because it served as an adjunct to the Shillong main market or lewduh which is one of the greatest bazars on the northeast. Nongkseh was also the centre of a great festival. It was also one great centres of goldsmithery, blacksmithery and weaving. Its importance became greatly diminished after it was partitioned into the Mylliem and Khyrim kingdoms with the former's headquarters first shifted to Lait-lyng-kot, then to Mylliem and finally to the present city and the latter's first to Lang-kyrdem then Nongkrem and finally to Smit.

The notable architectural models also abound at Sohra and Mhwsmai and Mawmuh lying contagiously. The first impression is that we come across same house constructions in stone solid structures or thatched with plam, parts of house compounds and pavements being structured with stones. At Mawsmai and Pamsohmen, Mawki-syiem, stone pillars are noticed and one of them at Mawsmai is found wearing a disc or crown. On the outskirts and graveyards, notices also the memorial pillars preserving the hollowed memory of the dead constructed in the traditional or modern fashion. We see also stone maunds serving as royal pyres used at State cremations. Immediately in Sohra's outskirts and inside its premises and extending over the southern frontiers beyond this kingdom and covering other state, the numerous state benches laid inside the ovens called *Kors* are seen which form haltages to travellers commemorating the memory of heroes and eminent personages. Near Lait-lyng-ew the once renowned centre of cool mining lying close to Sohrarim (the ancient Soh headquarters) there are collasal remain of bed- steads a very elaborate form of masonry and many of them have crumbled to ruins and which have ever existed as symbols of royal power. These architectural models in a brief highlight testify to their skills in masonry which have been conserved through the ages. Now the combination with the use of cement as well as the marble tiles and powder has become channelled to the multifarious constructions which have now flashed themselves in the towns and some villages existing side with the traditional patterns made of wood, bamboo and other accessories.

A typical example of the ancient palace exists at Smit, the walls structured and the house floored being made with the indigenous wood and wall plates, rafters, patterns, crossbeams and other pillars are of wood. The roof is thatched. Its courtyard is either a sand or gravelled pavement. The posts for construction are contributed by the royal house and some by the leading communes. The apartments are Shlur, a big hall, kyndong or bedrooms, Kynran and a room where goats are kept at state sacrifices, Kyndur or a bathroom, rympei a drawing room and bah, the main family residence. The house is occupied by Syiem Sad or a State priestess. The King's court and State establishment are housed in the other buildings attached to sad or palace. The shlur also serves as a durbar hall and venue of State prayers. It is one of the collasal house structures. There are smaller shlurs or sads located in a few interior Bhoi Syiemships also.

Traditional and urban trends with regard to the composition of towns, townships, and even the exposed roadside stations are seen to go hand in hand. Constructions and other complexes have evidently exhibited both the traditional and urban aspects of formation at some central places. Villages out of the reaches of roads are seen still to maintain their traditional outlook more uniformly.

As regards the composition of villages, houses are seen to be mostly aligned along the village streets, they face the main road; clusters of houses dominate the populous villages along the roadsides and houses so aligned are seen to skirt off in several directions. In largely-populated places, lack of space evidently taxes the house occupants. In some villages, townships and semi-urban complexes and very few houses are noticed to have spacious compounds and lawns; in some places, some house compounds are tightened up with the formidable clusters. Houses already congested can hardly leave now spaces kitchen gardening, and tree planting. Villages obviously owing to the extension of houses are no longer extended along the main village roadside; some villages spread in crossed directions, other villages are eagle-like in shape and some are in circuitous appearance. Owing to the congestion, a confused situation has arisen with regard to site locations and other factors.

Shillong evidently has become a great city. It started initially as the District headquarters about 1964-6 5. In 1869, the Jowai subdivision was constituted within the District. Circumstances favoured for the growth of Shillong as a provincial headquarters in 1874 in which the Chief Commissioner was stationed. However, the Governor of Assam substituted the chief commissioner in much more the later decade. The Governor held the administration of the province till the coming of independence. The powers and functions of the Governor have also been defined under the present Constitution. A station committee in the quarter of the past century was attached to the administration which advised Government on the matter relating to land acquisition and demarcation, allocation of forests, local road constructions and other issues. The syiem of Mylliem sat in it as its member. Later on the Shillong municipality under the Act entitling its formation was set up. The official and elected members sat in it and the Deputy Commissioner acted as its chairman.

The Deputy Commissioner had ever resumed his position as chairman, and it seems that the post of a Vice Chairman was filled by an elected member. It was since 1963 that a non-official member was entitled to act as chairman. Recently other changes were introduced in the Administrative set-up. The all weather roads leaving for Guwahati and Sohra and later on Mawphlang and Sylhet provided the infrastructure to the growth of the modern communications. The development of water supply, sanitation, public health and to some extent roads and education was taken up by the Municipality, the administrative issues at times had become intricate due to the working out of a tier administration. Hydroelectricity was introduced for the first time before 1930. Shillong became a great centrepot, and the centre of administration.

Now within the urban settlement confined to the Shillong municipality and semi-urban areas lying outside, most of the localities have been pressed hard with the problem of population congestion. Bazars, shopping and Industrial centres are all packed up everywhere. The natural beauty, to a great extent, has been marred.

Shillong on its suburbs holds certain potentials. There are picturesque scenes formed of the gentle hills; there are beautiful waterfalls, streams and rivers in its vicinity. The exhilarating golf links with their grassy lawns exists as a golf play ground encircled on their sides by rows of the elegant Pine trees. The Ward's lake lying in the heart of the city, the Lay Hyderi Park, and zoo and other parks and beauty spots are some of the attractions. The Umniam lake connected with the Hydel project provides a soothing and captivating sight. The State Secretariat, State Central Library and Museum are located in the ideal surroundings. The State Legislative Assembly on its main entrance, however, faces one of the most crowded places. There are hill tops which afford the good parking places at the Upper Shillong and Laitkor range above the city overlooking Shillong with its vast stretches of the localities and buildings on all sides radiating and ending in the boundary terminus where one can get a distant sight. It looks like a great circle of buildings and with its great towering circumference. As a result, the innumerable gorgeous buildings have come to stay and replaced the traditional patterns.

The Shillong lewduh or main bazar under the administration of Mylliem State has been greatly expanding during the recent years. Consequently, it has become more and more crowded with stalls and sheds stocking various crops, articles and goods. It has become largely expanded with poultry, vegetable, handicrafts, fish, tobacco flackes, spices, grains, arecanut, betel-vine, cloth and hosiery, grocery, essential commodities and many other stalls. It holds a volume of merchandise locally conserved and other articles brought from outside. There are small municipal markets also. The enhanced traffic and congestion has presented transport hazards to the movement of goods even within its premises, the local bus, taxi and public carrier stations lying nearby.

The other marketing centres are Police Bazar, Garikhana, Polo ground super market, Mawkhar Super Bazar and stalls are fairly distributed in the other localities.

Because of its matching scenery and salubrious climate and because it was once the centre of provincial administration, in spite of their complexes, it still holds a majestic splendour of its own. There are only a few Government wards and bulk of the localities comprised in the Shillong Cantonment and Municipality fall under the territorial jurisdiction of Mylliem state. It is anticipated that its population now has shot up to 23,06,069 persons approximately. There are several local clubs, societies, associations which operate cultural, sports and social entertainment programmes. Angkling is one of the favourite games. Local archery contest is one of the important sports. Sports of many kinds are undertaken. The Weiking dance where Shillong dancers and those from outside participate held during the spring time is a reinvigorating scene in a three-day dance. The Khyrim festival held at Smit in Shillong's neighbourhood provides means of recreation programme to' onlookers. The Hindus, the Muslims and other communities follow their own religious festivals. The Christian celebrations, however, have become more and more perceptible.

The tribal population has now been steadily increasing owing to the process of inter-district migration taking place now. These migration trends have become more noticeable nowadays. The youth power of the local population appears to be increasing. In these circumstances the more conventional standard of living is being catered to by the advanced sections of the population. Owing to the policy of divide and rule which seems to have become inherent in some ways, the individualistic temperament among the Khasi and non-Khasi population appears to have caused certain restraints to the growth of a corporal character. Moreover, certain nomadic habits seems to be largely permeating. Another confronting difficulty is that bulk of the government wards or lands have been acquired on a lease basis from private owners whose predecessors had allowed these rights to the authorities since 1862.

Jowai grew to importance after, a subdivision was formed. It was also storm centre of tribal resistance; in fact, U Kiang Nongban, a hero and martyr started the movement from Jowai in 1861. First development was the establishment of a Jowai thana under the charge of a Doroga which preceded the outbreak of the movement. The SDO after the subdivision formed primarily was concerned to regularise the government land-holdings acquired from the old Sutnga royal family, collection of house taxes, performance of a judicial duties and enforcement of the civil measures. It is one of the largely-populated villages and spreads out to a good number of localities. The river Myntdu winds the hills base upon which the village is located draining a number of wet rice lands spread on its bank. Subsequently, Jowai attracted a large number of residents from outside. Jowai on the establishment of Statehood was raised to the District. Subsequently branches of other District office establishments were-located besides which since the early times it was a centre of trade where traders from all nooks and corners moved through all along the frontier, visited the markets and hats located now in Bangladesh and Nowgong and performed transactions or merchandise. The transaction of goods was facilitated through the existence of ancient routes connecting Jowai, Jarain and Muktapur. At the spot which took off to Jaintiapur, an annual festival was held in which a couple of doves or pigeons were released and the direction the flight they made was taken to be auspicious. Other branch tracks existed with khyrim on the west and places lying eastward. Jowai was a great trade station lying eastward. Jowai was a great trade station lying on a trunk road existing since times immorial. The British Government had never constructed them originally. Because of these reasons, it is now one of the great administrative centres; its trade prospects have considerably been enhanced due to a considerable mining now being conducted in its vicinity. The local cultural clubs are Panaliar, Iongpiah and Shiliang Raid. Recently a town committee was constituted. It is also a headquarters of District Council. The town rises to a rousing jubilance during the celebration of Beh then-Khlam a great rain festive held in summer time. The concept of change has become more indispensable to our understanding.

On the progress of Adult Education within the confines of the Subdivision, Mondon Bareh many years ago reported.

"There are only 35 schools in the Jaintia Hills which cannot properly be designated as day schools or higher schools. In some of the villages... there was an ancient custom according to which all the male children and youths of the villages had to pass their night time in a sort of common house which served as their dormitory and also as a common resort place where social and religious gatherings were held. With the advent of Christianity and Education, school houses took the place of these common houses as dormitories of pupils. The school house should be of such size that it could contain all the children of the villages concerned and afford them sufficient room to sleep.

The school work of little children were carried on at night, as they had to start very early for field work, and the morning classes were attended only by little children. (The total enrolment of these 35 night institutions was 644). Jowai became a District headquarters after a century of its existence as 'a Subdivision.

The town' spreads over the gently spurs of hills. Located on a spacious table land it overlooks the valleys located downhill and on the further horizon, the other blue small ranges radiate around: On its exit, the hills and valleys glow with the grove of pine trees which usually characterise the hill terrain and these make their further extensions eastward.

Just before entering Jowai, on the outskirts of Ummulong, there are the beautiful grasslands which look like the sleeping valleys. It is in this direction that Thad-las-kern lake lies which provides a soothing sight. It was excavated hundreds of years ago by U Sajar Nangli, an artist, builder and sculptor of great repute. The Jowai's outskirt provides some interesting beauty spots. Another village Wahjajer, a centre of crafts and the adjunct of the once famous pottery is located near Ummulong with the cluster of beautifully-constructed houses lying along the main road and is another station on Shillong-Nartiang road. Raliang is another trade centre on the east.

Nongstoin which was a mere village decades ago has now become another district town. With the establishment of the Deputy Commissioner, West Khasi Hills, other district offices are located here since 1976. It was shortly after Meghalaya was born that the office and residential quarters of the administration were constructed. Consequently, new trades had sprung. It provided the motor road communication earlier to Sonapahar and now to Tura. Evidently Nongstoin is now one of the potential trade centres on the West. Transaction of goods *en route* Nongstoin has increased more than double in a decade. The headquarters of the Nongstoin Syiem is located in the town. Nongpyndeng a village lying above the district headquarters is perhaps still preserving some of its traditional characteristics.

Mairang

It lies in a road junction accessible to Shillong, Nongstoin and Nongkhlaw. Before independence it was only a village. The spread of administration, industry and trade had steadily brought Mairang to the limelight of business. Lewlangstieh a great market at Mairang is one of the market-day held. There is a cenotaph of Tirot and it forms the headquarters of the Nongkhlaw syiem.

Tura

It assumed its importance when it started as the first District headquarters nestled on the lower spury of Tura hill. It housed the first administrative and Mission establishments. The District having been bifurcated into the West and East Garo Hills Districts, Tura, the parent headquarters, has now remained the capital of West Garo Hills. Prior to the formation of Meghalaya, it was only a small town. Now a rapid expansion in the net work of communications, buildings and trade facilities has made Tura one of the centres of traffic and trade. The communications have been made easier over the roads skirting off over to various directions in the District and the State. There has been a great increase of educational and other institutions. Here the Wangala festival is celebrated enthusiastically annually. Constructions of houses with better materials have also taken place.

Williamnager

The name of the new District headquarters to East Garo Hills. Inception occurred in 1979. It lies parallel to Tura and eastward. The river Simsang with its upper reaches nearby follows near Williamnagar. It serves as an inter-road station and has access with Nongstoin and other places. A township has occurred due to the concentration of the new establishments.

Mendipathar

One of the nearest townships on the North-East to Assam. It started to grow only after a timber processing plant and industrial units were located in it.

Bagknrara

Lying west of Moheskhala in the Khasi Hills along with Dalu and Maliendraganj are the important places on the southern extremity bordering on Bangladesh and are like apexes located eastwardly, centrally and westwardly. The southern tract drained by famous rivers have its reputation for a variety of fish caught or fished out from them. The hills are open and do not form the sheer precipices as it is in the south Khasi Hills. The tract is also rich in different species of vegetation and the soil appears to have good potentials which can be conserved for different farming processes. There are many Garo Village markets and hats and attendance to them by batches of traders constitutes a typical scene. According to P.T. Marwein, Tman giri situated on the east "is famous for its handicraft in cane wood carving and bamboo works. There are a number of bachelors, house for each clan locally called Nokpantes. These houses are well-decorated by the youths with hand carvings on each post and pillar". The constitution of C.D. Blocks has evidently introduced the new social trends the traditional patterns of the village and house hold life have also their relevance to the present change.

Village scattered all over intimately linked up with their respective cultural, social and trade trends. The State evidently experienced an increase of population. Some villages which are like the strongholds of culture and folk life are yielding themselves to the educational impact. It is feared that the educational reconstruction at places falls short of responding to upkeep the local cultural and art requirements of the society as regularly and consistently. It is a healthy sign to see that some towns, townships and villages at places are maintaining the conscious elements of cultural continuity or awakening. At many places, therefore, the old village dances and festivals are held annually. The State represents the Christian and non-Christian sections of the population.

The latter are preserving their indigenous religion. Some of the roadside stations evidently have shown a great range of change structurally and materially. They have yielded themselves to the new economic trends in which new trades, practices and professions have loomed large. The situation has become inevitable that bulk of the villages are now included in Community Development Projects, barring some innovations made, agriculture is still run in traditional lines but in cities and towns, they have become linked up with the urbanised complex. We find that the scenery in Garo Hills is fairly distributed. It is broken by a series of rising peaks which demonstrate their sheer heights, by the jungle-clad hills and valleys, by the water falls which break forth through the ridges and by the barren hills. There are many caves, waterfalls and jungles which offer a natural phenomenon of their own.

Economic reconstruction is now the most important thing to alleviate the misery of poverty-ridden people, to create the wealth pattern and responding fully well to provide their cultural necessities. Much remains to be done to habituate our young people to develop their own arts, culture and society in the midst of the present complex and tension. The village markets and roadside depots have their basic roles to boost considerable measures to orient or improve the local economy. In the Khasi Hills, there are 16 ancient states. Excluding Mylliern all the Syiems' chieftains headquarters are located in the villages which serve the central places and preferably which have the accessible transport services.

Bibliography

Abbas, K.S.: *Census of India 2001: Meghalaya Administrative Atlas*, Controller of Publications, 2005.

Aggarwal, C.K.: *Ethnicity, Culture of Meghalaya. India,* Indus Publishing Company, New Delhi, 1996.

Agonkar, G.M.: *School Education in Meghalaya: Catholic Contribution,* Pius Varghese, Akansha Pub, 2009.

Ahmed, Mehtabuddin: *The Turbulent North East,* New Delhi, 1996.

Antrobus, H.A. : *A History of Meghalaya,* Edinbrough, 1975.

Baishya, A. J.: *Ferns and Fern Allies of Meghalaya,* Scientific Publications, 1991.

Bangladeshi Immigrants in Meghalaya: *Causes of Human Movement and Impact on Garo Hills: Sengjrang,* Sangma N., Anshah, 2005.

Barpujari, S. K.: *Meghalaya in the Days of the Company,* North Eastern Hill University Publications, Shillong, 1996.

Bhagabati, K. Abani and Kar, K. Bimal: *Survey of Research in Geography on North-East India 1970-1990,* Regency Publication, New Delhi, 1999.

Bhasak, R.G. : *History of North-eastern Fronetier,* Param Pub., Calcutta, 1917.

Bhattacharjee, J.B.: *North East Indian Perspectives in History,* Vikas Publishing House, New Delhi, 1995.

Bhattacharyya, N.N.: *Religious Culture of North-Eastern India,* Manohar Publishers & Distributors, New Delhi, 1995.

Bhattarcharjee, J.B. : *North-East India History,* NEHU Publications, Delhi, 2000.

Bhaumik, Subir: *Insurgent Cross Fire: North-East India,* Lancer Publishers, New Delhi, 1996.

Bhuyan, B. C.: *Political Development of the North East,* Omsons Publications, New Delhi, 1989.

Bordoloi, B. N.: *District Handbook: United Mikir and North Cachar Hills,* Tribal Research Institute, Shillong, 1972.

Brown, R. : *Statistical Account of the Native State of Manipur and the Hill Territory under its Rule*, Govt. Printing, Kolkata, 1873.

Burling, Robbins: *Rengsanggri: Family and Kinship in a Garo Village,* University of Pennsylvania Press, Philadelphia, 1963.

Chandra, Asok : *Federalism in India : A Study of Union State Relations,* MacMillan, London, 1965.

Chaube, S.K. : *Hill Politics in North-East India,* Calcutta, 1973.

Choudhury, P.C. : *The History of the Civilisation of the People of North-East to the Twelfth Century A.D.,* Concept Pub., Madras, 1959.

Clarke, C.B. : *On the Plants of Kohima and Muneypor,* London, 1889.

Dalton, Edward Tuite: *Descriptive Ethnology of Bengal,* Superintendent of Government Printing, Calcutta, 1960.

Dani, A.H. : *Pre-history and Protohistory of Eastern India*, Firma L. Mukhopadhay, Calcutta, 1960.

Das, K.N.: *Social Dimension of Garo Language,* Gauhati University, 1982.

Dash, K.H.: *Meghalaya District Gazetters*, Kumar Publication, Silong, 1999.

Datta, P.S.: *North East as I See It,* Omsons Publications, New Delhi, 1994.

Deep N. Pandey: *Van Kaa Viraat Roop: Use, Abuse and Proper Use of Forests* (in Hindi), Himanshu Publishers, 1996.

Dutta, N.C.: *Politics of Identity and Nation Building in North-East India,* South Asian Press, New Delhi, 1997.

Ethnobotanical Wisdom of Khasis: *Hynniew Treps of Meghalaya: Ayesha Ashraf Ahmed,* S.K. Borthakur, Bishen Singh Mahendra Pal Singh, 2005.

Eugene Thomas, D.: *Poverty and Rural Development in Meghalaya,* Akansha, India, 2004.

Flora of Jowai and Vicinity: *Meghalaya,* A Contribution Towards a Detailed Knowledge of the Flora of the Northeastern Region, India, 1981.

Garo: *Tribe of Meghalaya: S.H.M. Rizvi and Shibani Roy,* B R Pub, Achik, 2006.

Gassah, L. S.: *Traditional Institutions of Meghalaya: A Study of Doloi and his Administration,* Regency Publications, New Delhi, 1998.

Ghosh, S.P. : *Horticulture in North-East India*, Associated Publishing Company, New Delhi, 1984.

Gopalakrishnan, R. Jhunjhunwala, K. K.and Nongkinrih, A. K.: *Voluntary Organisations and Sustainable Rural Development in Meghalaya,* Regency Publications, New Delhi, 2001.

Grierson, George A.: *The Linguistic Survey of India*, Government of India, Delhi, 1967.

Jaintia Hills: *A Meghalaya Tribe : Its Environment*, Land and People, 2002.

Jamir, S. C.: *Reminiscences of Correspondences with A. Z. Phizo*, Published by the Author, Kohima, 1998.

Jaswal, I.J.S. : *Search for Early Man in North-Eastern India*, APH, New Delhi, 1998.

Jenkins, Nigel: *Through the Green Door: Travels Among the Khasis*, Penguin Books, New Delhi, 2001.

Jhunjhunwala, K. K.: *Voluntary Organisations and Sustainable Rural Development in Meghalaya*, Rehan Publications, Meerut, 2001.

Johri, B. : *Art and Culture of North-East India*, Publications Division, New Delhi, 1998.

Joshua, C. Thomas and Fiasta Diengdoh T.: *Ageing in Meghalaya*, Akansha Pub, 2009.

Khanna, S.K.: *Encyclopaedia of North-East India: Arunachal Pradesh, Assam, Manipur, Meghalaya, Tripura, Sikkim, Mizoram and Nagaland Tripura Sikkim*, Indian Pub, India, 1999.

Khasi: *Meghalaya: Past and Present: H.G. Joshi*, Mittal, 2004.

Khasi: *Tribe of Meghalaya : S.H.M.*, B R Pub, Meghalaya, 2006.

Kumar, Nikhilesh: *Survey of Research in Sociology and Social Anthropology in North-East India, 1970-1990*, Regency Publications, New Delhi, 1999.

Kynta, Hamlet Bareh Ngap: *The Economy of Meghalaya: Tradition to Transition*, Spectrum Publications, Delhi, 2001.

Kynta: *The Economy of Meghalaya: Tradition to Transition*, Spectrum Publications, Guwahati, 2001.

Laloo, Minimon: *Meghalaya Handbook: The Abode of Clouds 2001*, Laloo Brothers, Shillong, 2001.

Mackenzie, Alexander: *The North East Frontier of India*, Mittal Publications, New Delhi, 2001.

Majumdar, D.N.: A *Study of Culture Change in Two Garo Villages of Meghalaya*, Gauhati University Press, Gauhati, 1980.

Mali, D.D. : *International Development in North-East India*, Omson Pub., New Delhi, 1987.

Michell, J.F. : *Reports : Topographical, Political and Military on the North - East Frontier of India*, University of Kolkata, Kolkata, 1883.

Nag, Sajal: *India and North-East India: Mind, Politics and the Process of Integration 1946-1950*, Regency Publications, New Delhi, 1998.

Nayak, P. and Thomas, E.D.: *Human Development and Deprivation in Meghalaya*, Akansha, 2007.

Nepram, Binalakshmi: *South Asia's Fractured Frontier: Armed Conflict, Narcotics and Small Arms Proliferation in India's North East,* Mittal Publications, New Delhi, 2002.

Nibedon, N. : *North East India,* New Delhi, 1981.

Nuh, V. K.: *Struggle for Identity in North-east India: A Theological response,* Spectrum Publications, Guwahati, 2001.

Pakem, B. Shibani Roy and Arabinda Basu: *People of India: Meghalaya,* Seagull Books, 1994.

Pakem, B.: *Insurgency in North-East India,* Om Sons Publications, New Delhi, 1997.

Phukon, Girin: *Politics of Regionalism in Northeast India,* Spectrum Publications, Guwahati, 1996.

Power to People in Meghalaya: *Sixth Schedule and the 73rd Amendment,* L.S. Gassah and C.J. Thomas, Regency, 1998.

Purkayastha, R. K.: *Border Trade: North-East India and Neighbouring Countries,* Akansha Publishing House, New Delhi, 2000.

Querry, B. : *Studies in the History of North-east India,* MacMillan, London, 2000.

Rahman, S.A.: *The Beautiful India: Meghalaya,* Reference Press, India, 2006.

Rao, R.R.: *Ferns and Fern Allies of Meghalaya State (India),* Scientific Publications, 1988.

Rao, V.V. Thansanga, H. Hazarika N. : *A Century of Government and Politics in North-East India,* S. Chand and Co., New Delhi, 1987.

Rosamma Mathew and Nibedita Sen: *Records of the Zoological Survey of India : Studies on Caecilians (Amphibia : Gymnophiona: Ichthyophiidae) of North East India with Description of Three New Species of Ichthyophis from Garo Hills, Meghalaya (Occasional Paper No. 309): Additional Information on Ichthyophis Garoensis Pillai and Ravichandran - 1999,* Zoological Survey of India, India, 2009.

Roy, Sankar Kumar: *"Aspects of Neolithic Agriculture and Shifting Cultivation, Garo Hills, Meghalaya."* Asian *Perspectives,* 1981.

Sachdeva, Gulshan: *Economy of the North-East: Policy, Present Conditions and Future Possibilities,* Konark Publishers, Delhi, 2000.

Sen, S.N. : *Rulers of Tripura, Chunta of India: Northeastern India,* New Delhi, 1986.

Sharma, A.K.: *Emergence of Early Culture in North-East India,* A Study Based on Excavations at Bhaitbari, Meghalaya, 1993.

Sharma, T.C. : *Pre-historic Archaeology in North Eastern India : Its Problems and Prospects,* Dibrugarh University, Assam, 1974.

Singh, K. S.: *People of India: Meghalaya,* Seagull Books, Calcutta, 1994.

Srivastav, Nirankar: *Survey of Research in Economics on North East India 1970-1990,* Regency Publications, New Delhi, 2000.

Sujit Kumar Dutta: *Functioning of Autonomous District Councils in Meghalaya,* Akansha, 2002.

Susmita Sen Gupta: *Radical Politics in Meghalaya,* Problems and Prospects, Kalpaz, 2009.

Syiemlieh, R. David: *Survey of Research in History on North-East India 1970-1990,* Regency Publication, New Delhi, 2000.

Sylhet : *The North Cachar Hills,* Nagaland, 1998.

Tarapot, Phanjoubam: *Drug Abuse and Illicit Trafficking in North Eastern India,* Vikash Publishing House, New Delhi, 1997.

Tayang, J.: *Census of India, 1981,* Directorate of Census Operations, Shillong, 1981.

Thomas, C. Joshua: *Dimensions of Displaced People in North-East India,* Regency Publications, New Delhi, 2002.

Verghese, B.G.: *India's North East Resurgent: Ethnicity, Insurgency, Governance, and Development,* Konark Publishers, New Delhi, 1997.

Vishal, J.K.: *The Social History of Meghalaya,* Yamin Publication, New Delhi, 1983.

Wadhwa, A.K.: *Traditional Institutions of Meghalaya: A Case Study of Doloi and His Administration: L.S.* Gassah, Regency, 1998.

Zairema: *God's Miracle in Meghalaya,* Synod Press & Bookworm, Mizoram, 1978.

Zanne, M. : *Gazeetteer of Meghalaya,* Mittal Publication, New Delhi, 1979.

Index

❑❑❑